T0387690

Teaching and Learning Online: Science for Secondary Grade Levels

A Volume in:
Teaching and Learning Online

Series Editors:
Franklin S. Allaire
Jennifer E. Killham

Teaching and Learning Online

Series Editors:

Franklin S. Allaire
University of Houston-Downtown

Jennifer E. Killham
University of La Verne

Series Books

Teaching and Learning Online: Science for Elementary Grade Levels (2022)
Franklin S. Allaire & Jennifer E. Killham

Teaching and Learning Online: Science for Secondary Grade Levels

Franklin S. Allaire
Jennifer E. Killham

INFORMATION AGE PUBLISHING, INC.
Charlotte, NC • www.infoagepub.com

Library of Congress Cataloging-In-Publication Data

The CIP data for this book can be found on the Library of Congress website (loc.gov).

Paperback: 979-8-88730-127-3
Hardcover: 979-8-88730-128-0
E-Book: 979-8-88730-129-7

CONTENTS

Introduction: Teaching and Learning Online: Science for Secondary Grade Levels..ix
Franklin S. Allaire and Jennifer E. Killham

PART I
FRAMEWORKS

1. **Inquiry and Nature of Science in Digital Spaces** 3
   John L. Pecore and Lisa Martin-Hansen

2. **Crosscutting Concepts: The Common Thread Often Hidden** 15
   Patrick Enderle, Scott Cohen, and Marissa Murdock

3. **Issues of Diversity, Equity, and Inclusivity in Online Secondary STEM Education** 31
   Anne Mangahas

4. **Empowering Secondary Teachers to Use EQuIP Rubric to be Critical Conscious Users of Online Science Curricular Materials**... 45
   Amal Ibourk and Tina Cheuk

5. **Engineering Design as a Framework for Virtual Education in Inclusive Science Classrooms** 57
   Amanda L. Mazin and Jessica F. Riccio

6. **Bridging the Gap: Empowering Adolescent Girls in STEM Through Online Learning and Mentoring** 69
Leslie Ekpe and Sarah Toutant

7. **Supporting Claim-Evidence-Reasoning in Linguistically Diverse Secondary Science Classes** 91
Preetha K. Menon

8. **Giving Online Learning the Personal Touch: The Promoting Evidentiary Reasoning and Self-Regulation Online (PERSON) Framework**... 107
Robert B. Marsteller and Alec M. Bodzin

PART II
TEACHER'S JOURNEYS

9. **Using Educational Technology to Foster High School Students' Online Presence and Engagement as *Becomings:* An Integrated Stem Lesson on Trebuchets and Parabolas** 125
Sophia Jeong and Stephen T. Lewis

10. **A PhET Simulation Inquiry Lab on Energy Conservation: Modified for Remote Learning in High School**.................................. 143
Trish Loeblein and Katherine Perkins

11. **Active Learning at Home: Using 3D Virtual Reality Viewers to Explore the Human Heart for High School Students**........................ 159
Rebecca Hite, Gina Childers, and M. Gail Jones

12. **Citizen Science to Engage Youth in Pollinator Conservation for the Social Good**.. 171
Rita Hagevik and Kaitlin Campbell

13. **Where Did My Food's Food Come From? Nature Journaling as a Tool For Meaning-Making In Photosynthesis**................................. 183
Kelly Feille and Stephanie Hathcock

14. **Design Thinking and Mini-Maker Kits in Science Education: Frameworks for Creative Problem-Solving in Transitions to Online and Hybrid Learning** 197
Helen Douglass and Isaiah Darden

PART III
LESSON PLANS

15. **Exploring Regional Climates With 360-Degree Photo Spheres** 209
Matthew Clay

16. **Scientific Modeling in a Virtual Setting:
Floating and Sinking Pennies!** 225
Sophia Jeong and David Pauli

17. **Digging Into Rocks & Minerals Through Science Olympiad's
MY SO Program** 241
Lucas Gobel, John Loehr, and Katrina Pavlik

18. **A Look Inside the Atom: The Basic Building Block of Matter
and the Foundation in an Online Science Course** 259
Natasha Hillsman Johnson and Sophia Jeong

19. **When Things Move With Constant Velocity and Acceleration** 281
Philomena N. Agu

20. **Using Scaffolding to Develop Evidentiary Reasoning: A
Simulation-Based Approach to Teaching Biological
Evolution Online** 309
Robert B. Marsteller and Alec M. Bodzin

21. **Climate Crisis Issues in Our Community** 331
Amy Vo

22. **Exploring Digital Inclusive Pedagogy in Action in a High School
Physics Class: Analyzing and Interpreting Force and Motion** 347
Jessica F. Riccio, Amanda L. Mazin, and Ibrahim Dincer

23. **Stability and Change: Wildfires and Ecosystem Succession** 363
Marissa Murdock, Scott Cohen, and Patrick Enderle

24. **How Does CO_2 Interact With Water To Make It More Acidic?** 385
Lorna Otero, Juliet Octavius, Amanda L. Mazin, and Jessica F. Riccio

25. **A Case of Violet's GLUT1: What is Wrong with Violet?** 399
*Sophia Jeong, Jennifer Yauck, Sarah Robinson,
Patricia Zagallo, and Paula Lemons*

Biographies 421

Technology is nothing. What's important is that you have a faith in people, that they're basically good and smart, and if you give them tools, they'll do wonderful things with them.

—*Steve Jobs*

DEDICATION

FSA: To Sachie, Eleanor, Thomas, Kayla, and Coconut.
JEK: To Hal.

TEACHING AND LEARNING ONLINE

Science for Secondary Grade Levels

Franklin S. Allaire
University of Houston-Downtown

Jennifer E. Killham
University of La Verne

The hands-on aspect of science is what sets it apart from other disciplines. Whether it is titrating acids, investigating the properties of rocks and minerals, viewing muscle cells through a microscope, or swinging a bowling ball pendulum, the hands-on nature of science makes it fun and accessible for students of all ages, backgrounds, and abilities. Hands-on science activities engage students in the inquiry process and motivate them through the excitement that comes from discovering something new. However, the hands-on aspect of science instruction also makes it uniquely challenging when teaching science in virtual environments.

In his book, *Experience and Education* (1997), John Dewey discusses the need for making meaningful connections between experiences. He notes that experiences can be "agreeable or even exciting in itself" with each being "lively, vivid, and 'interesting'" (p. 26) and encourages educators to ensure that learning "arouses curiosity, strengthens initiative, and sets up desires and purposes" (p. 38). Yet,

Dewey warns of the consequences of disconnection between experiences and the negative educational outcomes that can result. While his philosophical discourse was on the analysis of "traditional" versus "progressive" education in the early 20th century, his emphasis on connection rings true for online education in the 21st century as well.

Teaching secondary science in online environments raises critical social, technological, and pedagogical questions. How do we, as science teachers, create meaningful connected experiences for our students in online environments? How do we deliver high-quality science instruction in an online environment that leads to age/grade-level appropriate science content knowledge and literacy? How do we engage science students online to foster collaborative experiences in the inquiry process and the nature of science?

As a society, we tend to envision secondary classrooms as face-to-face. However, online learning opportunities offered by schools and districts for secondary students have steadily increased (Killham, et al., 2014, 2016; Taie & Goldring, 2019). Since the 1990s, and even during economic and overall enrollment downturns, the adoption of online coursework across both secondary (Kennedy & Ferdig, 2018) and higher education (Darby, 2019) settings has steadily increased (Darby & Lang, 2019; Seaman et al., 2018).

The U.S. Department of Education and National Center for Education Statistics (2011) reported that approximately 6,400 middle/junior high students and over 214,000 high school students were enrolled in some type of technology-based distance education courses during the 2002–2003 school year. By the 2009–2010 school year, this number had increased to over 15,000 middle/junior high and 309,000 high school students. The Digital Learning Collaborative (2020) reported that, for the 2018–2019 school year, 375,000 students (up from 310,000 the previous year) were enrolled in fully online schools across 32 states, an additional 1,015,760 students enrolled in one of 21 state virtual schools, and supplemental online course enrollment, including credit recovery, was approximately 1.5 million students. Similar growth trends were cited by the National Education Policy Center (Molnar et al., 2019).

Similarly, enrollment in full-time virtual schools increased by nearly 30,000 students between 2017–2018 and 2019–2020 to include over 330,000 students, with over 239 district virtual schools and 238 charter virtual schools operating (Molnar et al., 2021). Further, reports indicated a steady rise in districts and charters with physical locations adopting hybrid/blended learning methods. This trend, in turn, has impacted hiring practices at the secondary level with teachers being hired exclusively to teach online within a brick-and-mortar secondary school or as part of a virtual school (Molnar et al., 2021; Taie & Goldring, 2019; U.S. Department of Education & National Center for Education Statistics, 2011).

Due to a greater emphasis on science content, secondary teachers' confidence and science teaching self-efficacy tend to be higher than their secondary colleagues (Azar, 2010; Brígido et al., 2013; Kaya, et al., 2021). The National Survey of Science and Mathematics Education (Banilower, et al., 2018) reported that 55% and 91% of middle and high school teachers, respectively, have degrees in science/engineering or science education as compared to only 3% for secondary teachers. While the level of science preparation is higher for secondary teachers, the same report details the varying levels at which secondary science teachers consider themselves very well prepared to teach science topics. For example, approximately 49% of middle school science teachers consider themselves very well prepared to teach biology/life science-related topics as compared to about 68% of their high school colleagues. On the other hand, 85% of high school science teachers feel prepared to teach chemistry-related topics compared to about 42% of middle school science teachers. However, both middle and high school teachers feel the least prepared to teach earth/space science (35% MS vs. 61% HS) and physics (26% MS vs. 54% HS).

We recognized these trends and how research on best practices has not mimicked the growth of online secondary learning. As a result, secondary teachers can feel under-equipped for online science teaching. *Teaching and Learning Online: Science for Elementary Grade Levels* (Allaire & Killham, 2022) was conceived of and assembled with secondary teachers, teacher candidates, and teacher educators in mind. Unlike other general and content-specific textbooks and supplementary texts focused on online learning, *Teaching and Learning Online: Science for Secondary Grade Levels* (Allaire & Killham, 2022) focuses on the unique needs and science-related experiences of secondary students and teachers in online environments. Additionally, other books and textbooks often include a technology chapter or attempt to integrate technology throughout the text. However, the technology integrated into these texts is usually limited to the use of hardware and equipment to support the inquiry process (e.g., using probes and sensors to collect data). *Teaching and Learning Online: Science for Secondary Grade Levels* (Allaire & Killham, 2022) differentiates itself from these texts in that it focuses exclusively on online environments for science teaching and learning.

COVID-19 AND TEACHING AND LEARNING ONLINE

The COVID-19 pandemic has thrust teaching and learning in online environments to the forefront of national educational discourse and given us a lot to reflect upon as we prepared this book. The spread of the SARS-CoV-2 virus (COVID-19) in Spring 2020 caused a rapid and dramatic shift in our personal and professional realities (Allaire, et al., In Press). Timelines and schedules for coursework, research, undergraduate field experiences, student teaching, weddings, birthdays, publications, conferences, and tenure were hastily changed or cancelled. Secondary educators, like their elementary and higher education counterparts (Allaire, et al., In Review; *Critical Storytelling During the COVID-19 Pandemic*, 2021), also faced a pedagogical reckoning due to the dramatic shift from face-to-face to online learning. Teachers around the world met this unprecedented moment in history and created or modified lessons, activities, and experiences for students in online environments. This book is not a "COVID-19 book"; however, its importance and relevance was made urgent by the pandemic. As a result, chapters and lessons in this book were, in part, generated through authors' pandemic-related experiences.

HOW TO USE THIS BOOK

Materials presented in *Teaching and Learning Online: Science for Secondary Grade Levels* are based on current research and best practices from the science, science teaching, and online learning communities. Section chapters and lesson plans were written by experts within the field of science teaching and online education with a focus on teaching and learning science at the secondary grade levels. All manuscripts had to undergo a rigorous multi-step peer review process. We firmly believe that the inclusion of the chapter/lesson plan authors in the review process was a significant contribution that strengthened the quality of this book.

Just like the previous elementary volume (Allaire & Killham, 2022), *Teaching and Learning Online: Science for Secondary Grade Levels* is comprised of three distinct sections: Frameworks, Teacher's Journeys, and Lesson Plans. Each section uniquely explores the current trends and the unique challenges facing secondary teachers and students when teaching and learning science in online environments.

1. The Frameworks Chapters link theory with best practices in the use of online technologies, methodologies, pedagogies, and environments to support secondary teachers as they strive to meet their students' science content-related needs.
2. Teacher's Journeys Chapters take a "deep dive" into the creative journey the authors took to develop new or transform face-to-face science lessons for online environments.
3. The Lesson Plan section provides readers with detailed practical lesson plans that are "classroom ready" for online learning environments.

All three sections include alignment with Next Generation Science Standards, tips and advice from the authors, resource notes, and discussion questions to foster individual reflection and small group/classwide discussion. Teacher's Journeys and Lesson Plan sections use the 5E model (Bybee et al., 2006; Duran & Duran, 2004). This model, which consists of engagement, exploration, explanation, elaboration, and evaluation phases, is dynamic and interactive for both teachers and students and was chosen because of its widespread use in the sciences. Each chapter and lesson plan also contains resource notes so that readers can access resources suggested by the authors. We hope the inclusion of resource notes encourages readers to integrate various websites, apps, simulations, and videos into their curriculum (e.g., Chandler & Hawley, 2017). It is also a way for us to model what we believe is a best practice in online education—providing students and teacher with multiple ways to access materials online. The resource notes include links to the primary website, a direct link to the resources cited by the authors, and directions on how to find a resource on the primary website, particularly in the event that a direct link changes or becomes inactive. Finally, it is crucial to acknowledge and celebrate the diversity—ethnic, social, language, and ability—of students in online learning environments (Allaire, 2018; Killham, 2017; Killham et al., 2021). Therefore, emphasis was placed on addressing the needs of diverse learners and fostering an inclusive learning space for all students.

ONE MORE THING...

Several different terms are used by authors in this book, in research, to describe teaching and learning "online." These include "virtual environments," "online learning," "distance learning," and "remote learning." Generally speaking, we define online, or any other term used in this book, as having instruction during which students and teachers are separated by time and/or location and interact via internet-connected computers or other electronic devices (U.S. Department of Education & National Center for Education Statistics, 2011).

REFERENCES

Allaire, F. S. (2018). Themes from a narrative analysis of Native Hawaiian experiences in science, technology, engineering, and mathematics. *Journal of Ethnographic and Qualitative Research, 12*, 173–192.

Allaire, F. S., Goltz, H. H., Beebe, R. S., & Gilmore, E. L. (in Review). Examining undergraduates' learning-related emotions at an urban university at the start of the COVID-19 pandemic.

Allaire, F. S., & Killham, J. E. (Eds.). (2022). *Teaching and learning online: Science for early childhood and elementary grade levels.* Information Age Publishing.

Allaire, F. S., Perrotta, K., & Killham, J. E. (2022). Living and teaching in the COVID era: A conversation with three teacher educators. In C. Scott & K. Varner (Eds.), *Corona chronicles 3.0: Learning to live living to lead with COVID.* DIO Press Inc.

Azar, A. (2010). In-service and pre-service secondary science teachers' self-efficacy beliefs about science teaching. *Educational Research and Reviews, 5*(4), 172–185. https://doi.org/10.5897/ERR09.243

Banilower, E., Smith, P., Malzahn, K., Plumley, C., Gordon, E., & Hayes, M. (2018). *Report of the 2018 NSSME+.* Horizon Research. http://horizon-research.com/NSSME/wp-content/uploads/2020/04/Report_of_the_2018_NSSME.pdf

Brígido, M., Borrachero, A., Bermejo, M., & Mellado, V. (2013). Prospective primary teachers' self-efficacy and emotions in science teaching. *European Journal of Teacher Education, 36*(2), 200–217. https://doi.org/10.1080/02619768.2012.686993

Bybee, R. W., Taylor, J. A., Gardner, A., Van Scotter, P., Powell, J. C., Westbrook, A., & Landers, N. (2006). *The BSCS 5E instructional model: Origins, effectiveness, and applications.* BSCS.

Chandler, P. T., & Hawley, T. S. (Eds.). (2017). *Race lessons: Using inquiry to teach about race in social studies.* Information Age Publishing.

Darby, F. (2019). How to be a better online teacher. *The Chronicle of Higher Education.* https://www.chronicle.com/article/how-to-be-a-better-online-teacher/

Darby, F., & Lang, J. (2019). *Small teaching online: Applying learning science in online classes* (1st ed.). Jossey-Bass.

Dewey, J. (1997). *Experience & education* (Touchstone ed.). Simon & Schuster.

Digital Learning Collaborative. (2020). *Snapshot 2020: A review of K–12 online, blended, and digital learning.* https://www.digitallearningcollab.com

Duran, L. B., & Duran, E. (2004). The 5E instructional model: A learning cycle approach for inquiry-based science teaching. *The Science Education Review, 3*(2), 49–58.

Hartlep, N. D., Stuchell, C. V., Whitt, N. E., & Hensley, B. O. (Eds.). (2021). *Critical storytelling during the COVID-19 pandemic.* Information Age Publishing.

Kaya, F., Borgerding, L. A., & Ferdous, T. (2021). Secondary science teachers' self-efficacy beliefs and implementation of inquiry. *Journal of Science Teacher Education, 32*(1), 107–121. https://doi.org/10.1080/1046560X.2020.1807095

Kennedy, K., & Ferdig, R. E. (Eds.). (2018). *Handbook of Research On K–12 Online and Blended Learning* (2nd ed.). ETC.

Killham, J. E. (2017). Has social media provided communities of color a platform for sharing counternarratives? In P. T. Chandler & T. S. Hawley (Eds.), *Race lessons: Using inquiry to teach about race in social studies* (pp. 341–360). Information Age Publishing.

Killham, J. E., Estanga, L., Ekpe, L., & Mejia, B. (2021). The strength of a tigress: An examination of first-generation college Latina students' tenacity during the rapid shift to remote learning. *Journal of Research on Technology in Education, 54*(sup1), S253–S272. https://doi.org/10.1080/15391523.2021.1962450

Killham, J. E., Saligman, A., & Jette, K. (2016). Unmasking the mystique: Utilizing narrative character-playing games to support English language fluency. *International Journal of Game-Based Learning (IJGBL), 6*(4), 1–21. http://doi.org/10.4018/IJG-BL.2016100101

Killham, J. E., Tyler, S. P., Venable, A., & Raider-Roth, M. (2014). Mentoring in an online simulation: shaping preservice teachers for tomorrow's roles. *Teaching and Learning, 28*(2), 62–79. https://link.gale.com/apps/doc/A388263516/PROF?u=ulv_gvrl&sid=bookmark-PROF&xid=21dad0ff

Molnar, A., Miron, G., Barbour, M. K., Huerta, L., Shafer, S. R., Rice, J. K., Glover, A., Browning, N., Hagle, S., & Boninger, F. (2021). *Virtual schools in the U.S. 2021.* National Education Policy Center. https://nepc.colorado.edu/publication/virtual-schools-annual-2021

Molnar, A., Miron, G., Elgeberi, N., Barbour, M. K., Huerta, L., Shafer, S. R., & Rice, J. K. (2019). *Virtual schools in the U.S. 2019.* http://nepc.colorado.edu/publication/virtual-schools-annual-2019

Seaman, J. E., Allen, I. E., & Seaman, J. (2018). *Grade increase: Tracking distance learning in the United States.* https://www.bayviewanalytics.com/reports/gradeincrease.pdf

Taie, S., & Goldring, R. (2019). *Characteristics of public and private elementary and secondary schools in the United States: Results from the 2017–18 National Teacher and Principal Survey First Look (NCES 2019-140).* U.S. Department of Education. https://nces.ed.gov/pubsearch/pubsinfo.asp?pubid=2019140

U.S. Department of Education, & National Center for Education Statistics. (2011). *Percentage of public school districts with students enrolled in technology-based distance education courses and number of enrollments in such courses, by instructional level and district characteristics: 2002–03, 2004–05, and 2009–10*. U.S. Department of Education. https://nces.ed.gov/programs/digest/d19/tables/dt19_218.20.asp

PART I

FRAMEWORKS

CHAPTER 1

INQUIRY AND NATURE OF SCIENCE IN DIGITAL SPACES

John L. Pecore

University of West Florida.

Lisa Martin-Hansen

California State University, Long Beach

Much of the general public struggles with ideas regarding what science is and how science works. Secondary science classrooms provide a place for students to develop critical thinking regarding nature of science concepts, which is a component of the Next Generation Science Standards and a requirement for scientific literacy. Recently, secondary science teachers have found themselves transferring their science teaching online. Therefore, typical teaching strategies must change for online instruction. Examples of instructional strategies and lessons for teaching nature of science online are illustrated with the central idea of an explicit focus on students' meaning-making versus simply passively giving information.

RATIONALE

Nature of science (NOS) is integrally tied to the general public's understanding, or failure to understand, what science is and how science works (Lombrozo et al., 2008). Misunderstandings of the enterprise of science lead to issues regarding trust in sound scientific (peer-reviewed) data and the need for appropriate skepticism of data and conclusions from questionable and biased sources. The second-

Teaching and Learning Online: Science for Secondary Grade Levels, pages 3–13.

ary science classroom allows teaching our students concepts in NOS– not only to meet national or state science standards—but more practically, to foster the development of critical thinking skills (Khishfe, 2012) so that our future voting citizens can make informed choices regarding policy and policymakers. Citizens should be able to consider the relationship of humans in their environment on Earth along with the exploration and discovery of new scientific ideas or reinterpretations of prior ideas. These ideas and issues are equally valid in digital spaces. As K–16 schooling transitions to online platforms and virtual learning schools, additional considerations must be made when converting tried-and-true activities into engaging virtual learning experiences.

The National Science Teaching Association (NSTA) identified NOS as an essential aspect of scientific literacy that improves students' understandings of science ideas and empowers them to make scientifically grounded decisions about personal and societal issues (NSTA Position Statement, Nature of Science, 2020, par. 1). NOS includes both characteristics of scientific knowledge and the development of scientific knowledge. Science practices or inquiry refers to how knowledge is developed, while NOS knowledge (NOSK) refers to the characteristics of scientific knowledge (Lederman & Lederman, 2019). Students often have considerable misconceptions about science stemming from popular media, prior experiences, and classroom teaching, which stresses known science facts over how science is known (McComas, 2020). Thus, many students develop an idea of science being an accumulation of facts following a scientific method void of imagination and creativity. All science teachers need to have a shared accurate view of NOS and teach NOS concepts explicitly.

THEORETICAL BACKGROUND

Explicit and reflective instruction is necessary for developing informed conceptions of inquiry and NOS. This approach provides learners with multiple opportunities to actively engage in science activities and reflect on the process and development of scientific knowledge. According to Lederman (2007), explicit discussion between activities and aspects of NOS is vital for teaching NOS effectively. Explicit and reflective instruction promotes metacognitive knowledge for encouraging critical awareness of the implicit values inherent in scientific endeavors and how scientific knowledge builds upon the collaborative work of scientists using scientific practices (Pandya & Dibner, 2018).

Teaching science and NOS in a virtual learning environment requires creativity and knowledge of instructional technology. Many inquiry and NOS activities need to be modified for the virtual classroom, and modifications will vary depending on the instruction method (asynchronous, synchronous, or hybrid). An important consideration is providing lessons and activities that depict aspects of inquiry and NOS and opportunities to intentionally reflect on those specific aspects, fostering metacognitive thinking (Lederman, 1992). Just as important as providing hands-on experiences is guiding students to reflect on their thinking.

INQUIRY AND NOS

Establishing the general components is an essential aspect of teaching NOS concepts within secondary science classrooms. According to Rutherford and Ahlgren (1991), NOS includes the scientific world view, scientific methods of inquiry, and the nature of the scientific enterprise. Teaching NOS should focus upon how a body of scientific knowledge is developed over time and the actions scientists take in this development. Additionally, the culture in which these actions occur must be considered since society influences science and vice versa.

The processes of doing science include scientific inquiry. In order to address the difficulty in understanding the nature of inquiry (Colburn, 2000; Martin-Hansen, 2002) and how to enact it within science classrooms, the Next Generation Science Standards (NRC, 2015) delineated practices that are part of scientific inquiry as well as other activities related to the scientific enterprise, such as argumentation and modeling, which all impact the development of scientific knowledge. Scientists pursue curious questions (basic science) or questions to solve a problem (applied science) in creative ways to gather data that can help to explain naturally occurring phenomena in our universe (Stokes, 1997).

Inquiry: Development of Scientific Knowledge

Science inquiry includes the development of scientific knowledge through process skills (i.e., observing, inferring, classifying, predicting, measuring, questioning, interpreting, and analyzing data) combined with scientific knowledge, scientific reasoning, and critical thinking. Scientific inquiry refers to the systematic approach used to answer questions of interest. Contrary to popular belief, scientific inquiry is not a universal step-by-step method. Teaching "the scientific method" (i.e., observe, question, research, hypothesize, experiment, analyze, conclude, report) presents a narrow and distorted view of scientific inquiry. There is no single fixed set or sequence of steps for conducting scientific investigations (Lederman et al., 2013).

Scientific investigations include observation, experiments, logical arguments, and skepticism in order to reach the best possible explanation about the natural world. The perception that experiments are the only way to explore scientific ideas is a common misunderstanding. Instead, many aspects of science do not fit into an experiment, such as investigations into galaxies' characteristics or questions about prehistoric animals' behaviors. Secondary teachers can model and discuss the various ways in which scientific inquiry is practiced.

Teaching Inquiry in Digital Spaces

In order to teach the inquiry process, it is not enough to model inquiry methods and one must also prompt students to think about how those methods are similar to what scientists do (National Research Council, 2000). Without the explicit discussion following an inquiry activity, students will view their experience simply as a school activity versus making connections to how scientists would use parallel processes in their scientific thinking. Furthermore, teaching science online creates new challenges, removing another step from a science lab setting with the materials and tools typically used for classroom instruction. By providing students with a kit of materials either assembled by the instructor, ordered through a curriculum company such as Lab-Aids (n.d.), or asking students to use typical materials from around the house or outside the house, they can engage in inquiry at home—either synchronous with the class online or asynchronous as an independent investigation outside of synchronous class time.

Science Inquiry Online Example: The Effects of Water of Earth Materials

While most students will have kitchen supplies (e.g., sugar, flour, rice) to use for an investigation, many students with food insecurity will not. Therefore, it is unacceptable to ask middle and high school students to investigate food that their families may desperately need. As a possible alternative, students could use dirt from outside, sand, or other found materials in place of kitchen supplies.

First, engage students in a phenomenon of a landslide (e.g., Norway landslide video, Bakkeby, 2020) and guide them in their exploration of earth materials and variables that might affect a landslide, such as slope, consistency, and water content. After completing a series of investigations to gather information, ask more questions, and discuss findings. Students create a claim of what factors are at play when landslides occur. Using evidence from their investigations, they can then describe the reasoning behind their thinking. Lastly, provide scientific explanations of the characteristics and physics behind landslides. This explanation allows the students to compare their ideas to scientists' consensus views and discuss additional questions about the phenomenon.

Immediately following the investigations is the time to enact a dialogue to think about how these investigations may have been similar (or different) compared to what scientists do to explore their ideas. Through this discussion, students can refer back to scientific processes and call out which processes they recognized as part of their investigation. Having a list of the NGSS Scientific and Engineering Practices is useful (NGSS Lead States, 2013). Through this discussion, students can become aware of their thinking and how they are thinking scientifically.

NOS: Characteristics of Scientific Knowledge

The real power of science is how science explains and predicts. NOSK refers to science as a way of knowing that encompasses the "values and beliefs inherent in the development of scientific knowledge" (Lederman, 1992, p. 331). The main characteristics of NOSK relevant to the K–12 curriculum are that scientific knowledge is a function of the relationship between theories and laws and is observational, subjective, tentative, durable, natural, creative, and cultural (Lederman, 2007). The following descriptions of each tenant of NOSK are derived from Lederman et al. (2013).

Laws and Theories

The distinction between scientific laws and theories is a critical NOS characteristic since students often have a simplistic, hierarchical order between the two, erroneously thinking that theories can become laws. One central idea to understand is that theories and laws are different kinds of knowledge and do not become the other; laws do not become theories and theories do not become laws. As Lederman et al. (2013) defined: "Laws are statements or descriptions of the relationship among observable phenomena...Theories, by contrast, are inferred explanations about observable phenomena" (p. 140).

Observational

Scientific knowledge is based on or derived from observations as evidence to support a scientific idea. Students need to understand the difference between observation and inference. Observations are descriptions of natural phenomena that are theory-laden. Inferences, however, are statements about observed natural phenomena and, thus, are also theory-laden.

Subjectivity

Scientists are human and, therefore, their work is influenced by human characteristics, qualities, and experiences to include personal bias and interpretation of observations. Scientific knowledge is subjectively influenced by scientists' theoretical commitments, prior experiences, knowledge, and training. These background factors provide the mindset for investigating scientific problems and how investigations are conducted, observations are made (or not made), and interpretations of observations. Scientists attempt to identify and avoid bias through accurate record-keeping and repeated checks with colleagues. Additionally, the peer review process assists with guarding against, but not guaranteeing, possible bias.

Durable yet Tentative and Well-established

Scientific knowledge, while durable, is tentative in nature. Core ideas of science, including facts, theories, and laws that are subjected to a wide variety of confirmations, are unlikely to change. However, scientific knowledge is subject to change as new evidence becomes available. Scientific hypotheses, theories, and laws cannot be absolutely proven.

Natural Explanations

Since science is empirically based upon evidence, science proceeds through curiosity and attempts to explain natural phenomena. Science cannot answer all questions, including questions about religion that are based on faith. Enacting scientific tests on supernatural beings would be difficult, if not impossible, to execute. Explanations of the natural world based on myths, personal beliefs, religious values, mystical inspiration, or superstition are not scientific.

Curiosity, Creativity, and Imagination

Science is both logical and creative, which involves creating explanations that require a great deal of imagination by scientists. Science proceeds creatively where scientists use their imaginations to ask questions, either curious questions or problems to solve, leading to scientific investigations. Many consider the creation of the procedure to be the only creative component when, in actuality, all of the components of scientific investigations are inherently creative (e.g., including data display and findings are creative components).

Social, Cultural, and Historical Events

Science proceeds through contributions from people of all cultures and consists of both social and cultural traditions. The human enterprise of science is thus culturally embedded and includes various elements of politics, socioeconomic factors, philosophy, and religion. Social and historical events influence scientific ideas, and scientific ideas, in turn, can influence society and culture. These aspects are some of the pieces in the body of knowledge regarding NOS necessary for our future citizens to understand when making decisions requires understanding how science works.

Teaching NOSK in Digital Spaces

Teaching NOS concepts involves similar issues as any instruction online. Students need to be mentally engaged for active learning to take place. While an instructor may simply attempt to be entertaining, a more successful approach is asking students to think and talk about their ideas as part of the class. Additionally, asking students to think about their thinking and reflect upon their learning (metacognition) is a valuable part of online learning. An at-home science kit (see Resources for examples) can help to facilitate collaborative investigations via digital spaces.

Teaching NOS to illustrate what science is and how science works can occur through both contextualized and decontextualized activities (Clough, 2006; Lederman & Lederman, 2019). Contextualized NOS instruction involves concrete applications in a real-life context, perhaps through reading or role-playing a historical vignette to illustrate specific points about NOS (Allchin, 2009; Clough, 2011, n.d.). For instance, students can learn that data exist, such as data about the mid-Atlantic rift zone and the stripes of rock with magnetic minerals aligning to magnetic north or magnetic south depending on the time when they were formed. Decontextualized NOS lessons focus solely on NOS ideas, excluding science concepts. For example, students can learn that science is tentative and subject to revision, subjective, and a human enterprise through the checks lab activity (Evolution and the Nature of Science Institutes [ENSI], n.d.). Both contextualized and decontextualized types of learning are effective. However, teaching with both types of strategies is recommended for deeper learning of concepts.

Decontextualized Lesson Example: Nature of Science Magic Bottle and Mystery Tube

In a decontextualized lesson, a video (developed for online instruction) about a so-called Magic Bottle (Kisiel, 2020) prompts discussion about what might be happening inside. Students can discuss in real-time in breakout groups or asynchronously on discussion boards how they might gather data about the phenomenon and how they could try to test their ideas. The most important point is that the answer is not shared since that would not be illustrative of scientific knowledge. We seldom get to pop off the top of a container to see the answer in science and no bell rings when we are right (McComas, 2020). A conversation about science not providing a definitive answer must be part of the discussion. Sadly, some of our tried-and-true hands-on explorations may be more difficult in an online setting. Students can be shown a NOS Tube (Caldwell & Lindberg, n.d.; Lederman & Abd-El-Khalick, 2002; National Academy of Sciences, 1998), and the strings can be pulled as students instruct, but that is very different from students feeling the tube, listening inside, and pulling the strings themselves.

Contextualized Lesson Example: Creating the Periodic Table of Elements

In a contextualized lesson, historical vignettes allow students to identify NOS examples. When teaching the periodic table of elements, students are first provided with a case paragraph on the early life of Mendeleev (available in Roskinsky, 2000) and discuss how his life might compare to theirs. Small groups of students are then given a set of element cards (available in Sterling, 1996) to arrange any way they want. Instead of physical cards that one would manipulate, it is relatively easy to create images of the cards placed in a set of Google Slides for use in digital spaces. Each group (or individual) can then manipulate the cards into an order that makes sense. The beauty of using a shared set of google slides where each student/group has their slide is that the instructor can view everyone's progress in real-time since the instructor (and students) can see the slides being manipulated. Students then explain the reasons for how they grouped the elements. The teacher then explains that Mendeleev probably grouped them much as they did until, after months of rearranging the cards, he proceeded with an arrangement he liked best. An explicit discussion can then follow with students reflecting on how this activity highlights that science is imaginative, proceeds through curiosity, and takes time. Student groups are then given another case paragraph to read and rearrange their elements based on Mendeleev's periodic table by atomic mass. Students notice that a few elements are missing. Next, another case paragraph is given to student groups to read that explains the missing elements because these elements had not been discovered at the time. In order to highlight the predictive NOS, students are to predict the properties of the missing elements. The following case paragraph explains the discovery of the missing elements and their properties. Students are then provided with a final case paragraph explaining how Moseley's modern periodic table, which arranges elements by atomic number and not atomic mass, fixes the few inconsistencies. Information from the final case paragraph provides an opportunity to explicitly reflect with students how this case highlights science's durable yet tentative nature. When teaching using contextualized NOS instruction, students not only learn science content, but they also learn the NOS.

SUMMARY AND REFLECTIONS

Traditional district curriculum pacing guides often dedicate the first week of instruction to scientific inquiry and NOS, which is typically taught through decontextualized instruction. It is important that NOS learning continues throughout the year. Teachers can then engage students contextually in activities and laboratory experiments to help further understandings of how science is done. Similarly, teachers engage students in contextualized NOS instruction when teaching various scientific discoveries. Being scientifically literate involves understanding what science is (NOS) and how science works (scientific inquiry), requiring engagement in explicit science activities and reflection on the process and development of scientific knowledge.

While some tried and true in-person activities for teaching science inquiry and NOS do not translate well into an online setting, many examples and strategies can be used productively in a virtual classroom. Any video example will translate easily into an online setting if the sharing capabilities allow for remote viewing. Some streaming providers like Netflix have been problematic due to sharing restrictions, so working through documentary sites or libraries is suggested. When asked about teaching inquiry and NOS, practicing teachers note higher periods of student engagement when providing small group instructional time in breakout groups before the whole-class discussion. Additionally, these same teachers note how the digital spaces require access to resources, especially for those individuals in underserved communities, such as prepackaged science kits (if possible), readily available kitchen equipment, or outdoor resources (e.g., playground or sports equipment; rocks, sand, and soil; leaves).

TIPS AND ADVICE

- Provide time for students to reflect on what science is and how science is done.
- Through synchronous online discussions or asynchronous discussion boards, make explicit connections to NOS and science inquiry during activities like the magic bottle, mystery tube, and laboratory experiments.
- In order to assist with student participation during synchronous online learning, like creating the periodic table of elements lesson, set up small

breakout groups for students to discuss ideas before leading a large group discussion.

- Embed inquiry and NOS using contextualized instruction throughout the school year.

RESOURCE NOTES

Name of Resource	Primary Website	How to Locate the Resource Online
The story behind the science: Bring science and scientists to life	https://www.storybehindthe-science.org	Go to the link https://www.story-behindthescience.org and click on "Stories of Interest."
Nature of science lessons	https://web.archive.org/web/20180305223402/http://www.indiana.edu/~ensiweb/natsc.fs.html	Go to the link https://web.archive.org/web/20180305223402/http://www.indiana.edu/~ensiweb/natsc.fs.html and click on "Nat. Science" on the left side links. Scroll down to the "Social Context" section and click on "Checks Lab."
A Mystery Moment	https://youtu.be/MaBznvZagho	Open an internet browser. In the browser search bar, type https://youtu.be/MaBznvZagho.
Hands-On@Home	https://store.lab-aids.com/kits-and-modules/details/hands-onhome-geological-processes-basic-package	Go to the link https://store.lab-aids.com/kits-and-modules/details/hands-onhome-geological-processes-basic-package and review the geological processes basic package material sets.
Landslide in Northern Norway	https://youtu.be/0y30hyMLJaY	Open an internet browser. In the browser search bar, type https://youtu.be/0y30hyMLJaY.
SHiPS Resource Center	http://www.shipseducation.net	Click on the link http://shipseducation.net and go to "Curriculum Modules." Select a historical reading of interest.
Understanding science: How science really works	http://www.undsci.berkeley.edu	Click on the link http://undsci.berkeley.edu. Click on the "For teachers" image. On the right side, click on "Resource database." In keyword(s), type "mystery tube" and click on the mystery tube resource.

DISCUSSION QUESTIONS

1. What types of nature of science concepts are more challenging to translate into digital spaces? What could be done to facilitate learning better?

2. All individuals involved in STEM teaching and learning should have a common, accurate view of the nature of science. What are some com-

mon, accurate characteristics of science and why are they important to teach?

3. What are additional digital learning resources available to teach NOS concepts?

4. How is contextualized instruction different from decontextualized instruction?

5. What is explicit and reflective instruction and how might this type of teaching be used to teach science inquiry and NOS in digital spaces?

REFERENCES

Allchin, D. (2009, January 12). *SHiPS Resource Center*. SHiPS. http://shipseducation.net

Bakkeby, J. E. (2020, September 12). *Landslide in northern Norway* [Video]. YouTube. https://www.youtube.com/watch?v=0y30hyMLJaY

Caldwell, R., & Lindberg, D. (n.d.). *Understanding Science: How science really works*. http://undsci.berkeley.edu

Clough, M. P. (n.d.). *The story behind the science*. https://www.storybehindthescience.org

Clough, M. P. (2006). Learners' responses to the demands of conceptual change: Considerations for effective nature of science instruction. *Science & Education, 15*(5), 463–494. https://doi.org/10.1007/s11191-005-4846-7

Clough, M. P. (2011). The story behind the science: Bringing science and scientists to life in post-secondary science education. *Science & Education, 20*(7–8), 701–717. https://doi.org/10.1007/s11191-010-9310-7

Colburn, A. (2000). An inquiry primer. *Science Scope, 23*(6), 42–44.

Evolution and the Nature of Science Institutes. (n.d.). *Nature of Science lessons*. https://web.archive.org/web/20170713075707fw_/http://www.indiana.edu/%7Eensiweb/natsc.fs.html

Khishfe, R. (2012). Nature of science and decision-making. *International Journal of Science Education, 34*(1), 67–100. https://doi.org/10.1080/09500693.2011.559490

Kisiel, J. (2020, September 12). *A mystery moment* [Video]. YouTube. https://www.youtube.com/watch?v=MaBznvZagho

Lab-Aids. (n.d.). *Hands-On@Home*. Lab-Aids. https://store.lab-aids.com/kits-and-modules/details/hands-onhome-geological-processes-basic-package

Lederman, N. G. (1992). Students' and teachers' conceptions of the nature of science: A review of the research. *Journal of Research in Science Teaching, 29*(4), 331–359. https://doi.org/10.1002/tea.3660290404

Lederman, N. G. (2007). Nature of science: Past, present and future. In S. K. Abell & N. G. Lederman (Eds.), *Handbook of research on science education* (pp. 831–880). Taylor & Francis Group. https://citeseerx.ist.psu.edu/viewdoc/download?doi=10.1.1.620.8583&rep=rep1&type=pdf

Lederman, N., & Abd-El-Khalick, F. (2002). Avoiding de-natured science: Activities that promote understandings of the nature of science. In *The nature of science in science education, rationales and strategies* (pp. 83–126). Kluwer Academic Publisher. http://dx.doi.org/10.1007/0-306-47215-5_5

Lederman, N. G., & Lederman, J. S. (2019). Teaching and learning nature of scientific knowledge: Is it Déjà vu all over again? *Disciplinary and Interdisciplinary Science Education Research, 1*(1), 1–9. https://doi.org/10.1186/s43031-019-0002-0

Lederman, N. G., Lederman, J. S., & Antink, A. (2013). Nature of science and scientific inquiry as contexts for the learning of science and achievement of scientific literacy. *International Journal of Education in Mathematics, Science and Technology, 1*(3), 138–147. https://files.eric.ed.gov/fulltext/ED543992.pdf

Lombrozo, T., Thanukos, A., & Weisberg, M. (2008). The importance of understanding the nature of science for accepting evolution. *Evolution Education & Outreach, 1*(3), 290–298. https://doi.org/10.1007/s12052-008-0061-8

Martin-Hansen, L. (2002). Defining inquiry. *The Science Teacher, 69*(2), 34–37.

McComas, W. F. (2020). Principal elements of nature of science: Informing science teaching while dispelling the Myths. In *Nature of science in science instruction* (pp. 35–65). Springer International Publishing. https://doi.org/10.1007/978-3-030-57239-6_3

National Academy of Sciences. (1998). *Teaching about evolution and the nature of science.* The National Academies Press. https://doi.org/10.17226/5787.

National Research Council. (2000). *Inquiry and the national science education standards: A guide for teaching and learning.* National Academies Press.

National Research Council. (2015). *Guide to implementing the next generation science standards.* National Academies Press.

NGSS Lead States. (2013). *Next generation science standards: For states, by states.* National Academies Press.

National Science Teaching Association. (2020). *Position statement: Nature of science.* National Science Teaching Association. https://www.nsta.org/nstas-official-positions/nature-science

Pandya, R., & Dibner, K. A. (2018). *Learning through citizen science: Enhancing opportunities by design.* The National Academies Press.

Roskinsky, N. M. (2000). Setting the table. *Odyssey, 9*(8), 11.

Rutherford, F. J., & Ahlgren, A. (1991). *Science for all Americans.* Oxford University Press.

Sterling, D. (1996). Discovering Mendeleev's model. *Science Scope, 20*(2), 26–30.

Stokes, D. E. (1997). *Pasteur's quadrant: Basic science and technological innovation.* Brookings Institution Press.

CHAPTER 2

CROSSCUTTING CONCEPTS

The Common Thread Often Hidden

Patrick Enderle, Scott Cohen
Georgia State University

Marissa Murdock
Rockdale County Public Schools, Georgia

Crosscutting Concepts (CCCs) are considered the more challenging aspect of the Three-Dimensional Learning for science teachers to teach. This chapter describes some insights about teaching with the CCCs gained from research and classroom experiences. We also share resources that we found helpful in online learning environments. Therefore, our recommendations in this chapter are relevant for both face-to-face and online teaching contexts. We describe an example science lesson sequence that consistently uses a focal CCC as a tool to explore an interesting phenomenon and support their engagement in scientific practices and learning of disciplinary core ideas.

RATIONALE

The release of the *Next Generation Science Standards* (NGSS; NGSS Lead States, 2013b), coupled with the guidance of *A Framework for K–12 Science Education* (National Research Council [NRC], 2012), spurred a significant shift in the way districts, schools, and teachers envisioned, designed, and implemented science

Teaching and Learning Online: Science for Secondary Grade Levels, pages 15–30.

instruction. Guided by a conceptual framework emphasizing science learning that focused on making sense of natural phenomena, these standards, and the various state-level adaptations they encouraged, broaden the view of what science learning should include. Rather than focusing on an extensive collection of concepts within each discipline while separately considering the historical, philosophical, and investigative aspects of science, the new vision for science education offered a more synthesized conceptualization known as Three-Dimensional Learning (3DL). 3DL environments engage students in "figuring out" explanations for various scientific phenomena by engaging students in several inquiry and explanatory practices. These practices are shared across science and engineering fields. As students engage in figuring things out, they leverage conceptual resources, including discipline-specific core ideas and broader ideas shared across the sciences, but with unique compositions based on the focal phenomenon (Schwarz et al., 2017).

The 3DL framework for science education presents a fundamental change for science education. Student-led activity and sensemaking are foregrounded through science practices. Historically positioned as the significant foci of learning, science concepts are reshaped into tools for these learning activities. Nevertheless, as with most significant change efforts, schools and teachers need time to learn deeply about this new vision in order to develop ways to plan and implement instruction that aligns with the 3DL framework (Fick et al., 2019a; Sinapuelas et al., 2019). A limited number of resources existed, so many teachers needed to learn how to adapt their curriculum to meet the 3DL vision. Driven by the emphasis on scientific practices, much work in science education research and resource development focuses on elaborating these practices' dynamics and knowledge functions and how to anchor instruction in them (Enderle et al., 2015; McNeill & Krajcik, 2011; Windschitl & Thompson, 2013). Although re-envisioned to focus on broader conceptual understanding rather than collections of factual knowledge, the disciplinary core ideas remain the most familiar dimension of the 3DL for most teachers (NGSS Lead States, 2013b). However, the third dimension, the crosscutting concepts, represents a challenge for many teachers and curriculum developers since all seven of these broad ideas are generically accessible but rarely focused on or addressed as teachers develop expertise in particular science disciplines (Rehmat et al., 2019).

In light of this challenge with the crosscutting concepts (CCCs), the first and second authors developed a new course that helps pre-service and in-service teachers develop deeper understandings of each of the seven crosscutting concepts identified in the *Framework* and *NGSS*. The third author was a teacher in this course who excelled in their work and growth, contributing to how teachers learn to incorporate the crosscutting concepts. So, the course could serve teachers in face-to-face and virtual programs, we intentionally designed the experience as an asynchronous, online course that could work with teachers' differing schedules. We had to develop a collection of resources useful in online learning environments for the teachers and us from this design decision. The examples and resources described later in the chapter are drawn from the work of this course and continued collaborations extending from that experience.

THEORETICAL BACKGROUND

The *Framework* (NRC, 2012) and the *NGSS* (NGSS Lead States, 2013b) describe seven different crosscutting concepts (CCCs) when exploring the third dimension of the 3DL framework. Appendix G of the *NGSS* provides further insight into the definition, elements, and developmental learning progressions associated with each crosscutting concept. The learning progressions are instrumental in helping teachers understand the depth and detail that should be addressed when using the CCCs in either elementary, middle, or high school grade bands. The CCCs include:

1. Patterns—The recognition and use of patterns drive much of the scientific enterprise, including identifying compelling phenomena and developing investigable questions to explore relevant relationships. Patterns also serve as the foundation for the predictive capabilities of scientific models, theories, and laws.
2. Systems and system models—All scientific work endeavors to study and understand the multitude of systems that comprise the natural universe. By identifying and defining essential elements of systems, scientists can develop models that focus on elements of interest related to their lines of inquiry, using these models to test and explain relationships among them.
3. Flows of energy and matter—As science endeavors to understand various systems, the fundamental components of energy and matter, both in various forms, move through those systems in particular ways. The movement and transformation of energy and matter in a system provide insight into other important relationships and capabilities.
4. Structure and function—The objects or "things" (e.g., organisms, stars, atoms, rocks, gases) that make up a system are structured in particular ways that determine their functional capabilities or characteristics (e.g., wings allowing for flight; hydronium/hydroxide structures in acids/bases; Sun, being the most prominent object and at the center, induces gravitation forces that shape the solar system).
5. Cause and effect—A large part of the scientific endeavor is to understand the nature of the relationships and interactions between different system elements. Exploring the causal relationships and their observed effects focuses on identifying the active mechanisms that connect the interactions to particular outcomes and using those relationships to predict and explain outcomes in other contexts.
6. Stability and change—Across the various systems that scientists explore, maintaining conditions in stable states and how periods and rates

of change emerge to provide a critical understanding of those systems, enhancing the explanatory and predictive qualities of the models developed for them.

7. Scale, proportion, and quantity—A fundamental aspect of any system and how they are described includes recognizing the level of scale involved (from subatomic to astronomical frames) and proportional relationships occurring at those different levels of scale, since system interactions at one scaler level (e.g., Atoms and molecules) will influence the functional dynamics of system structures (e.g., Cellular organelles and activities) and the nature of causal relationships among system components (e.g., Breaking of chemical bonds in ATP to release energy for cellular processes).

Although the seven concepts are listed separately, their overlap and the interconnectedness of their elements are evident in the descriptions provided above and elsewhere (NGSS Lead States, 2013b; NRC, 2012). Indeed, their interconnectedness, both with each other and the other dimensions of 3DL, serves as the reason for emphasizing them so that students can make connections across units and courses of study (Fick, 2018; Rivet et al., 2016). The more expansive role of the CCCs in connecting science activity and knowledge across multiple domains builds upon and enhances other conceptual collections that have been described in previous standards efforts (Common Themes; Rutherford & Ahlgren, 1991) and scholarly areas (Nature of Science; Flick & Lederman, 2004). As such, these big ideas are useful in helping students learn about aspects of science that are not readily apparent in the methods that science instruction has been traditionally implemented, both face-to-face and virtually (Duschl, 2012).

Rivet et al. (2016) described four different ways educators could view the functional role of the CCCs in science teaching and learning, which have direct implications for instruction. Teachers can use the concepts as *lenses* to explore various phenomena entails understanding the components of a particular crosscutting concept (e.g., systems have boundaries, inputs and outputs, and interactions of components that can be included in a system model), have students consider and describe those components for specific phenomena, and then use more discipline-specific concepts to elaborate the focal phenomenon further. Teachers can also use the CCCs as *bridges* to connect different curricular areas within and across scientific disciplines. (e.g., the atomic structure of different chemicals and the functional dynamics of chemical bonding determine their functions within organisms, which influences the cellular structures evolved to process those chemicals to support the functions of the overall organisms.) A third way of viewing the CCCs involves them being conceptual *tools* for students to use when engaged in scientific practice and sensemaking, using them to develop more sophisticated understandings of those practices in applied settings (e.g., when developing and evaluating the design of investigations, students consider how their investigation documents the flow of energy and matter within the system of interest and at what scale it is occurring).

The fourth metaphor Rivet et al. (2016) identified involves using the CCCs as *rules* for thinking and communicating about science, focusing on using the components of the CCCs to organize the ways they think about and communicate about particular phenomena. These ways of viewing the functions of the CCCs in the science classroom offer potential guidance for teachers when considering their use, understanding that all four views should be considered as teachers work on weaving CCCs throughout their instruction. Another caveat when planning for the CCCs involves always being mindful of using approaches that make the most sense for the students in their classrooms and the contexts in which they are applying them. That is, some CCCs and approaches to them may be better suited for certain phenomena/core ideas, times of the school year, or different student communities than others (Fick, 2018; Rivet et al., 2016).

A related challenge for helping science teachers implement 3DL instruction involves the lack of empirical research exploring the best ways to teach with and about the CCCs (Fick et al., 2019b). Researchers have determined that teachers tend to focus more on core ideas and practices, viewing the role of the CCCs as secondary to the other two (Rehmat et al., 2019). Some challenges with understanding the role of CCCs in science teaching and learning include critiques that this collection of ideas still implies a monolithic view of 'science' as a singular endeavor, rather than the rich and varied knowledge pursuits researchers engage in across the 'sciences' (Osborne et al., 2018). Chesnutt et al. (2019) identified a critical issue involving the more implied positioning of CCCs in standards documents than explicit identification of science practices and disciplinary core ideas. However, another finding from this group's work demonstrated the power of emphasizing CCCs. They determined a strong positive significant relationship between students' understanding of the CCC on scale and proportion and students' achievement on major science and mathematics assessments across grade levels.

CHAPTER FOCUS

We offer a few considerations for teachers to keep in mind as they work to implement CCCs into their lesson plans and instruction. Then, we describe some general resources that we find helpful for thinking about and teaching lessons emphasizing CCCs in conjunction with DCIs and SEPs. Finally, we describe an example lesson activity grounded in using a CCC as a 'lens' to begin exploring a relevant and engaging phenomenon.

Considerations for Teaching With the CCCs

The lens metaphor (Rivet et al., 2016) is particularly useful in planning and teaching science lessons with the CCCs. Using them as a lens positions these concepts as *tools* students can apply to a large variety of phenomena to begin making sense of them and pushing their thinking. Further, students will have some level of previously constructed understanding about these concepts through science learning experiences in the elementary grades and out-of-school experiences. We recommend that when a teacher first engages with a specific CCC at the start of the school year, they take the time to include some direct instruction about that CCC so that students can begin to understand some of the elements of that CCC. For example, the *Flows of Energy and Matter* includes understanding different types of matter and energy and understanding transformations, flows, and conservations.

If a teacher uses the NGSS directly, then the developers have already identified a particular CCC for each performance expectation. However, for teachers in many states (including where we work), the state education agencies and legislatures chose to develop their versions of science standards based on the *Framework*, so the NGSS performance expectations do not directly align. In such situations (and even in NGSS states), we suggest that science teacher assert their expertise and select one of the seven CCCs to focus on when developing a lesson sequence for a particular standard. One challenge with the CCCs noted by researchers and teachers alike concerns the fact that these concepts overlap together with the core ideas and practices and each other (Chesnutt et al., 2019; NGSS Lead States, 2013b; Rivet et al., 2016). Teachers often note how several CCCs apply in any particular lesson. We agree that this occurrence is challenging but also trust each teacher to use their professional knowledge to select the most accessible CCC for the lessons they develop and make sense to their students. As such, teachers should focus on one CCC per lesson sequence to make sure students have the opportunity to sincerely engage with that concept along with the core idea and relevant scientific practices.

Another consideration teachers should keep in mind as they teach the CCCs is that it is important to be clear in addressing them (Chesnutt et al., 2019; Nordine & Lee, 2021; Rehmat et al., 2019). Indeed, the NGSS also identifies this consideration as a challenge when developing 3DL instruction and asserts that CCCs must be evident in the instructional tools, pedagogical approaches used, and assessments (NGSS Lead States, 2013b). This need for explicitness can be facilitated by including specific items addressing the CCC in the various assessments and instructional plans they develop. When developing or adapting items to address the CCCs, teachers should be mindful of using terminology related to the focal CCC (Nordine & Lee, 2021).

Finally, the learning progressions developed in Appendix G of the NGSS (NGSS Lead States, 2013b) provide teachers guidance on what aspects of particular CCCs should be emphasized for elementary, middle, and high school learners. The statements in these learning progressions also indicate the depth to which students should learn about each of those aspects within those grade bands. However, a challenge arises that this guidance is only distinguished to the middle and high school grade bands rather than to specific grade levels (with the exception of elementary) or science disciplines. The NGSS performance expectations provide a small amount of information connecting the CCC to particular DCIs. Although these resources can help orient teachers as they plan and deliver their instruction, teachers' experience with their students, classrooms, and school communities also play a critical role in determining how to implement the CCCs in their lessons.

The phenomena selected for lessons serve as connections to students' lives. As such, certain CCCs may make more sense for certain phenomena within certain community contexts or times of the year. For example, if a teacher teaches the life cycles of plants or seasonal weather patterns during fall when leaves change colors, then she may want to use the Stability and Change CCC. However, some communities do not experience a very noticeable change in the color of plants, so that would not be a relevant phenomenon to use in those places, which may mean that the CCC of Structure & Function may be more useful to teach about plant life cycles. Thus, incorporating CCCs into science teaching will be uniquely shaped by grade level, discipline, and the communities where students live.

Resources for Teaching and Learning the CCCs

This NSTA resource our teachers found helpful with their growing CCC understanding includes videos of several recorded webinars provided by NSTA on their YouTube™ channel (Mendez, n.d.). Although a few years old, these presentations provide a rich overview of each CCC as they explore each CCC's general components and how they functionally apply across particular phenomena and contexts. These overview segments typically span the first 30–40 minutes of the presentation and then explore the learning progressions and some example lessons for the remainder of the webinar. Another excellent source for accessible videos about the CCCs is the *Bozeman Science* website (Anderson, n.d.). These brief videos, which are 10–15 minutes long, provide teachers a briefer overview of each CCC that can help orient a teacher to a CCC they are preparing to teach. If a teacher would like to use these videos during synchronous instructional time, they should consider identifying the particular segments they would like to use. These smaller segments are easier to weave throughout the phases of a lesson, such as during a 'bell ringer' or 'exit ticket' activity, particularly during the Engage or Explore phase. They could also be used for brief pauses during the body of a lesson in the Explain or Elaborate phase to provide 'just-in-time' teaching if students appear to be struggling with considering a CCC for a particular phenomenon during the lesson activities.

Another valuable CCC resource involves a set of graphic organizers that focus on each CCC. Published by Peacock & Peacock (2017), this set of eight Power-Point slides offers valuable tools that can be adapted for multiple uses in various online instructional approaches (Workosky, 2017). Although we focus on this specific resource, a general online search for CCC graphic organizers should produce several variations that teachers can evaluate for the appropriateness for their students. Each organizer begins with identifying the scientific phenomenon that is the foundation for a 3DL lesson and offers an intriguing context for students to explore while working towards the focus of the targeted learning standards. Each organizer contains multiple text boxes connected in different configurations suitable to the focal CCC. These collections of text boxes represent the components for each CCC and are mostly numbered to provide a suggested order in completing them.

As slides, these graphic organizers are easy to incorporate into presentations shared in synchronous virtual classrooms while also sharing them as virtual worksheets for students to complete individually, in small group work, or as a whole class activity. A graphic organizer could be expanded into a scaffolded activity by making each component text box (or pair depending on the CCC) an individual slide in a synchronous presentation or as activities/assessment checkpoints within a slide set, such as Nearpod™ with the digital whiteboard functionality.

STEM Teaching Tools is a free online resource helpful for developing 3D instruction includes a collection of question stems developed by a well-respected organization of science educators that publish numerous resource briefs for science teachers. These briefs synthesize extensive collections of research into 2-page research briefs focused on various topics, many of which contain links to access further resources across the internet. This particular brief, Brief #41, offers a collection of question stems that can be used to help students reflect on their understanding of the CCCs (Penuel & Van Horne, 2018). For each CCC, this resource identifies several instructional scenarios where teachers could incorporate one of the questions to have students reflect on how that CCC applies or helps explain the events in the scenario. For each scenario, the brief provides multiple question stems containing blank spaces where teachers would add more specific information from the lesson. These question stems can be helpful in planning several phases in the lessons, particularly as parts of 'bell ringers' and 'exit tickets,' to make the CCC more apparent and connected to the SEPs and DCIs.

An Example Lesson Activity

This lesson sequence was developed for an 8th grade Physical Science classroom. The overall unit addressed gravity, electricity, and magnetism concepts and used roller coaster design as the anchoring phenomenon for the entire unit. Several lessons prior to this example explored how roller coasters use the force of gravity to speed up the train of cars relying on transformations of potential and kinetic energy and how electricity was used to help the train overcome gravity. For this lesson, roller coasters that use electromagnets to propel the train were the investigative phenomenon to explore using the focal CCC of *Energy & Matter* and the DCI of *Forces & Interactions*.

The lesson begins by showing students a collection of pictures of different kinds of roller coasters, including those that rely on engine-powered chains to move the train and those that use electromagnets. These static pictures could also be replaced with a short video showing these types of roller coasters, which can help create a more dynamic online learning environment. Students are asked to connect back to previous lessons and ways they have previously discussed how so much matter (the train) can move so fast. They are asked to consider where the energy comes from to move all of that matter. In a face-to-face environment, students could be asked to turn and talk to their neighbors and be ready to share some responses. In online environments, these paired discussions can be a bit more challenging to facilitate if the virtual platform being used has limits on breakout room features. In those cases, the teacher can ask students to post comments in the chatbox feature. Students are also encouraged to share their experiences of what it feels like to ride in the different types of roller coasters. Teachers should have multiple students share their ideas and experiences and document them on a digital whiteboard or a notes document shared with the class. Teachers can begin focusing on ideas that show how students perceive the flow of energy and matter in the electromagnetic roller coaster to set the stage for the next phase.

After collecting students' ideas, the teacher focuses on the electromagnet roller coaster and asks students to remember how magnets act on matter and with each other (ex.—repulsion of similar poles). Building on this focus, the teacher can directly pose or use students' thinking to develop the question, 'How could we make an electromagnetic roller coaster go faster?' This larger question is then further elaborated using the focal CCC by posing two sub-questions: "How could the amount of matter in the roller coaster be changed?" and "What role might the flow of energy play in making it go faster?" These questions should be included in the presentation materials and any shared notes documents to anchor students' thinking and discourse in an online context. Again, teachers should rely on the online discourse structures and interactions their students are comfortable with, such as breakout rooms, chatbox postings, or sharing virtual whiteboard spaces. Students are given opportunities to talk and think with each other before sharing ideas with the whole class. As teachers collect these ideas and discuss them as a class, they can move the discussion to consider how matter and energy interact in electromagnets specifically.

The next phase of the lesson involves the teacher providing more direct instruction about electromagnets by using the lens of *Energy & Matter* to explain how they work. This direct instruction would address how electromagnets function using solenoid structures as an example, including how the directional flow of energy determines the direction of the magnetic field (e.g., the 'right-hand rule'). The teacher then explores how the electric current flowing around the solenoid produces a force that makes the magnetic domains of the atoms in the metal align in a particular direction. This alignment of the atoms produces the magnetic field, resulting in the metal core of the solenoid becoming magnetized, which the teacher can highlight as an interaction between the energy and matter in the system. The teacher should also point out that this interaction does not cause a physical change in the metal, demonstrated by the loss of magnetism when the electric current is stopped. For online classrooms, this information should be included in the presentation materials used, such as slide presentations or video resources preferred by the teacher, directly using the language of the CCC provided in Appendix G of the NGSS (NGSS Lead States, 2013a).

The direct instruction segment, framed through the lens of *Energy & Matter*, provides the framing for the next phase when the teacher demonstrates how an electromagnet can be made of simple household materials, including a battery, coated electrical wire, and an iron nail or rod. Using this model system, the teacher can ask students how to manipulate it to increase the electromagnet's strength. This question allows students to engage in the SEP of *Planning & Conducting Investigations*, and the teacher brings the lens of *Energy & Matter* back by asking to follow up questions like 'How could we change the energy and matter in this magnet to increase its strength?' and 'What data can we collect about energy and matter that would tell us how strong the magnet is?' In face-to-face classrooms, teachers guide students to consider measuring the number of paper clips picked up by the magnet to indicate the electromagnet's strength. Teachers can use a simulation for online spaces, such as the Magnets and Electromagnets simulation created by PhET™ Interactive Simulations (2001) to serve as that investigation context and tool. If using the simulation rather than physical materials, the teacher should let students explore the simulation and see how to make changes in energy (adjusting battery voltage) and matter (adjusting the number of coils of wire). Instead of using the number of paper clips picked up as an indicator of magnetic strength, the simulation includes meters that measure magnetic field strength.

Once students collect data from manipulating variables in the electromagnet, they can shift to engaging in the SEP of *Analyzing Data* while still using *Energy & Matter* as a lens to make sense of the data. This analysis aims to develop evidence that students can use to develop a claim to the original question concerning how to make an electromagnetic roller coaster go faster. That evidence includes the analysis of the data set, which should also contain an appropriate graphical representation, and an interpretation of the analysis that points to the relationships between energy and matter that emerge from the data set (e.g., as the number of coils of wire [matter]/voltage of the battery [energy] increase, so does the number of paper clips picked up by the magnet [magnet strength]). This analysis work includes students working with digital resources, such as a spreadsheet program to record their data and generate graphs.

Once students develop their evidence from their data, they can shift to the SEP of *Arguing from Evidence* while still using *Energy & Matter* to guide their reasoning towards developing a claim. Students develop their arguments on whiteboards using a common format for structuring scientific arguments, either C-E-R (McNeill & Krajcik, 2011) or C-E-J (Enderle et al., 2015). However, following the advice provided earlier, teachers should make clear to students that as they construct their reasoning/justification section of their whiteboard, they need to include how the concepts of energy and matter helped them develop their claim from their evidence. This guidance should be provided through talk and written elements on any anchoring material for this stage of activity.

Again, for online classrooms, the discourse structures (including argument whiteboards) to which students respond well should be used in place of physical whiteboards. Digital resources can include students developing a shared set of presentation slides that contain the information for each section of the arguments but could also include the development of short presentation videos where students explain the argument their group constructed. Typically, this investigation would shift to students presenting their group's argument board to their peers and having the groups engage with each other in a critique of their arguments. However, many online platforms are not well suited to this format of student interactions, so the teacher should consider what presentation/feedback interaction structures work well in their online classroom. These structures could involve having groups present to the whole class one by one or posting to a shared classroom space and having students leave digital comments and questions for the group to consider.

Following these phases of lesson activities that have mostly occurred within small student groups, the teacher may want to assess students individually on the understandings they have developed through the investigation. The graphic organizers described earlier (Peacock & Peacock, 2017) can be used in this way so that each student can describe the electromagnet system they used in the investigation. The *Energy & Matter* graphic organizer asks students to consider the energy and matter inputs and outputs of a system and the processes that connect them. Focusing on only the solid matter and energy boxes, the inputs (nonmagnetic iron rod/electrical current) and outputs (magnetized iron rod/magnetic energy) are connected by a process description highlighting how the flow of electricity forces the magnetic domains of iron atoms to align within the rod, resulting in a magnetic field. Follow-up questions in the graphic organizer provide students to demonstrate their understanding of different aspects of the *Energy & Matter* CCC in relation to this system, including conservation, flow, and transformations.

Reflections

Considering the example lesson sequence provided, we would like to draw attention to the various points where the CCC was used as a lens and supported the exploration of the phenomenon and engagement in SEPs using DCIs as well. Throughout the lesson, several different elements that could be considered assessment points also serve as points where the CCC is emphasized. The CCC is the foundation for several collections of question prompts that are used to access students' prior knowledge and drive their thinking about roller coasters and electromagnets. These questions also serve as opportunities for informal/formal formative assessments. The CCC also guided the design of an investigation into electromagnet strength by focusing students' attention on variables and data related to energy and matter. If teachers have students prepare an anchoring product for this phase, such as an investigation proposal (Enderle et al., 2015), items that focus on the CCC and its role in the design should be included in the product template.

The products students create from engaging in the explanatory SEPs (i.e., Constructing Explanations, Arguing from Evidence, and Developing & Using Models) also provide teachers more formal assessments where students can be asked to incorporate the focal CCC into their products. Just as the Reasoning/ Justification section of students' arguments in the lesson above needed to include statements addressing the role of energy and matter concepts, teachers can also highlight and include specific items asking students about how a CCC helps clarify parts of the explanatory product, such as different interactions represented in a student-developed model. Graphic organizers grounded in particular CCCs afford teachers tools for individual summative assessment opportunities for students to demonstrate their understanding. Thus, as teachers work to plan and implement CCCs more consistently throughout their science teaching, they should look to different assessment points in their lessons as access points to ensure the CCCs receive explicit attention.

A final reflection for this chapter concerns some issues teachers may encounter when working in online environments. The overarching challenge in online classrooms involves changes in the nature and quality of opportunities for students to talk and write with each other (discourse interactions). The design of the online platform and the mixture of synchronous/asynchronous instruction expected by districts shape how much teachers can implement such opportunities. The CCCs are often easily incorporated and used to frame these interactions, so teachers should be flexible in planning them but include explicit attention to the CCCs during them. This attention can be facilitated by including CCC-focused questions and items directly in the materials used to present and those students work with during the lesson activities.

SUMMARY AND REFLECTION

We sincerely hope that the resources, descriptions, and suggestions for the CCCs' usage in online contexts provided in this chapter will help support science teachers as they continue to develop innovative online instructional environments that explicitly address the CCCs in concert with disciplinary core ideas and scientific practices. The considerations and tips for teaching the CCCs should serve as guideposts for science teachers to follow and not strict rules. As seen from the overview of relevant research, researchers and educators are still in the early stages of investigating and developing evidence that highlights effective ways to teach the CCCs in concert with the other two dimensions of the 3DL framework. Therefore, we encourage science teachers to be creative, attempt different approaches, including ideas from other chapters in this book, and trust in their professional expertise to evaluate those attempts and adapt them in ways that further support their students' learning. By focusing on various CCCs across different contexts, teachers can help their students make deeper connections across topics and disciplines, helping them appreciate the dynamic way of knowing that we value and call Science!

TIPS AND ADVICE

- Focus on one CCC for each lesson sequence with multiple opportunities for students to engage with it.
- Be explicit by directly addressing the CCC throughout all phases of the lesson.
- Use formative assessment items to check for students' CCC understandings during the lesson.
- Take time, particularly at the beginning of the school year, to focus lesson segments on directly teaching about the CCCs themselves.
- What we assess shows what we value, so be sure to include CCC items in most of your assessments.

RESOURCE NOTES

Name of Resource	Primary Website	How to Locate the Resource Online
Appendix G of the Next Generation Science Standards	https://www.next-genscience.org/	Go to https://www.nextgenscience.org/. Scroll the mouse over The Standards, located on the top left-center, and click appendices—open appendix G. https://www.nextgenscience.org/sites/default/files/resource/files/Appendix%20G%20-%20Crosscutting%20Concepts%20FINAL%20edited%204.10.13.pdf
Bozeman Science CCC Videos	http://www.bozemanscience.com	Go to http://www.bozemanscience.com/. Scroll the mouse over the video on the top center screen and click on NGSS—Next Generation Science Standards. Click on one of the CCCs for the video. http://www.bozemanscience.com/next-generation-science-standards
Magnets and Electromagnets simulation created by PhET	https://phet.colorado.edu	Go to https://phet.colorado.edu. In the top right corner, use the search magnifying glass to search for Magnets and Electromagnets. https://phet.colorado.edu/sims/cheerpj/faraday/latest/faraday.html?simulation=magnets-and-electromagnets
NSTA YouTube Webinar Videos	https://www.nsta.org	Go to https://www.nsta.org. Enter NGSS Crosscutting Concepts Collection in the search bar, then click on the proper link. Scroll down to choose the archived webinar on the CCC of your choice. https://my.nsta.org/collection/46124
STEM Teaching Tools	http://stemteachingtools.org	Go to https://stemteachingtools.org. Click on the Tools button located on the top left-center. Scroll down until you find practice brief #41 http://stemteachingtools.org/brief/41

Name of Resource	Primary Website	How to Locate the Resource Online
Using the Crosscutting Concepts to scaffold student thinking & CCC Graphic Organizer	https://www.nsta.org	Go to https://www.nsta.org. Enter "Using the Crosscutting Concepts to scaffold student thinking" in the search bar, then click on the link matching the title. The graphic organizer can be found on this page by clicking on the Google Slides link on the first sentence of the third paragraph. https://www.nsta.org/blog/using-crosscutting-concepts-scaffold-student-thinking

DISCUSSION QUESTIONS

1. In what ways could you adapt the online resources you already regularly use with your students to directly address the crosscutting concepts in concert with disciplinary core ideas and scientific practices?
2. How have you learned about each crosscutting concept, and what can those reflections help you consider for your students' learning?
3. Considering your current assessment practices, what formative and summative assessments offer the most accessible way for you to incorporate explicit items addressing the crosscutting concepts?

REFERENCES

Anderson, P. (n.d.). *NGSS—Next generation science standards.* Bozeman Science. http://www.bozemanscience.com/next-generation-science-standards

Chesnutt, K., Jones, M. G., Corin, E. N., Hite, R., Childers, G., Perez, M. P., Cayton, E., & Ennes, M. (2019). Crosscutting concepts and achievement: Is a sense of size and scale related to achievement in science and mathematics. *Journal of Research on Science Teaching, 56*(3), 302–321. https://doi.org/10.1002/tea.21511

Duschl, R. A. (2012). The second dimension—Crosscutting concepts. *Science Teacher, 79*(2), 34–38.

Enderle, P., Bickel, R., Gleim, L., Granger, E., Grooms, J., Hester, M., Sampson, V., & Southerland, S. (2015). *Argument-driven inquiry in life science: laboratory investigations for grades 6–8.* NSTA Press.

Enderle, P., Schellinger, J., Hagan, C., Okan, O., Granger, E., & Bevis, T. (2021, April 7–10). *Which hat should I wear? Examining teacher positioning and engagement in professional development* [Paper presentation]. 2021 International Conference for the National Association for Research in Science Teaching (NARST), virtual.

Fick, S. J. (2018). What does three-dimensional teaching and learning look like?: Examining the potential for crosscutting concepts to support the development of science knowledge. *Science Education, 102*(1), 5–35. https://doi.org/10.1002/sce.21313

Fick, S. J., Barth-Cohen, L., Rivet, A., Cooper, M., Buell, J., & Badrinarayan, A. (2019a). Supporting students' learning of science content and practices through the intentional incorporation and scaffolding of crosscutting concept. In S. J. Fick, J. Nordine, K. W. McElhaney (Eds.), *Summit for examining the potential for crosscutting concepts to support three-dimensional learning* (pp. 15–26). University of Virginia. https://curry.virginia.edu/ccc-summit

Fick, S. J., Nordine, J., & McElhaney, K. W. (2019b). The need for a summit for examining the potential for crosscutting concepts to support three-dimensional science learning. In S. J. Fick, J. Nordine, K. W. McElhaney (Eds.), *Summit for examining the potential for crosscutting concepts to support three-dimensional learning*, (pp. 4–11). University of Virginia. https://curry.virginia.edu/ccc-summit

Flick, L. B., & Lederman, N. G. (2004). *Scientific inquiry and nature of science.* Kluwer Academic Publishers.

McNeill, K. L., & Krajcik, J. (2011). *Supporting grade 5–8 students in constructing explanations in science: The claim, evidence and reasoning framework for talk and writing.* Pearson Allyn & Bacon.

Mendez, F. (n.d.). *NGSS Crosscutting concepts collection.* National Science Teacher Association. https://my.nsta.org/collection/46124

National Research Council (NRC). (2012). *A framework for K–12 science education: Practices, crosscutting concepts, and core ideas.* National Academies Press.

NGSS Lead States. (2013a). *Appendix G—Crosscutting concepts.* National Academies Press.

NGSS Lead States. (2013b). *Next generation science standards: For states, by states.* National Academies Press.

Nordine, J., & Lee, O. (2021). *Crosscutting concepts: Strengthening science and engineering learning.* NSTA Press.

Osborne, J., Rafanelli, S., & Kind, P. (2018). Toward a more coherent model for science education than the crosscutting concepts of the next generation science standards: The affordances of styles of reasoning. *Journal of Research on Science Teaching, 55*(7), 962–981. https://doi.org/10.1002/tea.21460

Peacock, J., & Peacock, A. (2017, May 24). *Using the crosscutting concepts to scaffold student thinking.* National Science Teacher Association. https://www.nsta.org/blog/using-crosscutting-concepts-scaffold-student-thinking

Penuel, W. R., & Van Horne, K. (2018, February). *Prompts for integrating crosscutting concepts into assessment and instruction.* STEM Teaching Tool. http://stemteachingtools.org/brief/41

PhET Interactive Simulations. (2001). *Magnets and Electromagnets.* https://phet.colorado.edu/sims/cheerpj/faraday/latest/faraday.html?simulation=magnets-and-electromagnets

Rehmat, A. P., Lee, O., Nordine, J., Novak, A. M., Osborne, J., & Willard, T. (2019). Modeling the role of crosscutting concepts for strengthening science learning for all students. In S. J. Fick, J. Nordine, K. W. McElhaney (Eds.), *Summit for examining the potential for crosscutting concepts to support three-dimensional learning* (pp. 66–73). University of Virginia. https://curry.virginia.edu/ccc-summit

Rivet, A. E., Weiser, G., Lyu, X., Li, Y., & Rojas-Perilla, D. (2016). What are crosscutting concepts in science? Four metaphorical perspectives. In C. K. Looi, J. L. Polman, U. Cress, & P. Reimann (Eds.) *Transforming learning, empowering learners: The International Conference of the Learning Sciences (ICLS) 2016, Volume 2.* International Society of the Learning Sciences.

Rutherford, F. J., & Ahlgren, A. (1991). *Science for all Americans.* Oxford University Press.

Schwarz, C. V., Passmore, C., & Reiser, B. J. (2017). Moving beyond "knowing about" science to making sense of the world. In B. J. Reiser, C. V. Schwarz, & C. Passmore (Eds.), *Helping students make sense of the world using next generation science and engineering practices* (pp. 3–21). National Science Teachers Association.

Sinapuelas, M. L., Lardy, C., Korb, M. A., Bae, C. L., & DiStefano, R. (2019). Developing a three-dimensional view of science teaching: A tool to support pre-service teacher discourse. *Journal of Science Teacher Education, 30*(2), 101–121. https://doi.org/1 0.1080/1046560X.2018.1537059

Windschitl, M., & Thompson, J. (2013). The modeling toolkit: Making student thinking visible with public representations. *The Science Teacher, 80*(6), 63–69. https://stem-tlnet.org/sites/default/files/2021-11/The-Modeling-Toolkit_Full.pdf

Workosky, C. (2017, May 24). *Using the crosscutting concepts to scaffold student thinking.* National Science Teacher Association. https://www.nsta.org/blog/using-cross-cutting-concepts-scaffold-student-thinking

CHAPTER 3

ISSUES OF DIVERSITY, EQUITY, AND INCLUSIVITY IN ONLINE SECONDARY STEM EDUCATION

Anne Mangahas

University of La Verne

Much of education has been pushed to virtual environments for various reasons. Online STEM learning for secondary grade levels has proven particularly challenging due to technological access, equity in the curriculum, and the need to adapt content for neurodiverse learners. This chapter explores the impacts of (a) digital redlining on historically underserved groups and the need for accessible curriculum, (b) inclusive online secondary STEM curriculum, and (c) humanistic student-level supports through social-emotional learning and its role in secondary STEM curriculum.

Online secondary Science, Technology, Engineering, and Mathematics (STEM) education covers multiple facets. In order to promote its effectiveness in reaching all groups and prove to be an equitable platform by which all students are supported, various considerations need to be included. This chapter explores these various aspects of digital learning impacting students and provides solutions to these varied challenges. It further examines these elements, specifically technological access, equitable curriculum, and social-emotional learning.

Teaching and Learning Online: Science for Secondary Grade Levels, pages 31–44.

RATIONALE

STEM education has historically been perceived to be a values-free discipline. According to Lekka-Kowalik (2009), science is and cannot be laden-free since "relevant values are both cognitive and moral" (para. 1). The values embedded in sciences' ideological frameworks are based on the values and ideals of society and the scientists and educators that generate their interpretations of the natural world, making the practice less instrumental and more constructivist in its approach. In the same way, teachers' perspectives or beliefs may influence how scientific content is taught, spurred mainly from one's ideological mindsets (Mangahas, 2017). As such, STEM teachers need to approach how they teach science from a more inclusive framework.

According to Lichtenberger and George-Jackson (2012), students who took STEM courses at the secondary level and achieved better on science and math standardized tests "were significantly and positively related to an increased interest in STEM" (para. 1). Of this group, college aspirations were significant and those students with more interest in pursuing further education were more likely to major in a STEM field. Additionally, "male high school students were significantly more likely to have an early interest in STEM relative to their female peers, as were African-American high school students compared with White students" (para. 1). In contrast, students from low-income backgrounds were significantly more likely to be interested in STEM than their higher-income peers (Lichtenberger & George-Jackson, 2012).

Online learning has only amplified socioeconomic gaps because of various access issues. In addition to the content delivery platform, which may not be accessible to underserved populations due to several socioeconomic and systemic barriers, there is also how science has traditionally been taught through the lens of white-male-Eurocentrism, and the weed out culture promoting ableism that leaves students from marginalized groups at the younger ages finding it more challenging to connect with, gain interest, and achieve in the STEM disciplines. In this chapter, I hope to illuminate some of these areas in which progress can be made to address and mitigate the impacts of these factors that prohibit STEM achievement and provide solutions to enable greater access and inclusivity for online secondary curriculum.

THEORETICAL FRAMEWORK

Technological Redlining and Equitable Online Secondary STEM Curriculum

Digital platforming has caused millions of households to appreciate the importance of broadband. It has become the primary gateway in enabling access to a wide variety of services from school to work, telehealth, and connections with loved ones. Lack of access to these services particularly impacts historically underserved communities. The Pew Research Center estimates that those individuals without broadband access encompass over one-third of those individuals that identify as African-American or Black and over 40% as Latinx/Hispanic. According to current estimates, over 42 million people do not have such access to broadband, with approximately 75% of those households representing communities of color. In order to better understand how to improve remote learning access, it is relevant to explore the impacts of *digital redlining* on marginalized communities. According to the Robert Wood Foundation, the term refers to "major network providers systematically excluding low-income neighborhoods from broadband service—deploying only sub-standard, low-speed home Internet" (Lancaster, 2020, para. 2). One of the primary issues of households in underserved communities is a lack of choice amongst providers, with many having only one option for broadband. This lack of choice reduces competition and the opportunity to negotiate better service and more affordable options, leaving members of these underserved communities unable to receive upgrades (Lancaster, 2020). Reduced market competition in certain areas only highlights the systemic inequities present in the societal matrix, which more deeply perpetuate the disparities preventing marginalized communities from advancement. More than a renaming of the digital divide, *digital redlining* is distinct in that it represents a "set of education policies, investment decisions, and IT practices that actively create and maintain class boundaries through structures that discriminate against groups…whose consequences reinforce existing class structures" (Gilliard, 2019, para 10). Historical redlining that resulted from the National Housing Act of 1934 created disparities in access to schools, libraries, and homeownership. Digital redlining is integrated into educational technology in reproducing the same types of discriminatory practices. According to Brown (2018), this "lack of access to technology creates a technology divide that begins at the elementary educational level and impacts students' postsecondary educational careers. A more troubling issue is that a relationship exists between the use of digital media and student academic achievement" (para. 2). This lack of access thus exacerbates this digital divide, such that 90% of college graduates compared with 37% of non-high school graduates have high-speed Internet access at home (Zickuhr & Smith, 2013).

Collaborative Learning & Considerations in Online STEM Learning

As more learning in the pandemic era has been pushed to virtual contexts, considerations are needed regarding the impact of an inclusive STEM curriculum in helping engage students in online learning. There are considerable challenges in secondary STEM education, highlighting the need to incorporate collaborative learning and develop a more diverse and inclusive curriculum. In building their social and navigational capital, secondary students require the development of needed social capital to engage in a community as they transition from secondary to postsecondary education and the workplace. According to the National Inventors Society (2021), on the importance of collaboration in STEM:

> Educators have long known the importance of promoting a collaborative environment within their classrooms. By working in groups, or even as one connected learning community, students can simulate the style of work they will likely encounter when they enter the workforce—a place where teamwork is often expected. This collaborative work is crucial for STEM (science, technology, engineering, and mathematics) because complex problems require creative solutions. Rarely does one person have all the answers. Instead, it is more often the case that innovation is the product of many minds working in unison to achieve a shared goal. (para 1–2)

According to Rovai et al. (2005), a strong and active social life on campus can be "used to explain both high persistence and learning satisfaction" amongst learners and lower persistence rates of students in online courses are caused by a lack of social connectedness in that learning community (p. 4). However, this finding should be understood because not all students take courses strictly for social interaction alone. Thomson (2010) observed that many students had a desire to work independently and at a different pace than their peers, eliminating the need for the type of collaborative learning found in these settings and supporting the argument that students may be taking online courses for content over social interaction (Thomson, 2010). With the NGSS standards encouraging more opportunities in the curriculum to engage students in collaborative work, it is worthwhile for online secondary STEM teachers to consider these shifts as they build students' career and workforce readiness skills.

Inclusive Curriculum for Online Secondary STEM Content

An inclusive curriculum considers the specific needs of various learner populations. It ensures equal access to the material while including content that accurately represents the lived experiences of marginalized groups. It is widely known that culturally responsive teaching (CRT) promotes authentic engagement and rigor amongst culturally and linguistically diverse students (Hamedani & Darling-Hammond, 2015; Ladson-Billings, 1995). Additionally, culturally responsive teaching increases engagement and positive outcomes for diverse students with neurodiverse needs (Ford et al., 2014). Applied to STEM, culturally responsive teaching engages historically underrepresented groups in curriculum, instruction, and assessment. It places value in students' cultural practices and reflects their lived experiences (Community for Advancing Discovery in Research in Education, n.d.).

Cultural Representation

Developing an inclusive curriculum may help mitigate the widening opportunity gap as students progress through grade levels and into higher education. Bauer-Wolf (2019) noted that Latinx and African-American students leave the STEM fields at far higher rates than White peers. The White House Initiative on Educational Excellence for African-Americans found that in 2012 in science and engineering, only 11.2% of bachelor's degrees, 8.2% of master's degrees, and 4.1% of doctorate degrees were awarded to women of color. While women received over half of the bachelor's degrees awarded in the biological sciences, they received far fewer in the areas of computer science (17.9%), engineering (19.3%), physical sciences (39%), and mathematics (43.1%).

According to Gholston-Key (2010), cultural diversity in content presentation may be the key to engaging students of color into the STEM disciplines from the secondary levels and well into adulthood. Gholston-Key (201) wrote:

> Science curricula and science classrooms have been devoid of relevant cultural inclusion or multicultural education. Many science educators believe 'science is pure' and thus escapes the influences of current pedagogy, trends, and especially cultural influences. Even though science processes are generic or 'culture-free,' if students cannot and do not identify with information that is 'processing,' they may internalize the notion that they cannot perform science or are not expected to process scientific information. The process of validating and/or correcting perceived notions depends on one's culture. Multicultural science or culturally inclusive science is believed to be an enhancement for students of color. (p. 1)

According to Terada (2021), mathematics is often considered culture or values-free. Despite this façade of neutrality, STEM instruction is couched in a mainly male and Eurocentric system. To add to this fact, Jose Vilson, a veteran middle school teacher, explained that language operates similarly, adding that Math and STEM are centered around Whiteness. In Terada (2021), Jose stated:

> Whatever axioms have come to play, when it comes to Math, came from people. And people come in with their own biases. And this is layered across power. So, if America has serious racial issues, especially serious racist issues, then inherently what we're teaching is going to see manifestations of that racism. (para. 14–15)

Neurodiverse Student Needs

In order to better serve neurodiverse students at the secondary level, teachers will need to utilize effective strategies for making content accessible through universal design learning approaches (Basham & Marino, 2010) and consideration of 508 accessibility requirements. Section 508 of the Rehabilitation Act of 1973, as articulated by the U.S. Department of education, ensures electronic and information technologies are accessible to individuals with disabilities by enabling equal access to electronic information. With the move to online learning, all web-based educational institutions must comply with 508 standards in making content accessible for those individuals who qualify under ADA restrictions. According to University System of Georgia (n.d.), the standards state:

> Covered entities under the ADA are required to provide effective communication, regardless of whether they generally communicate through print media, audio media, or computerized media such as the Internet. Covered entities that use the Inter-

net for communications regarding their programs, goods, or services must be prepared to offer those communications through accessible means as well. (para. 10)

Encouraging motivation in an online course can pose an added challenge given the needs of neurodiverse students. Those students who may struggle with independent learning or autonomy were observed to have lower success rates than others who were more self-directed learners with higher self-responsibility and organization skills (Savenye, 2005). Others that had challenges with self-regulation were unable to apportion enough time for assignment completion, turning in lesser quality work, or late assignments (You & Kang, 2014). Students who lacked internal or external motivators easily lost sight of their original goals, becoming lost in the course and, in many cases, withdrawing (Chaney, 2001).

Humanizing Social-Emotional Learning for Secondary STEM Students

Social-Emotional Learning (SEL) has become an integral component of childhood education, particularly in the digital era. Much prior research has shown that schools that emphasize social-emotional development see increases in academic success, improved quality of relationships between teachers and students, and decreased problematic behavior (Durlak et al., 2011). Peterson et al. (2018) found that a STEM-based curriculum integrated with a Social Emotional Learning framework enhanced learning and overall student development and promoted an increased interest in STEM fields at the secondary level.

As we explore SEL in the context of the current Diversity, Equity, and Inclusivity (DEI) dialogs, it is critical to note the importance of humanization as a viable framework that may resolve some of the shortcomings of SEL in "repairing the cultural contempt of hegemonic miseducation" in its inability to "address the primary social forces" that "negatively impact the health and wellness of communities of color and their colonial relationship with inequitable social systems" (Camangian & Cariaga, 2021, para. 4). In addition, research has shown the effectiveness of whole-school approaches in SEL for addressing the needs of students from diverse backgrounds, including various racial and socioeconomic groups (Hamedani & Darling-Hammond, 2015).

CHAPTER FOCUS: PRACTICAL APPLICATIONS IN DEVELOPING A MORE INCLUSIVE ONLINE STEM CURRICULUM

Equal access to digital learning platforms is a significant issue in promoting equity in online education. Addressing equity and access issues is an important key in ensuring all students have the ability to succeed. In this section, I explore a few strategies that may mitigate the impacts of digital redlining on various subgroups to promote greater access and equity in education.

Strategies That Account for the Impacts of Digital Redlining

To even begin to address some of the impacts of digital redlining and account for the various issues of access to broadband Internet, the first step for online secondary STEM teachers is to acknowledge that such disparities in technological access do exist. Next, teachers need to consider these access issues that students from underserved communities may face and attempt to make content more accessible in various formats in order to allow students to access, view, and complete the work. Empathy in curriculum design with an emphasis on equity prevents the diminishment of student experiences and enables pathways to access the curriculum. This design allows secondary students to engage in the material meaningfully and expands navigational capital.

Collaborative Learning and Building Social Capital in Online Settings

In building students' social capital and preparedness for career and workforce settings, through the building of networks and exposure to various careers in the field, teachers can utilize digital platforms to bring access to these networks through guest speakers. Because content may seem more inaccessible due to digital instructional methods, interest or enthusiasm in science may dwindle. Researchers suggest the benefits of bringing in guest speakers to promote networking and role-molding, exposure to real-life applications of the content, and increased confidence in the presenter's field (Kamoun & Selim, 2007). Because of misconceptions about the nature of STEM content, such as its difficulty (Kim et al., 2018), need for advanced learning and requirement of higher education (Kim et al., 2018; Noonan, 2017), lack of altruism (Kim et al., 2018), and concepts seen as boring (Kennedy & Hefferon, 2019), including engaging speakers may promote greater interest in STEM content. In addition, the use of collaborative activities that help engage students in meaningful content application as found in preservice preparation programs (Tomas et al., 2015) may help increase interest in science learning since it provides more hands-on application for understanding the abstract nature of science better as students explore explanations of natural phenomena.

Developing Social Capital & NGSS Connections

In order to better engage students through the building of networks and exposure to the STEM fields, students can interact with speakers to learn more about their roles and develop a richer interest in STEM careers. Teachers can invite speakers located anywhere in the country or world to classroom sessions, expanding the array of guests that can help benefit the student learning experience. In helping students obtain as much information from the guest speaker, teachers can distribute speaker bios ahead of the synchronous session and ask students to investigate and explore their work. Students can then be tasked with coming to class prepared with questions to ask the speaker based on their Webquest research. Doing so helps better engage students and assists in developing their social capital through the building of network interactions. It builds student confidence as they interact with members of the scientific community. In this way, the Science and Engineering Practice of *Obtaining, Evaluating, and Communicating Information*, where students may be tasked to gather, read, and evaluate scientific/technical information from authoritative sources and communicate that information through multiple formats, can be elicited in this activity ((NGSS: 6–8, 9-12 Condensed Practices).

Another way to build this skill and promote more collaborative learning could be through the Science and Engineering Practice of *Developing and Using Models.* Here, students may be tasked with developing, revising, and using a model on evidence to illustrate or predict relationships between systems or components of a system. Coupled with the Crosscutting Concept of *Systems and System Models*, students could work on a collaborative *Jigsaw* project through synchronous breakout groups where students are asked to develop a model to predict the behavior of the biogeochemical cycle. Students can be given real-time data from NOAA that provides information on carbon dioxide levels in oceanic environments and develop an explanation to correlate coral bleaching and oceanic acidification due to these increased levels. Models can be developed using *GeoGebra*, a free math app, to generate graphs and illustrate the relationship of these factors and explain this phenomenon. After meeting in their collaborative groups, students can return to the main session and present their findings in a symposium-like format, mimicking the process in which researchers share their data. Student groups can ask clarifying questions and provide meaningful feedback. In this way, students can develop their skills in developing models and presenting technical information to their peers, thus improving collaboration and increasing engagement in advanced scientific concepts.

Culturally Inclusive Learning in Virtual Contexts

Eliciting more effective ways to engage secondary students in learning STEM content in online settings, teachers should reconsider the traditional science curriculum by including the cultures of students represented in the classroom. It is believed that culturally inclusive science can integrate the learner's culture into the academic and social context of the science classroom, aiding and supporting science learning (Baptiste & Key, 1996; Boisselle, 2016). Student achievement is influenced by several factors: student attitudes, interests, motivation, type of curricula, relevancy of materials, and the culture of the students (Banks & Banks, 1995). In addition, culturally inclusive learning brings value to the perspectives of Indigenous cultures since students are taught the sociocultural and sociopolitical impacts of human activity on the environment. Research findings also show that including the narratives of Indigenous groups' to promote greater sense of belonging might better address the underrepresentation of marginalized populations in STEM (Allaire, 2018). These practices, which aim to *decolonize* the curriculum, may promote greater engagement of secondary school students in STEM curriculum as they extend their learnings to multidisciplinary contexts in helping address and solve more complex issues as it regards ecological impact and other areas and how they can view diverse perspectives on related topics (Boisselle, 2016).

Cultural Inclusivity & NGSS Connections

In science, discoveries are often generated as researchers collaborate to develop explanations of the natural world. It is commonly understood that a variety of individuals have contributed to the totality of scientific knowledge. In applying culturally inclusive strategies to the Science and Engineering Practice of *Planning and Carrying Out Investigations*, particularly focusing on the planning and conducting of experiments to produce data in collaboration with peers (NGSS: 6–8, 9-12 Condensed Practices), the inclusion of the diverse array of perspectives and contributors could be brought into the dialog to reinforce these concepts better. In order to connect abstract scientific concepts to students, perhaps groups could be tasked with exploring the life stories of some of science's contributors who represent marginalized or underserved groups. Utilizing either a *Jigsaw* expert group through a Webquest activity or a presentation using multimedia of scientific figures, students could explore the life and journey of renowned individuals representing diverse groups who were or are significant contributors to the field. In this way, by presenting opportunities to explore the lives of scientific figures, some students may find more connection to the content through the lived experiences of those individuals.

Accessible Curriculum for Neurodiverse Students

Secondary STEM teachers should assist in building students' study and organizational skills by devising clear curriculum content access through learning management systems and other organizational systems, lowering the cognitive load through more easily accessible content. In addition, they should make themselves available through virtual office hours and field responses so that students do not feel they are navigating the course on their own. Some learners require higher levels of support in navigating in a more autonomous setting (Thomson, 2010).

Online assignments being more reading and writing intensive may cause challenges for neurodiverse learners. Students who struggle with reading may find the heavier text in the secondary STEM curriculum cumbersome (Donlevy, 2003). As such, teachers need to evaluate their curriculum for accessibility, making assignments meaningful and encouraging the development of career and workforce readiness.

UDL and NGSS Connections

In order to make content more accessible for students, teachers should consider utilizing a formal learning management system (LMS) if their school or district has not already adopted one. There are free varieties such as Google Classroom and limited free platforms like Schoology. Presenting organized material helps with asynchronous pacing and may encourage a more profound understanding of concepts since it lowers the cognitive load associated with navigating disorganized resources. In addition, Google Classroom and other LMS' can enable content to be differentiated for individuals or groups of students. There is also software that can be embedded in these systems, such as Snap & Read, which reads text aloud and provides access to those individuals with special needs.

In order to promote design-thinking and engineering mindsets amongst students, consider incorporating these strategies with the Science & Engineering Practice of *Engaging in Argument from Evidence*. As stated, the goals of this practice are to help students develop the ability to compare and evaluate arguments, evaluate claims, and present counter-arguments based on data and evidence (NGSS: 6–8, 9-12 Condensed Practices). In building this practice amongst secondary-aged students, groups may be presented with a topic to engage with on an online discussion forum on any learning management platforms mentioned earlier. Students should be encouraged to review the various perspectives uploaded to the unit folder in order to examine and critique opposing viewpoints and be tasked with defending a viewpoint they have been assigned. Then, as they build their arguments, they can respectfully provide and receive critiques on scientific arguments by the process of probing reasoning and evidence, while challenging ideas and conclusions and responding thoughtfully to diverse perspectives, all abiding within the rules established through the class's netiquette policies.

Social-Emotional Learning and Trauma-Informed Practices

Like the discussion regarding promoting equity in the approach to online secondary STEM curriculum began, I again look to its role in the advancement of SEL and its connection to supporting student learning. Here is highlighted the importance of engaging in social and emotional learning that also addresses the implicit biases of our everyday lives. In so doing, within the context of teaching secondary STEM curriculum in virtual settings, it is worthwhile for educators to examine how that content is presented, how students are treated as valued contributors to the class, and how developing safe spaces in online learning is prioritized to support the development and achievement of students.

SUMMARY AND REFLECTION

Through this discussion, various elements of equity have been presented in the teaching and curriculum development of online secondary STEM education, from digital redlining to the multidimensions of intersecting identities that require consideration in the development of equitable curriculum. In promoting greater access and opportunity for all students to engage in STEM content, it is critical that these particular areas are appropriately addressed. In order to lead within this context of next-generation teaching and learning, it requires from teachers a new and informed mindset that elevates the needs of students and celebrates their diversity as a learning community.

TIPS AND ADVICE

- Recognize that teaching for inclusivity promotes engagement and achievement for all students, not just target populations.
- Differentiate the learning and elicit the seven elements of culturally responsive teaching using technology promotes engagement and achievement for all students. The Seven Principles are as follows: (a) Students are affirmed in their cultural connections; (b) Teachers are personally inviting; (c) Learning environments are physically and culturally inviting; (d) Students are reinforced for academic development; (e) Instructional changes are made to accommodate differences in learners; (f) Classroom is managed with firm, consistent, loving control; and (g) Interactions stress collectivity as well as individuality.
- Demonstrating to students your willingness to learn about students' funds of knowledge encourages an environment in which students are more willing to take academic risks to achieve learning targets and approach mastery of concepts.
- Decolonizing one's teaching practices takes time, effort, and patience. It is ok not to get it right the first time so long as you commit yourself to a lifelong practice of learning.

RESOURCE NOTES

Name of Resource	Primary Website	How to Locate the Resource Online
Adapting Science Lessons for Distance Learning	https://www.edutopia.org/article/adapting-science-lessons-dis-tance-learning	Click on the article link. It will direct you to the source article.
Teach Engineering K–12	https://www.teachengineering.org/	In the middle of the page, use the search magnifying glass to search for various lessons and projects pertinent to the standards you will cover in class.
How Culturally Relevant Teaching Can Build Relationships While Students are at Home.	https://www.kqed.org/mind-shift/56450/how-culturally-rele-vant-teaching-can-build-relation-ships-while-students-are-home	Click on the article link. It will direct you to the source article.

DISCUSSION QUESTIONS

1. In developing inclusive online materials in science, is there an account of students' socioeconomic, emotional, cultural, and cognitive needs in selecting, creating, and presenting those resources?
2. Why is being a culturally-responsive educator critical in a field seen as values-free?
3. What steps can you take to become a more culturally inclusive science educator and bring a more significant sense of belonging to all your student groups?
4. How can you maintain academic rigor in developing culturally inclusive materials as you transition your teaching to virtual environments?

REFERENCES

Allaire, F. S. (2018). Themes from a narrative analysis of Native Hawaiian experiences in science, technology, engineering, and mathematics. *Journal of Ethnographic & Qualitative Research, 12*(3), 173–192.

Banks, J., & Banks, C. (1995). *Handbook of research on multicultural education.* Macmillan.

Baptiste, P., & Key, S. (1996) Cultural inclusion: Where does your program stand? *The Science Teacher*, 32–35.

Basham, J. D., & Marino, M. T. (2010). Introduction to the topical issue: Shaping STEM education for all students. *Journal of Special Education Technology, 25*(3), 1–2.

Bauer-Wolf, J. (2019) *Early departures.* Inside HigherEd. https://www.insidehighered.com/news/2019/02/26/latinx-black-college-students-leave-stem-majors-more-white-students

Boisselle, L. N. (2016). Decolonizing science and science education in a postcolonial space. *Sage Open, 6*(1), 1–11. https://doi.org/10.1177/2158244016635257

Brown, V. (2018). Technology access gap for postsecondary education: A statewide case study. *Promoting Global Competencies through Media Literacy* (p. 21).

Camangian, P., Cariaga, S. (2021). Social and emotional learning is hegemonic miseducation: Students deserve humanization instead. *Race Ethnicity and Education.* DOI: 10.1080/13613324.2020.1798374.

Chaney, E. G. (2001). Web-based instruction in a rural high school: A collaborative inquiry into its effectiveness and desirability. *NASSP Bulletin, 85*(628), 20–35.

Community for Advancing Discovery in Research in Education. (n.d.). *Culturally responsive STEM education.* http://cadrek12.org/culturally-responsive-stem-Education

Community for Advancing Discovery in Research in Education. (2018). *Creating inclusive prek–12 STEM learning environments.* https://files.eric.ed.gov/fulltext/ED590489.pdf

Donlevy, J. (2003). Teachers, technology and training: Online learning in virtual high school. *International Journal of Instructional Media, 30*(2), 117–121. http://search.proquest.com/docview/204262673?accountid=27700

Durlak, J. A., Weissberg, R. P., Dymnicki, A. B., Taylor, R. D., & Schellinger, K. B. (2011). The impact of enhancing students' social and emotional learning: A meta-analysis of school-based universal interventions. *Child Development, 82*(1), 405–432.

Ford, B. A., Stuart, D. H., & Shernavaz, V. (2014) Culturally responsive teaching in the 21ˢᵗ century classroom. *Journal of the International Association of Special Education. 15*(2), 56–62.

Gholston-Key, S. (2010). Diversity in science education. *Research Into Practice Science.* https://assets.pearsonglobalschools.com/asset_mgr/current/20109/Diversity_in_Science_Education.pdf

Gilliard, C. (2019, November 5). *Digital redlining, access, and privacy.* Common Sense Education. https://www.commonsense.org/education/articles/digital-redlining-access-and-privacy

Hamedani, M. G., & Darling-Hammond, L. (2015). *Social emotional learning in high school: How three urban high schools engage, educate, and empower youth* (pp. 1–15). Stanford Center for Opportunity Policy in Education. Research Brief.

Kamoun, F., & Selim, S. (2007). A framework towards assessing the merits of inviting IT professionals to the classroom. *Journal of Information Technology Education: Research, 6,* 81–103. https://doi.org/10.28945/203

Kennedy, B., & Hefferon, M. (2019, March 28). *What Americans know about science.* Pew Research Center. https://www.pewresearch.org/science/2019/03/28/what-americans-know-about-science/

Kim, A. Y., Sinatra, G. M., & Seyranian, V. (2018). Developing a STEM identity among young women: A social identity perspective. *Review of Educational Research, 88*(4), 589–625. https://doi.org/10.3102/0034654318779957

Ladson-Billings, G. (1995) But that's just good teaching: The case for culturally relevant pedagogy. *Theory Into Practice, 34*(3), 159–165. http://www.jstor.org/stable/1476635

Lancaster, C. (2020, August 14). *Digital redlining.* NC State University Institute for Emerging Issues. https://iei.ncsu.edu/2020/digital-redlining/

Lekka-Kowalik, A. (2009). Why science cannot be value-free. *Science & Engineering Ethics, 16*(1), 33–41. https://doi.org/10.1007/s11948-009-9128-3

Lichtenberger, E., & George-Jackson, C. (2012). Predicting high school students' interest in majoring in a STEM field: Insight into high school students' postsecondary plans. *Journal of Career and Technical Education, 28*(1), 19–38. http://doi.org/10.21061/jcte.v28i1.571

Mangahas, A. (2017). Perceptions of high school biology teachers in Christian schools on relationships between religious beliefs and teaching evolution. *Journal of Research on Christian Education, 26*(1), 24–43. https://doi.org/10.1080/10656219.2017.1282902

National Inventors. (2021). *The importance of collaboration in STEM.* https://www.invent.org/blog/trends-stem/collaboration-learning-STEM

Noonan, R. (2017). *Women in STEM: 2017 Update.* U.S. Department of Commerce. https://www.commerce.gov/sites/default/files/migrated/reports/women-in-stem-2017-update.pdf

Peterson, A., Gaskill, M., & Cordova, J. (2018, March 26). Connecting STEM with social emotional learning (SEL) curriculum in secondary education. In E. Langran & J. Borup (Eds.), *Proceedings of Society for Information Technology & Teacher Education International Conference* (pp. 1212–1219). United States: Association for the Advancement of Computing in Education (AACE). https://www.learntechlib.org/primary/p/182681/

Rovai, A. P., Wighting, M. J., & Liu, J. (2005). School climate: Sense of classroom and school communities in online and on-campus higher education courses. *Quarterly Review of Distance Education, 6*(4), 361–374. http://search.proquest.com/docview/231071527?accountid=27700

Savenye, W. C. (2005). Improving online courses: What is interaction and why use it? *Distance Learning, 2*(6), 22–28.

Teach Engineering. (n.d.) *Teach engineering: Ignite STEM learning in K–12*. https://www.teachengineering.org/

Terada, Y. (2021, March 26). *Why Black teachers walk away*. Edutopia. https://www.edutopia.org/article/why-black-teachers-walk-away#:~:text=In%20a%20new%20study%20published,wanted%20to%20leave%20the%20profession

Thomson, L. D. (2010). Beyond the classroom walls: Teachers' and students' perspectives on how online learning can meet the needs of gifted students. *Journal of Advanced Academics, 21*(4), 662–712. http://joa.sagepub.com.pluma.sjfc.edu/content/21/4/662.full.pdf+html

Tomas, L., Lasen, M., Field, E., & Skamp, K. (2015). Promoting online students' engagement and learning in science and sustainability preservice teacher education. *Australian Journal of Teacher Education, 40*(11), 79–107. http://dx.doi.org/10.14221/ajte.2015v40n11.5

University System of Georgia. (n.d.) *Higher education, The Americans with Disabilities Act and Section 508*. https://www.usg.edu/siteinfo/higher_education_the_americans_with_disabilities_act_and_section_508

You, J. W., & Kang, M. (2014). The role of academic emotions in the relationship between perceived academic control and self-regulated learning in online learning. *Computers & Education, 77*, 125–133. https://doi.org/10.1016/j.compedu.2014.04.018

Zickuhr, K., & Smith, A. (2013, August 26). *Home broadband*. Pew Research Center. https://www.issuelab.org/resources/15698/15698.pdf

CHAPTER 4

EMPOWERING SECONDARY TEACHERS TO USE EQUIP RUBRIC TO BE CRITICAL CONSCIOUS USERS OF ONLINE SCIENCE CURRICULAR MATERIALS

Amal Ibourk

Florida State University

Tina Cheuk

California Polytechnic State University, San Luis Obispo

This chapter shares how secondary science teachers can leverage the *Educators Evaluating the Quality of Instructional Products* (EQuIP) rubric (n.d.) as a tool that empowers them to be critical users of online science curricular materials and in online learning spaces. We outline ways in which science teachers can integrate this tool in their review, selection, and adaptation of online curricular materials in efforts of problematizing and desettling expectations of their normalized views and practices of disciplinary teaching and learning, using a variety of online application tools (e.g., Google Slides™, Mentimeter™, Zoom™ breakout rooms) while engaging in the 5E instructional model.

Teaching and Learning Online: Science for Secondary Grade Levels, pages 45–55.
Copyright © 2023 by Information Age Publishing
www.infoagepub.com

RATIONALE

One of the biggest levers that science teachers have on hand is the curriculum materials they use with their students. We recognize that teachers—as well as district leaders—are bombarded with choices around curricular materials. As a result, we argue that science teachers need practice in evaluating the vast array of accessible online secondary curricula available in the marketplace so they can be better consumers of curricular materials, attending to the strengths and priorities of their local contexts. Specifically, teachers need to develop a critical consciousness lens or adopt a lens where they question whether these online curricular materials are designed in ways that privilege some students over others. Adapted from Freire and Ramos' (1970) definition of critical consciousness, our role as teacher educators is to support future teachers in deepening their awareness and understanding their positionality and biases. In turn, teachers can make better decisions and actions against oppressive aspects of schooling through the instructional materials they use and scaffold for full and equitable participation in the culture of science and school science through curriculum, instruction, and assessment.

Online curricular materials in the hands of teachers can serve as an educative tool for learners (Ball & Cohen, 1996; Schneider & Krajcik, 2002), especially for secondary science teachers since they are often vetting, adopting, and adapting curricular materials in their classrooms. Since teacher educators train and support the next generation of science teachers, they must have the experience to critically

EQuIP Rubric for Lessons & Units: Science

I. Alignment to the NGSS	II. Instructional Supports	III. Monitoring Student Progress
The lesson or unit aligns with the conceptual shifts of the NGSS: A. Grade-appropriate elements of the science and engineering practice(s), disciplinary core idea(s), and crosscutting concept(s), work together to support students in three-dimensional learning to make sense of phenomena and/or to design solutions to problems. i. Provides opportunities to develop and use specific elements of the practice(s) to make sense of phenomena and/or to design solutions to problems. ii. Provides opportunities to develop and use specific elements of the disciplinary core idea(s) to make sense of phenomena and/or to design solutions to problems. iii. Provides opportunities to develop and use specific elements of the crosscutting concept(s) to make sense of phenomena and/or to design solutions to problems. iv. The three dimensions work together to support students to make sense of phenomena and/or to design solutions to problems. A unit or longer lesson will also: B. Lessons fit together coherently targeting a set of performance expectations. i. Each lesson links to previous lessons and provides a need to engage in the current lesson. ii. The lessons help students develop proficiency on a targeted set of performance expectations. C. Where appropriate, disciplinary core ideas from different disciplines are used together to explain phenomena. D. Where appropriate, crosscutting concepts are used in the explanation of phenomena from a variety of disciplines. E. Provides grade-appropriate connection(s) to the Common Core State Standards in Mathematics and/or English Language Arts & Literacy in History/Social Studies, Science and Technical Subjects.	The lesson or unit supports instruction and learning for all students: A. Engages students in authentic and meaningful scenarios that reflect the practice of science and engineering as experienced in the real world and that provide students with a purpose (e.g., making sense of phenomena and/or designing solutions to problems). i. The context, including phenomena, questions, or problems, motivates students to engage in three-dimensional learning. ii. Provides students with relevant phenomena (either firsthand experiences or through representations) to make sense of and/or relevant problems to solve. iii. Engages students in multiple practices that work together with disciplinary core ideas and crosscutting concepts to support students in making sense of phenomena and/or designing solutions to problems. iv. Provides opportunities for students to connect their explanation of a phenomenon and/or their design solution to a problem to their own experience. v. When engineering performance expectations are included, they are used along with disciplinary core ideas from physical, life, or earth and space sciences. B. Develops deeper understanding of the practices, disciplinary core ideas, and crosscutting concepts by identifying and building on students' prior knowledge. C. Uses scientifically accurate and grade-appropriate scientific information, phenomena, and representations to support students' three-dimensional learning. D. Provides opportunities for students to express, clarify, justify, interpret, and represent their ideas and respond to peer and teacher feedback orally and/or in written form as appropriate to support student's three-dimensional learning. E. Provides guidance for teachers to support differentiated instruction in the classroom so that every student's needs are addressed by including: i. Suggestions for how to connect instruction to the students' home, neighborhood, community and/or culture as appropriate. ii. Appropriate reading, writing, listening, and/or speaking alternatives (e.g., translations, picture support, graphic organizers) for students who are English language learners, have special needs, or read well below the grade level. iii. Suggested extra support (e.g., phenomena, representations, tasks) for students who are struggling to meet the performance expectations. iv. Extensions for students with high interest or who have already met the performance expectations to develop deeper understanding of the practices, disciplinary core ideas, and crosscutting concepts. A unit or longer lesson will also: F. Provides guidance for teachers throughout the unit for how lessons build on each other to support students developing deeper understanding of the practices, disciplinary core ideas, and crosscutting concepts over the course of the unit G. Provides supports to help students engage in the practices as needed and gradually adjusts supports over time so that students are increasingly responsible for making sense of phenomena and/or designing solutions to problems.	The lesson or unit supports monitoring student progress: A. Elicits direct, observable evidence of three-dimensional learning by students using practices with core ideas and crosscutting concepts to make sense of phenomena and/or to design solutions. B. Formative assessments of three-dimensional learning are embedded throughout the instruction. C. Includes aligned rubrics and scoring guidelines that provide guidance for interpreting student performance along the three dimensions to support teachers in (a) planning instruction and (b) providing ongoing feedback to students. D. Assessing student proficiency using methods, vocabulary, representations, and examples that are accessible and unbiased for all students. A unit or longer lesson will also: E. Includes pre-, formative, summative, and self-assessment measures that assess three-dimensional learning. F. Provides multiple opportunities for students to demonstrate performance of practices connected with their understanding of disciplinary core ideas and crosscutting concepts and receive feedback.

FIGURE 4.1. EQuIP Rubric for Lessons and Units: Science

evaluate the online curricula they have on hand or will be presented within their classrooms to maximize the learning opportunities for their learners (Mensah, 2019). Science teachers now have greater access to a myriad of online science curricula—a shift from previous generations where only *printed* copies were only available for teacher use.

The *Educators Evaluating the Quality of Instructional Products* (EQuIP) rubric for science provides criteria to assess how well lessons and units are designed for the Next Generation Science Standards (NGSS, 2013). This freely available online tool (see source notes) was developed by teachers, states, and leaders in science education research and organized by Achieve, an independent, nonpartisan U.S. nonprofit education reform organization that works with states to raise academic standards, improve assessments, and strengthen accountability. The rubric is comprised of three core elements: NGSS 3D Design, NGSS Instructional Supports, and Monitoring NGSS Student Progress. Within each major category are subcomponents that detail ways science teachers can examine lessons and units with a critical eye toward student learning. See Figure 4.1 for the EQuIP rubric overview.

THEORETICAL BACKGROUND

This chapter considers the wide variability of online science instructional materials for middle and high school instruction across the United States. Public school classrooms serve an increasingly diverse population of K–12 students and families who are bilingual, multilingual, or have immigrant origins (NCES, 2020). As teacher educators and former science teachers, we recognize that much of the existing science curricular materials continue to perpetuate stereotypical representations of historically marginalized groups, promote knowledge construction that is filtered through a White gaze, and erase narratives and contributions to science from non-dominant communities (Mensah & Jackson, 2018).

Also, in the following quote, the NRC Framework (2012) describes its vision of equity in science education as one that:

> requires that all students [be] provided with equitable opportunities to learn science and become engaged in science and engineering practices; with access to quality space, equipment, and teachers to support and motivate that learning and engagement; and adequate time spent on science. In addition, the issue of connecting to students' interests and experiences is particularly important for broadening participation in science. (p. 28)

The framework clearly emphasizes that making science relevant and inclusive to students is vital in expanding participation in science. We want our science teachers to understand that their students will learn best in classrooms that honor and reflect their cultures and ways of thinking, which in turn broadens and impacts their opportunities to participate in science. We counter dominant narratives by engaging and empowering our science teachers through practice in evaluating science curricular materials with a critical consciousness lens to disrupt the inequities in these materials. Part of empowering our science teachers and being critically conscious of online curricular materials includes deepening their understanding of how science teaching and learning occurs within a larger context of culture and community, as well as power and knowledge construction (Calabrese Barton & Tan, 2020). In other words, we want science teachers to critically examine how science curricula can marginalize some of their students when they are framed around a dominant culture and to understand the importance of selecting curricula that give voice to the varied cultural perspectives that exist in the classroom.

CHAPTER FOCUS

The EQuIP rubric components from this rubric (Figure 4.1) that align closely with developing science teachers' critical consciousness lens include identifying, evaluating, and improving upon instructional supports. These supports (1) are relevant and authentic to students, (2) elicit student ideas that provide learners with ample opportunities to express their thinking, and (3) are differentiated to learners' strengths and needs. While we recognize that these three components are by no means all-inclusive or an exhaustive list, we have chosen them strategically as high-leverage supports in the development and enactment of critical consciousness for beginning teachers in science classrooms.

In this section, we discuss our approach to using a 5E lesson planning framework (Bybee, 2006) as an instructional model for supporting science teachers to be critical users of curriculum materials for online learning using the criteria from EQuIP rubric. We recommend using three broadly accessible publishers who have made their units online in terms of secondary science curricula, including OpenSciEd, McGraw Hill, and Amplify. What is novel about our uses of EQuIP and these units is that publishers have begun to release their curricula online. As a result, science teachers can preview and evaluate these online curricula in an online learning space. However, we also recommend instructors learn what local districts and county secondary schools have adopted and are using in their middle and high school science classrooms.

Engage

In preparation for learning together, we recommend giving time for science teachers in going over the different categories in the EQuIP rubric and reviewing the unit's lessons, which can be done in the form of a pre-read prior to the lesson launch. At the start of class, teacher educators start by sharing with the science teachers the plethora of developed and state-adopted science curriculum materials that are available and NGSS-aligned and those materials that are used and *not* stated-adopted. We recommend also showing an example of a lesson/curriculum unit from the website *Teachers Pay Teachers* as an example of curricula materials that have not been vetted and do not consider the various ways of knowing and assets that students may bring into account in a science classroom. Examples of online curricular materials can be found in the Source Notes section at the end of this chapter. Science teachers are then asked to reflect on the following two prompts and engage in a class discussion about the role of instructional supports in curriculum materials in promoting social justice outcomes:

- Why is it important not to take curriculum materials wholesale (as is)?
- What might we promote when we teach in ways that do *not include a critical consciousness lens* in our decision-making?

As a class, we suggest using Google Jamboard™ or Mentimeter as an online tool to elicit student thinking to these prompts and ask them to generate possible instructional supports that would be important if we want social justice outcomes for our learners. See Figure 4.2 for an example. Google Jamboard and Mentimeter are both are interactive online tools that science teachers can use to respond to the questions.

Explore

Teachers are organized in triads in Zoom breakout rooms and provided with electronic links to folders of curriculum units and lessons to review and critique. (See Source Notes for sample curricula.) Before class, during asynchronous preparation, team members are tasked to preview their assigned curriculum and lessons to be ready for the discussion and application of the EQuIP rubric during synchronous class discussion.

The teacher educator would also loop back to the instructional supports from the Engage stage (see Figure 4.1) and review the three supports: relevance & authenticity, student ideas, and differentiated instruction (see Figure 4.3). The first support is relevance and authenticity, which "looks at how the lesson or set of les-

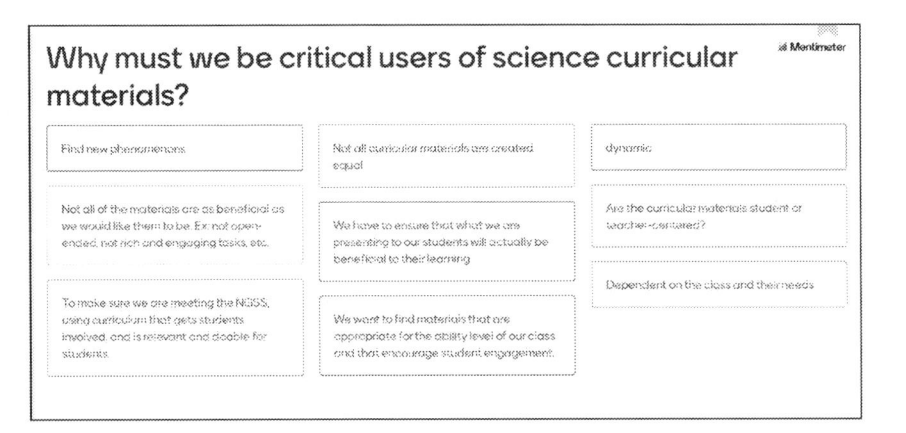

FIGURE 4.2.   Science Teachers' Responses Using Mentimeter Tool

Lesson and Unit Criteria Lessons and units designed for the NGSS include clear and compelling evidence of the following:	Specific Evidence From Materials (what happened/where did it happen) and reviewer's reasoning (how/why is this evidence)	Evidence of Quality?	Suggestions for Improvement
Relevance And Authenticity: Engages students in authentic and meaningful scenarios that reflect the practice of science and engineering as experienced in the real world. 1. Students experience phenomena or design problems as directly as possible (firsthand or through media representations). 2. Includes suggestions for connecting instruction to the students' home, neighborhood, community, and/or culture as appropriate. 3. Provides opportunities for students to connect their explanation of a phenomenon and/or their design solution to a problem to questions from their own experience.		☐ None ☐ Inadequate ☐ Adequate ☐ Extensive	
Student Ideas: Provides opportunities for students to express, clarify, justify, interpret, and represent their ideas and respond to peer and teacher feedback orally and/or in written form as appropriate.		☐ None ☐ Inadequate ☐ Adequate ☐ Extensive	
Differentiated Instruction: Provides guidance for teachers to support differentiated instruction by including: 1. Appropriate reading, writing, listening, and/or speaking alternatives (e.g., translations, picture support, graphic organizers) for students who are English language learners, have special needs, or read well below the grade level. 2. Extra support (e.g., phenomena, representations, tasks) for struggling students to meet the targeted expectations. 3. Extensions for students with high interest or who have already met the performance expectations to develop a more profound understanding of the practices, disciplinary core ideas, and crosscutting concepts.		☐ None ☐ Inadequate ☐ Adequate ☐ Extensive	

FIGURE 4.3. EQUIP Rubric Excerpt

sons engages students in authentic and meaningful scenarios that reflect the practice of science and engineering as experienced in the real world" (see Figure 4.3). The second support focuses on student ideas and looks at how the lesson or series of lessons provide "opportunities for students to express, clarify, justify, interpret, and represent their ideas and respond to peer and teacher feedback orally and/or in written form as appropriate" (see Figure 4.3). The last support differentiated instruction provides guidance for teachers to support differentiated instruction by including appropriate reading, writing, listening, and/or speaking alternatives (e.g., translations, picture support, graphic organizers) for students who are designated English learners, have special needs, or read well below the grade level (see Figure 4.3). The instructor would go through how they are defined and can use locally adopted high school science curricula to apply the EQuIP tool.

Explain

Teacher teams can select one science unit and critically analyze one lesson for their evaluation and improvement using a *modified* EQuIP rubric (Figure 4.2). Each team is given access to a set of editable Google Slides with the rubric template where they are tasked to review and critique their selected unit and lesson against criteria. At the same time, instructors can monitor group progress via shared Google Slides and move to and from online breakout groups to check in and troubleshoot. Figure 4.4 shows how one group reviewed and critiqued a sample lesson from *Amplify science curriculum* using the EQuIP rubric.

Elaborate

Once small groups have completed the majority of their review, a 'reporter' from each group is tasked to share key findings in a 'gallery walk' format when presenting their key findings using Google Slides. Members of the learning community are tasked to (1) ask clarifying questions, (2) identify an area of strength in the group review, and (3) suggest additional improvements. The *elaborate* portion of the lesson can be done during asynchronous work after class or, if time permits, synchronously after group work.

Evaluate

The science teacher educator reviews both the small group critiques as well as 'gallery walk' responses from their colleagues and leads the class in a closing discussion of patterns and trends that emerged from these engagements as well as ways this set of activities serves as practice as teachers apply their learning in their own science classrooms. This activity aims to strengthen future science teachers' knowledge and practice in improving and adapting published curriculum so that *all* students have access to and are empowered to learn science in improving the human condition. After this set of activities, teachers understand that published

Curriculum Chosen: Amplify: Metabolism: Body Systems: (Lesson 2.1: Exploring the classroom Body Systems Model)

Lesson *and* Unit Criteria Lessons and units designed for the NGSS include clear and compelling evidence of the following:	Specific evidence from materials (what happened/where did it happen) and reviewer's reasoning (how/why is this evidence)	Evidence of Quality?	Suggestions for improvement
Relevance and Authenticity: Engages students in authentic & meaningful scenarios that reflect the practice of science and engineering as experienced in the real world. i. Students experience phenomena or design problems as directly as possible (firsthand or through media representations). ii. Includes suggestions for how to connect instruction to the students' home, neighborhood, community and/or culture as appropriate. iii. Provides opportunities for students to connect their explanation of a phenomenon and/or their design solution to a problem to questions from their own experience.	1. The students experience a phenomena both firsthand and through media representations by hands on models and simulations with metabolism (oxygen passing through the body) and the teacher plays a video about the body systems for the students to watch. 2. The lesson focuses on how molecules of food and air get to all parts of the body so it's hard to connect that to the students' home and community. The lesson overall doesn't do that. 3. Through the homework and the simulations/model, the students are able to connect their explanation of the phenomenon to questions from their own experience. For example, through the different activities, the students can understand what's happening in their own bodies and understand how delicate the body systems.	☐ None ☐ Inadequate ☒ Adequate ☐ Extensive **We chose adequate only due to the fact that the lesson did not provide connection to instructions to the student home or neighborhood.**	The lesson would benefit from providing connections of instruction to the home/neighborhood, community and/or culture. If the lesson was able to explain the lesson in ways that connected to the student's community, the lesson would be labeled as extensive. The teacher could do this by talking about how when one part of the body system isn't functioning correctly, you can get sick/ why people in the students' homes and community get sick.

FIGURE 4.4. Critical Analysis of a Sample Lesson from Amplify Science Curriculum

science curricula are imperfect and they need to improve upon the lesson and units so that each of their learners can thrive in science.

We can see emerging evidence that students are using the criteria of differentiated instruction in critiquing the science lesson, which also serves to raise their critical consciousness. For one group who examined a lesson titled, *How does light help me see things and community with others?*, one pre-service teacher expressed: "Because this investigation requires vision, this activity might not work well for students with visual disabilities." This noticing and subsequent reflection in how science curricula could be designed to be inclusive of all learners is key—ensuring full and equitable participation of *all* students in science learning and not limiting opportunities for those individuals otherwise marginalized in this lesson around light.

SUMMARY AND REFLECTIONS

We have two main takeaways from the enactment of this activity. The first is around selecting sample secondary science curricula and the second is around the scaffolding needed so that the time teachers have with each other is used efficiently. Depending on your locale, we recommend sourcing a varied list of science curricula used by local science teachers. Cross-check this list with any state-adopted or approved science curricula if they are present. It is essential to showcase the wide variety of science curricula available for teachers and understand that they are of varying quality. The example shown in this chapter is from a curriculum of relatively high quality. Nevertheless, teachers were still able to make suggestions for improvement (see Figure 4.4).

We found that teachers benefited from clearly scaffolded instructions that guided their learning. These scaffolded instructions included understanding the rationale behind this activity, breaking down the components of the EQuIP tool into manageable parts for use, providing time to preview sample curricula, and including clear step-by-step instructions for group discussions and deliverables. All of these processes leveraged online tools (e.g., Google Jamboard and Slides, Mentimeter, Zoom breakout rooms) and required that the sample curricula be accessible online.

TIPS AND ADVICE

- Generate a list of state-adopted science curricula that have been approved by your state and what science curricula are most commonly used locally.
- If you are short on time, then break down this activity using the Jigsaw technique. Small groups are responsible for a subcategory of a larger topic and then teach it to the rest of the group or class. Leverage breakout rooms for group work and rotate 'experts' across rooms. See source notes for additional support on how to conduct Jigsaw.
- Make sure teachers know how to navigate Zoom, Google Slides, and Google Jamboard functions. If it is the first time using these online tools, then model the various available functions to your students.
- Ensure that Google Slides have clear directions for the group, including group norms, in edit mode.

RESOURCE NOTES

Name of Resource	Primary Website	How to Locate the Resource Online
Amplify	https://amplify.com/	Go to "Programs" in the top tab. Then go to "Programs by subject" and select "Science." Scroll down and select "Amplify Science." Click on Free Sample (and submit relevant information). https://amplify.com/programs/amplify-science/
Cult of Pedagogy	https://www.cultofpedagogy.com/	Go to the "search bar" within this site and type in "Jigsaw instructions." Hit return. Scroll down to the second item called "Jigsaw instructions" and hit "read more." https://www.cultofpedagogy.com/jigsaw-instructions/
McGraw Hill	https://www.mheducation.com/	Go to "PreK–12" in the top tab. Scroll down to "Science & Health." Go to "9-12 program." Click on "learn more." https://www.mheducation.com/prek–12/program/microsites/MKTSP-AIB05M0/9–12.html

Name of Resource	Primary Website	How to Locate the Resource Online
Mentimeter	https://www.mentimeter.com/	Sign up for a free account and create a presentation.
National Science Teachers Association (NSTA)	https://www.nsta.org/	Go to "Classroom resources." https://ngss.nsta.org/classroom-resources.aspx
NGSS	https://www.nextgenscience.org/	Go to "Instruction and Assessment" in the top tab. Then click down to "Evaluating NGSS Design." Scroll down the page to "Tools to evaluate instructional materials." Click on "EQuIP rubric for science." https://www.nextgenscience.org/resources/equip-rubric-science
NGSS	https://www.nextgenscience.org/	Go to "Instruction and Assessment" in the top tab. Then click down to "quality NGSS units" to access example online science units. https://www.nextgenscience.org/resources/examples-quality-ngss-design
Open SciEd	https://www.openscied.org/	Go to "instructional materials" in the top tab. Then click down to "Access the instructional materials" (1st tab) to access example online Open SciEd units. https://www.openscied.org/about-instructional-materials/

DISCUSSION QUESTIONS

1. What are the most common online science curricula that your school has adopted, district, or county?
2. How might these online science curricula align with the criteria found in the EQuIP rubric?
3. Where in the online curriculum do you find the need for the greatest improvement or adaptation to your local contexts?
4. How might the EQuIP tool be used to inform lesson and unit planning development?
5. How do the three criteria address the problematizing and expectations of normalized views and practices of disciplinary teaching and learning in science in the online curricula of your school district?

REFERENCES

Ball, D. L., & Cohen, D. K. (1996). Reform by the book: What is—or might be—the role of curriculum materials in teacher learning and instructional reform? *Educational Researcher*, 25(9), 6–14.

Bybee, R. (2006). *The BSCS 5E instructional model: Origins, effectiveness, and applications. Full Report for the Office of Science Education National Institutes of Health.* BSCS.

Calabrese Barton, A., & Tan, E. (2020). Beyond equity as inclusion: A framework of "rightful presence" for guiding justice-oriented studies in teaching and learning. *Educational Researcher, 49*(6), 433–440. https://doi.org/10.3102/0013189X20927363

Freire, P., & Ramos, M. B. (1970). *Pedagogy of the oppressed.* Continuum.

Mensah, F. M. (2019). Finding voice and passion: Critical race theory methodology in science teacher education. *American Educational Research Journal, 56*(4), 1412–1456. https://doi.org/10.3102%2F0002831218818093

Mensah, F. M., & Jackson, I. (2018). Whiteness as property in science teacher education. *Teachers College Record, 120*(1), 1–38. https://doi.org/10.1177%2F016146811812000108

National Center for Education Statistics. (2020, May). *English language learners in public schools.* The Condition of Education. https://nces.ed.gov/programs/coe/indicator_cgf.asp

National Research Council. (2012). *A framework for K–12 science education: Practices, crosscutting concepts, and core ideas.* National Academies Press.

NGSS. (n.d.). *EQuIP rubric for science.* https://www.nextgenscience.org/resources/equip-rubric-science

NGSS. (n.d.). *Quality examples of science lessons and units.* https://www.nextgenscience.org/resources/examples-quality-ngss-design

NGSS Lead States. (2013). *Next generation science standards: For states, by states.* National Academies Press.

NGSS Lead States. (n.d.). *The EQuIP rubric for science.* https://www.nextgenscience.org/resources/equip-rubric-science

Schneider, R. M., & Krajcik, J. (2002). Supporting science teacher learning: The role of educative curriculum materials. *Journal of Science Teacher Education, 13*(3), 221–245. https://doi.org/10.1023/A:1016569117024

CHAPTER 5

ENGINEERING DESIGN AS A FRAMEWORK FOR VIRTUAL EDUCATION IN INCLUSIVE SCIENCE CLASSROOMS

Amanda L. Mazin and Jessica F. Riccio
Teachers College, Columbia University

Differentiated content for all learners and adhering to the high standards of teaching and learning set forth by the NGSS Standards seems to be an improbable task for science teachers. Layered on top of these challenges has been an emphasis on remote teaching and learning. Collaboration at teacher education's preservice and in-service levels can provide a foundation for successful planning and instruction. This chapter will provide a framework for constructing collaborative co-teaching methods in science and special education using instructional practices determined to be evidence-based for students with disabilities and the NGSS Framework for essential scientific practices.

RATIONALE

Providing access to a high-level science curriculum for students with disabilities has historically been a challenge for science teachers (Spooner et al., 2014). Many students have been left without technology, and even when Wi-Fi and remote learning devices can be used, students with disabilities continue to struggle to access the curriculum in a meaningful way. In online learning environments, students experience learning barriers that are more pronounced than in the traditional classroom. Learning challenges typically arise for students with disabilities in these areas: academic areas, executive function, and learning behaviors. In the online environment, additional challenges arise in these three areas due to the lack of real-time guidance from teachers, lack of just-in-time support and feedback, and the need for students to manage instructional activities more independently (Rao et al., 2021). It is increasingly clear that students' social and emotional experiences influence their learning and that teachers must learn how to integrate these areas of development to be effective (Darling-Hammond & Hyler, 2020).

Teaching science is evidently and inevitably uncertain. No one can be sure which science teaching approach will be most successful with a particular group of students (Capobianco, 2011). Research has determined that collaborative models of instruction are effective in teaching academic skills to students with disabilities (Wexler et al., 2018). Professional collaboration is also associated with higher job satisfaction, self-efficacy, and the use of innovative practices, especially when instructional pivots are required (Gawronski, 2021). In addition to increased collaboration for teachers in districts, preparation programs also strengthen collaboration with different departments at their universities to support their teacher and leader candidates' social and emotional needs (Darling-Hammond & Hyler, 2020). The engineering design process has been proposed as an innovative approach to solving many of the issues presented in science classroom instruction (Capobianco, 2017). Using engineering design, connected to evidence-based practices in special education, collaborative experiences where teachers can work together to provide effective online experiences for all learners will be presented.

THEORETICAL FRAMEWORK

The theoretical framework to support the creation of virtual collaborative spaces for science and special education teachers is threefold, containing elements of inclusive pedagogies, Universal Design for Learning (UDL), and Social Constructivism. First, inclusive pedagogies draws attention to the fact that the varied approaches to inclusive science education must be reinforced and co-constructed in teacher education and in the school context with a hope and vision for students to see themselves and their communities reflected in the classroom, language, and content taught in school science (Mensah & Larson, 2018). Second, UDL draws from various research, including neuroscience, the learning sciences, and cognitive psychology. It is deeply rooted in concepts such as the Zone of Proximal Development, scaffolding, mentors, and modeling. The empirical base of UDL is neuroscience, which provides a solid foundation for understanding how the learning brain intersects with effective instruction. This alignment is further extended and clarified by the guidelines and checkpoints (CAST, 2018). The intersection of the learning brain with effective instruction addresses individual differences, multiple models, scaffolds, and varied techniques that should be offered so that students can identify, select, and use the techniques that are personally optimal. This process suggests the effectiveness of, and the strategies for, developing students' self-questioning, self-monitoring, and self-determination skills (Agran et al., 2008).

Third, Social Constructivist research is based on constructivist learning principles. The design models actively engage all stakeholders in the co-construction of its parts (Brooks & Brooks, 1993). The digital divide cannot be closed by removing the teachers' agency in this crisis by doing it for them. Navigation must be a multi-level and multi-lens process where all stakeholders explore inquiry together. The primary role is research and the development of new information. However, the relationship between teacher and student, including their voices and concerns, is within our project goals while providing a framework for success. Implicit in our process is modeling a gradual release protocol with our preservice teachers based on the Self-Regulated Strategy Development (SRSD) model (Graham & Harris, 1996) where the introduction of the intervention, modeling of the intervention, guided practice, and finally independent practice are explicitly taught.

These three distinct but interrelated concepts guided the development of collaborative experiences. UDL was the foundation for all experiences. The use of technology to provide access to curriculum and experiences and the development of differentiated curriculum was also directly linked to engineering design. Throughout these experiences, the overlap was a consistent reminder of the similarities in the concepts. By reflecting on the diversity of learners' experiences, knowledge, and goals, inclusive pedagogies guided representative experiences in science classrooms. Understanding the different ways learning can occur and

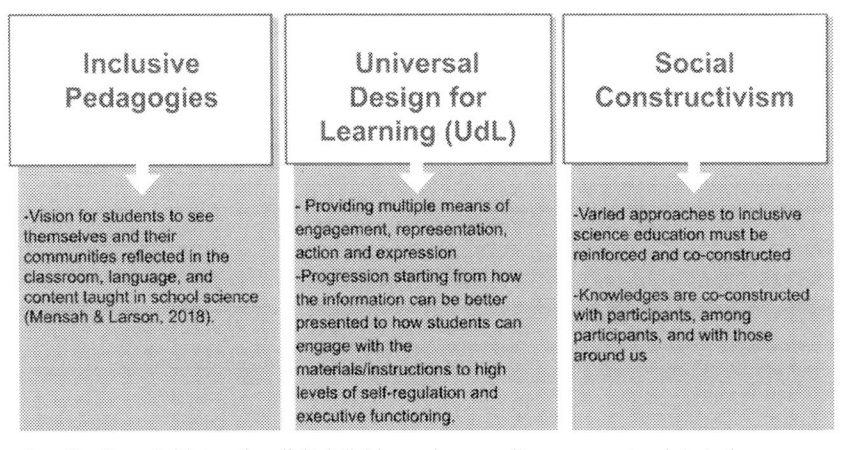

Application: bridging the digital divide and expanding access to global phenomena

FIGURE 5.1. Theoretical Framework

providing the tools for each learner to achieve their highest potential highlights the projects and the interconnectedness of the theoretical framework.

CHAPTER FOCUS

The Next Generation Science Standards (NGSS Lead States, 2013) have changed the science education landscape. Teachers can achieve equity for all students by providing appropriate supports to help students access and learn about their world within this framework (Spooner et al., 2014). By bridging the two disciplines in a research-supported learning environment, teachers will be better prepared for inclusive environments. With inclusive pedagogies at the center, opportunities for science and special education teachers to collaborate will follow an iterative structure grounded in social constructivism. Figure 5.2 highlights the continuous, nested interaction among stakeholders.

Creating Collaborative Virtual Experiences

This section highlights the relationship between the Science and Engineering Practices (NGSS Lead States, 2013) and UDL Guidelines (CAST, 2018) by presenting models of use where blending the practices occur. The relationship between these practices is shown in Figure 5.3. See Figure 5.4 for engineering design principles.

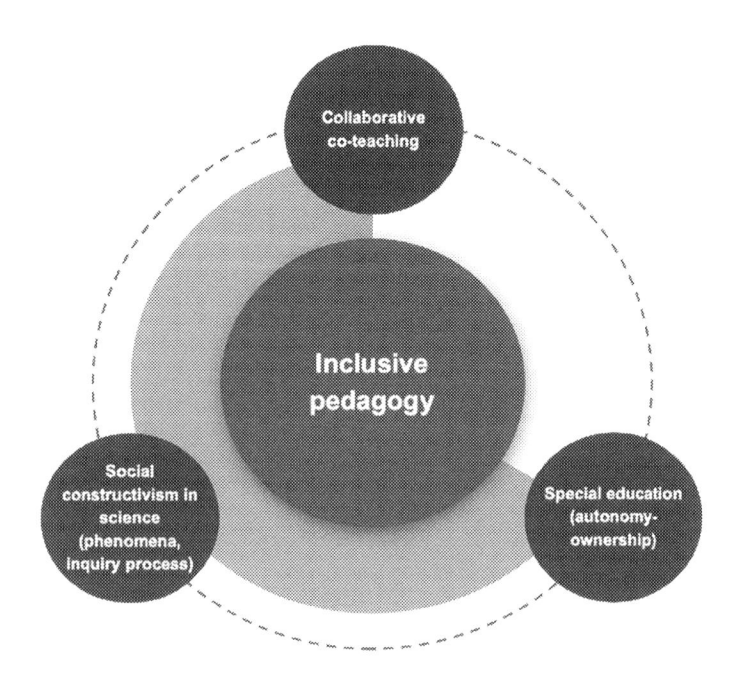

FIGURE 5.2. Model for Inclusive Digital Pedagogy

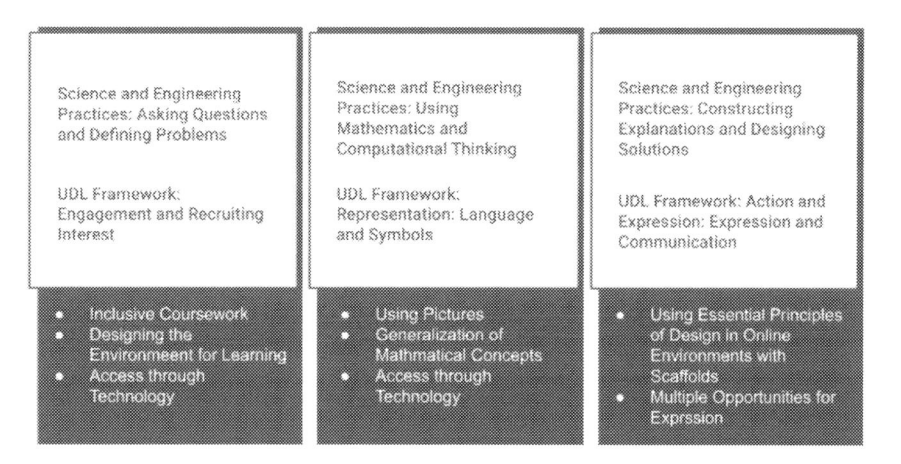

FIGURE 5.3.   Relationship of Science and Engineering Practices to UDL

Two examples of this process are presented below. They illustrate the process of science and special education teachers collaboration to differentiate high school curricula to participate in and create inclusive practices for online learning using the NGSS Standards (2013), UDL Guidelines (CAST, 2018), and following Social Constructivist Learning Principles (Brooks & Brooks, 1993). The examples contain sequential, collaborative teaching experiences. Example I: Constructing Explanations and Designing Solutions is focused on planning and implementing collaborative experiences. Action I is situated in the classroom and instructional design. By focusing on designing inclusive spaces, science and special education

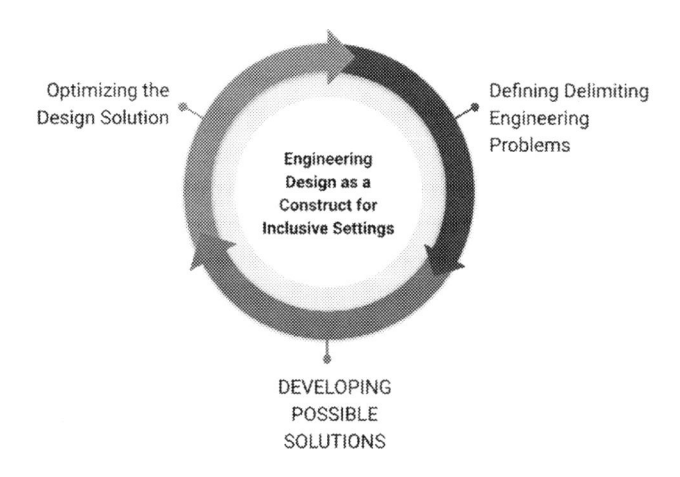

FIGURE 5.4.   Engineering Design Principles

teachers can lay the foundation for a productive learning environment. Action II is focused on the modification of the existing curriculum and practices. Using observation as the initial form of data collection, the teachers learn from each other. The teachers employ Engineering Design as a framework for planning. This framework begins the nested process of teaching and learning. Action III is collaborative lesson planning. Using elements of Engineering Design and specific NGSS to plan the lessons, the teachers can then focus on implementing the Principles of UDL to reach and teach all learners.

The proposed format for this lesson is online. Teachers collaborate to create a collaborative experience for the students in science classrooms. Example 2: Using Mathematics and Computational Thinking continues with the dual collaborative process. This example brings in research and reflection. By continuing to use Engineering Design as the foundation, NGSS Standards as instructional design, and UDL as the instructional method, teachers have created accessible lesson plans. The next step is to reflect on the process through teacher action research. This research is done using an interactive, simple four-step process that should be conducted in person and online. The mix of modalities allows for the Principles of UDL to be applied to all areas of collaborative instruction.

Example One

NGSS Standard: Constructing Explanations and Designing Solutions: Design a solution to a complex real-world problem based on scientific knowledge, student-generated sources of evidence, prioritized criteria, and tradeoff considerations. (HS-ETS1-2)

UDL Framework Ia. Engagement: Recruiting Interest: Information that is not attended to, that does not engage learners' cognition, is inaccessible. It is inaccessible both in the moment and future because relevant information goes unnoticed and unprocessed (CAST, 2018).

UDL Framework Ib. Representation: Language and Symbols: Inequalities arise when information is presented to all learners through a single form of representation (CAST, 2018).

Practice I. Inclusive Classroom Design and Planning

Action I. Setting the Stage: Using knowledge and experience to guide instructional decisions. This initial practice sets the stage for a productive relationship among all stakeholders. Using key elements of classroom design, collaborators will engage in decision-making surrounding the set-up and organization of the learning environment. The purpose is to *design* key elements of the learning space and instruction to recruit interest before learning occurs. Grounded in research, the focus should be on in-person and online teaching and learning. Specific, proactive, collaborative topics:

- Designing and organizing in-person classroom environments
- Designing and organizing online environments

- Engaging all learners in high-level curriculum online and in-person
- Differentiating curriculum to meet the diverse needs of learners with and without disabilities
- Providing access through technology
- Modifying curriculum, using graphic organizers, presenting material in new and innovative ways
- Classroom management techniques

Practice II. Teaching in Inclusive Environments

Action II. Instructional Decision-Making: These experiences are designed for in-person and online learning. This process necessitates rethinking the ways teachers could gain the same experiences while teaching and learning online. By applying the concepts of UDL, using an engineering framework, and social constructivist principles to engage teachers in the planning process, both teachers and students can learn in both environments. A collaborative online environment with a clear theoretical framework is needed to make this successful. Goals of teaching include:

- Modifying lesson plans to meet the needs of all learners in the classroom (virtual and in-person)
- Using technology to create more inclusive lessons
- Engaging students in large and small groups in online environments
- Data-based decision-making
- Observation and interviewing both science and special education teachers before instruction, during instruction, and after instruction
- Engaging in the planning process
- Ongoing conversations as key stakeholders (including students) in the process of teaching and learning

Practice III. Application of UDL in a science methods class (i.e., earth science; biology; physics; chemistry).

Action III. Collaborative Experiences: Using UDL, the teachers create a lesson plan that allows for the practice of collaborative skills. The use of a simple but explorative assignment allows teachers to focus on collaboration along with the essential principles of the design. The lesson plan is grounded in scientific processes and allows for collaborative creativity between instructors. The lesson includes designing an online lesson with only three pictures as the phenomena but creating scaffolded supports as a generalization of skills. The teachers will collaboratively design a lesson grounded in Engineering Design while specifically following the NGSS Standards and Principles of UDL. This assignment involves optimizing the design solution in which solutions are systematically tested and refined. The final design is improved by trading off less important features for those that are more important (NGSS Lead States, 2013). As students and teachers engage in iterations of asking questions, developing plans, designing prototypes or models, evaluating, and redesigning, they also have the opportunity to confront their understandings and misunderstandings of science concepts (Capobianco, 2011). This opportunity creates a nested process of continued learning. Goals of this lesson include:

- Application of specific evidence-based practices for students with disabilities
- Thinking about how different learners could access this assignment
- Engagement during an online lesson
- Linking concepts from special education literature and practice to this science lesson

Example Two

NGSS Standard: Using Mathematics and Computational Thinking: Use mathematical models and/or computer simulations to predict the effects of a design solution on systems and/or the interactions between systems. (HS-ETS1-4) Moreover, Constructing Explanations and Designing Solutions: Evaluate a solution to a complex real-world problem based on scientific knowledge, student-generated sources of evidence, prioritized criteria, and tradeoff considerations. (HS-ETS1-3).

UDL Framework. Action and Expression: Expression and Communication: It is crucial to provide alternative modalities for expression, both to level the playing field among learners and to allow the learner to appropriately (or easily) express knowledge, ideas, and concepts in the learning environment (CAST, 2018).

Practice I. Collaborative Teacher Action Research

Action I. Teacher Action Research Projects (in person)

In the teacher action research projects, an investigation into an aspect of classroom life that draws on the realities of the needs of the classroom to help understand learners' context and needs is conducted. Collaborative action research can reduce the amount of uncertainty teachers face and support teachers to better manage their uncertainties (Capobianco, 2011). It should:

- Draw upon the current research
- Be grounded in teaching experience
- Include teacher research (i.e., student interviews, innovative assessments, analysis of student work)
- Provide stakeholders an opportunity to explore the topic in a "real world" school-based experience.
- Follow the iterative four-step Teacher Action Research (reflect, plan, act, observe) process

Practice II. Collaborative Teacher Action Research

Action II. Teacher Action Research Projects (online)

This project includes the same fundamental concepts but will add fully remote collaboration and online/hybrid teaching. These action research projects partnered with engineering practices provide space for teachers to learn about the subject matter, pedagogy, and student learning uncertainties. When they "recognize and accept uncertainties and identify these as opportunities for growth, learning, and increased success over time" (Capobianco, p. 658, 2011), the change from passive to active participate in the online collaborative experience occurred.

SUMMARY AND REFLECTION

Over 70% of students who receive special education services spend more than 60% of their time in regular education classrooms (US Department of Education, OSEP, 2018). Federal law states that students with disabilities have access to the general curriculum to the maximum extent possible. However, content specialty teachers are unprepared to modify curriculum, enhance presentations and think about learning in terms of individual student needs. As a result, there is a need for coursework development to promote collaborative co-teaching with special education teachers and content specialty teachers, specifically in science.

Schools face increased pressure to help students with disabilities meet rigorous achievement standards across the content areas. However, science content remains a commonly overlooked academic content area for students with severe disabilities, despite recent research (Greene & Bethune, 2021). In addition to being required under the, Every Student Succeeds Act (ESSA, 2015), teaching students with disabilities science content allows for full educational opportunities within their school and highlights the fact that science instruction promotes understanding of the natural world, including providing a format for posing questions (Courtade et al., 2014; Spooner & Brown, 2011; Spooner et al., 2017). Science instruction for students with disabilities may have been pushed aside for several reasons, including that it has been previously thought that science concepts, particularly inquiry-based concepts, are too complex for students with disabilities (Mensah & Lawson, 2018; Spooner & Brown, 2011.).

By grounding opportunities in both a theoretical foundation and a real need in the field, we have created experiences that better prepare science and special education teachers for a collaborative experience. Historically, content specialty teachers knew their content and special education teachers knew their students. Current practice and understanding insist that all children, including those with severe disabilities, are taught academic skills, and EBPs are to teach those skills (Spooner et al., 2017). Teachers need to provide coursework and experiences in content areas with differentiated, individualized instruction. An emphasis on online teaching and learning highlighted the disparities in the educational system. By preparing science teachers to differentiate the curriculum to meet the needs of all learners and be active participants in the development of coursework and experiences, the nested model of teaching and learning continues. The key to successful online learning is collaborative experiences. Using the knowledge of all stakeholders and a clear foundation of understanding theory and practice related effective pedagogy allows teachers to make equitable decisions as part of their learning process.

TIPS AND ADVICE

- Leave room for social communication and opportunities to evolve as a team.
- Look to collaborate with colleagues in spaces that may not seem obvious.
- Identify an immersive rather than "add-on" approach to collaborative co-teaching.
- Provide multiple ways for students to access all information.
- Take time to pause and reflect. Model this behavior for students.

RESOURCE NOTES

Name of Resource	Primary Website	How to Locate the Resource Online
Appendix I—Engineering Design in NGSS	https://www.next-genscience.org/topic-arrangement/msengineering-design	To navigate from the NGSS page, click on download PDF in the upper right corner and scroll to the appendix. Direct link: https://www.nextgenscience.org/sites/default/files/Appendix%20I%20-%20Engineering%20Design%20in%20NGSS%20-%20FINAL_V2.pdf
UDL Guidelines	https://udlguidelines.cast.org/	This link is the main page for UDL information.
UDL Guidelines: Engagement	https://udlguidelines.cast.org/	Beginning at the main page, navigate to Engagement by clicking on the title on the top left of the navigation bar. Below is the direct link. https://udlguidelines.cast.org/engagement
UDL Guidelines: Representation	https://udlguidelines.cast.org/	Beginning at the main page, navigate to Representation by clicking on the title in the middle of the navigation bar. Below is the direct link. https://udlguidelines.cast.org/representation
UDL Guidelines: Action and Expression	https://udlguidelines.cast.org/	Beginning at the main page, navigate to Action and Expression by clicking on the title in the middle of the navigation bar. Below is the direct link. https://udlguidelines.cast.org/action-expression

DISCUSSION QUESTIONS

1. What is the impact of NGSS on science instruction for students with disabilities in virtual environments?
2. What collaborative strategies for teaching scientific processes to students with disabilities could benefit all learners while adhering to the standards set forth by the NGSS in both in-person and virtual teaching environments?
3. Describe the benefits of co-teaching for teaching students with disabilities in science and how methods can be developed to construct co-teaching environments to teach scientific processes.

REFERENCES

Agran, M., Wehmeyer, M. L., Cavin, M., & Palmer, S. (2008). Promoting student active classroom participation skills through instruction to promote self-regulated learning and self-determination. *Career Development for Exceptional Individuals, 31*(2), 106–114. https://doi.org/10.1177%2F0885728808317656

Brooks, J. G., & Brooks, M. G. (1993). *In search of understanding: The case for constructivist classrooms.* Association of Supervision and Curriculum Development.

Capobianco, B. (2011). Exploring a science teacher's uncertainty with integrating engineering design: An action research study. *Journal of Science Teacher Education, 22*(7), 645–660. http://www.jstor.org/stable/43156624

Capobianco, B., & Feldman, A. (2006). Promoting quality for teacher action research: Lessons learned from science teachers' action research. *Educational Action Research, 14*(4), 497–512. https://doi-org.ezproxy.cul.columbia.edu/10.1080/09650790600975668

CAST. (2018). *Universal Design for Learning Guidelines.* http://udlguidelines.cast.org

Courtade, G., Test, D., & Cook, B. (2014). Evidence-based practices for learners with severe intellectual disability. *Research and Practice for Persons with Severe Disabilities, 39*, 305–318. https://doi.org/10.1177/1540796914566711

Darling-Hammond, L., & Hyler, M.E. (2020) Preparing educators for the time of COVID…and beyond. *European Journal of Teacher Education, 43*(4). 457–465. https://doi.org/10.1080/02619768.2020.1816961

Every Student Succeeds Act, 20 USC § 6301 (2015).

Fouché, J. (2013). RETHINKING FAILURE: When getting it wrong can increase students' chances for getting it right. *The Science Teacher, 80*(8), 45–49. http://www.jstor.org/stable/43557846

Gawronski, J. H. (2021). Teaching during the time of COVID: Learning from mentor teachers experiences. *Journal of Digital Learning in Teacher Education, 37*(4), 217–233. https://doi.org/10.1080/21532974.2021.1965507

Graham, S., & Harris, K. R. (1996). Self-regulation and strategy instruction for students who find writing and learning challenging. In C. M. Levy & S. Ransdell (Eds.), *The science of writing: Theories, methods, individual differences, and applications* (pp. 347–360). Lawrence Erlbaum Associates, Inc.

Greene, A., & Bethune, K. S. (2021). The effects of systematic instruction in a group format to teach science to students with autism and intellectual disability. *Journal of Behavioral Education, 30*(1), 62–79. https://doi.org/10.1007/s10864-019-09353-6

Individuals with Disabilities Education Improvement Act, 20 USC 1400 et seq. (2004).

Mensah, F. M., & Lawson, K. (2018). *A summary of inclusive pedagogies for science.* Commissioned paper for Committee on Science Investigations and Engineering Design for Grades 6–12, Board on Science Education, Division of Behavioral and Social Sciences and Education, National Academy of Sciences, Engineering, and Medicine (NASEM). https://sites.nationalacademies.org/cs/groups/dbassesite/documents/webpage/dbasse_189501.pdf

National Research Council. (2012). *A framework for K–12 science education: Practices, crosscutting concepts, and core ideas.* Committee on a Conceptual Framework for New K–12 Science Education Standards, Board on Science Education, Division of Behavioral and Social Sciences and Education. National Academies Press.

NGSS Lead States. (2013). *Next generation science standards: For states, by states.* National Academies Press.

Rao, K., Torres, C., & Smith, S. J. (2021). Digital tools and UDL-Based instructional strategies to support students with disabilities online. *Journal of Special Education Technology 36*(2), 105–112. https://doi.org/10.1177/0162643421998327

Spooner, F., & Brown, F. (2011). Educating students with significant cognitive disabilities: Historical overview and future projections. In J. M. Kauffman & D. P. Hallahan (Eds.), *Handbook of special education* (pp. 503–515). Routledge.

Spooner, F., McKissick, B. R., Hudson, M., & Browder, D. M. (2014). Access to the general education curriculum in general education classes. In M. Agran, F. Brown, C. Hughes, C. Quirk, & D. Ryndak (Eds.), *Equity and full participation for individuals with severe disabilities: A vision for the future* (pp. 217–234). Brookes.

Spooner, F., McKissick, B. R., & Knight, V. F. (2017). Establishing the state of affairs for evidence-based practices in students with severe disabilities. *Research and Practice for Persons with Severe Disabilities, 42*(1), 8–18. https://doi.org/10.1177/1540796916684896

US Department of Education, Office of Special Education Programs. (2018). *40th annual report to congress on the implementation of the Individuals with Disabilities Education Act.* https://sites.ed.gov/idea/2018-annual-report-to-congress-on-the-individuals-with-disabilities-education-act/

Wexler, J., Kearns, D. M., Lemmons, C. J., Mitchell, M., Clancy, E., Davidson, K. A., Sinclair, A. C., & Wei, Y. (2018). Reading comprehension and co-teaching practices in middle school English Language Arts classrooms. *Exceptional Children, 84*(4) 384–402. https://doi.org/10.1177/0014402918771543

CHAPTER 6

BRIDGING THE GAP

Empowering Adolescent Girls in STEM Through Online Learning and Mentoring

Leslie Ekpe

Texas Christian University

Sarah Toutant

University of Southern California

Gender differences in science, technology, engineering, and mathematics (STEM) fields begin early; young girls report a lower degree of technical engagement and self-efficacy than primary schoolboys. Because of this nature, there is an existing need for opportunities to sustain young girls' interests in sciences. Online learning programs that provide more mentorship opportunities can inspire young girls to continue careers in STEM. This chapter illuminates the possible connections through online experiences that retain young girls' interests past the secondary school level in the science subject area.

The future of science is inclusive. Science, technology, engineering, and mathematics (STEM) will account for a significant portion of potential employment growth in the United States (National Academies, 2010). However, political, social, and personal influences consistently deter women from joining STEM industries, including pernicious assumptions and a lack of women in these working

Teaching and Learning Online: Science for Secondary Grade Levels, pages 69–90.

environments. Women have occupied less than 25% of STEM jobs in the last decade, while technical and mathematical occupations are consistently among the most highly paying careers (Cundiff & Vescio, 2016). If the study of STEM professions does not inspire young girls, then the gender disparity in these careers will continue to rise. Women are needed for economic needs and are also needed to create gender equality and social change. It is a question of social growth.

RATIONALE

According to Dasgupta and Stout (2014): "In childhood and adolescence, masculine stereotypes about STEM, parents' expectations of daughters, peer norms, and lack of fit with personal goals make girls move away from STEM fields" (pg. 21). The lack of women representation in STEM fields is nothing new based on the practices implemented historically. Sadker et al. (2009) explained:

> Here's how my 1960s high school chemistry class was taught: Boys were seated by male teacher on the side of the room with the teacher's desk. Girls were seated on the far side of the room. Girls were told to be quiet and not cause trouble, and they would not fail the class. When 'dangerous' experiments were conducted, the boys went into the lab while the girls watched through the window. (p. 49)

In American culture, gender inequality persists. Despite shifts in beliefs and subtler manifestations of sexism, gender disparities remain relatively easy to come by. Specific interest differs by gender as early as primary school, with girls showing less interest in and liking computers than boys (Cooper, 2006). In elementary and middle school, girls report having less confidence in their scientific and computer abilities than boys (Beghetto, 2007). Knowledge integration can be encouraged by online programming. Science and technology priorities are primarily formed by the end of elementary school (Maltese & Tai, 2010), indicating the importance of intervening earlier to promote their emergence. According to some theories, interest will progress from situational to individual interest (Hidi & Renninger, 2006).

Underrepresentation of women in STEM is a complex topic that must be considered as it relates to the future of science. According to the Women and Minorities in Science, Technology, Engineering, and Mathematics: Upping the Numbers (Burke & Mattis, 2007), "by the age of 12, children have already formed firm beliefs about the subjects at which they excel and those at which they fail" (p. 7). With the underrepresentation in computer science and engineering fields, young girls receive fewer chances to apply to and learn from these fields (Master et al., 2017). Although various interconnected variables affect the gender disparity in attendance, evidence shows that a gender difference in interest occurs in grade school (Ceci & Williams, 2010b). The cracked pipeline for women in the STEM field begins early. From middle school to post-secondary levels of education, girls are less confident and inspired in science and mathematics assessments than male students. Furthermore, many of these girls, who might otherwise become the next wave of scientists, engineers, and invention developers, lose their confidence, and do not pursue advanced classes and majors in the science field (Dasgupta & Stout, 2014).

Formal learning experiences face numerous problems that online learning programs can address. Our chapter will first explore the underrepresentation of girls in STEM by reviewing relevant literature. Next, we offer a framework that can be utilized for educators, teachers, and administrators alike to encourage, inspire, and empower adolescent girls who show interests in STEM, particularly in online environments. We end with tips and advice for how educational leaders can provide proper resources and support to close the gender gap in STEM.

DEFINITIONS

For this chapter, we utilize the following terms and their definitions:

- **Confidence**—Pajares et al. (2006) defines confidence as anticipating a successful outcome.
- **Mentoring**—the relationship of a person(s) who is more experienced and is purposed with developing and helping the mentee's career (Ragins & Cotton, 1991).
- **STEM**—Science, Technology, Engineering, and Mathematics. In this study, 'STEM' is used interchangeably with 'science fields.'

THEORETICAL BACKGROUND

Underrepresentation Influencing Gender Gaps

Girls are socialized to be communal (e.g., socially competent, and helpful) while being the nurturers of children and families, gravitating toward behaviors that emphasize interpersonal interactions, contrary to feminine gender position expectations (Konrad et al., 2000). Girls who express an interest in STEM are given less motivation at home and in the classroom than boys; there are fewer women in STEM role models, fewer STEM extracurricular programs, social gender role norms, and a computer community that favors male competence (Glick & Fiske.,1999; Herbert & Stipek, 2005). However, the reason for the underrepresentation of women in STEM fields has changed over time. Researchers in the early 20th century speculated that the genetic disparity between men and women might justify women's lower intellect, imagination, and scientific abilities, whereas men's mathematical ability was exemplified (Benbow & Stanley, 1980). We know this speculation is far from the truth.

The Commission on the Advancement of Women and Minorities in Science, Engineering, and Technology (CAWMSET) recognized the exclusion of underrepresented populations such as women, racially minoritized people, and persons with disabilities and called for a more inclusive approach to the representation of these populations. Despite the call to change, young girls and women continue to face difficulties pursuing STEM education and careers. There is no single or straightforward solution to the gender disparity problem. Notwithstanding, there is a desperate awareness needed to be centered when discussing a lack of women role models and mentors, social gender roles validated by peers, family, culture, and society, and a lack of trust due to internal feelings of inadequacy for women pursuing STEM (Besecke & Reilly, 2006; Cleaves, 2005). Advancement in STEM is critical for defense, prosperity, and economic development, whether it is looking back or looking forward (Burke & Mattis, 2007), and women are a critical part of such advancement.

Modern Context

STEM programs that bring together realistic experiences, role models, mentoring, and career exploration boost girls' self-assurance and engagement in science courses and careers (Campbell & Steinbrueck, 1996). Research further refers to numerous activities fostering a decent and balanced educational climate for girls and their continuity of quantitative disciplines such as science. The programming and resources provide group research, professional knowledge, a concentration on practical applications, and science teaching in a more integral and community-oriented way (Campbell et al., 2002). The variables correlated with girls' involvement in STEM and girls' success were proposed to various gender-based learning forms. Girls are more involved with software that offers teamwork, strategic thinking, and innovation (AAUW, 2000). Researchers have also found that computer programming expertise is connected to the computer divide between girls and boys. Furthermore, girls' programming abilities are a critical indicator of their sense of machine performance and university achievement (Sanders, 2002). Afterschool interest has grown considerably in the last decade as leaders, development workers, and parents view this time as an unusual challenge and opportunity (Dasgupta & Stout, 2014).

Other similar characteristics of many of these successful interventions include exposure to realistic, interactive activities; a correlation between the curriculum and the home; and less school-like settings where young girls seek assistance and build positive relationships with mentors. In order to manage an increasingly dynamic environment and globalized economy, STEM skills are increasingly required. Therefore, STEM education can provide activities after school and at the fingertips to enhance and expand opportunities for young women. The effect of these types of extended learning opportunities and off-school programs also illustrates young girls' achievement upgrades. It is vital to learn meaningful STEM, which stretches over one-shot interactions often experienced in the classroom. The provision of standard, coherent programming on STEM subject areas should be given close attention to online post-school programs. Moreover, whenever possible, programs, to optimize their effect on their STEM programs, must have a range of STEM learning opportunities to keep young girls engaged past the classroom.

Chapter Focus

When women continue to be underrepresented in STEM, what role do educators have in inspiring and empowering these women to persist within the field? At a time when technology is rapidly changing how we live, educators need to empower more young women. The decision about what field to pursue as an adolescent can be challenging, especially with the rigors of STEM careers. We encourage teachers and educators to spark curiosity for young women outside the classroom through online learning and mentoring.

CONCEPTUAL FRAMEWORK

Connectivism as a Learning Theory

As many classrooms have shifted from in-person to online, professors, teachers, and students alike have navigated a new learning environment. Traditionally classes are transitioning to common platforms, such as Zoom, as well as extracurricular activities (e.g., clubs and programs). This global shift to relying solely on online learning environments makes it even more pertinent to theorize. In order to discuss learning in the digital age, we lean towards Connectivism as a Learning Theory framework.

Connectivism is characterized as "the enhancement of how a student learns with the knowledge and perception gained through the addition of a personal network" (Duke et al., 2013, p. 7). Through such personal networks, people learn by being exposed to the diversity of thought. Connectivism also acknowledges that one person cannot know all there is to know, which is why they must tap into different databases and resources of knowledge to learn (Duke et al., 2013). Lastly, connectivism accounts for the new digital age of acquiring knowledge since it finds that where to find knowledge is more vital than answering the how or what (Duke et al., 2013).

Connectivism as a learning theory in the age of online learning and discovery helps theorize about girls in STEM since it accounts for their shift in learning. To explain, girls need new and exciting ways to be engaged with STEM in online environments. Connectivism acknowledges that girls will need (1) mentors to be connected with to enhance their intellectual thought processes, (2) the internet to acquire new forms of knowledge through online databases, and (3) the space to lean into online environments to take control of their futures in STEM. We must begin to envision this new digital age of technology as a new way to learn, network, and engage. By learning into connectivism as a learning theory, educational leaders can use online programming and mentoring to close the gender disparities in STEM.

ONLINE STEM LEARNING FOR ADOLESCENT GIRLS

Several factors need to be considered when adopting non-traditional plans for learning for young adolescent girls in the field of STEM. Despite a rising understanding of the importance of implementing STEM in the curriculum of the K–12, the systematic implementation of the classroom remains inconvenient. STEM education requires more interdisciplinary and collaborative approaches to learning and ability creation (Committee on STEM Education, 2018). The separated and fragmented conventional approach to teaching STEM disciplines ignores cross-cutting ideas and connections with real-world implementations (Rogers et al., 2015).

Exposure to non-traditional classroom environments of young girls to STEM will boost trust in their STEM identity. A mere emphasis on one age demographic cannot solve all social challenges that affect women's career choices. However, correcting the negative views of young girls will make them take up mathematics and science as they go to high school instead of avoiding subjects. Otherwise, young women would believe they had an error when facing the obstacles to completing a STEM major without knowing the resources open to mathematics and scientists. Online mentoring programming provides many ways of connecting, learning new skills, sharing imagination, and helping a healthier world for young girls.

Stoeger et al., (2013) explained that STEM mentorship brings different benefits. It gives girls suitable role models of women who are STEM experts (Dasgupta, 2011). Girls and women who have picked classes, curricula or careers in STEM emphasize the importance of decision-making of role models (Eccles-Parsons, 1984). The mentor's presence extends beyond the role models that they have. Female mentors also support their students through advice, encouragement, training, and information sharing (Stoeger et al., 2019). For example, mentors encourage their mentees to develop insight and successful options for action in STEM that can lead to learning and improvements in success. Mentors play a critical role in assisting mentees envisioning themselves in STEM careers.

Developing Identities in STEM

The period of adolescence to develop STEM identities is critical by aligning *who I am* with a STEM field, which I want to be. A clear STEM identity may also be a vital factor in helping young people to develop their future STEM careers. While certain aspects of identity may be based on indifferent development or even include completed biological maturity, like sexual identity, intrinsic to and established within a social environment is social identity (Kim et al., 2018). Online STEM programming provides a space for engaging critical thinking skills and further developing ones' identity in science through a nontraditional route. According to Steinke (2005), stereotypes of STEM professions have played a critical role in the construction, portrayal, dissemination, and propagation of stereotypes, but little is understood about how stereotypes affect STEM identity development. It is critical to women's progression to implement inclusive strategies connecting adolescent girls to their STEM identities.

Productive Mentoring

Mentoring is defined in myriad ways since no single definition exists and scholars have provided various definitions of mentoring (Brown et al., 2020). We borrow from Simmie and Moles' (2011) productive mentoring" framework for our conceptual framework. In this framework, the authors engage a learner-centered and democratic approach by utilizing theory to inform practice. Productive mentoring is unique since it promotes a mentoring relationship that involves an equal playing field "in which all participants are posited as competent and valued, regardless of experience in the field" (Simmie & Moles, 2011, p. 24). Productive mentoring is useful when examining girls' underrepresentation in STEM since it includes them as co-creators in their realities. Co-creating is vital because encouraging girls in STEM also means providing them the space to grow personally, academically, and, ultimately, professionally in collaboration with their mentors.

Productive mentoring also requires a philosophy of care, which means mentors think critically about aiding their mentee's learning (Simmie & Moles, 2011). This framework helps design innovative programs to improve girls' STEM education because it centers on the needs of students and creates space for mutually beneficial collaborative discussions. Specifically, this theoretical framework invites mentees, regardless of their age, to the table to participate in reflection and intellectual exercises. Such a framework does not assume that mentors cannot also learn from mentees. Nonetheless, it is imperative for educational leaders and beyond to understand that the youth have just as much knowledge—if not more—for the future of STEM. Their knowledge and intellectual and professional desires should be nourished and believed in through productive mentoring.

Productive Mentoring in Connected Online Learning

By utilizing connectivism and productive mentoring theories in conjunction, we can imagine the inventive ways the digital age and mentoring can shape girls' futures in STEM. It is not enough for programs for girls in STEM to transition to online spaces, but rather, programs should be intentionally designed for online learning. By moving towards this model, girls in STEM will have mentors who are knowledgeable about the benefits of online spaces, know how to mentor with technology and not against technology, and encourage girls to use online platforms to their learning advantage. Overall, we argue that these theories suggest that education leaders should not adapt to the digital times but should design with these times in mind.

Implications

According to Webb (1995), students learn more when the debate group has a wide variety of viewpoints and when students can both pose and answer questions. According to Dewey (1901), all learning is psychological and subsequent scholars have formulated advantages and processes for learning in a social context (Vygotsky, 1978). Students of all ages are expected to attend a form of education. As a result of this compulsory obligation, school accounts for a large portion of students' conscious hours. This study aims to offer innovative learning environments through online STEM learning programs. It illustrates that equal dialogue opportunities can be developed. It pushes science educators to think beyond the box to improve the reflective aspect of class dialogue and ensure that all voices are understood. This research is salient because it explores factors influencing the participation and trust of girls in mathematics and science in the sixth and 12th grades and suggests creative online programming. First, when describing the drivers that affect the desires of young girls, we should understand the STEM developmental experiences as these experiences contribute to the interests and trust in the subject of Mathematics. Social identities describe who belongs to a social group and what it means to be a member of that group. In addition, we use Social Identity Theory as a basis for analyzing how the online STEM learning atmosphere influences female students' efforts to stay in STEM while maintaining interest in their STEM identities.

One implication of online learning programming is that young girls may lose interest in signing in through a digital platform. However, the drive to participate is an ongoing topic in the online debate. When awarded, participants log in and comment, but some adopt a minimalist position only once. Most students do not consider the debate to be exciting and several efforts to inspire audiences to attend focus groups do not succeed. Many with hobbies or medical problems that are important for the participants tend to be the most popular parties. There is a need for more studies to identify approaches to inspire scientific discussions equally across all genders.

Another implication of online mentoring is the need for mentor training. Even the most skilled mentors may improve their mentoring skills with proper training. When mentor and mentee expectations are matched and each individual has the skills to maximize the mentoring opportunity, the most effective mentoring partnerships are established. As a result, maintaining an effective mentoring strategy will be a continual process of reflection and change.

Lastly, building online learning and mentoring opportunities for young women looks drastically different at all levels grade levels. For example, middle school level opportunities present themselves in ways such as taking part in video game design, exploring digital animation, experimenting with science toolkits, meeting and being paired with women role models in the STEM field, and more from the comfort of their homes. In comparison, upper-level opportunities for high school girls can include personal interactions with other young women at various schools to build community, a mix of lecture and hands-on activities, various coding opportunities, building confidence through independent practice, and receiving small-group and online tutoring from mentors. A benefit of online learning is that it allows young women who otherwise would not have access to STEM programs to participate. It also allows for the creation of communities that expand far beyond the classroom to collaborate and come together. Moreover, online learning and mentoring participation can help to strengthen healthy female-female relationships for young women ages 11 to 18. By creating STEM identity, we say a young woman comes to STEM to see their existing and potential future selves.

SUMMARY AND REFLECTIONS

Since there is no single reason for the leaky pipeline of girls and women into STEM sectors, there is no single solution. Learning and work experiences that promote belonging are much more likely to succeed in hiring, maintaining, and progressing girls and women in STEM than environments that feel isolated and homogeneous (Dasgupta & Stout, 2014). When correctly implemented, online mentoring can serve as a practice to mitigate the gender gap within the STEM field. Mentoring serves as an environmental factor that contributes to girls' poor involvement in STEM fields. Efficient mentoring requires structural and operational elements such as adequate mentoring duration, routine exchanges between mentee and mentor, and mentor supervision and preparation. The consistency of the partnership between tutor and mentee is a meaningful measure of effectively applied mentoring if these institutional and operational dimensions are met (Bayer et al., 2015).

The lack of representation of women and girls in STEM is a topic that continues to garner more attention. As the literature illustrates, girls and women are systemically guided away from STEM throughout their educational journeys, which limits their career options in adulthood. This chapter argues that to tackle gender disparities in STEM, we must start at an early age. Girls in K–12 education need to be provided the resources, mentors, and tools to envision themselves in STEM. Given the ever-changing digital world of which we are all a part, such supports must also consider how online learning intersects with tackling the underrepresentation of girls in STEM. To operationalize closing this gap, we suggest a connectivism and productive mentoring theoretical approach for classroom teachers, administrators, teacher educators, and others interested in empowering young women to pursue STEM courses at the high school and college levels.

In order to work towards closing the gender gap in STEM, it is also essential to consider the practical ways educators can contribute. Although STEM programs and initiatives aimed at improving the representation of girls are helpful, we must also provide educators and administrators with a guide to support these girls. Educators and administrators are at the frontline, serving students on a day-to-day basis. Given their proximity to young women in these spaces, it is also crucial that we empower educators to mentor, guide, and support our youth in STEM careers. Thus, this chapter has provided literature to trace the historical context of the gender disparity in STEM, suggested an inclusive framework to ground this work, and in the next section will provide more tips and advice for educators, teachers, and administrators to influence the gender gap in STEM fields. This work fits into the current body of knowledge about the relevance of identity in scientific education techniques for increasing females' persistence in STEM areas, particularly in the unique context of informal science settings. Overall, closing the STEM gap is a task that all professionals in the educational sector need to work toward. Although the gap will not be closed quickly, we are hopeful that, in the coming years, progress will continue.

TIPS AND ADVICE

Building a science identity is critical to developing young girls in STEM. Removal of gender bias in STEM may require self-reflection by teachers. When girls become aware of male supremacy in arithmetic through subtle and overt cultural signals, each contact with mathematics and technology becomes more difficult, causing self-doubt in even the most studious young girls. In order to counter this narrative of direct perception bias, educators must be attentive to how stereotypical threats occur for these girls. Teachers can assist in encouraging students to develop a growth mindset by emphasizing that dedicated work can increase achievement. Understanding that intelligence is not fixed is critical to young women's persistence in STEM. In mathematics and science, educating young women to continuously work towards developing their identities in STEM education ultimately establishes ways to maintain confidence and overcome adversities (Burns et al., 2016). Thus, we suggest three resilience strategies that mitigate stereotypes and cultural norms that dampen girls' interest in STEM. Instead, with these strategies, educators can play a part in mitigating the gender gap by influencing and dispelling stereotypes in STEM education.

Maintaining Confidence—Pedagogy and curriculum directly affect young girls' confidence in STEM-related fields. Creating possibilities for women to improve knowledge to function science in their methods (Carlone et al., 2014) enhances mathematics and science confidence. Remember, it is not a lack of confidence that is holding women back. It is gendered norms within the field that are pushing women away. In order to combat the gender inequality trend in STEM, teachers must equip girls with hands-on STEM experiences because STEM experiences at an early age can sustain confidence in STEM subjects and beyond. In addition, the process of planning, designing, failing, and retesting will teach young women that failure is a part of success.

Identity Development—The formation of one's identity can be a complex process. Girls and women long for a sense of belonging within the science field (Mooney et al., 2018). Sense of belonging is a critical determinant in developing STEM identity, especially for young girls. Knowing this fact, educators can positively influence the intent to pursue STEM domains by increasing involvement and mentoring possibilities for young girls. Identity development in STEM is critical to a young woman's persistence as a scientist.

Role Models—Girls and young women do not see examples of female scientists and engineers in books, in the media, and in popular culture. There are far fewer role models for women of color in mathematics and science. With the necessary efforts of parents, activists, and educators, women in STEM role models are essential to encouraging women to pursue careers in STEM. In addition, women with female STEM role models are more interested in STEM careers than those women without. As a result of having women role models in STEM disciplines and knowing the gender stereotypes associated with these disciplines, young women may look for influence outside of the traditional classroom. In general, women are less concerned about being compared to men in STEM; however, women are needed in STEM role model positions to mentor other women in maintaining interest in STEM, helping to close the gender and skills gap in the long run. As a result of these relationships, young women experience a positive sense of community in the STEM field; in other words, they are able to feel part of an ingroup. On the one hand, it is important to continue to support girls as they progress through high school with approaches to learning through non-traditional STEM programming such as online learning. On the other hand, our charge as educators is to intensify all efforts to dismantle the cultural norms of science-related fields to increase opportunities for young women to persist.

RESOURCE NOTES

Name of Resource	Primary Website	How to Locate the Resource Online
Tech-savvy: Educating girls in the new computer age	www.aauw.org	Go to www.aauw.org. Located in the top right corner, use the search engine to search for "Tech-savvy: Educating girls in the new computer age." Select the first project option to locate the recommended page. http://stelar.edc.org/publications/tech-savvy-educating-girls-new-computer-age
Using volunteer mentors to improve the academic outcomes of underserved students: The role of relationships	https://onlinelibrary.wiley.com	Go to https://onlinelibrary.wiley.com. Located in the middle of the page, use the search engine to search for "Using volunteer mentors to improve the academic outcomes of underserved students: The role of relationships." Select the first article to locate the recommended page. https://onlinelibrary.wiley.com/doi/abs/10.1002/jcop.21693
Does creativity have a place in classroom discussions? Prospective teachers' response preferences	https://psycnet.apa.org/	Go to https://psycnet.apa.org/. Located on the left of the page, use the search engine to do a "basic search" for "Does creativity have a place in classroom discussions? Prospective teachers' response preferences." Select the first article to locate the recommended page. https://psycnet.apa.org/record/2007-09541-001
Sex differences in mathematical ability: Fact or artifact?	https://www.jstor.org/	Go to https://www.jstor.org/. Located in the middle of the page, use the search engine to search for "Sex differences in mathematical ability: Fact or artifact?" Select the first article to locate the recommended page. https://www.jstor.org/stable/1684489

Name of Resource	Primary Website	How to Locate the Resource Online
Factors influencing career choice for women in science, mathematics, and technology: The importance of a transforming experience	https://awl-ojs-tamu.tdl.org/	Go to https://awl-ojs-tamu.tdl.org/. Located at the top left corner of the page, use the search engine to search for "Factors influencing career choice for women in science, mathematics, and technology: The importance of a transforming experience." Select the first article to locate the recommended page. https://awl-ojs-tamu.tdl.org/awl/index.php/awl/article/view/258
Creating, implementing, and redefining a conceptual framework for mentoring pathways for education doctorate students	https://files.eric.ed.gov	Go to https://files.eric.ed.gov. Located in the middle of the page, use the search engine to search for "Creating, implementing, and redefining a conceptual framework for mentoring pathways for education doctorate students." Select the first article to locate the recommended page. https://files.eric.ed.gov/fulltext/EJ1279828.pdf
Women and minorities in science, technology, engineering, and mathematics: upping the numbers	https://www.e-elgar.com	Go to https://www.e-elgar.com. Accept the cookies to navigate the page. Located in the upper right-hand corner of the page, use the search engine to search for "Women and minorities in science, technology, engineering, and mathematics: upping the numbers." Select the first book to locate the recommended page. https://www.e-elgar.com/shop/usd/women-and-minorities-in-science-technology-engineering-and-mathematics-9781845428884.html
Girls' interest in STEM	https://ieeexplore.ieee.org/Xplore/home.jsphttps://ieeexplore.ieee.org/abstract/document/7757645	Go to https://ieeexplore.ieee.org/Xplore/home.jsp. Located in the upper middle section of the page, use the "PDF." Use the search engine to search for "Girls' interest in STEM." Select the first article to locate the recommended page. https://ieeexplore.ieee.org/abstract/document/7757645
Upping the numbers: Using research-based decision making to increase the diversity in the quantitative disciplines	http://www.campbell-kibler.com/	Go to google.com. Located in the middle of the page, use the search engine to search for "Upping the numbers: Using research-based decision making to increase the diversity in the quantitative disciplines." Select the first article to locate the recommended page. http://www.campbell-kibler.com/upping_the_numbers.pdf
Striving for gender equity: National programs to increase student engagement with math and science	https://files.eric.ed.gov/	Go to google.com. Located in the middle of the page, use the search engine to search for "Striving for gender equity: National programs to increase student engagement with math and science." Select the second article to locate the recommended page. https://files.eric.ed.gov/fulltext/ED485720.pdf

Name of Resource	Primary Website	How to Locate the Resource Online
Becoming (less) scientific: a longitudinal study of students' identity work from elementary to middle school science	https://onlinelibrary.wiley.com	Go to https://onlinelibrary.wiley.com. Located in the upper section of the page, use the search engine to search for "Becoming (less) scientific: a longitudinal study of students' identity work from elementary to middle school science." Select the first article to locate the recommended page. https://onlinelibrary.wiley.com/doi/10.1002/tea.21150
Sex differences in math-intensive fields	https://www.ncbi.nlm.nih.gov/	Go to https://www.ncbi.nlm.nih.gov/. Located in the upper middle section of the page, use the search engine to search "Sex differences in math-intensive fields." Select the PubMed option to locate the first article on the recommended page. https://www.ncbi.nlm.nih.gov/pmc/articles/PMC2997703/
The formation of science choices in secondary school	https://www.tandfonline.com/	Go to https://www.tandfonline.com/. Located in the middle of the page, use the search engine to search for "The formation of science choices in secondary school." Select the first article to locate the recommended page. The full article will then be available. https://www.tandfonline.com/doi/full/10.1080/0950069042000323746
The digital divide: the special case of gender	https://onlinelibrary.wiley.com/	Go to https://onlinelibrary.wiley.com/. Located in the middle of the page, use the search engine to search "The digital divide: the special case of gender." Select the first article to locate the recommended page. The full article will then be available. https://onlinelibrary.wiley.com/doi/full/10.1111/j.1365-2729.2006.00185.x
Gender stereotypes influence how people explain gender disparities in the workplace	https://link.springer.com	Go to https://link.springer.com. Located in the upper section of the page, use the search engine to search for "Gender stereotypes influence how people explain gender disparities in the workplace." Select the first article to locate the recommended page. Use the "Download PDF" option to download the article. https://link.springer.com/article/10.1007/s11199-016-0593-2
Ingroup experts and peers as social vaccines who inoculate the self-concept: The stereotype inoculation model	https://psycnet.apa.org/	Go to https://psycnet.apa.org/. Located on the left of the page, use the search engine to do a "basic search" for "Ingroup experts and peers as social vaccines who inoculate the self-concept: The stereotype inoculation model." Select the first article to locate the recommended page. https://psycnet.apa.org/record/2011-28401-002

Name of Resource	Primary Website	How to Locate the Resource Online
Girls and Women in Science, Technology, Engineering, and Mathematics: STEMing the Tide and Broadening Participation in STEM Careers	https://journals.sagepub.com	Go to https://journals.sagepub.com. Located in the upper section of the page, use the search engine to search for "Girls and Women in Science, Technology, Engineering, and Mathematics: STEMing the Tide and Broadening Participation in STEM Careers." Select the first article to locate the recommended page. Use the "PDF" option to download the article. https://journals.sagepub.com/doi/full/10.1177/2372732214549471
The situation as regards the course of study	Amazon.com	Go to amazon.com. Located at the upper section of the page, use the search engine to search or "Journal of Proceedings and Addresses of the Fortieth Annual Meeting: Held at Detroit, Michigan, July 8–12, 1901 (Classic Reprint)." Select the first option to locate the recommended book. https://www.amazon.com/gp/product/1528333276/ref=as_li_tl?ie=UTF8&tag=forgobooks-20
Connectivism as a digital age learning theory	https://www.semantic-scholar.org	Go to https://www.semanticscholar.org. Located in the middle section of the page, use the search engine to search for "Connectivism as a digital age learning theory." Select the first article to locate the recommended page. Use the "[PDF] hetl.org" option to download the article. https://www.semanticscholar.org/paper/Connectivism-as-a-Digital-Age-Learning-Theory-Duke-Harper/9d499406ce42d07fc501c534eca528361ffe460f
Sex differences in mathematics participation	https://psycnet.apa.org/	Go to https://psycnet.apa.org/. Located on the left of the page, use the search engine to do a "basic search" for "Sexism and other "isms": independence, status, and the ambivalent content of stereotypes ." Select the first article to locate the recommended page.
Sexism and other "isms": independence, status, and the ambivalent content of stereotypes	https://psycnet.apa.org/	Go to https://psycnet.apa.org/. Located on the left of the page, use the search engine to do a "basic search" for "Sexism and other "isms": independence, status, and the ambivalent content of stereotypes ." Select the first article to locate the recommended page. https://psycnet.apa.org/record/1998-06496-008
Talking about science in museums	https://www.research-gate.net	Go to https://www.researchgate.net. Located in the upper section of the page, use the search engine to search for "Talking about science in museums." Select the first article to locate the recommended page. Use the blue "Download" option to download the article. https://www.researchgate.net/publication/227839652_Talking_About_Science_in_Museums

Name of Resource	Primary Website	How to Locate the Resource Online
The Emergence of Gender Differences in Children's Perceptions of Their Academic Competence	https://www.sciencedirect.com/	Go to https://www.sciencedirect.com/. Located in the upper middle section of the page, fill out the title section with "The Emergence of Gender Differences in Children's Perceptions of Their Academic Competence." Select the first article to locate the recommended page. https://www.sciencedirect.com/science/article/pii/S0193397305000171
The four-phase model of interest development	https://www.tandfonline.com/	Go to https://www.tandfonline.com/. Located in the middle section of the page, use the search engine to search for "The four-phrase model of interest development." Select the first article to locate the recommended page. The full article will then be available. https://www.tandfonline.com/doi/abs/10.1207/s15326985ep4102_4
Developing a STEM Identity Among Young Women: A Social Identity Perspective	https://journals.sagepub.com/	Go to https://journals.sagepub.com/. Located in the upper middle section of the page, use the search engine to search for "Developing a STEM Identity Among Young Women: A Social Identity Perspective." Select the first article to locate the recommended page. Use the grey "PDF" option to the right of the page to download the article. https://journals.sagepub.com/doi/full/10.3102/0034654318779957
Sex differences and similarities in job attribute preferences: a meta-analysis	https://pubmed.ncbi.nlm.nih.gov/	Go to https://pubmed.ncbi.nlm.nih.gov/. Located in the upper middle section of the page, use the search engine to search for "Sex differences and similarities in job attribute preferences: a meta-analysis." Select the first article to locate the recommended page. https://pubmed.ncbi.nlm.nih.gov/10900998/
Eyeballs in the Fridge: Sources of early interest in science	https://www.tandfonline.com/	Go to https://www.tandfonline.com/. Located in the upper middle section of the page, use the search engine to search for "Eyeballs in the Fridge: Sources of early interest in science." Select the first article to locate the recommended page. The full article will then be available. https://www.tandfonline.com/doi/full/10.1080/09500690902792385
Programming experience promotes higher STEM motivation among first-grade girls	https://pubmed.ncbi.nlm.nih.gov	Go to https://pubmed.ncbi.nlm.nih.gov. Located in the upper section of the page, use the search engine to search for "Programming experience promotes higher STEM motivation among first-grade girls." Select the "full text links" option. Click on the "FULL TEXT LINKS" pop-up window. From here, click on the "PDF" option located at the bottom right-hand corner of the page to download the article. https://pubmed.ncbi.nlm.nih.gov/28433822/

Name of Resource	Primary Website	How to Locate the Resource Online
Nobel Prize Women in science: their lives, struggles, and momentous discoveries	https://www.amazon.com	Go to https://www.amazon.com. Located in the upper section of the page, use the search engine to search for "Nobel Prize Women in science: their lives, struggles, and momentous discoveries." Select the first option to locate the recommended book. https://www.amazon.com/Nobel-Prize-Women-Science-Discoveries/dp/0309072700
Computer science identity and sense of belonging: A case study in Ireland	https://www.researchgate.net	Go to https://www.researchgate.net. Located in the upper section of the page, use the search engine to search for "Computer science identity and sense of belonging: a case study in Ireland." Select the first option to locate the recommended article. Use the blue "Download" option to download the article. https://www.researchgate.net/publication/326048649_Computer_science_identity_and_sense_of_belonging_a_casestudyinIreland
Rising above the gathering storm, revisited: Rapidly approaching category 5	https://www.nsf.gov	Go to https://www.nsf.gov. Located in the upper right section of the page, use the search engine to search for "Rising above the gathering storm, revisited: Rapidly approaching Category 5." Select the first option to locate the recommended article, which will automatically open the PDF. https://www.nsf.gov/attachments/117803/public/3b--RAGS_Revisited.pdf
Self-Efficacy Beliefs and Motivation in Writing Development	https://www.uky.edu	Go to https://www.uky.edu. Located in the upper left section of the page, use the search engine to search for "Self-Efficacy Beliefs and Motivation in Writing Development." Select the first option to locate the recommended article, which will automatically open the PDF. https://www.uky.edu/~eushe2/Pajares/Pajares2003RWQ.pdf
Easier said than done: Gender differences in perceived barriers to gaining a mentor	https://libgen.ggfwzs.net/	Go to https://libgen.ggfwzs.net/. Located in middle section of the page, use the search engine to search or "Easier said than done: Gender differences in perceived barriers to gaining a mentor." Select the first option to locate the recommended book. https://libgen.ggfwzs.net/book/75025558/0a0d7f
Using sustainability themes and multidisciplinary approaches to enhance STEM education	https://eric.ed.gov	Go to https://eric.ed.gov. Located in the upper middle section of the page, use the search engine to search for "Using sustainability themes and multidisciplinary approaches to enhance STEM education." Select the first option to locate the recommended article. https://eric.ed.gov/?id=EJ1064050

Name of Resource	Primary Website	How to Locate the Resource Online
Still failing at fairness: How gender bias cheats girls and boys in school and what we can do about it	Amazon.com	Go to amazon.com. Located at the upper section of the page, use the search engine to search or "Still failing at fairness: how gender bias cheats girls and boys in school and what we can do about it.." Select the first option to locate the recommended book. https://www.amazon.com/Still-Failing-Fairness-Gender-Cheats/dp/1416552472
Snatching Defeat from the Jaws of Victory: When Good Projects Go Bad. Girls and Computer Science	https://eric.ed.gov/	Go to https://eric.ed.gov/. Located in the middle section of the page, use the search engine to search for "Snatching Defeat from the Jaws of Victory: When Good Projects Go Bad. Girls and Computer Science." Select the first option to locate the recommended article. Use the "Download full text" option to the upper right-hand corner of the page to download the article. https://eric.ed.gov/?id=ED466701
Critical thinking, caring and professional agency: An emerging framework for productive mentoring	https://www.research-gate.net	Go to https://www.researchgate.net. Located in the upper section of the page, use the search engine to search for "Critical thinking, caring and professional agency: An emerging framework for productive mentoring." Select the first option to locate the recommended article. Use the blue "Download" option to download the article. https://www.researchgate.net/publication/254320174_Critical_Thinking_Caring_and_Professional_Agency_An_Emerging_Framework_for_Productive_Mentoring
Cultural representations of gender and science: portrayals of female scientists and engineers in popular films	http://citeseerx.ist.psu.edu	Go to http://citeseerx.ist.psu.edu. In the upper left of the page, use the search engine to search for "Cultural representations of gender and science: portrayals of female scientists and engineers in popular films." Select the first option to locate the recommended article. Use the "Cached Download Links" options on the far right to download the article. http://citeseerx.ist.psu.edu/viewdoc/download?doi=10.1.1.487.6117&rep=rep1&type=pdf
Online Mentoring for Talented Girls in STEM: The Role of Relationship Quality and Changes in Learning Environments in Explaining Mentoring Success	https://onlinelibrary.wiley.com/	Go to https://onlinelibrary.wiley.com/. Located in the upper middle section of the page, use the search engine to search for "Online Mentoring for Talented Girls in STEM: The Role of Relationship Quality and Changes in Learning Environments in Explaining Mentoring Success." Select the first article to locate the recommended page. The full article will then be available. https://onlinelibrary.wiley.com/doi/full/10.1002/cad.20320#:~:text=We%20found%20evidence%20that%20in,successful%20mentoring)%20was%20associated%20with

Name of Resource	Primary Website	How to Locate the Resource Online
The effectiveness of a one-year online mentoring program for girls in STEM	https://www.sciencedirect.com/	Go to https://www.sciencedirect.com/. Located at the upper middle section of the page, use the search engine to type in the title "The effectiveness of a one-year online mentoring program for girls in STEM." Select the first article to locate the recommended page. The full article will then be available. https://www.sciencedirect.com/science/article/pii/S0360131513002091
Mind in society: The development of higher psychological processes	Amazon.com	Go to amazon.com. Use the search engine in the upper middle section of the page to search for "Mind in society: The development of higher psychological processes." Select the first option to locate the recommended book. https://www.amazon.com/Mind-Society-Development-Psychological-Processes/dp/0674576292
Group collaboration in assessment: Multiple objectives, processes, and outcomes	https://journals.sagepub.com/	Go to https://journals.sagepub.com/. Located in the upper middle section of the page, use the search engine to search for "Group collaboration in assessment: Multiple objectives, processes, and outcomes." Select the first article to locate the recommended page. Locate the "Access Options" to gain access to the article. https://journals.sagepub.com/doi/abs/10.3102/0162373717002239?journalCode=epaa

DISCUSSION QUESTIONS

1. The Connectivism as a Learning Theory Framework serves as a foundation for change within the practices of STEM in order to mitigate the gender gap, which is presently widening. What are other ways in which the framework can be applied to online learning as it relates to STEM?

2. The framework, when used correctly, can assist in young girls developing a science identity. Because the barriers for women are present at a young age, it can be difficult to bring these girls back into the STEM field. These extra barriers to developing a positive STEM identity explain why merely offering access to these children does not necessarily result in greater persistence. In terms of STEM identity, how can educators create an all-girls online program that would assist in creating the enthusiasm and confidence for young girls to enter STEM? What would such a program look like?

3. One outcome of the Coronavirus (COVID-19) pandemic was the vigorous response by organizations, initiatives, and persons who develop, convert, and exchange online learning experiences and tools in the STEM education ecosystem. Thus, online learning is arguably one of the most critical topics education researchers have recently engaged. How can online learning help develop young girls' science identity?

4. Because fewer women study and work in STEM professions, these fields tend to sustain rigid, exclusive, male-dominated cultures that are neither welcoming nor appealing to women and racially minoritized people. Teachers and parents frequently underestimate girls' arithmetic abilities. Lower expectations and prejudices are thought to account for almost half of the gender accomplishment gap in arithmetic. How can teachers empower young girls to pursue STEM?

5. Online mentoring, when properly done, addresses both the human and environmental factors of women's low STEM participation rates. According to Stoeger et al. (2019), online mentoring for young girls offers an innovative solution to a historical problem with STEM. It is not dependent on participants' physical proximity and does not necessitate synchronous in-person encounters. What online mentoring format is most effective when engaging adolescent girls in hopes of forming their STEM identity?

6. In what ways do girls support the development of their scientific identities and how are these activities pursued within the online learning environment?

REFERENCES

American Association of University Women. (2000). *Tech-savvy: Educating girls in the new computer age.* Author.

Bayer, A., Grossman, J. B., & DuBois, D. L. (2015). Using volunteer mentors to improve the academic outcomes of underserved students: The role of relationships. *Journal of Community Psychology, 43*(4), 408–429. https://doi.org/10.1002/jcop.21693

Beghetto, R. A. (2007). Does creativity have a place in classroom discussions? Prospective teachers' response preferences. *Thinking Skills and Creativity, 2*(1), 1–9.

Benbow, C. P., & Stanley, J. C. (1980). Sex differences in mathematical ability: Fact or artifact? *Science, 210*(4475), 1262–1264. https://doi.org/10.1126/science.7434028

Besecke, L. M., & Reilly, A. H. (2006). Factors influencing career choice for women in science, mathematics, and technology: The importance of a transforming experience. *Advancing Women in Leadership*, 21. http://www.advancingwomen.com/awl/summer2006/Besecke_Reilly.html

Brown, R. D., Geesa, R. L., & McConnell, K. R. (2020). Creating, implementing, and redefining a conceptual framework for mentoring pathways for education doctorate students. *Higher Learning Research Communications, 10*(2), 20–37. https://10.0.73.182/hlrc.v10i2.1188

Burke, R. J., & Mattis, M. C. (2007). *Women and minorities in science, technology, engineering, and mathematics: upping the numbers.* Edward Elgar Publishing Limited.

Burns, H. D., Lesseig, K., & Staus, N. (2016). *Girls' interest in STEM* (pp. 1–5). IEEE Frontiers in Education Conference (FIE). https://doi.org/10.1109/FIE.2016.7757645

Campbell, P., Jolly, E., Hoey, L., & Pearlman, L. (2002). *Upping the numbers: Using research-based decision making to increase the diversity in the quantitative disciplines.* Education Development Center, Inc.

Campbell, P., & Steinbrueck, K. (1996). *Striving for gender equity: National programs to increase student engagement with math and science.* American Association for the Advancement of Science.

Carlone, H. B., Scott, C. M., & Lowder, C. (2014). Becoming (less) scientific: A longitudinal study of students' identity work from elementary to middle school science. *Journal of Research in Science Teaching, 51*(7), 836–869. https://doi.org/10.1002/tea.21150

Ceci, S. J., & Williams, W. M. (2010b). Sex differences in math-intensive fields. *Current Directions in Psychological Science, 19,* 275–279.

Cleaves, A. (2005). The formation of science choices in secondary school. *International Journal of Science Education,* 27(4), 471–486.

Cooper, J. (2006). The digital divide: the special case of gender. *Journal of Computer Assisted Learning, 22*(5), 320–334. https://doi.org/10.1111/j.1365-2729.2006.00185.x

Cundiff, J. L., & Vescio, T. K. (2016). Gender stereotypes influence how people explain gender disparities in the workplace. *Sex Roles: A Journal of Research, 75*(3–4), 126–138. https://doi.org/10.1007/s11199-016-0593-2

Dasgupta, N. (2011). Ingroup experts and peers as social vaccines who inoculate the self-concept: The stereotype inoculation model. *Psychological Inquiry, 22*(4), 231–246. https://doi.org/10.1080/1047840X.2011.607313

Dasgupta, N., & Stout, J. G. (2014). Girls and women in science, technology, engineering, and mathematics: STEMing the tide and broadening participation in STEM careers. *Policy Insights from the Behavioral and Brain Sciences, 1*(1), 21–29. https://doi.org/10.1177/2372732214549471

Dewey, J. (1901). The situation as regards the course of study. *Journal of the Proceedings and Addresses of the Fortieth Annual Meeting of the National Education Association.*

Duke, B., Harper, G., & Johnston, M. (2013). Connectivism as a digital age learning theory. *The International HETL Review, 2013* (Special Issue), 4–13.

Eccles-Parsons, J. (1984). Sex differences in math participation. *Women in Science,* 93–138.

Glick, P., & Fiske, S. T. (1999). "Sexism and other "isms": independence, status, and the ambivalent content of stereotypes. In W. B. Swann, J. H. Langlois, & L. A. Gilbert (Eds.), *Sexism and stereotypes in modern society: The gender science of Janet Taylor Spence* (pp. 193–221). American Psychological Association. https://doi.org/10.1037/10277-008

Haden, C. A. (2010). Talking about science in museums. *Child Development Perspectives, 4*(1), 62–67. doi:10.1111/j.1750-8606.2009. 00119.x

Herbert, J., & Stipek, D. (2005). The emergence of gender differences in children's perceptions of their academic competence. *Journal of Applied Developmental Psychology, 26*(3), 276–295. https://doi.org/10.1016/j.appdev.2005.02.007

Hidi, S., & Renninger, K. A. (2006). The four-phase model of interest development. *Educational Psychologist, 41*(2), 111–127. https://doi.org/10.1207/s15326985ep4102_4

Kim, A. Y., Sinatra, G. M., & Seyranian, V. (2018). Developing a STEM identity among young women: A social identity perspective. *Review of Educational Research, 88*(4), 589–625. https://doi.org/10.3102/0034654318779957

Konrad, A. M., Ritchie, J. E., Jr., Lieb, P., & Corrigall, E. (2000). Sex differences and similarities in job attribute preferences: a meta-analysis. *Psychological Bulletin, 126*(4), 593–641. https://doi.org/10.1037/0033-2909.126.4.593

Maltese, A., & Tai, R. H. (2010). Eyeballs in the fridge: Sources of early interest in science. *International Journal of Science Education, 32*(5), 669–685. https://doi.org/10.1080/09500690902792385

Master, A., Cheryan, S., Moscatelli, A., & Meltzoff, A. N. (2017)Programming experience promotes higher STEM motivation among first-grade girls. *Journal of Experimental Child Psychology, 160*, 92–106. https://doi.org/10.1016/j.jecp.2017.03.013

McGrayne, S. B. (2005). *Nobel Prize women in science: Their lives, struggles, and momentous discoveries* (2nd ed.). Joseph Henry Press.

Mooney, C., Becker, B., Salmon, L., & Mangina, E. (2018, May). Computer science identity and sense of belonging: A case study in Ireland. In *2018 IEEE/ACM 1st International Workshop on Gender Equality in Software Engineering* (pp. 1–4).

National Academies. (2010). *Rising above the gathering storm, revisited: Rapidly approaching category 5.* National Academies Press.

Pajares, F., & Valiante, G. (2006). Self-Efficacy Beliefs and motivation in writing development. In C. A. MacArthur, S. Graham, & J. Fitzgerald (Eds.), *Handbook of writing research* (pp. 158–170). The Guilford Press.

Ragins, B. R., & Cotton, J. L. (1991). Easier said than done: Gender differences in perceived barriers to gaining a mentor. *Academy of Management Journal, 34*(4), 939–951. https://doi.org/10.2307/256398

Rogers, M., Pfaff, T., Hamilton, J., & Erkan, A. (2015). Using sustainability themes and multidisciplinary approaches to enhance STEM education. *International Journal of Sustainability in Higher Education, 16*(4), 523–536. https://doi.org/10.1108/IJSHE-02-2013-0018

Sadker, D., Sadker, M., & Zittleman, K. R. (2009). *Still failing at fairness: How gender bias cheats girls and boys in school and what we can do about it.* Simon & Schuster, Inc.

Sanders, J. (2002). *Snatching defeat from the jaws of victory: When good projects go bad.* Girls and Computer Science.

Simmie, G. M., & Moles, J. (2011). Critical thinking, caring and professional agency: An emerging framework for productive mentoring. *Mentoring & Tutoring: Partnership in Learning, 19*(4), 465–482. https://doi.org/10.1080/13611267.2011.622081

Steinke, J. (2005). Cultural representations of gender and science: portrayals of female scientists and engineers in popular films. *Science Communication, 27*(1), 27–63. https://doi.org/10.1177/1075547005278610

Stoeger, H., Debatin, T., Heilemann, M., & Ziegler, A. (2019). Online mentoring for talented girls in STEM: The role of relationship quality and changes in learning environments in explaining mentoring success. *New Directions for Child and Adolescent Development, 168*, 75–79. https://doi.org/10.1002/cad.20320

Stoeger, H., Duan, X., Schirner, S., Greindl, T., & Ziegler, A. (2013). The effectiveness of a one-year online mentoring program for girls in STEM. *Computers & Education, 69*, 408–418. https://doi.org/10.1016/j.compedu.2013.07.032

Vygotsky, L. S. (1978). *Mind in society: The development of higher psychological processes.* Harvard University Press.

Webb, N. M. (1995). Group collaboration in assessment: Multiple objectives, processes, and outcomes. *Educational Evaluation and Policy Analysis, 17*(2), 239–261. https://www.jstor.org/ stable/1164563

CHAPTER 7

SUPPORTING CLAIM-EVIDENCE-REASONING IN LINGUISTICALLY DIVERSE SECONDARY SCIENCE CLASSES

Preetha K. Menon

Stanford University

The purpose of this chapter is to explore the use of the Claim-Evidence-Reasoning (CER) framework in online settings using language routines with a focus on multilingual learners. Since science content is taught in a language they are still learning, these students face unique challenges. The CER framework explained here enables all students to participate in science practices and crosscutting concepts while engaging with disciplinary core ideas. Teachers can use the language routines to engage their multilingual learners to enhance their sense-making and communication skills. The CER framework can be applied in online settings by integrating digital resources into these routines.

RATIONALE

The number of English Learners (children ages 5–17) who speak a language other than English at home rose from 3.8 million to 5 million (National Center for Education Statistics, 2018). By 2025, nearly one out of every four public school

Teaching and Learning Online: Science for Secondary Grade Levels, pages 91–106.
Copyright © 2023 by Information Age Publishing
www.infoagepub.com
91

students will be an English Learner. The term *multilingual students* (MLs) is used in this chapter to acknowledge English Learners' diversity. This population is diverse regarding their proficiency in their home language, English, prior schooling, and prior knowledge in content areas (Lee, 2019). In states where the number of MLs exceeds nine to ten percent of enrollment, a substantial proportion of teachers feel unprepared to teach MLs (Franco-Fuenmayor et al., 2015; Hansen-Thomas et al., 2016). According to Lopez et al. (2015), only 26.8% of public school teachers participated in ML-related professional development. Additionally, in science classrooms, the language demands integrated into the three dimensions of NGSS present additional challenges for MLs (Lee et al., 2013). Every Student Succeeds Act (ESSA, 2015), a federal mandate, recommends classroom-based professional learning, emphasizing specific instructional approaches to support all students. Therefore, there is an impetus for school districts with an increasing ML population to provide instructional supports that will help them.

This chapter describes a system of such instructional supports called language routines, "structured but adaptable formats for amplifying, assessing, and developing students' language" (Zwiers et al., 2017). Although intended for mathematics classrooms, this chapter outlines how to provide opportunities for students to use English and disciplinary language in science. This chapter describes how to integrate these language routines in NGSS science practices of constructing explanations, engaging in argumentation with evidence, and developing and using models. These practices often use claims that answer a scientific question supported by considerable evidence and link the claims and evidence using reasoning statement(s) to explain the science concepts (McNeill et al., 2006). Likewise, this chapter describes how the language routines are integrated into the claim-evidence-reasoning (CER) framework within online settings using digital resources. While these instructional supports in the form of language routines suit all students learning science, the main objective is to meet the needs of linguistically and culturally diverse students who are simultaneously learning science while acquiring English.

Theoretical Background

The idea of science language routines is rooted in the sociocultural perspectives on teaching and learning. In sociocultural theory, knowing is fundamentally social, and participation in discourse, for example, is a primary characteristic of learning and knowing (Gutiérrez & Rogoff, 2003; Lave & Wenger, 2002; Vygotsky, 1978), for which language plays a crucial role, especially for MLs (Lantolf et al., 2015). A perspective on language, which is gaining importance, is language as action (Lier, 2007). In a classroom context, an action-based perspective shows that students engage in meaningful activities (projects, presentations, investigations) that stimulate their interest and encourage language growth through interaction, planning, research, discussion, and co-construction of products of various kinds (van Lier & Walqui, 2012).

Another aspect of the sociocultural perspective of teaching and learning means studying the world as scientists do and "learning the socially learned cultural traditions of what kinds of discourses and representations are useful and how to use them" (Lemke, 2001, p. 298). Activities of the science classroom which ascribe to such practices are often multimodal and include oral explanations, reading text, writing science information, drawing and interpreting visual images, doing hands-on laboratory work (Lee et al., 2013; NGSS Lead States, 2013; Norris & Phillips, 2003; Yore et al., 2004). Engaging in these multimodal activities helps students appropriate the science classroom's language through the "multiple aspects of the oral and written channels through which language is used" in science and engineering practices (Lee et al., 2013, p. 8). A sociocultural approach allows teachers to examine the nuances of meaning made as students work with different modalities and generate insights into how students learn scientific concepts and develop content area literacy in the process (Ford & Forman, 2006). In this chapter, language routines are an "adaptive system of communicative actions to realize key purposes" (Hakuta & Santos, 2012, p. ii) of science learning for MLs. The language routines link the process of sense-making and communicating so students can experience different aspects of science practices while engaging in the various multimodal activities of science classrooms.

CHAPTER FOCUS

This section describes how language routines are used in multimodal online activities. Table 7.1 below describes the alignment of the CER framework with language routines used. It also shows the digital resources used, how students engage in different aspects of the three dimensions of NGSS, and how the routines particularly support MLs.

DIGITAL RESOURCES USED IN THE SCIENCE LANGUAGE ROUTINES

Computer-based activities enable MLs to communicate better by providing opportunities to engage and learn in different language domains (Warschauer & Meskill, 2000) and promote science understanding (Hillmayr et al., 2020; Ryoo & Bedell, 2017). Beyond language learning, computer-based activities promote meaningful discourse. The online technology resources described below (see Resources below) are accessible, user-friendly, and enable collaboration. It is best to create free login access and set up the technological resources according to the class and students' needs. They include:

a. Google docs™ and Google slides™ for collaborative writes and group presentations in English and students' native languages.
b. Google Jamboard™ for collaborative writes.
c. Frayer model graphic organizer.

TABLE 7.1. Summary of the Chapter Focus

CER Framework and Language routines used	NGSS practices and crosscutting concepts	Digital Resources used	Supports for MLs
Claim/ Three Reads	Identifying claims Asking questions	Frayer graphic Jamboard	Reading comprehension Meta-awareness of science ideas
Evidence/ Compare and connect	Examining patterns Predicting cause and effect relationships Constructing an explanation	Frayer graphic Three column graphic organizer	Structured conversations Developing metalinguistic awareness of science practices
Reasoning/ Stronger and Clearer	Developing and using models Predicting cause and effect relationships Constructing an explanation	Frayer graphic Three column graphic organizer Google slides	Structured conversations Developing metalinguistic awareness of science practices and science ideas

The online resources used are listed below, and the links are in the Resources section.

    a.   Text from the webpage *Lynx-Snowshoe Hare Cycle*.
    b.   TUVA™ Labs Preview—Explore patterns in population changes (hare and lynx).
    c.   TUVA™ Teacher guide—Explore patterns in population changes (hare and lynx).
    d.   TUVA™ Student handout—Explore patterns in population changes (hare and lynx).

NGSS Dimensions

The disciplinary core ideas highlighted in this chapter include the environmental interactions with living and non-living things in an ecosystem, how organisms compete for resources, how their growth is limited by access to resources, and how predatory interactions may also affect the populations of organisms. These topics of how and why organisms interact with their environment and their effects are often taught in middle and high school grades. The crosscutting concepts applied here include examining patterns and predicting cause and effect relationships.

The NGSS practices discussed in this chapter are asking questions, constructing explanations, arguing with evidence, and developing and using models. These practices are particularly language intensive (Hakuta et al., 2013). Herein, language is used to examine data and make sense of it as evidence, analyze patterns and models, dispute models, and propose explanations or solutions. Language is also used for sense-making as well as to accomplish specific communicative goals in these practices (Quinn et al., 2012).

This chapter describes how the Claims-Evidence-Reasoning (CER) framework allows students to develop scientific knowledge by understanding how knowledge is constructed and refined (Osborne, 2014). The language routines link the process of sense-making and communicating to experience different aspects of these language-intensive NGSS dimensions. Drawing on the multimodal potential of the online and digital resources, the CER acts as a framework for applying NGSS science practices and crosscutting concepts.

Claim–Evidence–Reasoning (CER)

This section describes each aspect of the framework, how it is implemented in an online activity using various multimodal resources, and how the language routines are integrated within the science practices and crosscutting concepts. As part of science, claims provide answers to specific questions and provide context for a focused argument. The concept of evidence is related to facts or data supporting or contradicting a claim or assumption, and reasoning is the process of connecting the evidence with the claims.

Claim

Claims must be justified by research, evidence, and scientific reasoning (McNeill & Krajcik, 2011) and provide answers to specific questions and provide context for a focused argument. In science classes, the claims that are made are limited to what is within a domain of inquiry or what is debated. The term "claim" is usually used to describe answers to questions that relate to facts, definitions, or predictions based on cause-and-effect mechanisms and comparative analysis of related facts. In K–12 settings, teachers and students mostly discuss claims that have already been investigated, and scientists have already provided answers.

Online Activity. As part of this activity, teachers utilize the article on the website *Snowshoe Hare—Lynx cycle* (see Resources) to introduce the fundamental concepts of interdependence in an ecosystem. The teacher identifies the main guiding question(s) for the lesson or activity. The following is a sample guiding question: "How do lynx and hare populations relate to each other in the boreal forest ecosystem?" Next, the teachers and students understand the types of habitats, animals, and factors affecting the organisms in the habitat by using the snowshoe hare populations and the lynx as examples. The teacher also uses the text to help students use inquiry questions to identify claims from the text. The digital resource used is the Google Jamboard, where students record the information during the language routine on three different frames of the Jamboard.

Language Routines. The language routine used here is a reading strategy, the three reads protocol, where students interact with language-rich scientific ideas in the text. One way to use this strategy is in a whole class setting with the teacher reading to the class and in a student-student pair setting with one student reading to the other until all have read the text three times. This strategy aims to support understanding scientific concepts and linguistic clues while utilizing authentic texts without oversimplification (Martinez et al., 2014).

In this lesson, the first read aims to better understand the context and big ideas. This lesson includes the ecosystem of the boreal forest and the living and non-living things in this ecosystem. First, the teacher reads the text in chunks, with each chunk focusing on one or two primary ideas. Following the reading of each chunk, the teacher waits for the student groups to organize the big ideas that they have understood on Google Jamboard. Students use the first frame of the Google Jamboard to record what they have understood from the first reading.

A second read involves understanding the language used to emphasize disciplinary core ideas such as the predator-prey relationship between lynxes and hares and how resource availability affects animal populations. During this activity, the teacher asks clarifying questions about the big ideas, and students highlight words or phrases unfamiliar to them. The teacher provides a Frayer-like graphic organizer (see Resources) in the second frame of the Google Jamboard to explore different facets of a keyword or concept. Students place their target words or phrases at the center of the Frayer model. The titles of each square of this Frayer model (see Figure 1) will be the following:

1. A sentence from the text containing the word
2. Description of the words or phrases
3. Describe the meaning of the word or phrase in everyday language
4. Other sentences using the words

During the third read, the students identify claims within the text. In order to assist students in identifying claims, inquiry questions are often used. Three types of inquiry questions are described below, with examples derived from the text described in the resource.

a. Claim as a definition or fact: Answers questions such as: What is it? What has happened?—(An observation or prediction or phenomenon). For example, "Some lynx cannot maintain their body fat reserves on this type of diet and become more vulnerable to starvation."

b. Claim as a cause and effect: Answers questions such as, What caused the effect? and What are the effects? For example, "When hares become scarce, lynx numbers also decline."

c. Claim as a comparison: Answers questions such as, What can be learned by comparing one subject to another? How can one thing be better understood by examining another? For example, "As hare numbers start

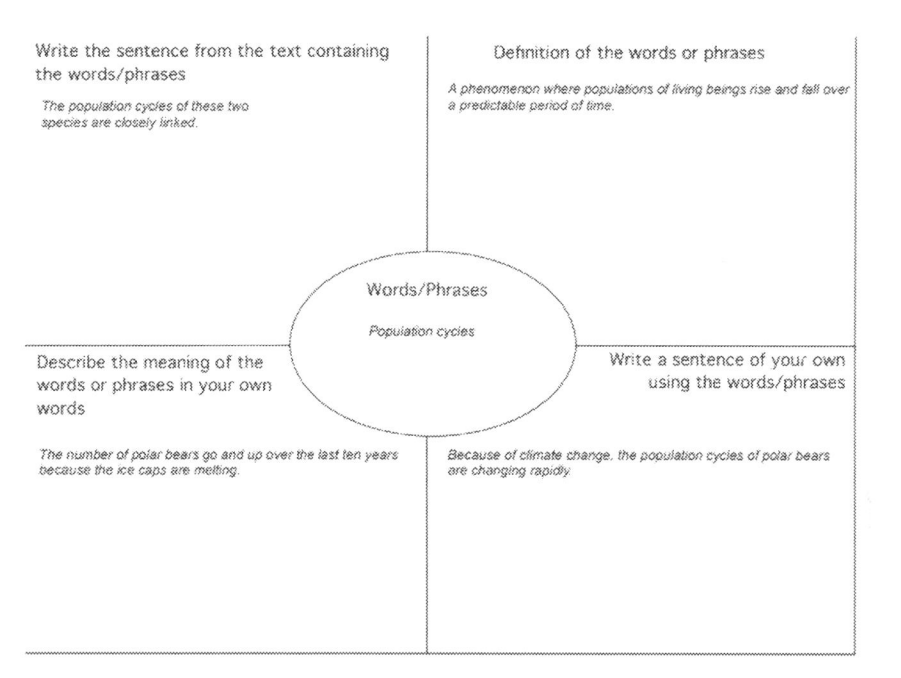

Write the sentence from the text containing the words/phrases

The population cycles of these two species are closely linked.

Definition of the words or phrases

A phenomenon where populations of living beings rise and fall over a predictable period of time.

Words/Phrases

Population cycles

Describe the meaning of the words or phrases in your own words

The number of polar bears go and up over the last ten years because the ice caps are melting.

Write a sentence of your own using the words/phrases

Because of climate change, the population cycles of polar bears are changing rapidly.

FIGURE 7.1. Frayer Model Template

to decline, lynx continue to eat well because they can easily catch the starving hares."

The teacher reiterates how the students' inquiry questions should relate to the central guiding question. Next, the teacher demonstrates how to construct an inquiry question using examples of the claims-based inquiry questions seen above. In pairs or groups, the students discuss and write their inquiry questions on the third frame of Jamboard. The students reread the text to identify the claims related to their inquiry questions. Examples of claims the students can identify from the text which are related to the central guiding question include:

- Hare populations across most of the boreal forest experience dramatic fluctuations in a cycle that lasts 8–11 years.
- Snowshoe hare is the primary food of the lynx. The population cycles of these two species are closely linked.
- The lynx population decline follows the snowshoe hare population crash after a lag of one to two years.

Through this specific application of the three reads strategy, students are exposed to text multiple times to assist with reading comprehension, develop a meta-awareness of the language of science, and understand the text's main ideas.

Evidence

Evidence generally refers to information, facts, or data supporting or contradicting a claim or assumption in science classrooms. The process of gathering evidence involves deciding what to measure, collecting or organizing the data, interpreting the data, and evaluating the data to develop explanations or refine arguments or models (NRC, 2007). Science teachers can emphasize the importance of evidence by placing it at the core of students' classroom experiences. As part of this activity, students determine if the data, a) are valid, b) analyze patterns in the data and use the patterns to build models, and c) construct explanations based on the evidence selected (Brown et al., 2010).

Online Activity. In order to participate in this activity, you will need to create a free account at TUVA labs™. In google classroom, the teacher assigns this online activity to students by clicking on "Assign" and provides the "Student handout—Patterns in Population Changes" (See Resources). The digital resources used for this activity include a three-column graphic organizer provided on google docs to help the students align their claims with the type of data analyzed. The first column has the 'Claims,' the second column the 'Evidence' or data, and the third column, the 'Science ideas.' The students can use this resource to participate in discussions in their group, enhance their ideas, and construct their explanations.

Language Routines. The students engage in the routine 'Compare and Connect' (Zwiers et al., 2017). They identify, compare, and contrast different forms of evidence needed to engage in this activity. Students often rely on their content knowledge and language skills to make accurate claims and cite sufficient data to support those claims (Sandoval & Millwood, 2005). In this online task, the students identify claims, find the appropriate data on the hare and the lynx population, and examine and analyze the patterns from the data. While engaging in this activity, students are prompted to reflect on and linguistically respond to the comparisons between the different types of data. This routine supports structured conversations and developing metalinguistic awareness of the practices.

Based on the main guiding question of the activity, student pairs or groups identify two or three claims from the text they would like to investigate in more detail and find the relevant evidence to support that claim. The students discuss the data types and the variables needed to analyze their identified claims in pairs or groups. They record all this information in the three-column organizer.

Next, they log onto the assigned task in the activity under "Explore Patterns in Population Changes" on the TUVA website and use the student handout (See Resources). They identify datasets on the hare and lynx populations from 1950 onwards. Next, they compare the variables or factors outlined in the claims they made earlier to the different data sets to find patterns in the data. Students look at a) what values in the graph are increasing or decreasing and b) whether they change over time for hare and lynx populations and complete the student handout.

After completing the online activity of identifying the data, the students compare and connect it with their identified claims using their three-column organizer.

The teacher needs to provide prompts and model how to engage in these discussions. Prompts such as, "How do you describe what you see?"; "How does this data compare to the other?"; and " How does this data help answer your claim?" will help students develop a metacognitive awareness of analyzing evidence. Other prompts include: "What do I say when I describe the graph?"; "How do I describe why I chose this graph?"; "What do I say when I compare two graphs?"; and "What do I say when I do not see any connection between the graphs and my claim?" When modeled, these prompts can help students develop meta-linguistic awareness of the type of language they use while describing evidence.

As they engage in this activity, each student in the pair/group should verbally describe their findings to their partner/others in the group. After listening to their partners, the students add more information to their assigned tasks on TUVA labs. The following sentence frames can help students connect the claim and evidence for their discussions and written descriptions.

- "My claim is ...."
- "I (we) found (describe evidence)."
- "This evidence supports my claim that (describe the claim)."

In the organizer, they describe the data and analyze the patterns across the data. The following sentence frames can be used to describe the data:

- "When I compared the year ___ data with year ___ counts, I noticed that..."
- "There are similarities [or differences] between years___ and years ___ "
- "I noticed a pattern when I looked at the data. The pattern is during years ___ the hare population is ___ and the lynx population is ___ "
- "One thing about the graph that surprises (or confuses) me is___ "

By selecting the best data they identified from the TUVA labs for their claim, the students learn to determine how accurately the data measures what is identified in the claim. This notion also supports students in understanding how to choose valid data. By participating in 'Compare and Connect' through the online activity, student handout, and the organizer, the students can understand how they compare the data, find the data that aligns with their claims and understand the type of language they can use to describe the evidence.

Reasoning

Based on the CER method, scientific reasoning takes various forms depending on the context in which it is used, like describing the results of experiments or choosing appropriate research methods. It is described as a strategy for finding relations between variables when evaluating one claim over another, comparing data sets, evaluating data patterns, testing hypotheses, and evaluating and using representations and models (Furtak et al., 2010). The extent to which students can differentiate between theoretical claims and the evidence to support a claim depends on their knowledge related to the science ideas (Berland & Reiser, 2009).

In this activity, the students use one claim for which they have identified data and use the TUVA labs website graph as the model that best represents the evidence to support their claim. They describe the model in detail and the patterns and then use reasoning to connect the claim and evidence in their explanations using the disciplinary core science ideas from the text. The digital resources used are the Jamboard they used for the first activity and the three-column graphic organizer provided on google docs in the second activity. Using these resources, the students align their claim, the type of data analyzed, and the science ideas they have highlighted from the text. They will write their explanations on google slides.

Online Activity. The teacher reiterates the main guiding question of the lesson to help the students identify the big ideas in the science text to write a complete CER explanation. The students write the first draft of their explanation on the first slide, with each student having their own set of slides. After discussions with their partners, the students make revisions on subsequent slides.

Language Routines. The language routine 'Stronger and Clearer' used in this activity enhances students' verbal and written communication skills (Zwiers et al., 2017). It is intended for students to discuss the CER response and then write it. Later in structured paired settings, students refine and clarify their responses through conversation, and finally, revise their initial written response. Students are encouraged to incorporate or address new ideas or language through the routine.

The students will create an explanation based on the claims-evidence-reasoning framework using information from previous activities—the Jamboard and the three-column organizer. First, students use the three-column organizer to write their claims and evidence. Next, the students work in pairs or groups to identify the science ideas on the Jamboard. The three reads identify ideas that may be relevant to the changes in lynx and hare populations. Each student writes an initial explanation and then engages in discussion with their partner to clarify their explanations. In order to engage in rich conversations, the teacher can use prompts to model these conversations. The prompts are intended to assist students in improving their language skills, utilizing science ideas, and asking each other for additional details.

The following prompts are examples of how students can expand and justify their reasoning:

- Explain what you know.
- How do you know that what you are saying is true?
- Explain how that idea is related to the claim and evidence.
- How does this idea make sense, can you tell me more?

Here are some examples of prompts to help students improve their language:

- What do you say when you choose to use science ideas to support your claim?
- What do you say when you are comparing science ideas?
- How would you write these science ideas to explain the claim?

Students are provided with the following sentence frames for completing their final written explanations:

- I (we) found (*describe the evidence*).
- The evidence provided here supports my claim that (*describe the claim*).
- It is (*scientific ideas you understand*) that (*connect claim and evidence*).

By participating in 'Stronger and Clearer' routine, using the digital resources (three-column organizer and Jamboard), the students understand engage in reasoning by justifying the claims they have identified to the evidence by using science ideas. This routine emphasizes the type of language they can use, enhancing their ideas from conversations with their peers to describe the evidence.

SUMMARY AND REFLECTIONS

This chapter illustrates how all the activities integrated within the CER framework support the synergistic relationship between science and language through the science practices, crosscutting concepts, and the disciplinary core ideas. By reiterating the same practices across different modalities, the students negotiate science and language learning from the graphs to the Jamboard and organizers. Reasoning using claims and evidence is a skill that takes practice. Students rarely write a good CER response in their first attempt and need guidance and support from teachers and peers to construct explanations. With the continued use of CER, students' writing can become more refined as they engage in activities similar to that of scientists. Schleppegrell (2004) contends that increasing both teachers' and students' awareness of linguistic choices will better participate in learning contexts. Through discussions and information about how students are reasoning, using evidence, and constructing explanations and arguments, science learning becomes visible and tangible.

RESOURCE NOTES

Name of Resource	Primary Website	How to Locate the Resource Online
Environment and Natural Resources. Lynx-Snowshoe Hare Cycle.	https://www.enr.gov.nt.ca/en/ services/lynx/lynx-snow- shoe-hare-cycle	Go to https://www.enr.gov.nt.ca/en/services/ lynx/lynx-snowshoe-hare-cycle. You can read the article Lynx-Snowshoe hare cycle.

Name of Resource	Primary Website	How to Locate the Resource Online
Frayer like graphic organizer	https://drive.google.com/file/d/16KAgWv4VlVRzDIB6r_1c38G6lBnx1jjE/view	A Frayer-like graphic organizer is used in the second frame of the Google Jamboard to explore different facets of a keyword or concept. The link provided shows an example of an organizer to be used during the three reads. Students place their target words or phrases at the center of the Frayer model. The titles of each square of this Frayer model include: 1. A sentence from the text containing the word 2. Description of the words or phrases 3. Describe the meaning of the word or phrase in everyday language 4. Other sentences using the words
Google Jamboard	https://jamboard.google.com/	Go to https://jamboard.google.com/ or use the search term "Jamboard" and click on the link. Sign in with your email address. Click on the plus sign in the lower right-hand corner. This will take you to a new Jamboard page. Have a Jamboard for each activity and label them based on the activity. Add frames to each Jamboard by clicking on the number above the title of the Jamboard. Each frame can be assigned to a student pair/group and label each frame with their names/group names.
TUVA labs Activity Preview	https://tuvalabs.com/datasets/lynx_and_snowshoe_hare_in_canada/activities/view/644/	Log into (https://tuvalabs.com) and create a free account in TUVA. The link provided here will give access to the science activity "Explore patterns in population changes." https://tuvalabs.com/datasets/lynx_and_snowshoe_hare_in_canada/activities/view/644 Alternatively, sign in to https://tuvalabs.com. Create a free account. Click on the tab Content Library, and then reach the content library page, click on Free and click on "Activities." Scroll till you see the Activity, "Explore patterns in population changes." Click on the title, and you will see the landing page of the activity. Click on the links on the lower right-hand side to access the student handout and teacher guide. Click on "Assign" to assign the activity to your class.

Name of Resource	Primary Website	How to Locate the Resource Online
Tuva Student Handout—Explore Patterns in Population Changes.	Tuva Student Handout—Explore Patterns in Population Changes. https://tuvalabs.com/docviewer/?title=Tuva%20Student%20Handout%20-%20Patterns%20in%20Population%20Changes%20(Gdrive)&embed_url=https://docs.google.com/document/d/1Cus_lei-HSxhZQCNpo_Ocv9gv-GY4cEP-UpaW9NBI_gME/edit?embedded=true	On the right-hand side of the webpage frame, students click on the tab "Review" to read background information regarding the activity. The graphs are located in the center of the webpage with x- and y-axes. Students may toggle between the graph types using a menu at the top of the frame. Depending on the activity, the students identify the most relevant graph. To plot the online graphs, students can drag and drop the relevant data files (year, population of hare, and lynx) from the case cards located on the left-hand side of the screen to the x and y axes.
Tuva Teacher Guide—Explore Patterns in Population Changes.	https://tuvalabs.com/docviewer/?title=Tuva%20Teacher%20Guide%20%20Patterns%20in%20Population%20Changes%20(GDrive)&embed_url=https://docs.google.com/document/d/1envATnFY69v7M62q380foMBAl8_3dWFY7ajsTdd3trg/edit?embedded=true	The teacher can model the above steps of this activity to help students navigate through the graphing activity. By referring to the link for "Teacher handout—Patterns in Population Changes," the teacher can model the steps of how to choose the graphs and plot the graphs.

TIPS AND ADVICE

- In order to promote students' interest and creativity, the teacher should provide opportunities for their students to investigate an ecosystem in the communities they live in and identify issues related to the populations of living organisms.
- After identifying the list of words/phrases in the Frayer model, the students should be encouraged to use them during their discussions and explanations.
- It is always helpful for the teacher to model a sample Claim-Evidence-Reasoning explanation with their students, using a familiar science topic.
- When discussing sample Claim-Evidence-Reasoning explanations, the teacher can create and use a checklist to help students write a concise one.
- Sentence frames are given to students struggling with the English language. The frames included here are for students to engage in Claim-Evidence-Reasoning in constructing explanations and describing models. Use these sentence frames only as scaffolds, and once students produce structured responses on their own, they need not be provided.

DISCUSSION QUESTIONS

1. Describe ways to engage students in the disciplinary core ideas of interdependent relationships of living and nonliving organisms within an ecosystem in the areas/communities they are living in. What types of resources will be helpful in this activity?
2. What are the limitations of using the language routines explained in this chapter? Will there be differences in how these routines are implemented in online settings versus classroom settings?
3. Discuss other ways to support students using the CER framework in online settings. What type of digital resources will you use?

REFERENCES

Berland, L. K., & Reiser, B. J. (2009). Making sense of argumentation and explanation. *Science Education, 93*(1), 26–55.

Brown, N. J., Furtak, E. M., Timms, M., Nagashima, S. O., & Wilson, M. (2010). The evidence-based reasoning framework: Assessing scientific reasoning. *Educational Assessment, 15*(3–4), 123–141.

Every Student Succeeds Act of 2015, Pub. L. No. 114–95 § 114 Stat. 1177 (2015).

Ford, M. J., & Forman, E. A. (2006). Chapter 1: Redefining disciplinary learning in classroom contexts. *Review of Research in Education, 30*(1), 1–32.

Franco-Fuenmayor, S. E., Padrón, Y. N., & Waxman, H. C. (2015). Investigating bilingual/ESL teachers' knowledge and professional development opportunities in a large suburban school district in Texas. *Bilingual Research Journal, 38*(3), 336–352.

Furtak, E. M., Hardy, I., Beinbrech, C., Shavelson, R. J., & Shemwell, J. T. (2010). A framework for analyzing evidence-based reasoning in science classroom discourse. *Educational Assessment, 15*(3–4), 175–196.

Gutiérrez, K. D., & Rogoff, B. (2003). Cultural ways of learning: Individual traits or repertoires of practice. *Educational Researcher, 32*(5), 19–25.

Hakuta, K., & Santos, M. (2012). Conference overview paper. *Commissioned Papers on Language and Literacy Issues in the Common Core State Standards and Next Generation Science Standards* (pp. i–ix). Stanford University. https://ul.stanford.edu/sites/default/files/resource/2021-12/UL%20Stanford%20Final%205-9-12%20w%20cover.pdf

Hakuta, K., Santos, M., & Fang, Z. (2013). Challenges and opportunities for language learning in the context of the CCSS and the NGSS. *Journal of Adolescent & Adult Literacy, 56*(6), 451–454.

Hansen-Thomas, H., Grosso Richins, L., Kakkar, K., & Okeyo, C. (2016). I do not feel I am properly trained to help them! Rural teachers' perceptions of challenges and needs with English-language learners. *Professional Development in Education, 42*(2), 308–324.

Hillmayr, D., Ziernwald, L., Reinhold, F., Hofer, S. I., & Reiss, K. M. (2020). The potential of digital tools to enhance mathematics and science learning in secondary schools: A context-specific meta-analysis. *Computers & Education, 153*, 103897.

Lantolf, J. P., Thorne, S. L., & Poehner, M. E. (2015). Sociocultural theory and second language development. *Theories in Second Language Acquisition: An Introduction, 1,* 207–226.

Lave, J., & Wenger, E. (2002). Legitimate peripheral participation in communities of practice. *Supporting Lifelong Learning: Perspectives on Learning, 1,* 111.

Lee, O. (2019). Aligning English language proficiency standards with content standards: Shared opportunity and responsibility across English learner education and content areas. *Educational Researcher, 48*(8), 534–542.

Lee, O., Quinn, H., & Valdés, G. (2013). Science and language for English language learners in relation to Next Generation Science Standards and with implications for Common Core State Standards for English language arts and mathematics. *Educational Researcher, 42*(4), 223–233.

Lemke, J. L. (2001). Articulating communities: Sociocultural perspectives on science education. *Journal of Research in Science Teaching, 38*(3), 296–316.

Lier, L. V. (2007). Action-based teaching, autonomy and identity. *International Journal of Innovation in Language Learning and Teaching, 1*(1), 46–65.

López, F., McEneaney, E., & Nieswandt, M. (2015). Language instruction educational programs and academic achievement of Latino English learners: Considerations for states with changing demographics. *American Journal of Education, 121*(3), 417–450.

Martínez, R. S., Harris, B., & McClain, M. B. (2014). Practices that promote English reading for English learners (ELs). *Journal of Educational and Psychological Consultation, 24*(2), 128–148.

McNeill, K. L., & Krajcik, J. S. (2011). *Supporting grade 5–8 students in constructing explanations in science: The claim, evidence, and reasoning framework for talking and writing.* Pearson.

McNeill, K. L., Lizotte, D. J., Krajcik, J., & Marx, R. W. (2006). Supporting students' construction of scientific explanations by fading scaffolds in instructional materials. *The Journal of the Learning Sciences, 15*(2), 153–191.

National Center for Education Statistics. (2018). *The condition of education, 2015.* U.S. Department of Education.

National Research Council. (2007). *Taking science to school: Learning and teaching science in grades K–8. Chapter 5. Generating and evaluating scientific evidence and explanations.* National Academies Press.

NGSS Lead States. (2013). *Next Generation Science Standards: For states, by states.* The National Academies Press.

Norris, S. P., & Phillips, L. M. (2003). How literacy in its fundamental sense is central to scientific literacy. *Science Education, 87*(2), 224–240.

Osborne, J. (2014). Teaching scientific practices: Meeting the challenge of change. *Journal of Science Teacher Education, 25*(2), 177–196.

Quinn, H., Lee, O., & Valdés, G. (2012). Language demands and opportunities in relation to Next Generation Science Standards for English language learners: What teachers need to know. *Commissioned Papers on Language and Literacy Issues in the Common Core State Standards and Next Generation Science Standards, 94,* 32–32.

Ryoo, K., & Bedell, K. (2017). The effects of visualizations on linguistically diverse students' understanding of energy and matter in life science. *Journal of Research in Science Teaching, 54*(10), 1274–1301.

Sandoval, W. A., & Millwood, K. A. (2005). The quality of students' use of evidence in written scientific explanations. *Cognition and Instruction, 23*(1), 23–55.

Schleppegrell, M. J. (2004). *The language of schooling: A functional linguistics perspective*. Routledge.

Tuva Student Handout. (n.d.). *Explore patterns in population changes.* https://tuvalabs.com/docviewer/?title=Tuva%20Student%20Handout%20-%20Patterns%20in%20Population%20Changes%20(Gdrive)&embed_url=https://docs.google.com/document/d/1Cus_leiHSxhZQCNpo_Ocv9gvGY4cEP-UpaW9NBI_gME/edit?embedded=true

Tuva Teacher Guide. (n.d.). *Explore patterns in population changes.* https://tuvalabs.com/docviewer/?title=Tuva%20Teacher%20Guide%20-%20Patterns%20in%20Population%20Changes%20(GDrive)&embed_url=https://docs.google.com/document/d/1envATnFY69v7M62q380foMBAl8_3dWFY7ajsTdd3trg/edit?embedded=true

van Lier, L., & Walqui, A. (2012). Language and the common core state standards. *Commissioned Papers on Language and Literacy Issues in the Common Core State Standards and Next Generation Science Standards, 94*, 44.

Vygotsky, L. S. (1978). *Mind in society: The development of higher psychological processes.* Harvard University Press.

Warschauer, M., & Meskill, C. (2000). Technology and second language teaching. *Handbook of Undergraduate Second Language Education, 15*, 303–318.

Yore, L. D., Hand, B. M., & Florence, M. K. (2004). Scientists' views of science, models of writing, and science writing practices. *Journal of Research in Science Teaching, 41*(4), 338–369.

Zwiers, J., Dieckmann, J., Rutherford-Quach, S., Daro, V., Skarin, R., Weiss, S., & Malamut, J. (2017). *Principles for the design of mathematics curricula: Promoting language and content development.* Stanford University, UL/SCALE. *http://ell.stanford.edu/content/mathematics-resources-additional-resources*

CHAPTER 8

GIVING ONLINE LEARNING THE PERSONAL TOUCH

The Promoting Evidentiary Reasoning and Self-Regulation Online (PERSON) Framework

Robert B. Marsteller
Delaware State University

Alec M. Bodzin
Lehigh University

The Promoting Evidentiary Reasoning and Self-Regulation Online (PERSON) framework uses scaffolded online simulations and case studies to develop evidence-based reasoning and argumentation while supporting skills for self-regulated learning. Several discipline-specific core content (DCI) and crosscutting concepts (CCs) related to the scientific practices (SEPs) of *arguing from evidence* are presented. A specific curriculum example based on Biological Evolution is described in more detail. However, the framework can be applied in various content areas and secondary grade levels and be used in various online formats. The importance of scaffolding learning with online simulations and providing appropriate support for student-centered learning in online environments are discussed.

Teaching and Learning Online: Science for Secondary Grade Levels, pages 107–122.
Copyright © 2023 by Information Age Publishing
www.infoagepub.com
107

RATIONALE

Promoting Evidentiary Reasoning and Self-Regulation Online (PERSON) is a design framework that synthesizes Bandura's (1977) social cognitive theory and Lave and Wenger's (1991) situated learning theory. The efficacy of this framework has been tested in multiple high school biology classrooms (Marsteller, 2017; Marsteller & Bodzin, 2015, 2019). When the framework was first developed, student enrollment in online courses increased (Queen et al., 2011). At that time, online courses disproportionally served students who had been unsuccessful in traditional classroom settings (Watson et al., 2014). Since the Fall of 2020, most K–12 students have participated in online learning (Burbio, 2020). We continue to hear reports of students struggling to succeed academically in online settings and of many students who do not show up (Diliberti & Kaufman, 2020). The PERSON framework was designed to support the development of scientific practices and self-regulated learning in various online environments that includes asynchronous, synchronous, and hybrid formats. Scientific practices, such as engaging in argument from evidence, are found across scientific disciplines, content areas, and grade levels (NRC, 2012). Further, self-regulated learning skills are needed by all students that are expected to learn independently online.

While significant attention has been given to the role of synchronous, video-based class meetings using tools such as Zoom (Widdicombe, 2020), this approach may not be the best option for struggling students. Asynchronous online learning environments allow learners increased time for reflection and thoughtful participation in coursework (Giesbers et al., 2014). The affordances of asynchronous online learning are effective for students that have difficulties in traditional classrooms, such as ESL learners (Bassett, 2011), students with learning disabilities (Graves et al., 2011), or students with a general reluctance to participate in face-to-face discussions (Bassett, 2011). However, asynchronous learning environments require more independence from learners than comparable synchronous environments (Giesbers et al., 2014). Because the same students that benefit from the unique affordances of asynchronous online learning environments often lack the skills to learn independently, special attention must be paid to supporting learner independence (Nandi et al., 2012).

Successful students have strategies to learn independently; less successful learners often lack these strategies (Hodges & Kim, 2010). These strategies are collectively known as self-regulated learning (SRL). Kitsantas and Zimmerman (2009) defined self-regulation of learning as the degree that students are metacognitively, motivationally, behaviorally, and actively responsible for their learning processes. SRL includes awareness of learning needs, effective learning strategies, and evaluating learning outcomes (Pata, 2009). While learning SRL through social interactions or within a community of practice is possible, it is important to actively promote these strategies and draw learners' attention to their efficacy. Support for self-regulation can make learners actively engage in the process of self-regulation (Al-Rawahi & Al-Balushi, 2015).

Developments in research about effective instruction in online learning environments have been concurrent with efforts to reform science instruction for K–12 students. The *Next Generation Science Standards* (NGSS; NGSS Lead States, 2013) integrate discipline-specific core content, scientific practices, and crosscutting concepts. Scientific practices are methods scientists use to understand the natural world (e.g., "analyzing and interpreting data" and "using computational thinking"). An example of a scientific practice is evidentiary reasoning (NGSS Lead States, 2013). Evidentiary reasoning is the process of collecting and organizing information to support inferences (Pellegrino et al., 2014). Previous research has found that K–12 students lack skills associated with evidentiary reasoning (Marsteller & Bodzin, 2015). Further, students do not seem to have many opportunities to develop those skills (Biggers et al., 2013). Consequently, it is necessary to create instruction that promotes evidentiary reasoning to meet the essential learning goals of the NGSS.

THEORETICAL BACKGROUND

Social cognitive theory states that learning occurs through shared experiences and observations in specific social settings (Bandura, 1977). Similarly, situated learning is a theoretical perspective that views learning through the lens of a specific environment where knowledge is used (Lave & Wenger, 1991). In this view, all knowledge is contextual and learning outcomes improve with an increased similarity between the learning environment and the practical environment (Lave & Wenger, 1991).

Social learning theory and situated learning theory complement each other by focusing on learners' interactions with each other and members of communities of practice. As learners engage in legitimate practices within a field, they can synthesize knowledge with existing cognitive structures relevant to their learning. Social learning theory and situated learning focus on the context of learning and how that context results in individual learning outcomes. Because teaching in online settings can appear impersonal or divorced from context, special attention is required to develop these essential features of instruction.

Eight key elements have been included in the design of the PERSON framework in order to develop the cognitive structures described in the previous paragraph. The key elements include *Foundational Knowledge*; *Simulation Study*; *Analyze and Extend*; *Case Study*; *Social Discourse*; *Scaffolding of Self-regulation*; *Scaffolding Evidentiary Reasoning*; and *Evaluation*. Facts and basic concepts are initially presented in the *Foundational Knowledge* section, followed by inquiry-based exploration in the *Simulation Study*. The *Analyze and Extend* element provides scaffolded problem solving and prepares students to engage with scientific practices in the *Case Studies*. Students use an asynchronous discussion forum to exchange ideas throughout the curriculum to promote *Social Discourse*. Students receive regular and consistent *Scaffolding of Self-Regulation* to develop skills necessary to learn independently. The skills of *Evidentiary Reasoning* are scaffolded and practiced continuously *and evaluation* provides formative and summative feedback.

KEY ELEMENTS OF PERSON

Evidentiary Reasoning

The evidentiary reasoning element contains scaffolded tasks that ask students to collect and analyze data to support scientific claims. *Engaging in argument from evidence* and *analyzing and interpreting data* are key scientific practices (NGSS Lead States, 2013). The online curriculum addresses the need for developing evidentiary reasoning skills by providing practice with fundamental science skills such as interpreting graphs and synthesizing information from multiple sources and providing students with a model of evidentiary reasoning (Brown et al., 2010) and prompted reflection. Throughout the curriculum, students participate in the structured practice of evidentiary reasoning. Students complete a handout with scaffolding prompts and areas to record evidence from the simulation and responses to formative assessment prompts during classroom implementation.

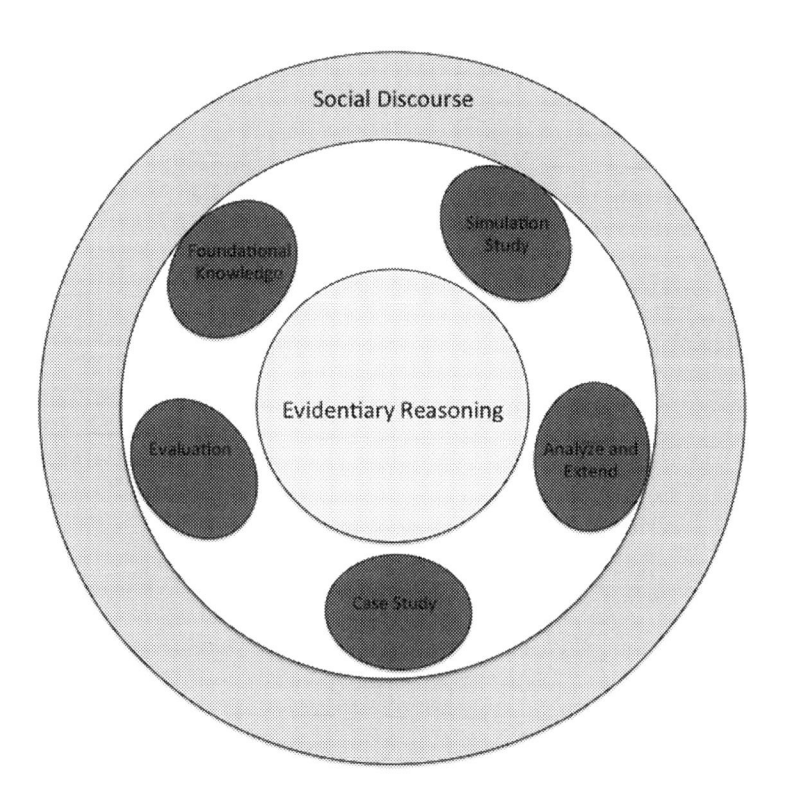

FIGURE 8.1. Key Elements of the PERSON Framework

Students can be guided through an evidentiary reasoning task by first asking them to collect meaningful data and then asking a question that draws their attention to relevant features of the data. Next, students can create an explanation for patterns they have recognized while focusing on the data they have collected. Then, students can attempt to develop a rule that would explain similar patterns in other related but distinct scenarios. Finally, students can apply this rule to a new situation. When using simulations to generate initial data, this last step could be to make predictions about the real world.

Here is an example of how to guide students through an evidentiary reasoning task related to Island Biogeography. Students are asked to work through these questions while using the Island Biogeography simulation (Figure 8.2). Teachers could use this model with any of the simulations provided at the end of the chapter. For this example, we asked the following questions:

In the Island Biogeography simulation, release 25 red butterflies and 25 green butterflies. Record the number of individuals in each population once the simulation is complete.

Aside from color, what is the difference between the green and red islands?

Based on your data, what can you determine about the relationship between red and green butterfly populations and the locations of the red and green islands?

Make a statement about the relationship between island location and the probability of migration from the mainland.

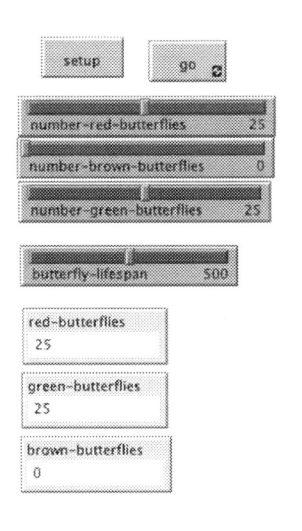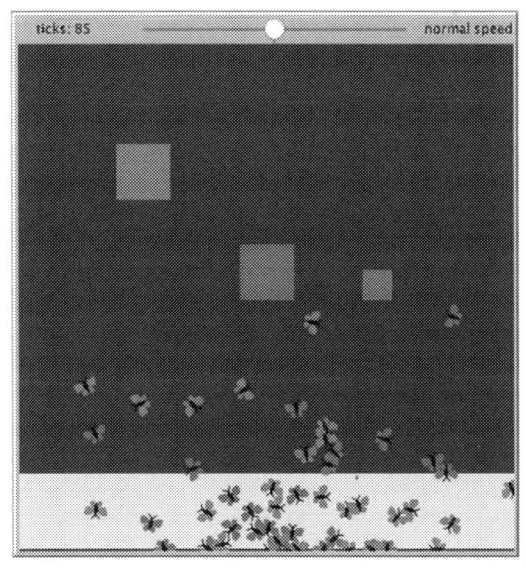

FIGURE 8.2. Screen Capture of the Island Biogeography Simulation

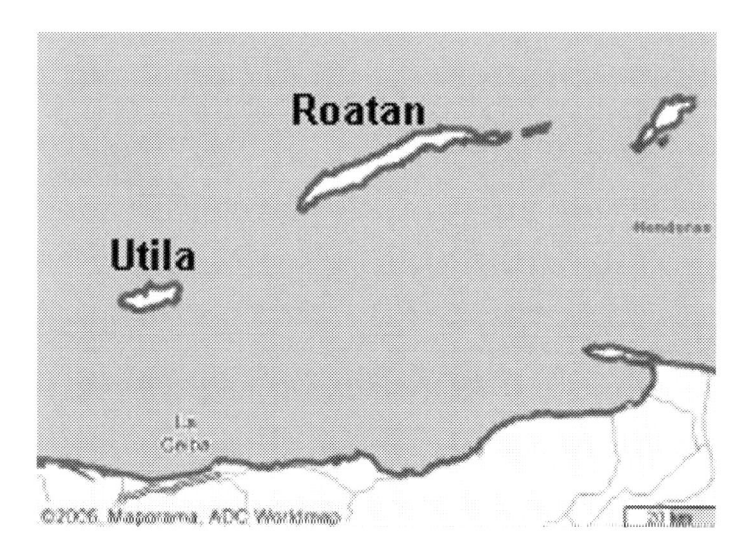

FIGURE 8.3. Map of Two Islands for Comparison. http://www.aboututila.com/Maps/WPhotos/Bay-Islands-Map.gif

Use the map in Figure 8.3 to predict the comparative likelihood of finding migratory animals from the mainland on each island.

Foundational Knowledge

Videos are provided to introduce fundamental concepts, terminology, and models of how information is structured in science. Videos utilize a combination of narration, titles, and images to introduce students to the complex vocabulary associated with science content. Presenting complicated terminology with both text and narration is an effective strategy for vocabulary acquisition (Clark & Mayer, 2003). In a hybrid setting, foundational knowledge could be presented in a traditional lecture but videos offer some options for more inclusive differentiated instruction. Videos provide the ability to pause in order to adjust pacing or the ability to repeat the video to review content. In the foundational knowledge video for the Island Biogeography simulation, students were introduced to the basic vocabulary of island biogeography and the challenges of migration across large bodies of water.

Simulation Study

Students are given structured activities that revolve around several Web-based simulations. This component is the primary means students can engage in the NGSS Science and Engineering practices of *developing and using models, planning and carrying out investigations*, and *analyzing and interpreting data* (NGSS Lead States, 2013). Particularly in regard to topics such as evolutionary biology, geology, or astronomy, simulations manage to bypass the budgetary and time constraints associated with the study of phenomena that occur across substantial amounts of time (Latham & Scully, 2008). The specific simulation platform used in our example was NetLogo. NetLogo allows users to observe and make predictions about complex phenomena by manipulating agent-based models (Tisue & Wilensky, 2004). There are a wide variety of web-based simulations freely available to science teachers that cover a broad scope of science content. Some of these sources are presented later in this chapter.

Analyze and Extend

The Analyze and Extend component of the online curriculum requires students to apply foundational knowledge in combination with experiences from simulations and readings to create and defend scientific positions and to critique the arguments of others. The NGSS practices include *constructing explanations* and *engaging in argument from evidence* (NGSS Lead States, 2013). The "analyze" learning tasks are scaffolded to support the development of analytical skills. Initial items provide concepts and data directly, while subsequent items require students to refer to foundational videos, simulations, or readings. The "extend" learning tasks ask students to transfer conceptual understandings from examples they have encountered to novel scenarios that share similarities with prior examples. The Analyze and Extend learning tasks also complement previous components of the online curriculum by allowing for scaffolding that directs and focuses student attention to relevant details that novice learners may miss.

Case Study

In the case study component, students are asked to examine realistic scenarios and apply the critical thinking practiced in the Analyze and Extend component of the curriculum. Students are given open-ended tasks with limited information to develop scientific understandings from basic concepts to complex, realistic scientific practices. Students are directed to authoritative sources that provide evidence focused on particular examples of science content. For example, in a unit studying evolutionary biology, students would explore cases about MRSA or the spread of the gene for lactose tolerance. If middle school students were studying geologic time scale, then they could explore fossils to establish the dates of geologic strata. Students are asked to apply evidence from the cases to build arguments that refine their conceptual understanding of science content. For example, students are asked to cite specific evidence from readings to indicate if MRSA infection rates were increasing or declining and then explain the change in infection rates. Alternatively, students could use fossil evidence to construct their geologic time scale. Students are asked to explain how to determine if their proposed explanation is accurate.

Social Discourse

Students are provided with a forum area to post questions and communicate with peers and the course instructor to promote social discourse. Students are prompted to create and support positions with evidence from course materials. Students are also encouraged to support or challenge each other's assertions with evidence of their own. Social discourse promotes engagement and motivation in what can otherwise be an isolating learning environment.

For example, students in a high school physics class could be challenged to propose materials to act as sound insulation for the band room. Asking students to support their proposal might not immediately elicit evidence-based claims about sound waves and the media through which they pass. In this case, the instructor would remind students of PhET simulations of wave properties.

Support for Self-Regulation

Two approaches are used to support self-regulation in this online curriculum framework: self-regulation mini-lessons and progress monitoring checklists. Self-regulation mini-lessons occur at the beginning of a task set, including introducing and practicing a specific self-regulatory skill, such as planning, monitoring, control, and reflection. As each activity within a task set continues, students use progress monitoring checklists for reflective comments about their learning process.

If you had a middle school class engaging in an engineering design task where your goal was for students to evaluate competing designs to insulate a home (using the *Convection in a House* simulation from the Concord Consortium), then the teacher could enforce a schedule and hold students to that schedule. However, if we want to develop self-regulation skills, then students could be asked to develop their schedules and monitor and adjust them as they engage in the design process. Ask a question before students begin the design process, such as "How long will it take to design and test a prototype?" This question can be followed up by questions such as "Was your estimated schedule accurate? Did you need more or less time than you expected? What factors contributed to the differences between your expectation and experience?"

Evaluation

In addition to assessing content knowledge, students are required to complete performance-based assessments that allow them to work with content knowledge to solve problems that do not have a single, correct answer and highlight their evidentiary reasoning skills. Teachers should refer to the performance expectations provided with the NGSS standards to develop assessments for their science content. Here is a performance expectation from the high school Earth and Space Sciences as an example:

HS-ESS1-5. Evaluate evidence of the past and current movements of continental and oceanic crust and the theory of plate tectonics to explain the ages of crustal rocks.

In this example, students would be directed to the USGS Earthquake map, which includes tectonic boundaries. They would be given data about the ages of crustal rocks from various locations that could be connected to plate tectonic activity. Students would then be challenged to connect the activities of tectonic plates, as measured by earthquake activity, to construct explanations for the rocks' ages.

ALIGNMENT TO NGSS

The purpose of this framework is to develop the ability of students to engage in evidentiary reasoning while supporting self-regulation of learning. This focus allows teachers to address the key components of the NGSS. Table 8.1 highlights how our examples align with key NGSS components.

SUPPORTING LEARNING WITH ONLINE/REMOTE LEARNING ENVIRONMENTS

These science topics are unified because they consider natural phenomena that cannot be perceived through firsthand experience. The mechanics of heredity and geologic time, or the process of evolution occur at scales that are well beyond unmediated human perception. The PERSON framework promotes the use of online simulations that allow students to engage with these phenomena in active learning experiences. Further, students can grasp how scientists study phenomena where direct observation is difficult or impossible. A teacher no longer needs to be the sole source of information for students. Instead, the role of a teacher in online learning environments is to facilitate the thoughtful and productive use of the many resources available. A teacher will create effective instructional scaffolding that is responsive to the needs of their students. A teacher will draw students' attention to the most relevant features and correct misunderstandings as they arise. The freely available simulations presented below are from the Netlogo (Tisue & Wilensky, 2004) and PhET (Podolefsky et al., 2010) projects, respectively. The United States Geological Survey (USGS) Earthquake map is a regularly updated record of earthquake activity worldwide. The scale of global geologic activity remains beyond the limits of firsthand experience but this resource shows actual data of phenomena occurring in the present. The Resource Notes section below presents a summary of freely available online simulations.

Critiques and Considerations

If you were to search the internet for simulations related to scientific topics, then your search would most likely return simulations that are demonstrative rather than interactive. The simulations recommended above curate opportunities for learners to manipulate phenomena and collect resulting data. Most of these

TABLE 8.1. NGSS Alignment of Examples

| Example | Science & Engineering Practice | | Engaging in Argument from Evidence |
	Disciplinary Core Ideas	Crosscutting Concepts	Performance Expectation
Evidentiary Reasoning: Island Biogeography	HS-LS4-5 Biological Evolution	Cause and Effect	Evaluate the evidence supporting claims that changes in environmental conditions may result in (1) increases in the number of individuals of some species, (2) the emergence of new species over time, and (3) the extinction of other species.
Case Study: MRSA	HS-LS3-2 Heredity	Cause and Effect	Make and defend a claim based on evidence that inheritable genetic variations may result from (1) new genetic combinations through meiosis, (2) viable errors occurring during replication, and/or (3) mutations caused by environmental factors.
	HS-ESS1-5 Earth's Place in the Universe	Patterns	Evaluate evidence of the past and current movements of continental and oceanic crust and the theory of plate tectonics to explain the ages of crustal rocks.
Case Study: Geologic Time Scale	MS-ESS1.C The History of Planet Earth	Scale, Proportion, and Quantity	Construct a scientific explanation based on evidence from rock strata for how the geologic time scale is used to organize Earth's 4.6-billion-year-old history.
Social Discourse: Band Room Insulation	HS-PS4.A Wave Properties	Cause and Effect	Use mathematical representations to support a claim regarding relationships among the frequency, wavelength, and speed of waves traveling in various media.
Support for Self-Regulation: Home Insulation	MS-ETS1.B Developing Possible Solutions		Evaluate competing design solutions using a systematic process to determine how well they meet the criteria and constraints of the problem.
Evaluation: Tectonic Plates and Rock Age	HS-ESS2.B Plate Tectonics and Large-Scale Interactions	Patterns	Evaluate evidence of the past and current movements of continental and oceanic crust and the theory of plate tectonics to explain the ages of crustal rocks.

simulations are robust tools with multiple options for manipulating them. However, these simulations could overwhelm students or make it difficult to focus on features relevant to a given problem. In order to ensure that students get the most out of these simulations, they must be provided with appropriate guidance. We contend that offering guidance to students embedded within instructional materials promotes self-regulated learning in an online environment. As with the theories of Bandura (1977) and Lave and Wenger (1991), learners must have models for how to behave when they encounter novel learning environments. To this end, it is essential to scaffold learners' experiences with simulations in order for them to understand how that learning tool functions and how it can be used to produce evidence to support a scientific argument.

SUMMARY AND REFLECTION

Scaffolded simulations provide an opportunity for students to engage in legitimate practices of evidentiary reasoning that support the acquisition of disciplinary core ideas and crosscutting concepts. Students can have firsthand experiences that are more engaging than viewing a demonstration or taking notes from a lecture. The use of simulations to gather and interpret data is at the heart of this framework. Subsequently, students can apply their developing understandings to a case study based on real-world scenarios. The case studies allow students to see how theoretical knowledge can be utilized.

Engaging students with simulations to generate data for evidence-based inquiry, leading to application in real-world case studies, is an approach that can be used in many middle or high school science content areas. In the examples shared above, we see how this framework could support learning in life, physical and Earth sciences, and engineering. The degree of support for independent, self-regulated learning will vary across grade levels and between students. A successful classroom teacher will possess the knowledge and skills to determine the needs of their students and respond accordingly. Some students may struggle to learn in this manner. However, we contend that our framework can be successfully applied in various online settings, including asynchronous, synchronous, and hybrid environments, with the proper support.

During testing of this framework, students expressed hesitation about beginning work with simulations before learning the associated content. While the literature supporting inquiry as an effective teaching tool is substantial (see, for example, Bybee, 2006; Margunayasa et al., 2019), it is still used infrequently in most classrooms (Sheffield, & McIlvenny, 2014). Providing scaffolding alleviates this hesitancy while helping students focus on appropriate experimental design principles. After successful initial experiences with highly scaffolded simulation studies, the degree of scaffolding was reduced. However, in testing this framework, we have been unable to eliminate the need for scaffolding. Eliminating all scaffolding resulted in very low assessment scores relative to items related to work with higher degrees of scaffolding. This decline in scores was likely due to the brief deployment period. Students likely required scaffolding to persist for a longer period of time or a more gradual schedule of elimination. It will be the responsibility of the course instructor to monitor assessment data and adjust the degree of scaffolding provided.

The role of self-regulated learning in online environments can be substantial. This framework has been tested with two distinct sample populations that can be described as academically successful students and academically struggling students. Academically successful students often possess various skills related to self-regulation of learning, while those students who struggle do not. Teachers will need to consider the population of students they are working with to determine how much support for self-regulation is required. The study conducted with academically struggling students did not produce significant improvements in self-regulated learning skills but the support provided likely contributed to improvements in metrics of academic achievement. Implementation research indicates that time is a factor when developing self-regulated learning skills. It is unreasonable to expect students to make significant progress in developing these skills across a single lesson. There is a need for future research to determine how long self-regulated learning must be supported in order to produce significant improvements. There may be differences in the length of support required in online or face-to-face learning environments.

TIPS AND ADVICE

- Support evidentiary reasoning: Most school-based learning focuses on knowledge-oriented testing (Pellegrino et al., 2014). Students may struggle to use evidence to support their conclusions. Providing a written structure for evidence-based reasoning such as EBRF (Brown et al., 2010) or the Claim Evidence Reasoning framework (McNeill & Krajcik, 2011) can be effective. Still, students will require adequate practice in using these tools. The PERSON framework provides opportunities for students to practice evidence-based reasoning. Structures like EBRF or CER can be presented in Foundational Knowledge videos and reinforced through scaffolding in Evidentiary Reasoning, Scaffolding, or Analyze and Extend activities.
- Split up compound questions: Some students struggle when asked to answer questions with multiple parts, such as providing an answer and supporting that answer with evidence. Consider asking students these questions as distinct questions (e.g., #1 and #2) rather than as multiple questions within a single item. Splitting up compound questions is especially important in online learning environments where students may work independently without immediate access to their teacher. If student responses to questions are reviewed asynchronously, then it is crucial to ensure all your questions are clear.
- Find the scaffolding sweet spot: Too much can be stifling, not enough can leave unprepared students directionless and dependent on their teacher. Use formative assessments to determine the appropriate level of support for your students. In online learning environments, teachers may not have access to the wealth of informal assessments that we sometimes take for granted in face-to-face teaching and learning environments. It is important to be deliberate about collecting formative assessment data and adjusting instructional scaffolding accordingly.
- Support self-regulated learning as needed. Students with a high degree of self-regulatory ability may consider keeping records of their planning and

monitoring burdensome and distracting. Use formative assessments to determine how much support your students need. Self-regulated learning can be challenging to assess in an online setting where you cannot observe your students working. You will need to be deliberate in collecting this information. Ask your students to make their thinking visible. Periodically asking your students to track their planning, monitoring, and evaluation processes will provide appropriate assessment data.

- Provide opportunities for students to interact: Working independently in online learning environments can be isolating but interactions must be meaningful and appropriate. One implementation study of this framework relied on discussion forums to provide social interaction. Still, surveys of student participants indicated that the speed of response and lack of meaningful interactions with peers made these forums ineffective (Marsteller, 2017).

RESOURCE NOTES

Name of Resource	Primary Website	How to Locate the Resource Online
Concord Consortium STEM resources	https://learn.concord.org/	Go to https://learn.concord.org/. Menus are located on the left side of the page that allows you to filter interactive STEM activities. Select content areas from the first menu and grade levels from the second menu. An alphabetic list will appear to the right of the menus.
Netlogo	https://ccl.northwestern.edu/netlogo/	Go to https://ccl.northwestern.edu/netlogo/. Select "Library" in the menu on the left side of the page. Scroll down to find a list of simulations organized by content area. https://ccl.northwestern.edu/netlogo/models/index.cgi
PhET	https://phet.colorado.edu/	Go to https://phet.colorado.edu/. Mouse over "SIMU-LATIONS" at the menu at the top of the page. A drop-down menu will appear that allows users to select a content area. Selecting a content area will allow you to browse related simulations. Once you have selected a content area, users can use the options on the left side of the page to filter simulations by grade level, technical specifications, or accessibility features. https://phet.colorado.edu/en/simulations/filter?type=html&sort=alpha&view=grid
United States Geological Survey	https://earthquake.usgs.gov/	Go to https://earthquake.usgs.gov/. Select "Latest Earthquakes" on the right side of the page. You will arrive at an interactive map that shows recent earthquake activity. Options on the left side of the page allow you to select between formats and to sort data. https://earthquake.usgs.gov/earthquakes/map/?extent=10.48781,-148.62305&extent=58.63122,-41.39648

DISCUSSION QUESTIONS

1. The PERSON framework requires effective scaffolding to support learners in online environments. What is an optimal level of scaffolding? How can instructional materials be designed for diverse learners and support their changing needs?

2. Feelings of isolation can develop for some learners in asynchronous online learning environments. How can we optimally promote effective social discourse in an online environment when using the PERSON framework?

3. The PERSON framework uses case studies to connect simulated online learning to the real world. How can you effectively use case studies with students of varying academic capabilities to use evidence in order to develop scientific conceptual understandings?

4. Simulations are a central feature of the PERSON framework. How can you engage your students in online data collection if a simulation that fits your needs is unavailable?

5. Simulations may have an array of variables that can be manipulated. The PERSON framework relies on a scaffolded approach to inquiry to ensure students focus on particular variables. What benefits could exist for students if you provide less scaffolding when using simulations? How could you prepare students for a more learner-centered approach to inquiry learning using simulations?

REFERENCES

Al-Rawahi, N. M., & Al-Balushi, S. M. (2015). The effect of reflective science journal writing on students' self-regulated learning strategies. *International Journal of Environmental & Science Education, 10*(3), 367–379.

Bandura, A. (1977). *Social learning theory.* Prentice-Hall.

Bassett, P. (2011). How do students view asynchronous online discussions as a learning experience? *Interdisciplinary Journal of E-Learning & Learning Objects, 7*(1), 69–79.

Biggers, M., Forbes, C. T., & Zangori, L. (2013). Elementary teachers' curriculum design and pedagogical reasoning for supporting students' comparison and evaluation of evidence-based explanations. *The Elementary School Journal, 114*(1), 48–72. https://www.jstor.org/stable/10.1086/670738

Brown, N. J., Furtak, E. M., Timms, M., Nagashima, S. O., & Wilson, M. (2010). The evidence-based reasoning framework: Assessing scientific reasoning. *Educational Assessment, 15*(3–4), 123–141. https://doi.org/10.1080/10627197.2010.530551

Burbio. (2020, October 21). *Press: In reversal, more than 60% of U.S. K–12 public school students will be attending schools with in-person options by election day.* https://info.burbio.com/press/

Bybee, R. W. (2006). *Scientific inquiry and science teaching.* In *Scientific inquiry and nature of science* (pp. 1–14). Springer.

Clark, R. C., & Mayer, R. E. (2003). *E-learning and the science of instruction: Proven guidelines for consumers and designers of multimedia learning.* John Wiley & Sons, Inc.

Concord Consortium. (2021). *STEM resource finder* [Computer software]. https://learn.concord.org/

Diliberti, M. K., & Kaufman, J. H. (2020). *Will this school year be another casualty of the pandemic? Key findings from the American Educator Panels Fall 2020 COVID-19 Surveys.* Rand Corporation. https://doi.org/10.7249/RRA168-4

Giesbers, B., Rienties, B., Tempelaar, D., & Gijselaers, W. (2014). A dynamic analysis of the interplay between asynchronous and synchronous communication in online learning: The impact of motivation. *Journal of Computer Assisted Learning, 30*(1), 30–50. https://doi.org/10.1111/jcal.12020

Graves, L., Asunda, P. A., Plant, S. J., & Goad, C. (2011). Asynchronous online access as an accommodation on students with learning disabilities and/or attention-deficit hyperactivity disorders in postsecondary STEM courses. *Journal of Postsecondary Education and Disability, 24*(4), 317–330. https://onlinelibrary.wiley.com/doi/abs/10.1111/jcal.12020

Hodges, C. B., & Kim, C. (2010). Email, self-regulation, self-efficacy, and achievement in a college online mathematics course. *Journal of Educational Computing Research, 43*(2), 207–223.

Kitsantas, A., & Zimmerman, B. J. (2009). College students' homework and academic achievement: The mediating role of self-regulatory beliefs. *Metacognition Learning, 4,* 97–110. https://link.springer.com/article/10.1007/s11409-008-9028-y

Latham, L. G., II, & Scully, E. P. (2008). CRITTERS! A realistic simulation for teaching evolutionary biology. *American Biology Teacher, 70*(1), 30–33.

Lave, J., & Wenger, E. (1991). *Situated learning: Legitimate peripheral participation.* Cambridge University Press.

Margunayasa, I. G., Dantes, N., Marhaeni, A. A. I. N., & Suastra, I. W. (2019). The effect of guided inquiry learning and cognitive style on science learning achievement. *International Journal of Instruction, 12*(1), 737–750.

Marsteller, R. B., & Bodzin, A. M. (2015). The effectiveness of an online curriculum on high school students' understanding of biological evolution. *Journal of Science Education and Technology, 24*(6), 803–817. https://link.springer.com/article/10.1007/s10956-015-9565-5

Marsteller, R. B. (2017). *Making online learning personal: Evolution, evidentiary reasoning, and self-regulation in an online curriculum* (Publication No. 10278376) [Doctoral dissertation, Lehigh University]. ProQuest Dissertations Publishing.

Marsteller, R. B., & Bodzin, A. (2019). Examining the implementation of an online curriculum designed with the person theoretical framework on student's evidentiary reasoning and self-regulated learning. *The Electronic Journal for Research in Science & Mathematics Education, 23*(3).

McNeill, K. L., & Krajcik, J. S. (2011). *Supporting grade 5–8 students in constructing explanations in science: The claim, evidence, and reasoning framework for talk and writing.* Pearson.

Nandi, D., Hamilton, M., & Harland, J. (2012). Evaluating the quality of interaction in asynchronous discussion forums in fully online courses. *Distance Education, 33*(1), 5–30. https://www.tandfonline.com/doi/abs/10.1080/01587919.2012.667957

National Research Council. (2012). *A framework for K–12 science education: Practices, crosscutting concepts, and core ideas.* National Research Council.

NGSS Lead States. (2013). *Next generation science standards: For states, by states.* National Academies Press. https://doi.org/10.17226/18290.

Pata, K. (2009). Modeling spaces for self-directed learning at university courses. *Educational Technology & Society, 12*(3), 23–43. https://www.jstor.org/stable/10.2307/jeductechsoci.12.3.23

Pellegrino, J. W., Wilson, M. R., Koenig, J. A., & Beatty, A. S. (Eds.). (2014). *Developing assessments for the next generation science standards.* National Academies Press.

Podolefsky, N. S., Perkins, K. K., & Adams, W. K. (2010). Factors promoting engaged exploration with computer simulations. *Physical Review Special Topics-Physics Education Research, 6*(2), 1–11.

Queen, B., Lewis, L., & Coopersmith, J. (2011). *Distance education courses for public elementary and secondary school students: 2009–10.* National Center for Education Statistics. https://files.eric.ed.gov/fulltext/ED526879.pdf

Sheffield, R., & McIlvenny, L. (2014). Design and implementation of scientific inquiry using technology in a teacher education program. *International Journal of Innovation in Science and Mathematics Education, 22*(6), 46–60. http://openjournals.library.usyd.edu.au/index.php/CAL/article/viewFile/7560/8440

Tisue, S., & Wilensky, U. (2004, May). *Netlogo: A simple environment for modeling complexity* [Paper presentation]. International Conference on Complex Systems (ICCS 2004), Boston, MA.

United States Geologic Survey. (n.d.). *USGS magnitude 2.5+ earthquakes, past day.* https://earthquake.usgs.gov/earthquakes/map/

University of Colorado Boulder. (n.d.). *PhET.* http://phet.colorado.edu/

Watson, J., Pape, L., Murin, A., Gemin, B., & Vashaw, L. (2014). *Keeping pace with K–12 digital learning: An annual review of policy and practice.* Evergreen Education Group. http://www.kpk12.com/wp-content/uploads/EEG_KP2014-fnl-lr.pdf

Widdicombe, L. (2020, April 2). *The great zoom-school experiment.* The New Yorker. https://www.newyorker.com/news/our-local-correspondents/the-great-zoom-school-experiment

PART II

TEACHER'S JOURNEYS

USING EDUCATIONAL TECHNOLOGY TO FOSTER HIGH SCHOOL STUDENTS' ONLINE PRESENCE AND ENGAGEMENT AS *BECOMINGS*

An Integrated Stem Lesson on Trebuchets and Parabolas

Sophia Jeong and Stephen T. Lewis
The Ohio State University

Teachers share a lived experience of the struggles of online integrated science, technology, engineering, and mathematics (STEM) instruction during the pandemic. Teachers realized that engaging students in an online learning environment was challenging and required different instructional approaches. This chapter offers a new way of thinking about students' online presence and engagement as becomings. This relational, ontological concept helps us think about students being part of an assemblage that is always organized, re-organized, assembled, and reassembled. Second, we share our journey during which we as classroom teachers practiced diffractive noticing during our integrated science, technology, engineering, and mathematics (STEM) lessons to support our students' becomings and support them to become differently.

Teaching and Learning Online: Science for Secondary Grade Levels, pages 125–142.

We aimed to teach an integrated STEM lesson on trebuchets and parabolas in an online setting, which was traditionally taught in person. We realized that instructional approaches that we utilized in an in-person setting could not simply be transferred to a synchronous online setting. A rectangular box with only the letters of the students' names removed social cues (both verbal and visual) that would have typically been used to gauge the level of our students' presence and engagement in an in-person classroom environment. Even when we saw a rectangular box with a student's name on the participants list, evaluating if the student were "present" or "in" the synchronous classroom was challenging. If we had been in an in-person setting, then we would have received verbal and visual feedback from the students to assess the students' presence and engagement. We realized that facilitating interactions between the teacher and the students and between the students with their peers had to be intentional. Most importantly, we had to un-learn and then re-define what would count as "students' presence" in an online learning environment.

Our chapter does not aim to provide our fellow secondary science teachers with a prescribed 5E synchronous lesson plan that "worked" per se. Nor is it our intention to provide a "ready-made" synchronous lesson plan. Instead, our purpose is to offer a new way of thinking about students' online presence and engagement as becomings. We accomplish this goal by sharing our journey during which we as teachers practiced diffractive noticing during our integrated STEM lessons and how we supported our students to become differently.

Student Engagement and Presence Through Becomings

Student engagement is considered a multidimensional concept, including behavioral, emotional/affective, and cognitive. Other studies broadened the definition of student engagement to include dimensions such as social-behavioral, agentic, volitional (Hoskins, 2012). Some scholars have critiqued the broad definition of student engagement in the literature. Recently, Fortney et al. (2019) called for an expanded definition of equity in STEM education. In response, we argued that equitable STEM instruction should not condition learners to a single being; instead, we should foster multiplicities of their becoming whose relational ontology is always and already changing. Thus, we found the broad and somewhat ill-defined concept of student engagement more fluid in allowing multiplicities of students' becomings. We aimed to investigate diverse ways and locations of possibilities (Brandt, 2008) for students to become differently in an online learning environment in ways that have yet to be thought. To this end, we examined how students' online presence and engagement were produced through their relations with other entities in an online environment.

Diffractive Noticing: A Novel Theoretical Approach Helps Us to "See" Differently

Conceptualizing students' online presence and engagement through the lens of a becomings (Barad, 2007) produced a different kind of change in practice based on relational ontology. These ideas based on relational ontology were not anything new, per se. (Jeong et al., 2018). However, these concepts worked as new tools to help us re-think and re-imagine students' online presence and engagement that was emergent and relational.

In order to re-imagine our students' becoming, we needed to "see" things differently. Examining the students' day-to-day interactions with other entities in an online environment required the teacher to "notice" classroom practices that could foster multiplicities of students' online presence and engagement. Goodwin (1994) theorized the concept of professional vision as "socially organized ways of seeing and understanding events that are answerable to the distinctive interests of a particular social group" (p. 606). In our chapter, we apply this framework to conceptualize teachers' "diffractive noticing." Diffraction is an optical metaphor for an effort to see the world differently and consider what we would do with the differently-way-of-becoming. This chapter will be the first to theorize as "diffractive noticing" (Jeong & Lewis, this chapter), a useful framework that will be important in helping teachers to differently become and "see" new possibilities for students' online presence and engagement.

Employing diffractive noticing, we opened ourselves to "see" our teaching practices differently and map the paths we have taken to consider possible ways to provide hybrid learning spaces (see Calabrese Barton et al., 2008), offering new possibilities of students' becomings. As such, after each integrated STEM lesson, we remained on Zoom to immediately discuss aspects of the lessons that were memorable, surprised us, stood out, and "glowed." We paid attention to the events, interactions, or moments that "glowed" (MacLure, 2013). We located moments in the classroom that opened us up to new ways of thinking and becomings for both ourselves and students. We began to develop our professional vision as we diffractively noticed our teaching practices through the subjectivities and experiences of others, juxtaposing, comparing, contrasting, challenging, and contesting our practices as a collective experience.

As we engaged in the dialogic reflexivity process (Sherman et al., 2021), our diffractive noticing emerged from four dialogic encounters[1]: 1) Articulate, 2) Reflect, 3) Analyze, and 4) Re-articulate. We articulated our assumptions, values, ideas, beliefs about our students, what we noticed, what we wondered, and what we felt, experienced, and encountered. We reflected on our articulations by engaging in dialogues as we identified tensions as well as resonances. In our nonlinear, rhizomatic dialogues, our roles and positionings were fluid concerning one another. When appropriate, one of us framed and analyzed the events to create productive tensions by juxtaposing the differences and similarities in what we noticed. We then re-articulated the bricolage of our students' becomings and further reflected in our dialogic encounters. The first author brought her science

---

[1] We have mutated and adapted the four dialogic encounters that emerged from the Nonlinear Theories Conference supported by the 2021 Dean's Emerging Seed Grant, "Cultivating innovative methodologies and transdisciplinarity through dialogic reflexivity" at The Ohio State University.

education experiences, while the second author contributed perspectives from his mathematics background. We opened ourselves to "seeing" each other's different perspectives during our dialogic encounters, internalizing our discussions, finding ways to respond to what we noticed about our students, and engaging in productive conversations towards change in practice.

Synchronous Integrated STEM Lessons

In this chapter, we share different components of a synchronous integrated STEM unit on trebuchets and parabolas to provide the teaching context for how we enacted diffractive noticing. We also illustrate examples of how we supported students' diverse ways of online engagement and presence and their becomings. Our goal is for our fellow teachers to use our lesson narratives to imagine possibilities to open up new ways of thinking about their students' online engagement and presence during an integrated STEM lesson.

CONNECTIONS TO NGSS AND THREE-DIMENSIONAL LEARNING

In our synchronous integrated STEM unit, we aimed to leverage the three-dimensional learning outlined by NGSS. For SEPs, we tried to elicit three practices asking questions, using mathematics and computation thinking to solve a problem, constructing explanations, and designing possible solutions. For DCIs, we identified the three science ideas that students would need to master to complete the designing of their trebuchets and parabolas. For CCCs, we addressed the concept of systems thinking and system models during the lessons.

Students' Performance Expectations

- **Code:** HS-ETS1 (Engineering Design)
- **Domain:** Engineering, Technology, and Applications of Science (ETS)
- **HS-ETS1-2:** Design a solution to a complex real-world problem by breaking it down into smaller, more manageable problems that engineering can solve.
- **HS-ETS1-4**: Use a computer simulation to model the impact of proposed solutions to a complex real-world problem with numerous criteria and constraints on interactions within and between systems relevant to the problem.

Science and Engineering Practices

Asking Questions and Defining Problems (HS-ETS1-1)

- Analyze complex real-world problems by specifying criteria and constraints for successful solutions.

Using Mathematics and Computational Thinking (HS-ETS1-4)

- Use mathematical models and/or computer simulations to predict the effects of a design solution on systems and/or the interactions between systems.

Disciplinary Core Ideas

Defining and Delimiting Engineering Problems (ETS1.A)

- Criteria and constraints also include satisfying any requirements set by society, such as taking issues of risk mitigation into account, and they should be quantified to the extent possible and stated in such a way that one can tell if a given design meets them.

Developing Possible Solutions (ETS1.B)

- When evaluating solutions, it is important to consider a range of constraints, including cost, safety, reliability, and aesthetics, and to consider social, cultural, and environmental impacts.

Optimizing the Design Solution (ETS1.C)

- Criteria may need to be broken down into simpler ones that can be approached systematically and decisions about the priority of certain criteria over others (trade-offs) may be needed.

Crosscutting Concepts

Structure and Function (ETS1-2)

- Models (e.g., physical, mathematical, computer models) can be used to simulate systems and interactions—including energy, matter, and information flow— within and between systems at different scales.

LESSON NARRATIVE

Engage

The Engage segment was utilized to "hook" the students' interests. The focus of this segment is to elicit their prior knowledge about the physics and mechanics of simple machines. This segment could be taught synchronously.

Teacher Moves

We presented a Youtube video [6], "NOVA Medieval Siege Excerpts Part 1," and a design challenge to build a mini trebuchet. During the Engage segment, we fostered students' interests by sharing how trebuchets were used during medieval times. We made explicit connections to how science, technology, engineering, and mathematics (STEM) concepts behind a trebuchet launch were still being used and applied in our lives today, such as airplanes, highways and bridges, and satellites. We asked questions such as: "Who knows what a trebuchet is? What do you think a trebuchet was used for? Have you seen a trebuchet used in our everyday lives? What do you notice about the different parts of a trebuchet?" We used different pedagogical approaches to provide students time to think about these questions and share.

Student Moves

Students entered into the online chat their ideas to these questions or unmuted themselves to share their responses. Students shared what they already knew about the topic in response to the prompts. Students engaged with peers in dialogues.

Diffractive Noticing

Provoking student responses were met with silence in the form of muted microphones and black rectangles. As teachers, we felt we talked at our students more than ever. We realized we had to un-learn our initial notions of and assumptions about our students' presence and engagement that were heavily dependent on students' talk and what we could observe of their facial expression and body language: these notions failed to work.

In our Zoom class, our students had to turn their videos off due to slow internet and limitations of Chrome book. We articulated our old notions of student engagement and presence regarding what we could see and hear physically and we expected as much in our online learning environment. As we were reflecting on the challenges of online instruction, we were beginning to "see" differently how these factors played a role in how our students could participate. Without a visual cue which we were accustomed to in an in-person setting, we were beginning to rely on students' verbal cues and their verbal participation (such as responding to our questions). Then, one of us pointed out a pattern where only a select few students or the same student were verbally participating. In that moment of reflection, we had to re-think how students might be interacting with their technology. We began to consider how our students might be interacting with the technology in this virtual, Zoom space. We had to think of ways to entangle ourselves with our students (to become differently) to "see" their online presence and engagement in a different way. We began to ask the students to type in their responses, thoughts, ideas into the chat. We also began to brainstorm and re-articulate ways to "see" our students differently, leveraging the affordances of technology in our next Zoom class.

Explore

The Explore segment was where students had the opportunities to explore the mechanics of simple machines as well as the physics and mathematical concepts that they needed to learn to build and launch a trebuchet (e.g., the relationship between the weight of the counterweight of the trebuchet and the weight of its projectile). The lesson background and concepts include but should not limited to 1) basic components of a trebuchet such as a lever and a wheel-and-axel, 2) science concept related to force that more force means more speed and more distance, 3) mathematics concepts related to parabolas that different factors such as launch angle, the position of the object, the mass of the object, air resistance, impact the projectile motion and the shape of the graph such as vertex height or axis of symmetry. We could choose any of the concepts or the topics and determine the sequence of the concepts to address during the Explore segment. Within our context, transitioning to address the mathematical concept of parabolas was most appropriate. This segment can be taught synchronously.

Teacher Moves

We presented a simulation-based activity on the "Phet Interactive Simulations" website hosted by the University of Colorado, Boulder. The simulation activity is called "Projectile Motion." Using this simulation, we provided an opportunity for students to become familiar with the path of a projectile that would follow the shape of a parabola. We encouraged the students to manipulate the height of the canon on the PhET simulation, angle of the launch, and the mass of the object. Students had to work independently to determine which parameter values impacted the ability to hit the target within these tasks. Students independently recorded their responses but their responses were captured on a shared google document. Each student shared their screen showing their simulations when they had achieved hitting the target with the projectile.

Following the Phet simulation [8], we used another web-based tool for students to explore the concept of a parabola using a basketball illustration, which could be found at geogebra.org. The activity was called "Basketball Parabola" [2]. We asked the students to imagine that they were at a basketball game, and one of the players was about to make a buzzer shot. We posed the question to students: "Can you predict if the ball will go in or out or hit the rim?" We used a web-based whiteboard (such as Awwapp [1] or Jamboard) and asked students to log in to write, type, or document their predictions. We were able to observe and read aloud some of the students' predictions and asked students to share out loud their predictions by unmuting their microphones. Then, we asked the students to manipulate the sliders for variables a, b, and c to simulate the basketball's path and test their predictions. Using the web-based whiteboard, we created a table for students to fill in (Figure 9.1). An example of the table and exemplar answers are below. We gave time for students to work on the table independently. Afterward, we asked the students to share out their responses.

Student Moves

Students verbally participated in making their predictions about whether the basketball player would make or miss the shot or type in their responses in the chat. Students manipulated the sliders for the variables on the "Basketball Parabola" activity. Students began to fill in the chart.

Diffractive Noticing

As teachers, we had our initial expectations of how our students would participate. However, we realized that the instructional approaches we utilized in an in-person setting could not simply be transferred to a synchronous online setting. Our reasons for choosing instructional strategies and activities mediated by technology in a synchronous online environment had to be intentional and deliberate. Most importantly, we had to have a clear understanding of the different types of cognitive demands required of our students. Since the beginning of this unit, we have been brainstorming ways to leverage the affordances of a web-based whiteboard to observe and monitor students' work and reveal student thinking, and thus we implemented Awwapp.

First, to effectively integrate technology into our lesson, we guided the students to become familiar with the technology. We chose Awwapp with a deliberate intention because we knew we would be able to see and monitor students' work in real-time. We had the students log in to Awwapp and spend one to two minutes simply playing with the different buttons (for drawing lines, text boxes). Students took the time to explore how Awwapp worked. When we saw that students were comfortable using Awwapp (e.g., drawing animals and becoming creative on the drawing board), we guided them to the instruction at hand with the Basketball Parabola. As students filled out the Basketball Parabola chart, we could see and monitor who was doing well and who was struggling with the activity. Each of us provided additional assistance to the students who were struggling. It was about a month into the semester when our students were starting to use technology with more ease. Based on this finding, we decided we were going to plan for time to support students' "technology fluency," which we loosely define as knowing when and how to use education technology tools to enhance learning (Plair, 2008).

Explain

The Explain segment was where students constructed explanations and we guided the students to generate sources of evidence to support their explanations. Our chapter illustrated what the student-centered Explain segment looked like following the Basketball Parabola lesson in the previous Explore segment. This segment could be taught synchronously or asynchronously but we recommend synchronous instruction when possible in order to create opportunities for students to engage in dialogues with each other.

Teacher Moves

A successfully integrated STEM lesson is built on solid mathematical foundations. We helped students connect what they explored during the Basketball Parabola activity with the mathematical concepts they needed to understand. We asked students to explain why they thought the basketball player would make the shot or not. We guided the students to use the mathematical terms and the data from the table to generate their explanations. To ensure that all students generate their explanations, we purposefully and intentionally integrated an educational technology, Flipgrid, and instructed students to take a few minutes to record their verbal explanations. Using their phone, they could point, highlight, emphasize different parts of their data table to generate their explanations. The videos were posted on Flipgrid. We chose a few videos to share in a larger class. Alternatively, in a smaller class, everyone's videos could be shared. As students listened to the videos of their classmates' explanations, we facilitated dialogues between the students and asked questions such as: "Does anyone have anything to add to Sophia's explanations?" Next, we introduced students to another online learning platform, Desmos [3], where we imported video stills of the basketball mid-shot. Using the general equation for a parabolic function, we helped students manipulate the parameter values using the dynamic features of Desmos to justify their prediction from the Explore segment (e.g., Can you predict if the ball will go in or out or hit the rim?). This activity with prompts from us allowed students to understand how the parameter values in a quadratic equation related to the projectile's maximum height, trajectory, and path. Furthermore, the discussions among the students helped the students connect the projectile motion equations previously explored and general quadratic functions.

Student Moves

An exemplar explanation from students would entail that the variable a changed the width of the parabola and up or down of concave; variable b changed the vertex's x value; variable c changed the vertex's y value, and vertex was the turning point of the parabola. Following our instruction to use Flipgrid, students filmed themselves explaining whether the basketball player would make the shot or not while incorporating the terms from the data table. As the class was listening to students' videos of explanations, they had the opportunity to participate and build on their peers' responses verbally.

Diffractive Noticing

We realized the importance of establishing a routine for our students to be consistent in developing their technology fluency. For example, before using these technologies, we provided opportunities for students to become familiar with using Flipgrid before we started to leverage the affordances of the technology to engage students with content. We were then consistent with the application of educational technology. We used Awwapp to monitor students' work and their progress on the datasheet in real-time. We used Flipgrid for students to generate explanations that became artifacts of classroom discussions. We used PheT Projectile Motion simulations to explore the path of a projectile and how adjusting parameters impacted the path. Finally, we used Desmos to help students relate the exploration with the mathematics of parabolic functions. Each educational technology was used deliberately to achieve specific learning tasks, requiring different types of cognitive demands.

After several lessons in using FlipGrid, students became accustomed to creating their explanations and sharing their videos. We had a class where one of our students asked to create a FlipGrid video in Spanish and we encouraged the student to use whichever language was preferred. The student created a Flipgrid video using both Spanish and English. Toward the end of the semester, we perceived increased students' online presence and verbal participation, which was noted by a school administrator who came to observe our class. When students were asked to build on their peers' FlipGrid videos, more students volunteered to add to the explanations contributing to productive classroom dialogues. We saw more "back-and-forth" conversations between students when we centered class discussions using students' FlipGrid videos.

In a different class period, another student struggled to fill out the datasheet on Awwapp. The same student who created a FlipGrid video in Spanish began to explain how to fill out the datasheet to the other student in Spanish while the teacher was attending to other students in class. These "side conversations" between peers happened to the delight of the teachers! Both the first and second authors remember this "glowing moment" when we were pleased to see this type of conversation and help between the students. This moment was not an interruption to what was happening with the rest of the class. This type of "side conversation" would occur in an in-person environment where students are engaged in the lesson while helping each other in a group dynamic. We were excited to see these peer-to-peer conversations happening in a synchronous environment and we are cautiously optimistic that it can be a good starting benchmark for students' online presence and engagement in a virtual learning environment culminating our efforts to integrate and leverage technology to provide ways for students to be "present" and "engaged."

Elaborate

In the Elaborate segment, scientific modeling was emphasized. We continued to address the science and mathematical concepts that students would need to learn to design and build their mini trebuchet to launch a hypothetical canon (e.g., marshmallow). One of the challenges of implementing an engineering design process in an online environment was that we had to modify the inquiry-based, hands-on session where students would typically build a real trebuchet using materials. Instead, we used a trebuchet simulator, "VirtualTrebuchet 2.0," to provide an opportunity for students to extend their understanding of how different variables (mass of an object, launch angle—See Explore segment) can impact the launch. This segment could be taught synchronously. The Elaborate segment was where we further pushed students to generate explanations using models. We began working with students to develop their understanding of a scientific model that would serve as the basis of their initial design of a mini trebuchet.

Teacher Moves

We asked the students to imagine that they were a team of engineers who had been challenged to design a mini trebuchet out of everyday items. Their challenge was to launch a marshmallow to accurately land on a target from as far a distance as possible. However, first, we reminded the students that they needed to develop a scientific model of their initial design.

We guided the students through the engineering design process, starting with the planning stage, determining which materials to use, and applying science and mathematical concepts to calculate the distance launch angle. We asked a prompting question: "What is engineering and how can engineering be used to teach science?" We prepared to follow up questions to elicit and build on students' responses. We anticipated an exemplar response that made the connection that engineering was an effective science teaching tool where the concepts of science and mathematics are applied to solve a real-world problem. We then reviewed the concepts of forces, energy, and interactions. Although we had to modify the inquiry-based, hands-on activity, we mailed a list of everyday items to the students that they could manipulate at home: pencils/pens (popsicle sticks might be helpful), straws, tape, string or dental floss, AA battery as a dead weight, a mechanical hex nut (any size but smaller will work better) or marshmallow, a hot glue gun (optional but useful), paper clips, and rubber bands (not for launching but to hold things together), tape, and string or yarn. We asked students to explore their manipulatives as well as the simulator. We pointed to the simulator's different components (counterweight, beam, sling, projectile, frame). We made explicit that students understood that these different variables would impact the launch and how far a marshmallow would fly.

Second, we worked with the students on developing their understanding of a scientific model. According to NGSS Lead States (2013): "A practice of both science and engineering is to use and construct models as helpful tools for representing ideas and explanations. These tools include diagrams, drawings, physical replicas, mathematical representations, analogies, and computer simulations" (p. 19). To this end, we asked the students to develop a diagram that represented their initial design of the mini trebuchet. In order to provide multi-modal ways of showing us their understanding, we allowed time for students to build a mini trebuchet using the materials we provided.

During this lesson segment, we wanted to ensure that students developed a strong understanding of how their scientific models could explain and predict the projectile trajectory of their marshmallow when it is hypothetically flung. Using the Flipgrid, we instructed students to videotape and explain their thinking that went into their initial design of their mini trebuchet. We guided students to develop their own explanations about how the different components of the design would make a trebuchet launch possible and what variables would be needed to make the launch the farthest. We then asked their peers to compare and contrast their models with each other. We also helped students apply their mathematical knowledge of the parabolas to explain that their marshmallows would follow a projectile trajectory and how far they would be launched.

Student Moves

Students demonstrated their understanding by producing an initial diagramed model of a mini trebuchet. They also could film their physical model they created using the materials that were mailed to them in advance. They explained the different components of the design that would make a trebuchet launch possible and predicted how far a marshmallow would fly. Students compared and contrasted their designs and noticed the differences on how they might be able to improve their models. Students should present their projectile trajectory of their marshmallow and explain why their design allows for it to fly the furthest. Students were expected to apply their mathematical knowledge about the parabolas to support their claims.

Diffractive Noticing

As teachers, we paid close attention to students' explanations of how their initial scientific model of a trebuchet worked and their predictions of how far their hypothetical marshmallow would launch. Building on what we had been doing in our class, we facilitated a class discussion where students listened to their peers' explanations of the design process and participated in evaluating their peers' claims. Alternatively, scientific modeling could be integrated earlier in the Explain segment. This integration would be at the discretion of the teacher. In the Explain segment above, we chose to teach the mathematical concept earlier in the example of "Basketball Parabola" to build a solid mathematical foundation. To that end, mathematical modeling was implied in the Explain segment as students generated their explanations for their predictions. We would encourage STEM teachers to use these "chunks" of lessons in the most appropriate ways for their teaching context. Scientific modeling could also be utilized in the Explain segment earlier, emphasizing claims, evidence, and reasoning (CER) exercise to generate explanations based on the scientific model that students created and engaging students in scientific argumentation. What we were trying to do in the Explain and Elaborate stage was help students to generate their explanations or claims and use models to support their claims.

Evaluate

The Evaluate segment was an extension of the Elaborate segment in that we had the opportunity to implement the performance-based assessment. In the Evaluate segment, we facilitated the design challenge presented to the students in the Engage segment. The Evaluate segment required that we create a kit with the everyday items for students to either pick up or mail home. The everyday items included pencils/pens (popsicle sticks might be helpful), straws, tape, string or dental floss, AA battery as a dead weight, a mechanical hex nut (any size but smaller will work better), hot glue guns (optional but useful), paper clips, and rubber bands (not for launching but to hold things together). In case the kits could not be prepared, a trebuchet simulator, "VirtualTrebuchet 2.0" [9], could be used as an alternative activity. In the Elaborate segment, students had an extended opportunity to engage in a design process to create and improve their physical model of a mini trebuchet and then test their model. Students improved their model after seeing their classmates' designs and sharing feedback. Then they were given the opportunity to test and launch their trebuchet to see how far their marshmallow would be flung. This segment could be taught synchronously or asynchronously.

Teacher Moves

We reminded the students of their challenge, which was to launch a "hypothetical canon" (e.g., marshmallow) so it could accurately land on a target from as far a distance as possible. We fostered students' enthusiasm (as we had done during the Engage segment) that they were finally ready to put their scientific model to work and to put their mathematical calculations to the test.

We provided time so that students could work on building their model asynchronously. In order to accomplish this step, we provided an "off-Zoom" time so that students could log off to create their physical model of a trebuchet and return to "Zoom" once finished. We instructed students to test out their physical models and fill out the data table (Figure 9.1). The data table was created on Awwapp or Jamboard so that we could monitor students' work. We used these educational technologies and implemented pedagogical approaches at our discretion and based on the context. We instructed the students to use Flipgrid to film the launch (a minimum of three takes) of a marshmallow and explain their design. Their explanations included the weight of the counterweight, sling length, placement of the arm's pivot point, other materials that the students chose to include other than what was provided and why.

Once the launch takes were complete and the data table was filled out, we provided a formative assessment where students needed their responses to the questions such as "Did you succeed in creating a trebuchet that could launch a marshmallow to land on a target accurately? If so, what was the maximum distance you achieved? If not, why do you think the trebuchet failed to launch or land accurately on the target? If you were to revise your model, what would you change?" A sample lesson on building a model of trebuchet can be referenced from "TryEngineering" [4] or "TeachEngineering" [5, 7]. This activity could be done synchronously and the questions could be used to facilitate a class discussion. The Flipgrid videos could be used as an anchoring point for students to compare, contrast, evaluate their peers' claims, ideas, and designs.

Alternatively, when the online trebuchet simulator was used, we pointed to the different components on the simulator. We made explicit that students understood that these different variables impacted the launch and how far a "hypothetical" marshmallow would fly. The engineering design process and scientific model building component could still be emphasized when using the online simulator. Students could still use the online trebuchet simulator to fill out the data table.

Student Moves

Using the kit with the everyday items, students designed their physical model of a mini trebuchet. Students then tested the trebuchet to launch a marshmallow. Using the Flipgrid, students videotaped their launch takes and explained the thinking that went into their design. The students filled out the data table on Awwapp or Jamboard. During synchronous class time, students viewed the videos of their peers and compared, contrasted, and evaluated their peers' claims, ideas, and designs.

Diffractive Noticing

As teachers, we paid close attention to students' explanations of how their trebuchet worked and their predictions of how far their marshmallows launched and why. Building on what we have been doing in our class, we facilitated a class discussion where students listened to their peers' explanations of their experimental results from the launch takes and participated in evaluating their peers' claims. See Figure 9.1.

[Student's Name]

Basketball Takes	Guess (Make or Miss)	Parabola Equation $a(x-b)^2+c$ $a=$ $b=$ $c=$	Vertext (___, ___)	Axis of Symmetry $x=$___	Zero 1 (___, 0)	Zero 2 (___, 0)
Take 1	Make	$a(x-b)^2+c$ $a = -0.23$ $b = 5.1$ $c = 4.7$	(5.1, 4.7)	(5.1, 4.7)	(5.1, 4.7)	(5.1, 4.7)
Take n						

FIGURE 9.1. An Example of Student-Facing Work on Mini Trebuchet

SUMMARY AND REFLECTIONS

Diffractive noticing sections after each of the 5E segments illustrate the four over-arching actions: 1) Articulate, 2) Reflect, 3) Analyze, and 4) Re-articulate. We think it would be more beneficial for our teachers to read what we noticed and reflect on our lesson, following each of the 5E segments for cohesiveness as a way to see the lesson through our perspective but also through their own. We approached STEM teaching and learning through a new lens. We first had to un-learn our initial assumptions about students' online presence and engagement and then re-define them. We had to re-think how students might be interacting with their technology. Students were interfacing with technology, their peers, and us as their teachers in this virtual, Zoom space. We had to think of ways to entangle our-selves with our students (to become differently) in a different way than we have been in an in-person setting. In doing so, we began to "see" their online presence and engagement differently. To this end, we paid careful and localized attention to how students interacted with the actors (both human and nonhuman) in an on-line classroom environment: these actors were the locations of new possibilities that would impact our students and our teaching practices. Following students' interactions was where students' presence and engagement emerged that started to work for us. As teachers, we were able to work with what we were seeing dif-ferently and found ways to engage students where we felt and believe our students were participating in our lessons, engaged and present.

As we illustrated during our integrated STEM lesson, creating multiple op-portunities for students' becomings was critical. These spaces were created as we leveraged the affordances of educational technology, which helped foster a more student-centered, synchronous online environment. From an outsider's perspec-tive, it might be easy to assume that students who connect to Zoom meetings without video cameras or working microphones are disengaged or not participat-ing. To be honest, we felt our students had become "Zoombies" where we were met with silence when we tried to elicit students' participation in the way we have always known it (J. Masty, personal communication, April 20, 2020). How-ever, our experience taught us that a deliberate selection of digital resources and implementation of educational technologies was important. Deliberate pedagogi-cal decisions helped create a space where students could stay engaged through an inquiry-based, hands-on activity and sharing their work through multi-modal platforms (such as FlipGrid, Phet Interactive Simulations, Desmos/Geogebra, or AWWapp/Jamboard) gave students an alternative means for engaging in STEM learning and opportunity to demonstrate their understanding (such as verbalize their ideas and reasoning in their mother-tongue language). These tools provided a means to support how we believed students were present and participating in their learning, contrasting conventional means typically seen during in-person learning. We knew that our students were resilient, but so were we as teachers. The pandemic has forced us to think differently, become differently, and be far more creative than we could have ever thought. We are all part of a giant assemblage and we are evermore evolving.

TIPS AND ADVICE

- Pay attention to "ah-ha" moments that stand out to you during your interaction with your students. These moments will be your students' moments of becomings.
- Students' becomings take on many forms. Structure and restructure your class as you diffractively notice your classroom interactions to allow for students to show you who they can be differently and be ready to be pleasantly surprised.
- Diffractive noticing takes on four actions: 1) Articulate, 2) Reflect, 3) Analyze, and 4) Re-articulate.
- Take the time to articulate your assumptions, reflect on them, analyze what happened in your "ah-ha" moments, re-articulate your assumptions based on your dialogues with your colleagues, and improve your approaches for the next time you teach your lesson.

RESOURCE NOTES

Name of Resource	Primary Website	How to Locate the Resource Online
AwwApp	https://www.awwapp.com	Go to the main page of www.awwapp.com. Sign up to create a whiteboard account for your class to use as needed.
Basketball Parabola	https://www.geogebra.org	Go to the main page of Geogebra.org. In the search bar that says "search classroom resources," type in "Basketball Parabola." Choose the classroom resource authored by Kelly G, and the topic is Parabola. https://www.geogebra.org/m/dbv93PhP
Desmos	https://www.desmos.com	Go to the main page of Desmos.com. Click the drop-down menu of "Math Tools" and select graphing calculator. This page is where you will first add by clicking on the "+" sign an image of a basketball shoot in a still motion. Then you will add by clicking on the "+" sign the parabola equations: $y = a(x-b)2 + c$, $a = 1$, $b = 0$, $c = 0$. https://www.desmos.com/calculator/kn1luamsvd
IEEE Lesson Plan: Trebuchet Toss	https://tryengineering.org	Go to the main page of https://tryengineering.org. In the search bar, type in "IEEE Lesson Plan: Trebuchet Toss." https://tryengineering.org/wp-content/uploads/trebuchet-toss.pdf
Launch into Learning: Catapults!	https://www.teachengineering.org	Go to the main page of https://www.teachengineering.org. In the search bar, type in "Catapults." Choose the Lesson titled "Launch into Learning: Catapults!" https://www.teachengineering.org/lessons/view/cub_catapult_lesson01

Name of Resource	Primary Website	How to Locate the Resource Online
NOVA Medieval Siege Excerpts Part 1	http://youtube.com	Go to the main page of Youtube. In the search bar, type in "NOVA Medieval Siege Excerpts Part 1." https://youtu.be/ZR_inE836lE
Physics of the Flying T-Shirt	https://www.teachengineering.org	Go to the main page of https://www.teachengineering.org. In the search bar, type in "Physics." Choose the Lesson titled "Physics of the Flying T-Shirt." https://www.teachengineering.org/lessons/view/cub_flyingtshirt_lesson01
Projectile Motion	https://phet.colorado.edu	Go to the main page of PheT Interactive Simulations. In the search bar, type in "Projectile Motion." Under the list of "Simulations," select "Projectile Motion" to access the simulation. https://phet.colorado.edu/sims/html/projectile-motion/latest/projectile-motion_en.html
Virtual trebuchet simulator 2.0	https://virtualtrebuchet.com	Go to the main page of https://virtualtrebuchet.com. This site is the only webpage that houses the virtual trebuchet simulator 2.0. https://virtualtrebuchet.com/#Simulator

DISCUSSION QUESTIONS

1. How do we create and foster a student-centered synchronous science and mathematics learning environment?
2. How do we use the affordances of educational technology to interact with students that lead to consistent online student presence and productive student engagement?
3. How do we use the affordances of educational technology to illuminate student thinking in a synchronous, online learning environment?

REFERENCES

Barad, K. (2007). Meeting the universe halfway: Quantum physics and the entanglement of matter and meaning. *Isis, 99*(4), 879–882. https://www.jstor.org/stable/10.1086/597741

Brandt, C. B. (2008). Discursive geographies in science: Space, identity, and scientific discourse among indigenous women in higher education. *Cultural Studies of Science Education, 3*(3), 703–730. https://doi.org/10.1007/s11422-007-9075-8

Calabrese Barton, A., Tan, E., & Rivet, A. (2008). Creating hybrid spaces for engaging school science among urban middle school girls. *American Educational Research Journal, 45*(1), 68–103. https://doi.org/10.3102/0002831207308641

Fortney, B. S., Morrison, D., Rodriguez, A. J., & Upadhyay, B. (2019). Equity in science teacher education: toward an expanded definition. *Cultural Studies of Science Education, 14*, 259–263. https://doi.org/10.1007/s11422-019-09943-w

Goodwin, C. (1994). Professional vision. *American Anthropologist, 96*(3), 606–633. https://doi.org/10.1007/978-3-531-19381-6_20

Hoskins, B. J. (2012). Connections, engagement, and presence. *The Journal of Continuing Higher Education, 60*(1), 51–53. https://doi.org/10.1080/07377363.2012.650573

Jeong, S., Britton, S., Haverkos, K., Kutner, M., Shume, T., & Tippins, D. (2018). Composing new understandings of sustainability in the Anthropocene. *Cultural Studies of Science Education, 13*(1), 299–315. https://doi.org/10.1007/s11422-017-9829-x

MacLure, M. (2013). Researching without representation? Language and materiality in post-qualitative methodology. *International Journal of Qualitative Studies in Education, 26*(6), 658–667. https://doi.org/10.1080/09518398.2013.788755

NGSS Lead States. (2013). *Next generation science standards: For states, by states.* National Academies Press.

Plair, S. K. (2008). Revamping professional development for technology integration and fluency. *The Clearing House: A Journal of Educational Strategies, Issues and Ideas, 82*(2), 70–74. https://doi.org/10.3200/TCHS.82.2.70-74

Sherman, B. J., Bateman, K. M., Jeong, S., & Haudek, L. (2021). Dialogic meta-ethnography: troubling methodology in ethnographically informed qualitative inquiry. *Cultural Studies of Science Education, 16*, 279–302. https://doi.org/10.1007/s11422-019-09961-8

CHAPTER 10

A PHET SIMULATION INQUIRY LAB ON ENERGY CONSERVATION

Modified for Remote Learning in High School

Trish Loeblein and Katherine Perkins

University of Colorado Boulder

PhET interactive simulations provide free meaningful opportunities for teachers to engage students in STEM practices in online learning environments. From planning investigations to collecting data to arguing from evidence, the simulations address a wide range of NGSS standards through guided-inquiry activities. This chapter describes the modification of an in-class inquiry lab using PhET's *Energy Skate Park: Basics* simulation for remote learning with high school students. We describe research-based strategies for using PhET simulations that provide rich opportunities for student discourse and facilitated feedback (synchronous and asynchronous) where students work independently to use inquiry practices and meet NGSS standards.

As a high school physics and chemistry teacher, I (Trish Loeblein) have written 128 inquiry-based lessons using the interactive simulations (sims) developed by the PhET Interactive Simulations team at the University of Colorado Boulder

Teaching and Learning Online: Science for Secondary Grade Levels, pages 143–158.

Copyright © 2023 by Information Age Publishing

www.infoagepub.com

(https://phet.colorado.edu). I discovered PhET sims in 2004, and with their ability to support inquiry learning, these digital tools quickly became a mainstay in my classroom. Each PhET sim creates an open exploratory environment where students can engage in STEM practices, connect multiple representations, and discover key concepts (Wieman et al., 2008). I have used these tools in my classroom labs, discussions, and homework.

As an openly-licensed (free) online resource, PhET sims are a natural tool to support student engagement in STEM content and practices in the context of online learning. Indeed, since the growth of online learning in 2020, the use of PhET sims has nearly doubled from 120 million sim runs per year to 250 million sim runs per year. This chapter describes and reflects upon my strategies to modify a PhET sim lesson for the remote teaching environment. My co-author (Katherine Perkins) expands the perspective with connections to the underlying research and discussion of adaptations for various online teaching scenarios.

We ground our discussion in the specific example of a guided-inquiry remote lab titled "Energy Skate Park Basics: Mechanical Energy Lab" (Loeblein, 2021). This lab uses PhET's *Energy Skate Park: Basics* sim and follows a 5E lesson structure to help students with standards about conservation of energy in two dimensions. Before this lab, students would have completed my lab using the PhET's *Masses and Springs* sim, which addresses similar standards but in one dimension. The lab is designed for high school students but can be adapted for middle school. After making a free teacher account, the student lab activity—both the in-class and remote versions—and lesson plan can be downloaded from the PhET website.

PhET's Energy Skate Park: Basics Sim

Engaging students in the science practices—from designing and conducting experiments to interpreting data to argue from evidence—and doing so in ways in which students perceive and have agency over their learning is a challenge when teaching in-person (Weiss et al., 2003) and even more so teaching online. Yet, it is a critical aspect of the Next Generation Science Standards (NGSS Lead States, 2013). PhET sims are carefully designed to help educators simultaneously address multiple learning goals, including content, practices, and affective goals (Lancaster et al., 2013).

The *Energy Skate Park: Basics* sim includes three screens—Intro, Friction, and Playground (PhET Interactive Simulations, 2014). Students are constrained to choose between three specific pedagogically-valuable scenes (a skate pipe, a ramp, and a double well, all frictionless) but are otherwise free to explore. They can place the skater anywhere, observe the resulting motion, and use multiple energy and speed representations to investigate relationships and collect data. A grid can be added to support systematic investigation and a slider allows students to vary the skater's mass. The Friction screen is identical, but now with the ability to change friction from "none" to "lots." Finally, the Playground screen allows students to build their skate track shape (loops are a favorite) and investigate using the now-familiar representations from the prior screens.

PhET sims utilize implicit scaffolding to create an environment in which students perceive significant control over their exploration and which also—through careful choice and design of controls, representations, and feedback—simultaneously encourages productive exploration (Paul et al., 2013; Podolefsky et al., 2013a). The presence of implicit scaffolding within the sim supports educators moving away from explicit instructions to use more open-ended questions and create a more student-centered learning environment (Atabas et al., 2020; Perkins et al., 2012).

Design of the In-Class Guided-Inquiry Lab

In my classroom, students work in groups sharing a computer to do PhET labs. We do 15–18 PhET labs each semester, so my students are familiar with exploring sims and designing experiments to test their ideas. I scaffold my inquiry-based hands-on labs and PhET labs such that the first few labs students do during the year help them learn to explore and design experiments. This lab would come midway through the year, so the structure and instructions assume students' skills for exploring and designing are fairly well developed.

At the beginning of each PhET lab, I have students openly explore the sim for a few minutes, often with a prompt to help them begin thinking about a learning goal. During a class discussion following this open play, students share features and initial findings using a large interactive whiteboard. Students take turns on the whiteboard to demonstrate something they found interesting as they explored the sim. When PhET lessons begin with "open play," research finds students engage in productive exploration (Moore et al., 2013) and they develop substantial agency and will take ownership of their learning as they move on engaging in more challenging tasks within the sim (Podolefsky et al., 2013b).

I employ many of PhET's recommended strategies for leveraging the implicit scaffolding in the sim to craft more open questions and prompts in the lab (Perkins et al., 2012; PhET Interactive Simulations, 2018b), designing them to help students meet the learning goals which are listed for students at the beginning of the lesson. Each group will write or make a digital document to answer questions, and not every question requires writing. Sometimes the group is directed to discuss, share ideas, or draw something. Other times students must show me something using the sim and I sign their paper for the credit.

My lesson facilitation approach is student-centered. As each group works at its own pace, I walk around the room, visiting with students about their discoveries and ideas and helping groups that need support. If many groups have similar difficulties during a lab, then I hold short class discussions using an interactive whiteboard or verbal sharing.

During and following a sim lesson, I often use multiple-choice concept questions and peer discussion with a student response system (clickers), a research-based instructional strategy pioneered by Eric Mazur (Mazur, 1997). PhET sims naturally pair with this instructional strategy—e.g., with prediction questions—and, as research has shown, sim-based "clicker questions" can lead to productive student and classroom discussions and improved learning (Keller et al., 2007). For instance, if there are sections in the lab that I know students must understand before proceeding, then I will facilitate a series of clicker questions to measure students' progress. As we discuss the questions, I use the sim with interactive discussion to model how it can help develop understanding. After the lab, sometimes at the beginning of the next class period, I use more clicker questions to check for understanding of the learning goals. For this particular lab, I wrote 15 questions to evaluate student learning that I could use during the lab or afterward.

Modification of the Lab for Remote Learning

I teach in a rural area with intermittent internet, so I made modifications to support a fully asynchronous learning experience that students could complete at their own pace and schedule. I retained my goals of engaging students in the science practices and emphasizing student reasoning but understood students would be working independently. Thus, I needed some additional signposts and support as they completed the lesson. Critical goals are lost in this context: student engagement in discourse and the benefits and feedback that come with peer-to-peer discussion and teacher facilitation. In the Summary and Reflections section, we discuss alternative options for the synchronous online environment.

Three pieces of my in-class lab needed to be modified for the asynchronous remote learning scenario, namely aspects of the inquiry prompts, the collaboration prompts, and the evaluation approaches. I also employed PhET's collaboratively-developed set of instructional strategies to support remote learning activities using PhET sims (PhET Interactive Simulations, 2020). Throughout the lesson narrative, I highlight the specific strategies employed in each of the 5E sections.

Open exploration of the sim remained an essential aspect of my inquiry lab approach. When teaching in the classroom, I can show the students how to navigate to the sim and then to the screen of interest. Furthermore, if students get on the wrong screen, then I can see their problem and help them get back to the screen of interest for that section of the lab. In order to minimize such start-up issues in the remote lab, I use section-specific links that directly open the sim showing only the screen of interest for that section. The "?screens=#" query parameter appends to the end of the sim URL to scaffold student interactions in this way, hiding the navigation bar so students cannot inadvertently navigate to the wrong screen (PhET Interactive Simulations, 2018a).

My in-class lab collaboration strategies include opportunities for learners to talk, share with the class, and compose a group paper. I modified the prompts for the remote lab to address the asynchronous learning scenario, where the students are learning independently. For instance, I replaced "Talk with your partner about how the buttons help you make observations. Be prepared to share your ideas with the class in a group discussion" with "Describe how these buttons help you make observations." and added images of the control buttons from the sim. In another place, I replaced "talking about" with "paying attention" and added hints about essential tools with images to find and use.

Finally, I modified the evaluation approach by adding the concept questions in the evaluate section with requirements that make the students self-evaluate. These concept questions often ask students to make predictions about scenarios, requiring them to apply their conceptual understanding and engage in qualitative reasoning to predict the outcome. The lesson narrative provides additional detail and examples of these modifications.

CONNECTIONS TO NGSS AND THREE-DIMENSIONAL LEARNING

As stand-alone digital tools, PhET sims are NGSS-ready, meaning a PhET sim can be leveraged in many ways to support the integrated three-dimensional learning experience central to the Next Generation Science Standards (NGSS Lead States, 2013). Still, it is how the sim is used—the lesson, learning goals, activity tasks, and facilitation—that ultimately determine if a sim-based lesson is aligned with the NGSS. I find it helpful to write explicit lesson-level learning goals, which are clear about how students will demonstrate their learning about each part of a standard. For example, "Predict position or estimate speed from Energy Bar and Pie Charts" is one goal for HS-PS3-2.

The "Energy Skate Park Basics: Mechanical Energy Lab" described below engages students in the three-dimensional learning of the NGSS. Students build towards performance expectations while they simultaneously engage in science practices and work with disciplinary core concepts and cross-cutting concepts. The specific NGSS standards addressed are detailed below.

Students' Performance Expectations

- **Code:** HS-PS3 (High School Energy)
- **Domain:** Physical Sciences (PS)
- **HS-PS3-2:** Develop and use models to illustrate that energy at the macroscopic scale can be accounted for as a combination of energy associated with the motion of particles (objects) and energy associated with the relative positions of particles (objects).
- **HS-PS3-3:** Design, build, and refine a device that works within given constraints to convert one form of energy into another form of energy.

Science and Engineering Practices

Developing and Using Models (HS-PS3)

- Develop and use a model based on evidence to illustrate the relationships between systems or between components of a system.

Planning and Carrying Out Investigations (HS-PS3)

- Plan and conduct an investigation individually and collaboratively to produce data to serve as the basis for evidence.

Constructing Explanations and Designing Solutions (HS-PS3)

- Construct explanations that are supported by student-generated sources of evidence consistent with scientific ideas, principles, and theories.

Disciplinary Core Ideas

Definitions of Energy (PS3.A)

- Energy is a quantitative property of a system that depends on the motion and interactions of matter and radiation within that system. That there is a single quantity called energy is due to the fact that a system's total energy is conserved, even as, within the system, energy is continually transferred from one object to another and between its various possible forms.

Conservation of Energy and Energy Transfer (PS3.B)

- Energy cannot be created or destroyed, but it can be transported from one place to another and transferred between systems.
- Mathematical expressions, which quantify how the stored energy in a system depends on its configuration and how kinetic energy depends on mass and speed, allow the concept of conservation of energy to be used to predict and describe system behavior.

Relationship between Energy and Forces (PS3.C)

- When two objects interacting through a field change relative position, the energy stored in the field is changed.

Crosscutting Concepts

Energy and Matter (HS-PS3)

- Changes of energy and matter in a system can be described in terms of energy and matter flows into, out of, and within that system.
- Energy cannot be created or destroyed—only moves between one place and another place, between objects and/or fields, or between systems.

LESSON NARRATIVE

The "Energy Skate Park Basics: Mechanical Energy Lab" follows a 5E lesson structure. Every time I write a lab, I include a basic lesson plan. I find that articulating students' prior experience and knowledge, my tips for the sim use, and a basic outline of what will happen helps me run the lab more smoothly. Below are some excerpts from the lesson plan for this lab.

> **Student prior experience and knowledge:** My students generally know about the conservation of energy. For example, they can tell you that energy comes from the sun and is converted by plants into food. Additionally, my students will have completed a lab using Masses and Springs PhET simulation https://phet.colorado.edu/en/contributions/view/2845 with these Learning Goals: Students will be able to explain the Conservation of Mechanical Energy concept using kinetic, elastic potential, and gravitational potential energy. Masses and Springs are one-dimensional, and Energy Skate Park is two-dimensional, making a sensible progression.

> [...]

> **In-class Lab:** Have the students use the lab sheet for guidance. After #2a, I have a class discussion encouraging students to share features they have found in the sim. After #6, I also have another class sharing time (or I check in with each group if the class is working at different rates) when they play with building their track to make sure they can use the features on the Playground screen. When students are working on 6a, building a track, I check with each group to ensure they have "no friction."

> **Remote lab:** This version can be used with students working remotely. I have included some helpful ideas in the directions for asynchronous situations and some ideas for modifying the directions if the lab is done synchronously.

> [...]

For each of the 5Es, I describe my thinking about my design, highlight the online writing strategies used from PhET's Remote Learning with Simulations document, list the NGSS standards, and provide examples of activity prompts.

Engage

In the engage section (below), I want to provide a hook for the students by encouraging them to begin to think about how their everyday experiences and prior knowledge of physics will help them make predictions for a skater on a two-dimensional track. The prompt encourages students to see physics in their everyday lives by providing several examples and asking students to use models from 4-PS3-1 Energy, MS-PS3-2 Energy, and HS-PS3-2 Energy, which they should have developed during the previous lab. However, I do not expect them to have accurate predictions; the idea is to make predictions and explain their present understanding.

Throughout the lesson, students will test their ideas and confirm, adjust, or correct their understanding. Three online writing strategies used include:

- Use screenshots to help students recognize things in your directions.
- Use table scaffolds for qualitative data collection.
- Include headers to help students to know what is expected in each part of the activity.

Explore

For the exploration part for this lab, students interact with the first screen of the sim using several inquiry practices: planning and carrying out investigations, analyzing and interpreting data, constructing explanations, and communicating information. The PhET sims with multiple screens are designed so that the first screen enables basic learning goals and has constraints that allow straightforward inquiry, so I always start the explore section using the first screen. In the first prompt, students are encouraged to play with the sim for specific goals and describe a few observations to help them develop ownership of their learning and build confidence in using the sim controls and visual representations.

I prompt students to design tests for their predictions from the engage section addressing the same three content standards in this lab. Then, students begin to carry out investigations that they design to confirm, adjust, or correct their understanding. I created this investigation so that students could answer all four questions after one trial with the chart, graph, and speed selected. The image I used for the engage section shows all the options selected, but I did not include the part of the screen that shows the controls checked because I want them to find the controls and choose their visualizations. One of the benefits of PhET sims is that students make choices to drive their understanding instead of just looking at a visual like in a PowerPoint or text. Therefore, in the explore prompt, I use an image of the sim as it opens with none of the boxes checked and the skater is in a start position. Students will have to play with the sim to figure out how to make the skater move to run trials, like if they were doing a real lab with a toy car or ball. They will have to decide where to place the skater and choose the visualizations that help them understand.

As students fill out the table, they will analyze and interpret data, construct explanations, and communicate information. For the online lab, I have students include images from the sim as evidence to support their reasoning because I cannot actively probe for understanding and evidence as I would in class. The screen captures serve to help students' self-evaluation, much like checking answers in a textbook. Some students might have more than one screen capture if they chose to check only one box at a time. Choosing one visual at a time can help students focus on one question, which may help them with their understanding. The online writing strategies I used for the explore prompts include:

- Limit students to a specific screen using "?screens=."
- Use Screenshots to help students recognize things in your directions.
- Invite students to play with the sim as an introduction.
- Use table scaffolds for qualitative data collection.
- Include headers to help students to know what is expected in each part of the activity.
- Use challenge prompts to engage students in STEM practices, rather than explicit instruction on using the sim.
- Have students take screenshots of the sim as evidence and add supporting explanations to explain their ideas.

TABLE 10.1. Engage by Using Your Knowledge of Physics in Your Everyday Life:

Think about things that go up and down when you play. For example, you might throw a ball in the air, ride a skateboard, or a swing at the playground. Look at this skater going down a frictionless track and use your experiences to fill in Table 10.1.

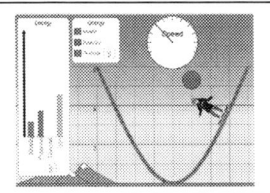

		Prediction	Describe Your Thinking
1	Will the speed increase, decrease or stay the same?		
2	Will the kinetic energy increase, decrease or stay the same?		
3	Will the potential energy increase, decrease or stay the same?		
4	Will the thermal energy increase, decrease or stay the same?		

The first prompt and the table (Table 10.2) help students organize their observations and ideas. In order to promote productive experimentation with the sim, the students are asked to insert images from the sim as evidence to support their claims. Following this prompt, two more explore prompts have students explore mass and position using the same practices.

Explain and Elaborate

I use the same writing strategies in these sections, prompting students to complete the learning goals. These sections enable students to meet more complex learning goals and standards. They will continue to use practices from their previous explorations and be asked to use higher-level practices. In the explain section, I have made direct references to specific learning goals to be more aware of how the lab prompts relate to the specific goals. The learning goals for all activities are listed in my class and my students recognize that tasks help them meet the goals. They appreciate when I put references to the goals in directions to help them monitor their progress. In one prompt, I have the students look for connections to help them support their reasoning because I find students feel more confident when they see that their understandings match accepted science.

TABLE 10.2. Explore to Develop your Understanding

Play with Energy Skate Park: Basics—Intro Screen to observe how the energies and speed change as the skater moves.

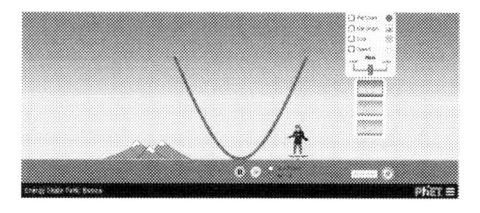

Design experiments to test your predictions from Table 10.1. Fill in Table 10.2 and then insert an image(s) from the simulation for evidence.

		Result of Test	Describe Your Thinking
1	Will the speed increase, decrease or stay the same?		
2	Will the kinetic energy increase, decrease or stay the same?		
3	Will the potential energy increase, decrease or stay the same?		
4	Will the thermal energy increase, decrease or stay the same?		

[Insert an image(s) from the simulation for evidence here]

In the elaborate section, I have the students move to a more complex sim screen to design their virtual skate park. I included an opportunity to play with the sim again to help the students feel comfortable with the sim controls and visual representations. I included some tips about using the essential controls because I have seen some student confusion on the more complex sim screens. By designing and testing a skate park, the students can partially meet an engineering goal in an online environment. As a follow-up in class, I have students use a Hot Wheel track to build a toy park to complete the engineering goal. Students must understand the differences between a virtual engineering design and a real-world build. Below, I included prompts for explaining and elaborating to demonstrate how the directions can be concise yet use more complex standards.

Explain your understanding of learning goal A:

3. For each question, make your prediction and explain your reasoning. Then, check your ideas using the simulation, describe how your ideas are supported or changed, and insert images for evidence.
   a. If the skater's speed is zero, what would you predict the bar and chart would look like?
   b. Where might the skater be when the speed is zero?
   c. What do you predict the speed, bar, and pie chart will look like when the skater is at the low point, as shown?

   d. Where might the skater be when the energies are equal?
   e. Summarize the relationship between position, energies, and speed.

[...]

Elaborate on your ideas by designing a skate park.

6. Play with Energy Skate Park Basics—Playground Screen paying attention to how the energy information can help you make a fun track and what tools help you run repeating trials.

Here are a few key tools you should have found and will need to proceed with the simulation. The track is built by dragging track pieces onto the playground and dragging the red circles to make track pieces change 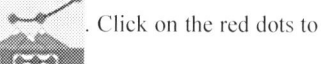. Click on the red dots to make more edits [image].

a. Explain how you could use your understanding of Conservation of Mechanical Energy to plan a track that is fun, challenging, and relatively safe. The track must have no friction [image].

b. Use your explanation in 6a to design a track using all five pieces of track. Test your track to make sure the skater will ride the entire track. Make edits to your thinking in 6a if you need. Insert images of your track showing the skater at the beginning and end of the ride.

Evaluate

For the evaluation of the online lab, I used the writing strategy of concept questions to demonstrate understanding of the learning goals. I added the questions we would have done in class with clickers and peer discussion, making the online students more responsible for self-evaluation using the same inquiry practices as in the other parts of the lab. I have written questions addressing each learning goal with images from the sim to reinforce the visual scientific representations referenced in the performance expectations. Below is the prompt and one example of a sim-based concept question.

Evaluate your ability to demonstrate the learning goals: Predict your answer and support your answer with an explanation for each question. There is no friction on any tracks. Then use *Energy Skate Park: Basics* to verify and add images for evidence to your explanation.

1. Do you think the skater will make it over the hump when starting on the left?

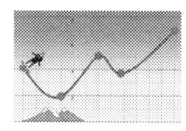

A. No, because his potential energy will be converted to thermal energy.
B. No, because he does not have enough potential energy.
C. Yes, because all of his potential energy will be converted to kinetic energy.
D. Yes, because some of his energy will be potential and some kinetic.

Prediction and explanation with support:

Extension

Some teachers include a sixth E, Extension, in lessons. For this lab, I have included an extension focused on the third sim screen, Friction. This section addresses the same PEs with thermal energy effects and uses the same writing strategies prompting students to explore, explain, and evaluate.

SUMMARY AND REFLECTIONS

PhET sims are free interactive simulations designed to support inquiry learning aligned with NGSS standards, particularly inquiry practices. On the PhET website, teachers can find many strategies for using the sims in classroom teaching, based on education research of how students learn and research using the sims (PhET Interactive Simulations, 2018b). The sims and lesson materials on the PhET website are open educational resources available under the Creative Commons Attribution 4.0 license.

This chapter shared my journey modifying an in-class lab for an online asynchronous teaching environment. I drew from my years of experience teaching with PhET sims in-class and assigning sim-based activities as homework, as well as tips from the PhET team. I have not had the opportunity to test this remote lab personally since I am retired. However, many teachers who have used my remote lessons, which are available on the PhET website, have sent positive feedback, providing some support for their usefulness in today's remote learning environment. Altogether, I modified or wrote 36 labs for remote and online instruction. While I purposely wrote for the asynchronous learning scenario, this context is missing the many significant benefits and immediate feedback that come with peer-to-peer discussion and synchronous teacher facilitation.

Synchronous online learning environments, when an option, provide great potential for adding these student discourse and feedback opportunities into the lesson. Using Zoom's capabilities for breakout rooms, screen sharing, polling, and annotation combined with Google Docs, facilitation can almost mirror the in-person class experience. In the Engage section, the teacher can facilitate a whole-class discussion, sharing real-world images and soliciting student thoughts and ideas. The teacher can then pair students in breakout rooms to complete the Engage and Explore sections of the activity, assigning students roles where one student is sharing their screen with the sim. They can work together in a shared lab Google Doc, or each student can work in their document. The teacher can move between breakout rooms, listening to and facilitating the conversation, and in doing so, gain early insight on student ideas. Following the Explore, the teacher can then bring the students back together, project the sim, ask students to share their findings, and use prompts to solicit more specific student observations that she wants to communicate across the class. Students can divide back into breakout rooms to continue the Explain and Elaborate portions of the lesson. The teacher can follow up with whole-class discussion and use the Zoom polling feature to facilitate clicker questions.

TIPS AND ADVICE

- Use ideas from PhET's Remote Learning with Simulations (PhET Interactive Simulations, 2020).
- Make a free teacher account on the PhET site so that you can view PhET's teacher resources and activities shared by other teachers.
- Browse the collection of PhET teacher-contributed activities for more remote labs shared by other teachers. Look for the Gold star ones which leverage inquiry practices.

RESOURCE NOTES

Name of Resource	Primary Website	How to Locate the Resource Online
PhET Energy Skate Park Basics: Mechanical Energy Lab Lesson Plan	https://phet. colorado.edu	Go to https://phet.colorado.edu. Located in the top right corner, sign in or register for a free teacher account. Then use the magnifying glass to search for "Loeblein Mechanical." Select the first choice title under the Activities category, "Energy Skate Park Basics: Mechanical Energy Lab." https://phet.colorado.edu/en/contributions/view/6375
PhET Energy Skate Park: Basics Simulation	https://phet. colorado.edu	Go to https://phet.colorado.edu. Click on "Simulations" then "Physics" in the navigation menu. Scroll down and click on "Energy Skate Park: Basics." https://phet.colorado.edu/en/simulations/energy-skate-park-basics
PhET Quick Tips: Custom Screens Video	https://www. youtube.com/	Go to https://www.youtube.com/. In the search box at the top of the page, search for "phet custom screens" and click on the first choice, "PhET Quick Tips: Custom Screens." https://www.youtube.com/watch?v=FCnORSSiBbE
PhET Remote Learning with Simulations	https://phet. colorado.edu	Go to https://phet.colorado.edu. Click "Teaching" then "Tips for Using PhET" in the navigation menu. Then scroll down and find "Remote Learning with PhET" link https://docs.google.com/document/u/1/d/e/2PACX-1vQMwNbLNOtwTdS4sWbXx4dXnJHDoENTgyv-Vl4Vwrq6NbC3ijlCrpPncSTItitHFRv9mp6-FFCL2u-Yp8/pub
Tips for Using PhET	https://phet. colorado.edu	Go to https://phet.colorado.edu. Click on "Teaching" then "Tips For Using PhET" in the navigation menu. https://phet.colorado.edu/en/teaching-resources/tipsForUsingPhet

DISCUSSION QUESTIONS

1. Compare and contrast the NGSS standards and the lab learning goals. Download the lab lesson plan at https://phet.colorado.edu/en/contributions/view/6375.

2. Download the in-class and remote versions of the labs and analyze the similarities and differences. How will the differences in activity and context impact student experiences with each activity?

3. Which of the modifications to make a lab remote seem most helpful for students?

4. What additional ideas might you try to make this remote lab more effective?

5. What do you think are the benefits and challenges of using simulations for secondary science teaching and learning?

REFERENCES

Atabas, S., Schellinger, J., Whitacre, I., Findley, K., & Hensberry, K. (2020). A tale of two sets of norms: Comparing opportunities for student agency in mathematics lessons with and without interactive simulations. *The Journal of Mathematical Behavior*, *58*, 100761. https://doi.org/10.1016/j.jmathb.2020.100761

Keller, C. J., Finkelstein, N. D., Perkins, K. K., & Pollock, S. J. (2007). Assessing the effectiveness of a computer simulation in introductory undergraduate environments. *AIP Conference Proceedings*, *883*(1), 121–124. https://doi.org/doi:10.1063/1.2508707

Lancaster, K., Moore, E. B., Parson, R., & Perkins, K. K. (2013). Insights from using PhET's design principles for interactive chemistry simulations. In *Pedagogic roles of animations and simulations in chemistry courses* (Vol. 1142, pp. 97–126). American Chemical Society. http://dx.doi.org/10.1021/bk-2013-1142.ch005

Loeblein, T. (2021). *Energy skate park basics: Mechanical energy lab*. https://phet.colorado.edu/en/contributions/view/6375

Mazur, E. (1997). *Peer instruction: A user's manual*. Prentice-Hall.

Moore, E. B., Herzog, T. A., & Perkins, K. K. (2013). Interactive simulations as implicit support for guided-inquiry. *Chemistry Education Research and Practice*, *14*(3), 257. https://doi.org/10.1039/c3rp20157k

NGSS Lead States. (2013). *Next generation science standards: For states, by states*. National Academies Press.

Paul, A., Podolefsky, N., & Perkins, K. (2013). Guiding without feeling guided: Implicit scaffolding through interactive simulation design. *AIP Conference Proceedings*, *1513*, 302–305. https://doi.org/10.1063/1.4789712

Perkins, K., Moore, E., Podolefsky, N., Lancaster, K., & Denison, C. (2012). Towards research-based strategies for using PhET simulations in middle school physical science classes. *AIP Conference Proceedings*, *1413*(1), 295–298. https://doi.org/10.1063/1.3680053

PhET Interactive Simulations. (2014). *Energy Skate Park: Basics*. https://phet.colorado.edu/en/simulations/energy-skate-park-basics

PhET Interactive Simulations. (2018a). *PhET quick tips: Custom screens*. https://www.youtube.com/watch?v=FCnORSSiBbE

PhET Interactive Simulations. (2018b). *Tips for using PhET*. https://phet.colorado.edu/en/teaching-resources/tipsForUsingPhet

PhET Interactive Simulations. (2020). *Remote learning with simulations*. https://docs.google.com/document/u/1/d/e/2PACX-1vQMwNbLNOtwTdS4sWbXx4dXnJH-DoENTgyvVl4Vwrq6NbC3ijlCrpPncSTItitHFRv9mp6-FFCL2uYp8/pub

Podolefsky, N. S., Moore, E. B., & Perkins, K. K. (2013a). Implicit scaffolding in interactive simulations: Design strategies to support multiple educational goals. *ArXiv:1306.6544 [Physics]*. http://arxiv.org/abs/1306.6544

Podolefsky, N. S., Rehn, D., & Perkins, K. K. (2013b). Affordances of play for student agency and student-centered pedagogy. *AIP Conference Proceedings, 1513*(1), 306–309. https://doi.org/10.1063/1.4789713

Weiss, I. R., Pasley, J. D., Smith, P. S., Baniflower, E. R., & Heck, D. J. (2003). *Looking Inside the Classroom: A Study of K–12 Mathematics and Science Education in the United States* (pp. 1–356). Horizon Research, Inc.

Wieman, C. E., Adams, W. K., & Perkins, K. K. (2008). PhET: Simulations That Enhance Learning. *Science, 322*(5902), 682–683. https://doi.org/10.1126/science.1161948

CHAPTER 11

ACTIVE LEARNING AT HOME

Using 3D Virtual Reality Viewers to Explore the Human Heart for High School Students

Rebecca Hite, Gina Childers
Texas Tech University

M. Gail Jones
North Carolina State University

High school science students need active learning experiences that are both immersive and interactive. Using a simple cardboard 3D virtual reality (VR) viewer and the *Living Heart for Cardboard VR* from the Google Play™ app, we provide a 5E lesson plan on science concepts related to homeostasis and form to function relationships found in complex systems of the human heart and circulatory system. We discuss ways to help students use VR technologies safely and responsibly while at home and consider issues of equity and accessibility when utilizing 3D VR technologies for remote and online science teaching and learning.

Science activities in which students can carefully observe while actively involved in the design and direct manipulation of their experiments demonstrate how exciting science can be for K–12 learners. Both involvement and interaction with scientific phenomena typify active learning, a process that is vital to constructivist, student-centered, and student-driven learning activities (Cattaneo, 2017; Demirci,

Teaching and Learning Online: Science for Secondary Grade Levels, pages 159–170.
Copyright © 2023 by Information Age Publishing
www.infoagepub.com
159

2017; Freeman et al., 2014). Students enjoy measuring plant growth when they can manipulate the nutritive variables, viewing objects as they fall to the Earth from heights of their choosing, and observing chemical reactions when they get to select the reagents.

However, active learning has its limitations when phenomena of interest are *inaccessible*. What happens when students want to manipulate nutritive variables of plants that are too costly to purchase for the classroom? What if students want to change the gravitational force so they can observe how objects fall on Mars, Venus, or Pluto? What if the experiment students want to conduct requires chemicals that are too dangerous or hazardous to do on their own? What if the face-to-face classroom itself is inaccessible due to a global crisis and they are now learning from home? Inaccessible phenomena are too abstract (smaller than can be viewed with a microscope and too large to be viewed with a telescope), too expensive, or too hazardous for students to have direct involvement or interaction.

Virtual reality (VR) experiences can help restore the immersive and interactive aspects of active learning when actual phenomena are inaccessible, either due to the nature of the scientific phenomena being explored or having to engage in science learning remotely and online. However, inaccessibility is not the same as unfeasible; teachers and students should not use virtual experiences when viable real-world options are available, albeit challenging to access. For example, Harron et al. (2019, p. 702) created a virtual reality field trip (VRFT) using a 3D VR viewer of a Texas science museum for a preservice science teacher education class. They found that preservice science teachers noted VRFTs could be a viable alternative for low-income students if they were unable to participate in in-person field trips due to constraints related to finances or time. However, this finding leads to the proposal of two questions: "Could the use of VRFTs reproduce educational inequities that are already present in the system? Furthermore, could the use of VRFTs unintentionally justify the lack of access to in-person field trips, particularly with low-income populations?" These questions suggest that science-focused VR technologies should enhance science experiences rather than supplant important real-world science activities, with their peers, in face-to-face settings. Although smart mobile devices are relatively ubiquitous in U.S. homes (Pew Research Center, 2017), it is crucial to ensure that all students have access to these technologies in order to participate in the activity successfully and learn about phenomena that might be inaccessible.

One such inaccessible phenomenon is the human heart, a vital organ in maintaining health and homeostasis through diet and exercise. The heart's function is part of students' primary science education to form a solid understanding of this vital organ (Kavey et al., 2003; Menard & Liu, 2020). In high school, students are tasked with in-depth learning of the heart, including its appearance and parts (anatomical form) and pulmonary circulation (physiological function). In order to meet these learning outcomes, students typically view the 2-D structure of the heart in a textbook, identifying and memorizing the various cardiac components.

Other instructional activities may include watching a video or examining a plastic model of the heart to infer form to function. What if high school science students could view, in 360°, the human heart pumping blood in real-time while being able to alter the heart rate, to reveal (rather than infer) form to function from their own home?

This chapter is about bringing VR experiences, centered on cardiac form and function, to high school students' homes using a simple, low-cost device (cardboard construction 3D VR viewer), ubiquitous technologies (a smart mobile device), and a free software download (application or app). Research suggests virtual and augmented realities help students engage in active learning through rich sensorial involvement and enhanced user-directed interactions. Students can better access and understand abstract and complex scientific phenomena, like the human heart (Gnidovec et al., 2020; Hite et al., 2022).

CONNECTION TO NGSS AND THREE-DIMENSIONAL LEARNING

There are several *Next Generation Science Standards* (Lead States, 2013) related to learning the human heart. This activity would be appropriate in any high school biology unit about human body systems, maintaining homeostasis, multicellularity, and evolutionary discussions regarding form and function.

Students' Performance Expectations

- **Code:** HS-LS1 (High School Life Science)
- **Domain:** From Molecules to Organisms: Structures and Processes
- **HS-LS1-2**: Develop and use a model to illustrate the hierarchical organization of interacting systems that provide specific functions within multicellular organisms.
- **HS-LS1-3**: Plan and investigate to provide evidence that feedback mechanisms maintain homeostasis.

Science and Engineering Practices

Constructing Explanations and Designing Solutions (HS-LS1-1)
- Construct an explanation based on valid and reliable evidence obtained from a variety of sources (including students' investigations, models, theories, simulations, peer review).

Developing and using models (HS-LS1-2)
- Develop and use a model based on evidence to illustrate the relationships between systems or between components of a system.

Disciplinary Core Ideas

Structure and Function (LS1.A)

- Feedback mechanisms maintain a living system's internal conditions within certain limits and mediate behaviors, allowing it to remain alive and functional even as external conditions change within some range. Feedback mechanisms can encourage (through positive feedback) or discourage (negative feedback) what is going on inside the living system.

Crosscutting Concepts

Systems and System Models (HS-LS1-2)

- Models (e.g., physical, mathematical, computer models) can be used to simulate systems and interactions—including energy, matter, and information flows—within and between systems at different scales.

Stability and Change (HS-LS1-3)

- Feedback (negative or positive) can stabilize or destabilize a system.

LESSON NARRATIVE

This lesson describes an asynchronous online activity using a stereoscopic 3D VR viewer headset, such as Google Cardboard™. Stereoscopic viewers have both immersive and interactive elements of 3D images and interactive virtual environments that have been shown to support active learning (Adi Badiozaman et al., 2021; Stojšić et al., 2016). These devices use a single button and the user's head movements to select or toggle elements in the 3D virtual learning environment. Although desktop systems and head-mounted displays offer more affordances in user immersion and interaction, their hardware costs tend to be prohibitive compared to 3D VR view headsets. The 3D VR viewer case can be, at minimum, made

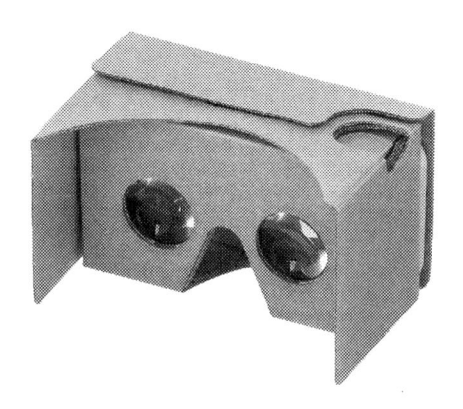

FIGURE 11.1. Google Cardboard VR Headset by Evan-Amos (2015)

at home from cardboard and two inexpensive lenses. Since American households have more smart devices than computers (Pew Research Center, 2017), 3D VR viewers have wider utility and usability for remote and online learning.

Preparing this activity for students to complete at home requires a one-time purchase of a 3D VR viewer (e.g., google cardboard) or the materials for students to make at home. The latter will require two biconvex lenses (45mm focal length recommended), four Velcro strips and a rubber band (to hold the smart mobile device in place), and an 8.75 inches (22 cm) by 22 inches (56 cm) and 0.06 inch (1.5mm) thick corrugated cardboard sheet (E flute thickness recommended) to cut into the viewer design (see Google, n.d. for design specifications and instructions). The mobile device will need some connectivity to the internet to download the app *Living Heart for Cardboard VR* from Google Play (2016); see Dassault Systèmes (2021) on how the app was made. Once the app is downloaded and the 3D Viewer is constructed, the student is ready to engage in active learning using a VR human heart. In this app, students can look inside the heart to explore the four chambers and observe and regulate blood flow.

Using the 5E process, we describe what students can learn from the heart through active learning processes with a 3D VR viewer. First, before this lesson, the students must have access to the app, the constructed 3D viewer headset, and a smart device to run the app. It is helpful for the students to use the 3D viewer before the lesson to be familiar with the setup and the expectation of the experience before the lesson begins. Second, provide the *Human Heart Graphic Organizer* (Figure 2) to your students, depending on how they access the activity. If students are at home (asynchronous), then they can use paper copies or an electronic copy of the activity in a word processing application. If they are remote but engaging with other students synchronously, then you can create a digital cloud-based document for active online collaboration among students. If using in-class, then consider providing a means for students to view and share their observations, such as a whiteboard (face-to-face) or shared screen function (hybrid or online) to document students' responses to Questions 1, 2, 3, 10, and 11 on the *Human Heart Graphic Organizer*. Third, ensure that the video links and digital materials used within the lesson are accessible and appropriate for your students. You may add other materials as needed to support the specific learning objectives targeted for this lesson.

Engage

Students will be asked to record their ideas and thoughts in the Human Heart Graphic Organizer to capture student interest and *prior background knowledge on the human heart graphic organizer.* First, ask your students to respond to Question #1 prompt: "*What do you know about the human heart?*" on the *Human Heart Graphic Organizer*. Once students have written a response to this question, ask students to share their responses with the classroom. The recommendation is to document their responses in a space that students can see in the classroom dur-

Engage			
Question #1: What do you know about the human heart?	Add your answer here!		
Question #2: While watching the video, write what you found interesting about the human heart.	Write what you found interesting about the human heart here!		
Question #3: What do you want to know about the human heart?	Add your answer here!		
Explore			
Question #4: What do you notice about the human heart when using the VR viewer?	Add what you noticed here!		
Question #5 (video): Describe the job or function of arteries, veins, and capillaries.	What do arteries do?	What do veins do?	What do capillaries do?
Question #6 (video): Label the structures of the heart.	You will label the following structures on the image below: right ventricle, left ventricle, right atrium, left atrium, tricuspid valve, pulmonary valve, pulmonary artery, pulmonary vein, bicuspid valve, and aortic valve. Image Source: https://commons.wikimedia.org/wiki/File:Heart_normal.svg		
Question #7 (video): Why is the heart pumping blood? What is the importance of pumping blood to the body?	Add your answer here!		
Explain			
Question #8: Explain how blood flows through the human heart and lungs. Provide a step-by-step description that includes how the blood is flowing and which structures of the human heart are being used.	Add your detailed descriptions of how blood flows through the human heart here!		
Elaborate			
Question #8: Research three heart-related issues and describe how doctors can treat these issues.	Coronary Artery Disease Description: Treatment:	Arrhythmia Description: Treatment:	Myocardial Infarction (Heart Attack) Description: Treatment:
Question #9: How might technology, like the VR viewer you used in this lesson, help people with heart-related issues?	Add your answer here!		
Question #10: What activities or strategies will support a healthy heart?	Add your answer here!		
Evaluate			
Question #11: What did you learn about the human heart?	Add your answer here!		
Question #12: What additional questions do you have about the human heart?	Add your answer here!		

FIGURE 11.2. Human Heart Graphic Organizer.

ing this time. Asking clarifying or probing questions during this time can help you address misunderstandings or enable students to expand on their initial responses. Next, introduce a video about the human heart that they watch and record what they thought was interesting on the *Human Heart Graphic Organizer* (Question #2 prompt). An example video that connects to learning goals and captures students' attention is found in the American Heart Association (2018) video. After watching the video, ask students to share with a partner (or a small group) about what they found interesting in the video, then open the sharing to the classroom. Record the students' responses in visual space in the classroom. Lastly, instruct the students to respond to the Question #3 prompt: "*What do you want to know about the human heart?*" on the *Human Heart Graphic Organizer*. Afterward, ask students to share their questions with the class while recording their responses in a visual space.

Explore

Students should explore, examine, investigate, and question information about the human heart within a collaborative learning space during this phase. The *Living Heart for Cardboard VR* will be used to model students to examine the human heart. First, students should be allowed to form collaborative pairs or groups. Instruct the students to access the VR app and viewer (please see teacher preparation notes above regarding this step) and allow students to experience the human heart models within the VR viewer system. During this time, students will respond to Question #4 (*What do you notice about the human heart when using the VR viewer?*) on the *Human Heart Graphic Organizer*. Sharing what was noticed among students within the collaborative groups is highly encouraged.

Once students have explored with the VR viewer and recorded their responses to Question #4, the next activity will require students to examine blood flow and the structure and function of the heart. In the first step, students will watch a video depicting the structure and function of the human heart and the flow of blood within the human heart and record their responses to Questions 5–7 on the *Human Heart Graphic Organizer*. A recommended video is found in Amoeba Sisters (2020) video. After completing the video and answering the questions, ask the students to share their answers to Question #7 (*Why is the heart pumping blood? What is the importance of pumping blood to the body?*). This multimedia presentation will support the transition from the exploration phase to the explain phase.

Explain

This section focuses on students explaining the flow of blood within the human heart based on exploring the structures in the previous exploration phase. Students begin by recording each step of blood flow within the human heart (and lungs) on their *Human Heart Graphic Organizer* (Question #8). It is recommended that the students continue to work in their collaborative groups for this section and be able to access the materials used in previous sections to support the construction of their answers (VR viewer and videos). Additional materials may be added to support your specific learning objectives. Afterward, review the flow of blood within the human heart to address any misunderstandings of students. Next, encourage students to add or revise their response to Question #3 (*What do you want to know about the human heart?*). Then, you will be able to facilitate a group discussion on new questions generated from the students.

Elaborate

During this phase, students will play the role of cardiovascular researchers and investigate heart-related issues connected to the structure, function, and flow of blood in the human heart system. Students will research three heart-related issues by describing the problem and explaining how to treat the issue (see Question #8 on the *Human Heart Graphic Organizer*). Next, students will consider how technologies, such as the VR viewer, can help individuals design approaches to address heart-related issues or problems. This reflection period allows the students to connect specific technologies they are using to real-world applications outside of the classroom. Afterward, students explore activities that support a healthy heart and record their responses on the *Human Heart Graphic Organizer* (Question #10). Once students have answered Question #10, have them share what activities or strategies will support a healthy heart and record their responses on a visual space in the classroom.

Evaluate

Students' evaluations and reflections on the learning experiences and processes allow them to connect what they learned to the learning objectives. On the *Human Heart Graphic Organizer*, Questions #11 and #12 ask students to reflect on their learning experiences and generate new questions related to the lesson. Once the students complete their responses to Questions #11 and #12, have students share what they learned and record their responses on a visual space in the classroom. Afterward, address new questions generated (from Question #12) or existing requests documented in Question #3. The *Human Heart Graphic Organizer* can be reviewed as a formative or summative assessment, a journal prompt, or outlined learning notes.

SUMMARY AND REFLECTIONS

This activity utilizes 3D viewer technology for students to explore the form and function of the human heart at home and online. Even though students use this VR technology independently and remotely, students must be prepared to use the VR safely and responsibly. Adults and adolescents have reported symptoms similar to motion sickness with VR technologies known as *VR sickness* or *cybersickness*. According to Geršak et al. (2020, p. 14492), "the difference between cybersickness and motion sickness is that the user is often physically stationary but has a compelling sense of self-motion because of moving visual imagery." A likely culprit of cybersickness is due to the *stereoscopic* effect of the 3D VR viewer technology (Guna et al., 2019). Stereoscopy is the illusion of depth created by two offset images, one to the left and one to the right eye.

Given that humans have binocular vision, these images combine in the brain to create the illusion of depth and, consequently, 3D images (Baños et al., 2008). Therefore, motion disorientation coupled with the eye strain from viewing double images over time contributes to cybersickness (Guna et al., 2019). You should let students know that they should remove the 3D VR viewer from their faces and take deep breaths if they feel disorientated or nauseated. Removing themselves from the 3D VR environment and deep breathing will help to mitigate the two symptoms of motion sickness. Cybersickness can also occur when using the 3D VR viewer for long periods of time. Students should be instructed to be seated (instead of standing) and use the technology for short periods of time to start (e.g., five minutes); they may gradually increase their time as they become accustomed to the stereoscopic effect. Students should be cautioned not to exceed 30 continuous minutes using the 3D VR viewer, taking breaks as needed, especially when experiencing mild cybersickness symptoms.

As shared in the teacher preparation notes in the lesson narrative section, students should have time before the lesson to become acquainted with the VR viewer system so that a teacher can address any technological issues (*is it working?*) or cybersickness (as described above). This lesson also requires other technology tools such as videos and online research sources. Ensuring that the students have access to these tools is vital for the smooth facilitation of the lesson's activities. Referring to the lesson's activities, make sure to capture students' thoughts and learn throughout the lesson's progression. The graphic organizer helps collect this information while also aligning with the 5E lesson plan structure to ensure that students engage in exploration, examination, and reflection when learning about the human heart.

TIPS AND ADVICE

- We recommend giving students a short technology survey (see Common Sense Media (2010) for a template) to determine the prior knowledge, comfort level, and current access to mobile smart devices.
- Just because students have access to and use their own smart mobile devices, they may not be familiar with VR apps. Students will need practice and additional scaffolding from their teacher (e.g., prior experiences in using the technology, guidance in their safe use) to ensure students are comfortable and ready to learn science with 3D VR viewers actively.

RESOURCE NOTES

Name of Resource	Primary Website	How to Locate the Resource Online
American Heart Association	www.youtube.com	Go to YouTube video and search for "Kids Heart Challenge Heart Facts," which can also be found directly at https://www.youtube.com/watch?v=2PFWpd_pxm8.
Amoeba Sisters	www.youtube.com	Go to Youtube.com and search for "Circulatory System and Pathway of Blood Through the Heart," which can also be found directly at https://www.youtube.com/watch?v=_vZ0lefPg_0.
Common Sense Media	https://www.commonsensemedia.org	Go to https://www.commonsensemedia.org/ and search for "Student Media and Technology Survey," which can also be found directly at https://www.commonsensemedia.org/sites/default/files/uploads/pdfs/student-survey-program.pdf.
Dassault Systèmes	http://www.3ds.com/heart	Go to http://www.3ds.com/heart to locate The Living Heart Project.

DISCUSSION QUESTIONS

1. Why do immersion and interaction both matter for active learning in science?

2. How does having a virtual experience with a "live" heart provide unique learning affordances students cannot receive from textbooks, videos, and models?

3. What are some equity considerations in the ethical use of virtual technologies when the real world (and experiences therein) are available but not convenient?

4. This chapter describes the use of VR technology for high school students. What are the challenges and benefits of using this technology in a middle school science class?

5. What virtual reality experiences are available for use with other grade levels? For other science disciplines?

REFERENCES

Adi Badiozaman, I. F., Segar, A. R., & Hii, J. (2021). A pilot evaluation of technology-enabled active learning through a hybrid augmented and virtual reality app. *Innovations in Education and Teaching International*. https://doi.org/10.1080/14703297.2021.1899034

American Heart Association. (2018, Oct. 31). *Kids heart challenge heart facts* [Video]. YouTube. https://www.youtube.com/watch?v=2PFWpd_pxm8

Amoeba Sisters. (2020, Aug. 26). *Circulatory system and pathway of blood through the heart* [Video]. YouTube. https://www.youtube.com/watch?v=_vZ0lefPg_0

Baños, R. M., Botella, C., Rubió, I., Quero, S., García-Palacios, A., & Alcañiz, M. (2008). Presence and emotions in virtual environments: The influence of stereoscopy. *CyberPsychology & Behavior*, *11*(1), 1–8. https://doi.org/10.1089/cpb.2007.9936

Cattaneo, K. H. (2017). Telling active learning pedagogies apart: From theory to practice. *Journal of New Approaches in Educational Research (NAER Journal)*, *6*(2), 144–152. https://www.learntechlib.org/p/180107/

Common Sense Media. (2010). *Student media and technology survey*. https://www.commonsensemedia.org/sites/default/files/uploads/pdfs/student-survey-program.pdf

Dassault Systèmes. (2021). *The living heart project*. http://www.3ds.com/heart

Demirci, C. (2017). The effect of active learning approach on attitudes of 7th grade students. *International Journal of Instruction*, *10*(4), 129–144.

Evan-Amos. (2015, December 12). *A google cardboard VR headset* [Photograph]. Wikipedia. https://en.wikipedia.org/wiki/Google_Cardboard#/media/File:Google-Cardboard.jpg

Freeman, S., Eddy, S. L., McDonough, M., Smith, M. K., Okoroafor, N., Jordt, H., & Wenderoth, M. P. (2014). Active learning increases student performance in science, engineering, and mathematics. *Proceedings of the National Academy of Sciences*, *111*(23), 8410-8415. https://doi.org/10.1073/pnas.1319030111

Geršak, G., Lu, H., & Guna, J. (2020). Effect of VR technology matureness on VR sickness. *Multimedia Tools and Applications*, *79*(21), 14491–14507. https://doi.org/10.1007/s11042-018-6969-2

Gnidovec, T., Žemlja, M., Dolenec, A., & Torkar, G. (2020). Using augmented reality and the structure-behavior-function model to teach lower secondary school students about the human circulatory system. *Journal of Science Education and Technology*, *29*(6), 774–784. https://doi.org/10.1007/s10956-020-09850-8

Google. (n.d.). *Get your cardboard*. https://arvr.google.com/cardboard/get-cardboard/

Google Play. (2016). *Living heart for cardboard VR* [Software]. https://play.google.com/store/apps/details?id=com.DS.Cardboard_LHP&hl=en_US&gl=US

Guna, J., Geršak, G., Humar, I., Song, J., Drnovšek, J., & Pogačnik, M. (2019). Influence of video content type on users' virtual reality sickness perception and physiological response. *Future Generation Computer Systems*, *91*, 263–276. https://doi.org/10.1016/j.future.2018.08.049

Harron, J. R., Petrosino, A. J., & Jenevein, S. (2019). Using virtual reality to augment museum-based field trips in a preservice elementary science methods course. *Contemporary Issues in Technology and Teacher Education*, *19*(4), 687–707. http://www.learntechlib.org/p/184159/

Hite, R. L., Jones, M. G., Childers, G. M., Ennes, M. E., Chesnutt, K. M., Pereyra, M., & Cayton, E. M. (2022). The utility of 3D, haptic-enabled, virtual reality technologies for student knowledge gains in the complex biological system of the human heart. *Journal of Computer Assisted Learning*, *38*(3), 651–667.

Kavey, R. E. W., Daniels, S. R., Lauer, R. M., Atkins, D. L., Hayman, L. L., & Taubert, K. (2003). American Heart Association guidelines for primary prevention of atherosclerotic cardiovascular disease beginning in childhood. *Circulation*, *107*(11), 1562–1566. https://doi.org/10.1161/01.CIR.0000061521.15730.6E

Lead States. (2013). *Next Generation Science Standards*: For states, by states. The National Academies Press

Menard, A., & Liu, L. A. (2020, December 26). *A look at the human heart.* ACLS Training Center. https://www.acls.net/a-look-at-the-human-heart.htm

Pew Research Center. (2017, May 25). *A third of Americans live in a household with three or more smartphones.* https://www.pewresearch.org/fact-tank/2017/05/25/a-third-of-americans-live-in-a-household-with-three-or-more-smartphones/

Stojšić, I., Džigurski, A. I., Maričić, O., Bibić, L. I., & Vučković, S. Đ. (2016). Possible application of virtual reality in geography teaching. *Journal of Subject Didactics, 1*(2), 83–96. https://doi.org/10.5281/zenodo.438169

CHAPTER 12

CITIZEN SCIENCE TO ENGAGE YOUTH IN POLLINATOR CONSERVATION FOR THE SOCIAL GOOD

Rita Hagevik and Kaitlin Campbell

University of North Carolina at Pembroke

In a time when computer screens and indoor learning are the standard for our youth, more than ever, there is a need for tandem outdoor experiential learning. Citizen science employs the collective strength of communities and the public to engage in scientific discovery while solving environmental problems. A discourse of social good and social justice through environmental citizen science projects can lead to environmental stewardship, justice, and promotion of social good. This chapter describes how to use citizen science (iNaturalist and the Great Sunflower Project) to engage youth in pollinator conservation through collecting data on native bees and wildflowers.

INTRODUCTION

A key challenge of virtual environmental science education is maintaining outdoor experiences that foster attitudes and motivations promoting environmental stewardship. Studies show that the attitude of youth toward conservation is great-

Teaching and Learning Online: Science for Secondary Grade Levels, pages 171–182.
Copyright © 2023 by Information Age Publishing
www.infoagepub.com

ly enhanced by outdoor experiences (Ernst & Theimer, 2011) and connectedness to nature (Frantz & Mayer, 2014). How, then, do we maintain experiential outdoor learning in an online environment? This chapter describes the value of citizen science using iNaturalist (iNaturalist.org, 2021) and the Great Sunflower Project (2021) to engage in pollinator conservation. It highlights their inclusive nature for engaging diverse audiences in the virtual and real environment in scientific investigations for the social good.

Citizen Science for the Social Good

Citizen science, also termed community science, is a valuable approach for gathering data that encourages the general public (non-scientists) to become involved in scientific research projects through data collection and discovery. For scientists, citizen science expands the geographic range of projects and the number of observations and creates data sets for long-term monitoring (Tulloch et al., 2013). From the public's perspective, citizen science projects are enjoyable pastimes that engage communities through experiential learning and increase awareness and understanding of scientific processes and conservation initiatives (Bonney et al., 2009; Dickinson et al., 2012).

An advantage of citizen science is that it engages diverse and underrepresented youth with stimulating science experiences around key conservation initiatives that promote sustainability and environmental justice for social good through an online crowd-sourced platform. While there are thousands of citizen science projects with many different goals, an ecocitizen science project is designed to contribute to science and at the same time benefit the child's development through participation in environmental stewardship and ecojustice (Makuch & Aczel, 2019). The social good is addressed through environmental justice and inclusion of and attention to diversity in age, gender, race, ethnicity, and social class when addressing issues of importance to underrepresented communities (Makuch & Aczel, 2020). Immersion and participation through global (virtual) communities to a local (real) community where youth live and go to school empowers youth to connect to others around issues of importance to their future, such as climate change.

Ecocitizen science projects are designed for all ages, so adaptation to the local or real community is organized by the teacher or the local community leader(s). Likewise, commitment to following protocols carefully and regular participation is critical and controlled by the teacher leader. Therefore, participation does take time and some organization by the individuals involved at the local level is required. However, on the citizen science websites, there are many helpful tips on ways to complete this task. According to the European Citizen Science Association (2015), there are 10 principles of citizen science which include publications, learning, enjoyment, satisfaction, and policy influence. However, changes in attitudes and values are missing from this list (Jørgensen & Jørgensen, 2020). Involvement in citizen science activities that cultivate environmental citizenship and change attitudes for the social good are called ecocitizen projects. Scientists and others engage with the community on a deeper, more holistic level. In science education, this deeper engagement is called culturally relevant science teaching (CADRE, 2021).

Ecocitizen Pollinator Conservation Projects

Many ecocitizen projects focus on essential pollinators, especially bees, to identify key flowers for promoting pollinators and to monitor bee populations (Jørgensen & Jørgensen, 2020). The Great Sunflower Project (greatsunflower. org) tracks visitation rates of pollinators to different flowers. The Great Pumpkin (Squash) Project (2021, scistarter.org/the-great-pumpkin-project) documents insects (pests and pollinators) and microbes (diseases) of squash. At the same time, Bumblebee Watch (2021, bumblebeewatch.org) and iNaturalist (inaturalist. org) allow citizen scientists to contribute distribution and biodiversity information through image uploads and a collaborative identification and verification process. These high-quality ecocitizen projects offer help and tutorials for teachers online. In this chapter, we focus on the Great Sunflower Project to promote pollinator conservation and iNaturalist to aid in identifying and verifying the observations. We involved the local community to cultivate environmental citizenship through awareness and enacting change.

Insect biodiversity is essential for functioning ecosystems because insects play vital roles as pollinators, predators, prey, and herbivores. Recent studies have noted a 75% decrease in insect biomass and diversity (Hallmann et al., 2017; Wagner, 2020) and dramatic pollinator declines (Potts et al., 2010). Insects are valuable educational subjects because they are ubiquitous and diverse, easily collected and observed, and inexpensive to study. However, they are mysterious and fascinating in their habits, often carrying a creep factor that excites people of all ages. Additionally, pollinator declines have resulted in more people wanting to learn about and help pollinators since the fate of human agriculture is closely tied to the fate of our pollinators (Oberhauser & Prysby, 2008; Penn et al., 2020; Wilson et al., 2017). The public, teachers, and students think globally by gathering distribution and diversity data with citizen science and act locally by promoting bee diversity in their local community and their own backyards. North America is home to over 4,000 bee species, of which the honeybee represents only a single, non-native species. Ecocitizen projects organize these concerns into actions around pollinator conservation (Oberhauser & Prysby, 2008; Wilson et al., 2017).

CONNECTIONS TO NGSS AND THREE-DIMENSIONAL LEARNING

Students' Performance Expectations

- **Code:** MS-LS2
- **Domain:** Ecosystems: Interactions, Energy, and Dynamics

- **MS-LS2-1:** Analyze and interpret data to provide evidence for the effects of resource availability on organisms and populations of organisms in an ecosystem.
- **MS-LS2-2**: Construct an explanation that predicts patterns of interactions among organisms across multiple ecosystems.

Science and Engineering Practices

Analyzing and Interpreting Data (MS-LS2-1)
- Analyze and interpret data to provide evidence for phenomena.

Constructing explanations and designing solutions (MS-LS2-2)
- Constructing explanations and designing solutions supported by multiple sources of evidence.

Disciplinary Core Ideas

Ecosystems dynamics, functioning, and resilience (LS2.C)
- Ecosystems are dynamic in nature. Biodiversity describes the variety of species found.

Biodiversity and humans (LS4.D)
- Changes in biodiversity can influence humans' resources, such as ecosystem services that humans rely on.

Crosscutting Concepts

Patterns (MS-LS2-2)
- Patterns can be used to identify cause and effect relationships.

LESSON NARRATIVE

Ms. H. is teaching a student-directed series of lessons focused on investigating biodiversity, ecosystem dynamics, and functioning using a combination of online and outdoor learning strategies. The driving question is the following: "How can we help our community to support biodiversity and sustainability." Additionally: "How do animals and plants survive and adapt to environmental change?"

Engage

Students first investigate the biodiversity of their local neighborhood ecosystem by capturing images of flowers and pollinators. The students were introduced to iNaturalist (iNaturalist, 2021) and practiced collecting data using the app (see Figure 1 below). Students discussed what pollinators might need in order to be successful based on their observations. Students interviewed others at school, at home, and in the community on their views regarding pollinators, bees, wildflowers, gardens, and biodiversity. The students explored different places (on the

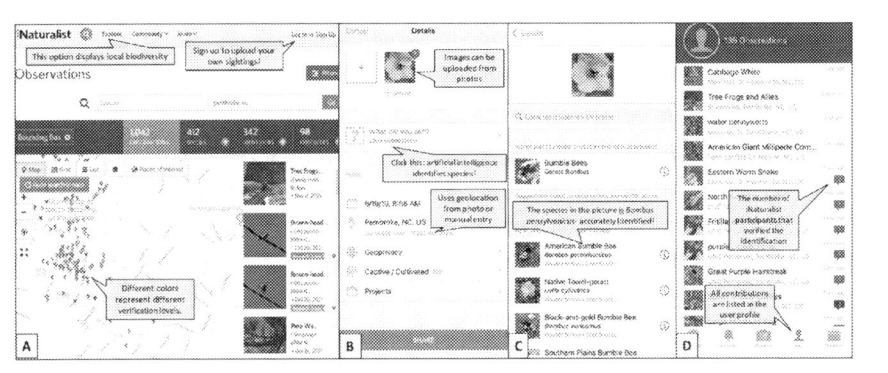

FIGURE 12.1. Screenshots of iNaturalist Interface as Seen with Browser (A) and Smartphone Application (B-D)

school grounds, at a local park, or their own homes), took pictures of flowers and insects with their smartphone or iPad, and uploaded them to iNaturalist. iNaturalist has an option through the browser (not the app) to follow people. The teacher and students can share usernames to see each other's observations of flowers and pollinators. Students considered what the needs are of pollinators and why they are important based on where they were or were not found.

Students discussed with their family members what they knew about bees and pollinators and their importance to plants and crops and reported back to the group. The students discussed ways to support pollinators and key ideas emerged: planting more flowers and providing more places for pollinators to live. The students asked the following questions: "What bees live here?"; "What flowers do they like best?"; "How can we help pollinators?"; and "Why is biodiversity important?" Students began to explore their ideas asynchronously and reported back to the group as a whole in a synchronous discussion. Students explained their thoughts using their observations or evidence about what they found during this initial investigation. Students compared their observations to what others found around them using the "Explore" tool on iNaturalist (see Figure 1A).

Explore

Ms. H. next introduced the students to the Great Sunflower citizen science project. Students used the single observation data table provided on the Great Sunflower citizen science site to complete five-minute observations of pollinators found on individual flowers (see Figure 2 below). A pollinator field guide is provided on the Great Sunflower project site. However, Ms. H. also had students use the *Kaufman Field Guide to Insects of North America* (Eaton & Kaufman, 2007) and *The Bees in Your Backyard: A Guide to North American Bees* (Wilson & Carril, 2015). In addition, Ms. H. had her students record basic weather data such as

FIGURE 12.2.   Screenshots of The Great Sunflower Project Browser Data Entry Interface

temperature, cloud cover, and wind using the protocols located on the GLOBE website (2021). Students used their smartphones to record the latitude and longitude or location of the observations. The information collected was uploaded to the Great Sunflower citizen science project website. Students used the location and weather data information to look for patterns in the data. They were able to compare what they found to what others found by using the citizen science sites.

Explain

In order to better understand why pollinators are so critical to humans, students read the book *The Reason for a Flower: A Book About Flowers, Pollen, and Seeds* (Heller, 1999) that clearly explains the reproduction of a flower from the perspective of pollen and pollinators. They also read *Bees are the Best!* (Van Orman & Wilson, 2020) and *Next Time you See a Bee* (Morgan, 2019) to better understand the role that bees play in pollination. The students developed interview questions to gain further insight regarding pollinators and their importance to the environment and biodiversity. Some examples of student-generated survey questions included: 1) Why are pollinators important to humans? 2) What do pollinators need to survive and thrive? 3) Are all pollinators equal, and are some better pollinators than others? 4) Are some specialists while others are generalists? 5) Are some flowers more popular than others? 6) Does the size or color of the flower make a difference? 7) Are pollinators having problems? 8) What can people do to help pollinators? and 9) Who might benefit if we help pollinators? They conducted video and audio interviews of local community experts, school staff, parents, and other teachers and shared them through their online learning platform. Throughout, Ms. H. guided the students in asking technical and social aspects of the problem. Students discussed the results of their interviews with others, continued to define the problem further, and discussed what additional data might be essential to collect now and in future work. The students discussed the importance of the diversity of native pollinators and why this is so important to the quality of life for all people. What would happen if these native pollinators were missing or even some of them were missing, for example? Throughout the activity, the teacher prompted the students to explain their choices based on their observations, research, interviews, and data.

Elaborate

The teacher continued the discussion by mapping the school grounds and the community to investigate how much green space, hard surfaces (pavement and buildings), and water were present. The green space was divided into the grass, trees, and agricultural land to further investigate the relationship of the landscape to pollinators. The teacher and students used Beescape (2021) to better understand how the landscape affected the bees. Another option is to use google maps (Horton et al., 2013) or ArcGIS online (ESRI, 2021) to study the landscape surrounding the students' observations.

As students made monthly observations of the flowers, trees, and water features on their school campus from the spring and then, into the summer and fall, they continued to look for other pollinators, take pictures, and participate in the two citizen science projects. Students noticed trends in their data and started formulating possible solutions regarding biodiversity and pollinators on their school grounds and in their communities. Students learned from community members, for example, the types of wildflowers and pollinators that were seen in the past where they lived. Students considered which community members were most interested in their investigation and why. They discussed who is most affected by this problem and the solutions they were enacting and exploring. Students gained perspectives on sustainability and its importance through surveying, interviewing, discussions, and evidence not only from their experiences, but also from the experiences of others of all ages and expertise.

Evaluate

The students discussed their ideas with knowledgeable others and experts, including other students, teachers, and staff (especially those individuals who manage the school grounds), about where they wanted to plant more wildflowers or how to care for and provide water for the flowers and pollinators. Information about pollinator gardens can be found at the Xercus Society for Invertebrate Conservation (2021). Wildflowers can be planted from seed in containers or small raised beds. Wildflowers are hardy and need little continued care; perennial wildflowers will come back year after year. We recommend that you plant native wildflowers from your area if possible.

Students asked: "Are there any strategies that might be taken to enhance the habitat for these pollinators and for the social good?"; "How can we honor all voices and perspectives in what we might plan to do?"; and "How can we get additional feedback about our plans from individuals in our school and community and beyond through the citizen science projects?" Ms. H. prompted the students to predict and make plans for the spring by going back to the original question: "How can we help our community support biodiversity and sustainability, and how do animals and plants survive and adapt to environmental change?" Students created a list of key things pollinators needed and actions others can take to help them. Students created digital and hard copy posters and infographics to distribute to the community. The students decided to become bee ambassadors and created an outreach booth, blog, or webpage to tell others in their community about bees, pollinators, wildflowers, and pollinator conservation.

SUMMARY AND REFLECTIONS

In the form of collaborative online environments, games, or augmented reality, the use of technology to encourage children to get outside and look closer at the environment is an innovative idea that is growing in popularity as more apps become available. For example, through its Every Kid in the Park initiative, the US Forest Service has developed a game called Agents of Discovery (2021) to be used outside to encourage family participation in parks (Alvarado, 2021). Pokémon GO is an example of a popular augmented reality game that can occur out of doors. Kawas et al. (2020) used an app called NatureCollections, similar to iNaturalist. They found an increase in curiosity and an increase in conversations between parents and children as a result. Despite this promise, there are few examples of how teachers can effectively blend these technologies with outdoor learning (Kawas et al., 2020). In these lessons, we used an online data collecting environment (iNaturalist and the Great Sunflower project), online research, video interviewing, digital survey data collection, digital posters and infographics, and scientific data collection and analysis to increase curiosity and conversation and facilitate problem-solving.

Environmental justice and inclusion, two central elements of social good, are an important part of ecocitizen science. Citizen science allows the local to be connected to the global (Trautmann et al., 2021). Using ecocitizen science for the social good and community ethnography as a method, teachers can make sure that all voices are heard equally (Schenkel et al., 2020).

We have found that when students and adults take a closer look at connectedness within the environment, they begin to understand the extraordinary diversity of native pollinators living in their local ecological communities. Students become more connected to their communities and ecosystems and, in so doing, realize that they are not above nature, but a part of it. The students notice that small changes make a difference and that they, as individuals, play a part in sustainability through environmental stewardship and action (Schenkel et al., 2020).

RESOURCE NOTES

Name of Resource	Primary Website	How to Locate the Resource Online
Agents of Discovery	https://agentsofdiscovery.com/	Go to https://agentsofdiscovery.com. Located in the middle of the page is schools: Information for teachers. Click here and go to https://agentsofdiscovery.com/schools/ to request a free trial and engage in an augmented reality game around parks.
Beescape	https://app.beescape.org/	Use GIS in an online app just for bees in the landscape. Go to the upper left corner and use the search to find your location using your zip code. Explore the crop layer as well as your forage and nesting quality score. You can read about the methodology or log in and participate in the data collection.
Bumble Bee Watch	https://www.bumblebeewatch.org/app	Go to www.bumblebeewatch.org. Click on home and go to "how to submit a sighting" to get started.
Community for Advancing Discovery Research in Education	http://cadrek12.org	Go to http://cadrek12.org. In the top right corner, use the search magnifying glass to search for "Culturally Responsive STEM Education." Select the first project spotlight option to locate the recommended page. From that page, click on the resources under "Spotlight" and peruse "Featured Projects." http://cadrek12.org/culturally-responsive-stem-education
Environmental Systems Research Institute (ESRI)	https://www.esri.com	Got to https://www.esri.com. In the top right corner, use the search magnifying glass to search for "ArcGIS for Student Use Overview." Select the first choice titled, "ArcGIS for Student Use	GIS Software, Data & Training for Students." https://www.esri.com/en-us/arcgis/products/arcgis-for-student-use/overview

Name of Resource	Primary Website	How to Locate the Resource Online
Globe	www.Globe.gov	Go to https://www.globe.gov/do-globe/globe-teachers-guide/atmosphere/data-exploration-learning-activities. Go to the atmosphere GLOBE data exploration activities. Go to the links on the left-hand side to get the protocols for air temperature, clouds, and wind.
Great Sunflower Project	https://www.greatsunflower.org/	Go to https://www.greatsunflower.org/quickguide to learn how to count the pollinators. In the far right at the top, you can register so that you can begin to add your own data. The data sheets are available at the downloads tab at the top.
iNaturalist	www.inaturalist.org	Go to https://www.inaturalist.org/pages/getting+started to get started and to learn about iNaturalist. Use the tabs on the top of the page to discover how to make and explore your observations. Use the compare tool https://forum.inaturalist.org/t/add-compare-tool-to-the-uploader/22928. On the left-hand side, the links will provide additional information on ways to manage projects.
The Great Pumpkin Project	http://studentsdiscover.org/lesson/the-great-pumpkin-project/	Go to the "students discover" page of the great pumpkin project at http://studentsdiscover.org/lesson/the-great-pumpkin-project/ and scroll down to the middle of the page under the summary to how to participate. Here you will find the directions and how to sign up.
Xerces Society	https://www.xerces.org/	Go to https://www.xerces.org/pollinator-conservation to find the pollinator conservation program. Scroll down the page to conserving pollinators in your landscape. Click on yards and gardens at https://www.xerces.org/pollinator-conservation/yards-and-gardens, and scroll down to get started.

DISCUSSION QUESTIONS

1. How do citizen science projects promote social good?
2. How can you do citizen science in the online environment and at the same time incorporate a real or offline component?
3. How can you bring community ethnography into your science classroom using citizen science?
4. How can you create community using ecocitizen projects around a common issue of interest to all involved?

REFERENCES

Agents of Discovery. (2021, November 15). *Rediscover learning.* https://agentsofdiscovery.com/

Alvarado, Y. (2021, August 3). *Creating environmental awareness with augmented reality technology.* Forest Service, US Department of Agriculture. https://www.usda.

gov/media/blog/2017/12/12/creating-environmental-awareness-augmented-reality-technology

Beescape. (2021, November 15). *Home page*. https://beescape.org/

Bonney, R., Cooper, C. B., Dickinson, J., Kelling, S., Phillips, T., Rosenberg, K. V., & Shirk, J. (2009). Citizen science: a developing tool for expanding science knowledge and scientific literacy. *BioScience, 59*(11), 977–984. https://doi.org/10.1525/bio.2009.59.11.9

Bumblebee Watch. (2021, November 15). *Home page.* https://www.bumblebeewatch.org/.

Community for Advancing Discovery Research in Education. (2021, November 11). *Home page.* http://cadrek12.org/

Dickinson, J. L., Shirk, J., Bonter, D., Bonney, R., Crain, R. L., Martin, J., Phillips, T., & Purcell, K. (2012). The current state of citizen science as a tool for ecological research and public engagement. *Frontiers in Ecology and the Environment, 10*(6), 291–297. https://doi.org/10.1890/110236

Eaton, E. R., & Kaufman, K. (2007). *Kaufman field guide to insects of North America.* Houghton Mifflin Company.

Environmental Systems Research Institute. (2021, November 15). *Home page.* www.esri.com

Ernst, J., & Theimer, S. (2011). Evaluating the effects of environmental education programming on connectedness to nature. *Environmental Education Research, 17*(5), 577–598. https://doi.org/10.1080/13504622.2011.565119

European Citizen Science Association. (2015). *Ten principles of citizen science.* https://ecsa.citizen-science.net/wp-content/uploads/2020/02/ecsa_ten_principles_of_citizen_science.pdf

Frantz, C. M., & Mayer, F. S. (2014). The importance of connection to nature in assessing environmental education programs. *Studies in Educational Evaluation, 41*, 85–89. https://doi.org/10.1016/j.stueduc.2013.10.001

GLOBE Program. (2021, November 15). *Home page.* https://www.globe.gov/

The Great Pumpkin Project. (2021, November 15). *Students discover page.* http://studentsdiscover.org/lesson/the-great-pumpkin-project/

Great Sunflower Project. (2021, November 9). *Home page.* https://www.greatsunflower.org/

Hallmann, C. A., Sorg, M., Jongejans, E., Siepel, H., Hofland, N., Schwan, H., Stenmans, W., Müller, A., Sumser, H., Hörren, T., Goulson, D., & de Kroon, H. (2017). More than 75 percent decline over 27 years in total flying insect biomass in protected areas. *PLOS One, 12*(10), 1–21. https://doi.org/10.1371/journal.pone.0185809

Heller, R. (1999). *The reason for a flower.* Puffin Books

Horton, J., Hagevik, R., Adkinson, B., & Parlmy, J. (2013). Get connected. *Science and Children, 50*, 44–49.

iNaturalist. (2021, July 20). *Home page.* https://www.inaturalist.org/

Jørgensen, F. A., & Jørgensen, D. (2020). Citizen science for environmental stewardship. *Conservation Biology, 35*, 1344–1347.

Kawas, S., Kuhn, N., Tari, M., Hiniker, A., & Davis, K. (2020). "Otter this world": Can a mobile application promote children's connectedness to nature? *The Information School.* https://doi.org/10.1145/3392063.3394434

Makuch, K. E., & Aczel, M. R. (2019). Eco-Citizen science for social good: Promoting child well-being, environmental justice, and inclusion. *Research on Social Work Practice, 30*(2), 219–232. https://doi.org/10.1177%2F1049731519890404

Morgan, M. (2019). *The next time you see a bee.* NSTA Kids.

Oberhauser, K. S., & Prysby, M. D., (2008). Citizen science: creating a research army for conservation. *American Entomologist, 54,* 103–105.

Penn, H., Penn, J., Hagan, M., & Hu, W. (2020). The buzz about bee campuses: Student thoughts regarding pollinator conservation. *American Entomologist, 66*(4), 54–61. https://doi.org/10.1093/ae/tmaa055

Potts, S. G., Biesmeijer, J. C., Kremen, C., Neumann, P., Schwieger, O., & Kunin, W. E. (2010). Global pollinator declines: trends, impacts and drivers. *Trends in Ecology and Evolution, 25*(6), 345–353. https://doi.org/10.1016/j.tree.2010.01.007

Schenkel, K., Bliesener, S., Calabrese Barton, A., & Tan, E. (2020). Community ethnography. *Science Scope, 43*(7), 56–64. https://www.jstor.org/stable/27048051

Trautmann, N., Branch, L., Wingerden, R., Watkins, M., Ort, J., & Deal, K. (2021). From local to global. *Science Teacher, 88*(5), 36–42.

Tulloch, A. I. T., Possingham, H. P., Joseph, L. N., Szabo, J., & Martin, T. G. (2013). Realizing the full potential of citizen science monitoring programs. *Biological Conservation, 165,* 128–138. https://doi.org/10.1016/j.biocon.2013.05.025

Von Orman, J., & Wilson, J. (2020). *Bees are the best!* The Bees in Your Backyard.

Wagner, D. L. (2020). Insect declines in the Anthropocene. *Annual Review of Entomology, 65,* 457–480. https://doi.org/10.1146/annurev-ento-011019-025151

Wilson, J. S., & Carril, O. M. (2015). *The bees in your backyard: A guide to North American bees.* Princeton University Press.

Wilson, J. S., Forister, M. L., & Carril, O. M. (2017). Interest exceeds understanding in public support of bee conservation. *Frontiers in Ecology and the Environment, 15*(8), 460–466. https://doi.org/10.1002/fee.1531

Xercus Society for Invertebrate Conservation. (2021, November 15). *Home page.* https://www.xerces.org/.

CHAPTER 13

WHERE DID MY FOOD'S FOOD COME FROM?

Nature Journaling as a Tool For Meaning-Making In Photosynthesis

Kelly Feille

University of Oklahoma

Stephanie Hathcock

Oklahoma State University

Students can sometimes get lost in the details of photosynthesis and the related chemical equations and fail to see the fundamental importance of these big science ideas to daily existence. This 5E series of middle-school life science lessons connect students' lived experiences to a foundational understanding of photosynthesis. These learning experiences focus on the practical application of the process of photosynthesis and energy cycling through nature journaling in online instructional settings. Incorporating nature journals into science teaching is a way to support meaning-making through drawing and the scientific practices of observation, recording data, asking questions, and constructing explanations from evidence.

Science education reform in the US calls on science teachers to engage their learners in authentic science learning experiences through science and engineer-

Teaching and Learning Online: Science for Secondary Grade Levels, pages 183–195.

183

ing practices across scientific disciplines (NGSS Lead States, 2013). We describe middle-school life science learning experiences that can be delivered online. These learning experiences incorporate constructivist work where students engage authentically with the natural world while constructing profound understandings of the process of photosynthesis

Meaning-Making and Nature Journaling

Meaning-making is considered learning in action (Lave, 1996). Meaning-making is the process learners go through as they assimilate new knowledge into their schema. Nature journaling has the potential to bridge 3-dimensional, standards-based instruction with natural phenomena in students' place of the schoolyard.

The pedagogy of utilizing outdoor areas for instruction includes engaging activities that use the environment to promote learning with academically engaged students. Drawing is a form of meaning-making, focused on the process, involving close observation, analytical thinking, and creativity. Drawing has historically been misinterpreted as a professional skill instead of a human practice, which has led to it not being used as a tool for learning (Dowd, 2018).

There is a multitude of research on students' learning with visual representations, such as those representations encountered in textbooks. More recently, a focus on learning occurs when students generate their representations to think about, construct knowledge, and communicate findings (Tippett, 2016). Nature journaling involves observing and interacting with the natural world through pictures, words, and numbers (Leslie & Roth, 2000). While nature journaling is currently experiencing a lot of interest and growth (Laws, 2016; Leslie & Roth, 2000), the act of journaling about nature has been a regular practice for scientists and naturalists for centuries, such as Aristotle, Leonardo da Vinci, Charles Darwin, Henry David Thoreau, John Muir, Rachel Carson, and Jane Goodall.

Previous studies have found that nature journaling at the early childhood level led to an increased sense of wonder and connection to nature (Johnson, 2014). A teacher-based research project with sixth graders led to an increased understanding of the environment (Cormell & Ivey, 2012). Nature journaling has also been shown to support literacy advances combined with readings about the natural world (McMillan & Wilhelm, 2007). As people journal, they engage in the meaning-making process through place-based learning and can serve as a bridge towards meaning-making in the schoolyard by incorporating science and art practices (Feille & Hathcock 2021; Feille, 2019).

Nature Journaling for Online Teaching

In place-based education, the local environment and community become focal points of teaching (Sobel, 2004). Place-based education includes principles of experiential learning, problem-based learning, democratic education, and community-based education (Gruenewald, 2003). When education becomes place-based, learners can capitalize on a social constructivist environment through collaborative inquiry. Nature journaling is a tool to support meaning-making in one's place. We have found that moving science instruction to an online learning environment has provided a diversity of opportunities for students to interact with their place.

When science instruction moves online, nature journaling can serve as a tool to connect learners with the outdoor natural environment around them. The approach of integrating nature journaling practices into online teaching environments supports a connection to scientific practices employed by naturalists and bench scientists alike. Nature journaling tasks invite learners to disconnect from the digital realm and engage in the natural world as scientists make personal connections to formal and complex science content understandings. We find that pairing nature journaling tasks with online teaching supports meaning-making for our students and creates a holistic science learning experience.

CONNECTIONS TO NGSS AND THREE-DIMENSIONAL LEARNING

Students' Performance Expectations

- **Code:** MS-LS1-6, MS-LS2-3 (MS Life Science)
- **Domain:** Life Science (LS)
- **MS-LS1-6**: Construct a scientific explanation based on evidence for the role of photosynthesis in the cycling of matter and flow of energy into and out of organisms.
- **MS-LS2-3**: Develop a model to describe the cycling of matter and flow of energy among living and nonliving parts of an ecosystem.

Science and Engineering Practices

Constructing Explanations and Designing Solutions (MS-LS1-6)
- Constructing explanations and designing solutions in 6–8 builds on K–5 experiences and progresses to include constructing explanations and designing solutions supported by multiple sources of evidence consistent with scientific knowledge, principles, and theories.

Developing and Using Models (MS-LS2-3)
- Modeling in 6–8 builds on K–5 experiences and progresses to developing, using, and revising models to describe, test, and predict more abstract phenomena and design systems.

Disciplinary Core Ideas

Organization for Matter and Energy Flow in Organisms (LS1.C)
- Plants, algae (including phytoplankton), and many microorganisms use the energy from light to make sugars (food) from carbon dioxide from

the atmosphere and water through the process of photosynthesis, which also releases oxygen. These sugars can be used immediately or stored for growth or later use.

Cycle of Matter and Energy Transfer in Ecosystems (LS2.B)
- Food webs are models that demonstrate how matter and energy are transferred between producers, consumers, and decomposers as the three groups interact within an ecosystem. Transfers of matter into and out of the physical environment occur at every level. Decomposers recycle nutrients from dead plant or animal matter back to the soil in terrestrial environments or to the water in aquatic environments. The atoms that make up the organisms in an ecosystem are cycled repeatedly between the living and nonliving parts of the ecosystem.

Crosscutting Concepts

Energy and Matter (MS-LS1-6, MS-LS2-3)
- Within a natural system, the transfer of energy drives the motion and/or cycling of matter.
- The transfer of energy can be tracked as energy flows through a natural system.

LESSON NARRATIVE

This series of lessons will build on students' prior understanding of the scientific process of photosynthesis. An understanding of the chemical processes involved should be well-established by the teacher before this series of lessons. This series of lessons is designed to illustrate the practical application of an understanding of energy cycling through photosynthesis related to the food we eat. You may consider using a photosynthesis simulation such as Chloroplasts and Food from Open Sci Ed to review the elements of photosynthesis. Additionally, you may have students use the resources from CK-12 Photosynthesis FlexBooks to review.

This lesson series also relies heavily on students' drawn work in paper journals or notebooks. We encourage the use of physical drawing tools as simple as colored pencils and a piece of paper. While students have demonstrated they can do these drawing tasks digitally (for example, on a tablet or iPad), we argue that it is the physical act of creating the nature journaling tasks on paper that contributes to their meaning-making and would discourage the use of entirely digital tools.

Engage

The Engage portion of the lesson should be introduced synchronously to allow time for student discussion over plant- vs. animal-based products and to clarify expectations for the nature journal entry.

Synchronous. Display or share the image "School Lunch" (see Figure 13.1). Have students identify all food items from plants (they should exclude any food items that come from animals, such as dairy products or meat). Consider using NearPod™ or similar presentation software that allows students to annotate directly on the image. For synchronous online work, facilitate conversation to help students identify plant- versus animal-based food items.

Next, students should pick one plant-based food item to trace back to the source. Using online resources such as USDA Plants Database or other resources and plant guides, students should research their chosen food's plant source to prepare their first nature journal entry, My Secret Plant. For example, if a student chooses cucumber salad, they should research the garden cucumber plant, *Cucumis sativus L,* for their journal entry. Encourage student argumentation for identifying plant-based food items. Encourage students to use evidence and prior knowledge to the reason for their chosen food item. (While students may make the case that animals eat plants for energy and should be considered plant-based, for this lesson, encourage them to choose an item that is more directly plant-based.)

Before moving to asynchronous, clarify the nature journal entry directions below with students. Brainstorm with them the types of clues they might want to

FIGURE 13.1.　School Lunch. Note. Creative commons use from https://www.nytimes.com/2020/02/10/opinion/universal-free-school-lunch.html

include in their entry by asking the class to consider what clues might help them identify their secret plant. Remind students that although you are asking them to draw, the goal of the activity is not a work of art—it is an act of scientific communication. If they feel hesitant to draw, then encourage them to include more words and numbers than drawn pictures. If they feel hesitant to include written words, then encourage them to add more detailed drawings or diagrams.

Asynchronous: My Secret Plant **(adapted from Laws & Lygren, 2020).** Create a treasure hunt for your classmates in your journal using words, drawing pictures, and numbers to describe your chosen secret plant. While your plant description should include words, pictures, AND numbers, you may rely more on one form of description than the others. Because you are creating a treasure hunt for your classmates, you will not include your plant's name. However, what clues would be helpful and guide your classmates to identify your plant? As you research your plant and prepare your journal entry, consider the essential question: *Where does the plant get its energy, and how do I get energy from the plant?*

Students should post a picture of their My Secret Plant entry to a class discussion board or forum. In response to classmates' My Secret Plant entries, students should try to guess (1) the plant and (2) the food item represented in the image, School lunch.

Synchronous. Facilitate a small group or class discussion where students consider and discuss (1) what clues they found the most helpful while trying to guess their classmates' secret plants, (2) what details they wish they had included about their plant but did not, (3) what patterns they notice among the different secret plants (e.g., forms of growth, flower shape, fruit presence, leaf color or shape, growing environment or conditions), (4) what ways they might categorize the various secret plants, (5) what are the important structures of the secret plants, and (6) how the plant structures may help the plant get energy. A helpful strategy may be to break students into smaller groups or pairs using breakout rooms or collaboration boards (e.g., NearPod or Jamboard™) and discuss one question at a time or assign student groups or pairs one discussion question to consider in-depth and then share with the class.

Explore

Synchronous. Revisit the essential question, *"Where does the plant get its energy, and how do I get energy from the plant?,"* focusing on the first half. If students do not bring up photosynthesis, then reintroduce them to the term and ask them what they remember about the process from prior learning. Create a class board with initial/review thoughts and ideas about the process of photosynthesis. Challenge students to find out more information about the lifecycle of their chosen plant and the inputs and outputs of energy by completing their second nature journal entry, Timeline. (It will be helpful for students to continue to work with the plant they chose in My Secret Plant as they should already be familiar with much of the structure of the plant, but this is not required.) Students can use web searches to get a general idea of a plant life cycle, but they will also need to determine the specific life cycle of the plant they choose. In order to help students understand timelines, show them timelapse videos on plants such as wheat, cucumber, and an apple tree from a site such as Youtube™. Facilitate a group discussion comparing and contrasting the lifecycle of each type of plant. Students can also use books, web pages, or videos of plants to see the complete lifecycle. Discuss the nature journal entry directions with students (Timeline, below). Brainstorm with them the information they might want to include in their entry that will show all of the stages of the plant's life, such as major structures and their functionality.

Asynchronous: Timeline **(adapted from Laws & Lygren, 2020)**. Create a timeline of your secret plant to show each of its stages of life. While your timeline should include words, pictures, AND numbers, you may rely more on one form of description than the others. Begin by finding a representation of your plant that is fully matured and draw and describe it in the center of your page. Next, find the oldest and youngest versions of the plant and draw them to the left and right of the page. Then, find as many intermediate stages as you can and draw them on the page by filling them in sequentially. Use outside resources such as books, web searches, and videos to fill in the remaining stages of the plant's life cycle. Finally, identify inputs and outputs throughout the lifecycle of the plant. National Geographic's Photosynthesis Resource Library may help consider inputs and outputs.

Students should post a picture of their Timeline entry to an online resource such as Flipgrid™ and create a video describing the various stages of the plant's lifecycle. Assign students to groups of three to four to view each other's videos to prepare for class discussion. They should focus on looking for patterns among the inputs and outputs of the timelines they viewed.

Explain

Synchronous. Facilitate a small group or class discussion where students identify their noted patterns as they view their classmates' videos. Focus the discussion on Crosscutting Concepts related to the topic, such as (1) plant structures and challenge students to consider the functions of each of these structures as they relate to photosynthesis, (2) cause and effect related to the plant stages and effects on food production (i.e., throughout the life cycle, how is the plant producing food?), (3) what parts of the plant changed and what parts stayed the same, and (4) how the structures of the plant at each stage contribute to the cycling of energy and matter. Ultimately, refocus on the essential question: *Where does the plant get its energy and how do I get energy from the plant?*

In order to formatively assess how students are applying their understandings of photosynthesis to the plants found in their school lunch, propose puzzling statements and allow students to debate their opinions as supported by evidence and scientific understanding (an example statement follows): *In the winter, there are no leaves or apples on an apple tree. Do you think apple trees can get food in the winter? Explain your reasoning.* Have students use an online collaboration tool (such as Nearpod Collaborate Slide or Jamboard™) to collectively construct a model showing *where the plant gets its energy from and how I get energy from the plant*. Drawing on previous understandings of the chemical processes of photosynthesis, co-construct a "Gotta Have It" checklist to support the class constructed model and facilitate a consensus explanation. A "Gotta Have It" checklist is a set of ideas that cues students to what should be included in final explanations and models to express the relationships among the concepts (Windschitl et al., 2018). Your class model should represent the level of knowledge appropriate for your students' previous understanding of the chemical processes of photosynthesis and the connections made between the structure and function of the plants they have investigated up to this point. Feel free to add your input into the Gotta Have Its checklist to push your students to construct deeper conceptual understandings of the processes of photosynthesis and energy cycling in the life cycle of the represented plants.

Elaborate

Asynchronous. In order to apply new understandings related to energy flow and cycling through the process of photosynthesis, students will construct an Event Comic nature journal entry. Before presenting the task to the students, show them several different images of pages from comic books (or better yet, ask them to show examples) and ask them to identify the tools used to tell a story, such as page layout, color, arrows, perspective shifts, action words. Create a public record of these tools and encourage students to incorporate as many as possible in their nature journal entries.

Event Comic *(adapted from Laws & Lygren, 2020)*. Considering the essential question, *Where does the plant get its energy and how do I get energy from the plant?*, students should use a series of panels and visual elements (e.g., arrows, perspective shifts, and action words) to tell the story of photosynthesis for a plant that they find in their surrounding outdoor space. The chosen plant should be one they are familiar enough with to identify the structures that support the function of photosynthesis. (You may adapt this to focus students back to their secret plant or another plant identified in the Engage and Explore phases.) The event comic should span at least one full page and should include the details of photosynthesis, including how plants use energy from the sun to make sugars from carbon dioxide from the atmosphere and water, resulting in the release of oxygen and the storing of sugars by the plant for growth or later use. The details should include the chemical reaction and highlight the energy and molecular inputs and outputs. After creating the nature journal entry, students should use a tool such as Apple Clips™ or Flipgrid to tell the story of their Event Comic using images from their nature journal and voice-over narration. The resulting video stories should then be shared with the teacher and classmates through course management software discussion posts, Wiki pages, or Flipgrid.

Evaluate

Synchronous. Students will work in small groups to determine a "Gotta Have Its" checklist (Windschitl et al., 2018) for answering the essential question: *Where does the plant get its energy, and how do I get energy from the plant?* It may help to review the Gotta Have It checklist and resulting model from the Explain phase with the class. Small groups should develop four to five ideas that will help guide students' toward complete answers. As students work, the teacher should facilitate by moving among the groups to listen and ask questions to help students clarify and extend their ideas. Once small groups have generated their "Gotta Have Its" checklist, the teacher should lead a whole group discussion of the "Gotta Have Its," in which students share and then decide on the four to five statements. You can read more about scaffolding students to make changes to their thinking visible over time at the Ambitious Science Teaching website and in Chapter 12 of the companion book (Windschitl et al., 2018).

For the final evaluation piece, students will construct an infographic where they answer the essential question. An infographic includes words, numbers, and pictures to provide a detailed description. Consider showing students examples of digital infographics like those found on the Graphic Mama website. For the infographic, students need to consider the layout of their journal entry before beginning to ensure they have enough space and design features to share their understanding and meet the expectations shared in the "Gotta Have Its" checklist.

Asynchronous: Infographic **(adapted from Laws & Lygren, 2020)**. Revisit the lunch plate picture from the Engage portion of the lesson. Explain the flow of energy from the plant to your mouth by creating an Infographic that synthesizes your understanding about the essential question: *Where does the plant get its energy, and how do I get energy from the plant?* Start by drawing and writing observations about your chosen food and the plant from which it originates. A fully described Infographic will explain the relationships listed in the class generated "Gotta Have It" checklist. It may also be helpful to refer to the class model generated in the Explain portion of the lesson as you construct your Infographic.

SUMMARY AND REFLECTIONS

Incorporating nature journals into online science teaching is a way to support meaning-making through drawing and the scientific practices of observation, recording data, asking questions, and constructing explanations from evidence. However, students often experience discomfort when asked to draw due to their own identities as an artist or not an artist. In order to alleviate this discomfort, we begin by reading the book *Ish* by Peter H. Reynolds with our students (Reynolds, 2004). We remind them that their "ishly" recorded drawings are enough and encourage the use of words, numbers, and symbols to communicate their findings in their nature journals. Because the purpose of nature journaling in science teaching is to support meaning-making, we are careful to focus student attention and praise on the science that their nature journal communicates rather than the quality or artistic merit of the entry. To that end, if students struggle to explain what they have recorded in their nature journal, then we encourage them to add descriptive elements to enhance meaning-making.

Finally, this series of lessons focuses on the practical application of the complex process of photosynthesis and energy cycling. We have found that students get lost in the details of photosynthesis and related chemical equations and fail to see the fundamental importance of these big science ideas to their daily existence. These learning experiences will connect your students' lived experiences to their pre-existing foundational understanding of the process of photosynthesis.

TIPS AND ADVICE

- The best way to teach using nature journaling is to keep a nature journal yourself (celebrate the "ish-ness" of your work too!).
- Providing access to simple drawing tools such as high-quality pencils, watercolors, and color pencils will enhance the nature journaling experience.
- Paper can make a difference. While copy paper or notebook paper is perfectly acceptable, a higher-grade paper may result in greater student buy-in. We recommend using unlined paper to encourage creativity in the composition of the nature journal entry.
- It may be helpful to watch John Muir Laws videos on journal page layout and structure and journal page composition.
- Provide students with Naturalist Tools Journal Insert to help them with estimates and measuring.
- Focus student attention and praise on the science of the nature journal rather than the artistic merit
- The importance of photosynthesis can get lost in the chemical formula and this lesson brings the practical importance of photosynthesis front and center.

RESOURCE NOTES

Name of Resource	Primary Website	How to Locate the Resource Online
Ambitious Science Teaching: Gotta Have Its	https:// ambitiousscienceteaching.org/	Go to https://ambitiousscienceteaching.org/. Click on Tools in the top right corner, then Face to Face Tools. Click on the Written guide to face-to-face tools: http://ambitiousscienceteaching.org/wp-content/uploads/2014/09/Guide-Face-to-Face-Tools.pdf
Apple Clips	https://www.apple.com/clips/	

Name of Resource	Primary Website	How to Locate the Resource Online
CK-12 FlexBooks: Photosynthesis	https://www.ck12.org/student/	Go to https://www.ck12.org/student/. Click on Explore in the middle band, then Flex-Books 2.0. Scroll to Science, then choose CK-12 Middle School Life Science 2.0. Next, choose 2. Cell Biology, then finally, click on 2.13 Photosynthesis: https://flexbooks.ck12.org/cbook/ck-12-middle-school-life-science-2.0/section/2.13/
Flipgrid	https://info.flipgrid.com/	
Google Jamboard	https://jamboard.google.com/	
Graphic Mama: Inforgraphic	https://graphicmama.com/blog/	Go to https://graphicmama.com/blog/, then click on Insights on the top band. Scroll to find the Infographic insight: https://graphicmama.com/blog/what-is-infographic/
John Muir Laws: Journal Page & Structure Video	https://johnmuirlaws.com/	Go to https://johnmuirlaws.com, then search the site for Journal Page Composition. Click on the Journal Page & Structure video link: https://johnmuirlaws.com/journal-page-layout-and-structure-video/
John Muir Laws: Journal Page Composition	https://johnmuirlaws.com/	Go to https://johnmuirlaws.com, then search the site for Journal Page Composition. Click on the Journal Page Composition link: https://johnmuirlaws.com/journal-page-composition/
John Muir Laws: Naturalist Tools Journal Insert	https://johnmuirlaws.com/	Go to https://johnmuirlaws.com, then click on the Store and scroll to Art & Naturalist Supplies, then click on Naturalist Tools Journal Insert: https://johnmuirlaws.com/product/naturalist-tools-journal-insert/
National Geographic's Photosynthesis Resource Library	https://www.nationalgeographic.org/society/	Go to https://www.nationalgeographic.org/society/. Click on the three bars on the left side, then choose "Learn with Us." Next, choose Education Resources. Scroll down to choose Resource Library, then scroll or search to find the Photosynthesis encyclopedic entry: https://www.nationalgeographic.org/encyclopedia/photosynthesis/
Nearpod	https://nearpod.com/	

Name of Resource	Primary Website	How to Locate the Resource Online
Open Sci Ed: Chloroplasts and Food	https://www.openscied.org/	Go to https://www.openscied.org/. On the top banner, click on Instructional Materials, the Simulation Library. Find the simulation entitled, Matter Cycling—Chloroplasts and Food: https://www.openscied.org/wp-content/uploads/2019/07/Chloroplasts-and-Food.html
USDA Plants Database	https://plants.usda.gov/home	
YouTube Timelapse Videos	https://www.youtube.com/	Go to https://www.youtube.com/ and use the Search box to search for timelapse videos such as Apple Tree, Cucumber, and Wheat.

DISCUSSION QUESTIONS

1. How does using nature journaling enhance student meaning-making of photosynthesis?
2. What additional content could be integrated into this lesson to support student meaning-making?
3. How does using nature journaling enhance student meaning-making of photosynthesis?
4. What additional content could be integrated into this lesson to support student meaning-making?

REFERENCES

Cormell, J., & Ivey, T. (2012). Nature journaling. Enhancing students' connection to the environment through writing. *Science Scope, 35*(5), 38–43.

Dowd, D. B. (2018). *Stick figures: Drawing as a human practice*. Spartan Holiday.

Feille, K. (2019). A framework for the development of schoolyard pedagogy. *Research in Science Education*, 1–18. https://doi.org/10.1007/s11165-019-9860-x

Feille, K., & Hathcock, S. (2021). Schoolyard pedagogy: Engaging preservice teachers in outdoor learning experiences. *Innovations in Science Teacher Education, 6*(1). https://innovations.theaste.org/supporting-schoolyard-pedagogy-in-elementary-methods-courses/

Gruenewald, D. A. (2003). The best of both worlds: a critical pedagogy of place. *Educational Researcher, 32*(4), 3–12. https://doi.org/10.1080/13504620802193572

Johnson, K. (2014). Creative connecting: Early childhood nature journaling sparks wonder and develops ecological literacy. *International Journal of Early Childhood Environmental Education, 2*(1), 126–139.

Lave, J. (1996). The practice of learning. In S. Chaiklin & J. Lave (Eds.), *Understanding practice: Perspectives on activity and context* (pp. 3–32). Cambridge University Press.

Laws, J. L. (2016). *The Laws Guide to nature drawing and journaling*. Heyday Books.

Laws, J. M., & Lygren, E. (2020). *How to teach nature journaling.* Heyday Books. https://doi.org/10.5840/teachphil20131015

Leslie, C. W., & Roth, C. E. (2000). *Keeping a nature journal: Discover a whole new way of seeing the world around you.* Storey Publishing.

McMillan, S., & Wilhelm, J. (2007). Students' stories: Adolescents constructing multiple literacies through nature journaling. *Journal of Adolescent & Adult Literacy, 50*(5), 370–377. https://doi.org/10.1598/JAAL.50.5.4

NGSS Lead States. (2013). *Next generation science standards: For states, by states.* National Academies Press.

Reynolds, P. (2004). *Ish.* Candlewick.

Sobel, D. (2004). *Place based education: Connecting classrooms and communities.* The Orion Society.

Tippett, C. D. (2016). What recent research on diagrams suggests about learning with rather than learning from visual representations in science. *International Journal of Science Education, 38*(5), 725–746. https://doi.org/10.1080/09500693.2016.1158435

Windschitl, M., Thompson, J., & Braaten, M. (2018). *Ambitious science teaching.* Harvard Education Press.

CHAPTER 14

DESIGN THINKING AND MINI-MAKER KITS IN SCIENCE EDUCATION

Frameworks for Creative Problem-Solving in Transitions to Online and Hybrid Learning

Helen Douglass and Isaiah Darden
University of Tulsa

This chapter shares the journey, frameworks and contexts the authors used to integrate design thinking, maker experiences, and introductory science and engineering lessons for those in an education course exploring the Next Generation Science Standards (NGSS) and teaching in formal and informal spaces. We discuss design thinking and mini-maker experiences across other subjects. Although a swift transition to online and hybrid platforms (and back to online at times) was difficult, it provided an opportunity for integrating design thinking and elements of maker education with the NGSS to center student experiences and places of learning.

The increase in online and hybrid learning opportunities has provided the opportunity to rethink maker education and design thinking in undergraduate teacher preparation courses. Students who would become formal and informal educators at the secondary level were left without the same experiences they would have had, had classes been conducted in a traditional way. However, moving to an

Teaching and Learning Online: Science for Secondary Grade Levels, pages 197–205.
Copyright © 2023 by Information Age Publishing
www.infoagepub.com
197

online format allowed for students to leverage their places of learning and experiences while utilizing a new way to participate in preparing lessons to be used in secondary learning both in and out of school time.

Students in an introductory STEM education course and preparing to work in secondary school contexts, as well as the course instructor, had to examine how they were preparing their lessons and where they had fallen short of the desired learning outcomes as well as looking for affordances the online and hybrid environment provided. The course learning objectives had to be achieved and yet students were not all in the same physical space. However, this shift provided an opportunity for creating take home maker kits for integrating making, design thinking, and lesson preparation that went far beyond the learning objectives. This context also provided for strengthening the frameworks used to plan and prepare experiences, especially the science teaching experiences, and to examine ways to be more equitable and inclusive in preparing future educators.

In designing and teaching classes to both pre-service teachers and those who will be informal educators (vis a vis tutoring, sponsoring clubs, and hosting camps), it is imperative to provide opportunities to explore implicit biases, stereotypes, and behaviors that marginalize many students and future students who will occupy professional teaching spaces and those individuals that will occupy professional science spaces. In a constant drive to remove barriers to science teaching and learning and to integrate more of the reform-based practices from *A Framework for K–12 Science Education: Practices, Crosscutting Concepts, and Core Ideas* and NGSS into student experiences, the move to online education created an unexpected outcome-that of allowing for individual, student-centered experiences while integrating engineering practices, design thinking and maker-space opportunities (Lead States, 2013; National Research Council, 2012).-

As the teaching corps seeks to become more diverse, and as our public schools' students are now representative of many ethnicities, cultural backgrounds, and languages, centering students and their experiences becomes more and more crucial as we seek to democratize science learning for all, in order for myriad participation and career options to be experienced. Whether or not a student becomes a professional science teacher or a science professional, access to science content and experience, and seeing themselves and their experiences as part of science education for the 21st century is vital. This approach sees students and their lived experiences as central and asset-based (Moll et al., 1992). We support a student-centered approach to the NGSS, specifically looking at Engineering, Technology and the Application of Science (ETS), integrated with design thinking and mini-maker kits. This shift provided a way to center student experiences and expand on science teaching in remote/online environments. Although undergraduate students who would become formal or informal educators explored the ETS, including using accessible materials and leveraging home contexts and supplies during hybrid and online learning, the frameworks and standards addressed apply to secondary students and the preparation of their learning experiences as well.

Frameworks

Design Thinking

We employ tenets of design thinking as enacted by Stanford University's dSchool, IDEO.Org and CreatEdu (https://dschool.stanford.edu/programs/k12-lab-network; IDEO.org, 2015; CreatEdu.org). In brief, design thinking is described as a human-centered approach to problem-solving and includes phases of empathy, problem definition, ideation, prototyping and test/feedback. Design thinking is one way to introduce and enact science and engineering practices that includes all student voices and experiences.

Makerspaces

Makerspaces are places where students can build and make to model what they have learned in the context of science learning. Physical makerspaces can have student choice at the center of the making experience and have consumable and non-consumable technological materials available. We see makerspaces (and as we adjusted for online and hybrid learning, mini-maker kits) as a place to center student experiences and provide both the materials and mindsets for problem-solving and model making that are relevant to student lives and communities and representative of a variety of perspectives and contexts.

Together, employing design thinking and maker education, we found a space that allowed for a more student-centered approach that could be done in a students' place of living and learning. With multiple ways to approach problem solving and practices, we were aligning with NGSS. Without the design constraint of moving to online teaching and learning, we would not have had to problem solve in this way. Design thinking, plus individual maker kits, provided new avenues to enrich and deepen science lesson planning and delivery.

CONNECTIONS TO NGSS AND THREE-DIMENSIONAL LEARNING

The journey shared in this chapter is the student-created lesson from the Disciplinary Core Idea (DCI) of Engineering, Technology and Application of Science (ETS). The focus is on ETS1.A and how to also address ETS1.B and C, using design thinking and mini-maker kits. The performance expectation (PE) was MSETS 1-1 "Define the criteria and constraints of a design problem with sufficient precision to ensure a successful solution (taking into account relevant scientific principles and potential impacts on people and the natural environments that may limit possible solutions)." Following the successful completion of MS ETS1-1, MS ETS1-4 "Develop a model to generate data for iterative testing and modification of a proposed object, tool, or process such that an optimal design can be achieved" is then undertaken. See Figure 14.1 for more information.

Students' Performance Expectations

Code: MS-ETS1-1 (MS Engineering Design)
Domain: Engineering, Technology, and Applications of Science (ETS)

- MS-ETS1-2. Evaluate competing design solutions using a systematic process to determine how well they meet the criteria and constraints of the problem.
- MS-ETS1-3. Analyze data from tests to determine similarities and differences among several design solutions to identify the best characteristics of each that can be combined into a new solution to meet the criteria for success better.
- MS-ETS1-4. Develop a model to generate data for iterative testing and modification of a proposed object, tool, or process such that an optimal design can be achieved

Science and Engineering Practices

- **Asking Questions and Defining Problems MS-ETS1-1**
  - ○ Students ask questions and define problems using given materials and design constraints.
- **Developing and Using Models (MS-ETS1-4 Engineering Design)**
  - ○ Using a variety of materials students construct, critique and refine models based on possible solutions to design problems.
- **Analyzing and Interpreting Data (MS-ETS1-3 Engineering Design)**
  - ○ Given information verbally and in writing, students make sense of data and apply results.
- **Engaging in Arguments from Evidence (MS-ETS1-2)**
  - ○ Students use a variety of evidence to craft and defend arguments related to design problems.

Disciplinary Core Ideas

- **Defining and Delimiting Engineering Problems (ETSA1-A)**
  - ○ Students use design constraints and contexts to determine problem to solver
- **Developing Possible Solutions (ETS1.B)**
  - ○ Designs can be conveyed using materials from many sources, including the mini-maker kits to construct models conducive to sharing and explaining problems and solutions.
- **Optimizing the Design Solution (ETS1.C)**
  - ○ Students compare and discuss multiple solutions to design problems, providing critique and feedback to improve solutions.

Crosscutting Concepts

Influence of Engineering, Technology and Science on Society and the Natural World (ETS1-1)

- Engineering, Technology and Science are used in the context of people and problems among a variety of possibilities and can be applied and critiqued to improve human existence.

FIGURE 14.1.   Next Generation Science Standards Addressed

LESSON NARRATIVE

We describe the first lesson undergraduate students in an education class for majors and non-majors had to plan and create. Undergraduate students, as novices, had to navigate the standards, choose a standard(s), and then plan and execute a lesson for their peers. Many lessons and standards were demonstrated, but this chapter highlights a student-created lesson from the DCI of Engineering, Technology and the Application of Science (ETS).

Mini-maker kits are how we integrated both design thinking and experiences students may have in a physical maker space that were not possible in the online and hybrid learning environment. Mini-maker kits consisted of a large resealable bag filled with consumable prototyping materials such as sticky notes, paper plates, pipe cleaners, wooden sticks, string, and other items the students contributed to from their homes and that were supplied by the instructor (Maker Ed Staff, 2020). This lesson introduces many students to ETS standards, but it was planned for middle school students. As undergraduate students work with design thinking and maker education, the mindsets, materials, and practices of design thinking and using mini-maker kits are applicable across many other standards in DCI's, CC, and SEP. See Figure 14.2, shown in a container, not bag, for photographic purposes.

Engage

The lesson began with a scenario of fictional community members needing to build a way to cross landmasses for daily activity. Paper strips with labels of monetary value and paper landmasses were the materials. The problem related to people needing to complete a bridge for their daily activities was presented to students. Students were issued a challenge to construct the bridge safely and economically. The paper strips and landmasses allowed for a low-tech use of materials while providing a collaborative experience with an engineering problem to

FIGURE 14.2.   Mini-Maker Kits (shown in a container, not bags, for photographic purposes)

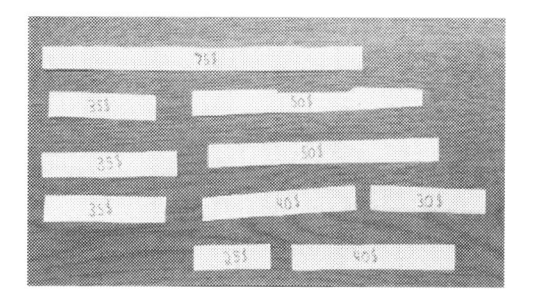

FIGURE 14.3.   Example of Paper Strips for Lesson

solve. These materials were accessible to all students and came from the lead peer teacher's supplies from home and the mini-maker kits. The first encounter was in person, and then carried over to online platforms. See Figures 14.3–14.5.

Explore

Students' initial preparations and executions of potential solutions with design constraints were extended in the form of a competition (ETS1-2). Time, cost, and scenarios were prescribed as constraints. Students were collaborating, including how to use the materials, what the performance expectation was, and how they would know they met it, in addition to completing the activity.

Explain

The undergraduate student acting as the peer teacher used observations as a formative assessment, adjusted instructions, and answered questions while students worked. The peer teacher had to explain the use of materials, pose questions to stimulate thinking, and prompt creative problem solving related to the initial materials and challenge. They also demonstrated use of the materials, if needed. This phase, depending on the students, may be done in person or online.

FIGURE 14.4.   Example of Blank Landmass for Lesson

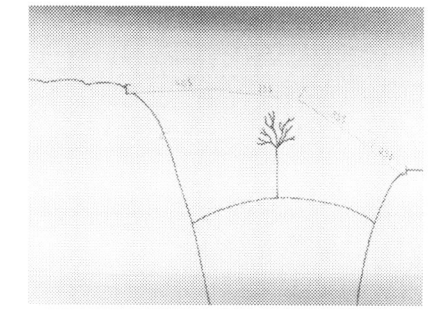

FIGURE 14. 5.   Example of Completed Iteration of Lesson

Elaborate

After the initial PE was met, students used their mini-maker kits to extend and improve the models. They each had their kit and were able to construct individually and then share collaboratively to improve on the process. This step allowed for both meeting the PE, utilizing design thinking and their maker kits, and allowing for individual and collaborative work.

For the online environment, students were given a picture for them to create the materials used in an in-person environment. They had access to each other and the instructor via a collaborative online learning platform. Two approaches were used in the online learning space. One was the instructor was in the breakout rooms of the learning management system with a set of materials like the students had. The students told the instructor what they did with their materials, and the instructor followed the lead to build the bridge. After the initial model, different students could be the moderator and do the same thing until a consensus was formed on which bridge model was agreed upon as meeting the PE.

Evaluate

As a second (or further) iteration, the students had the mini-maker kits. They could further the development of the model, increasing in sophistication, testing materials and theories, and creating a more advanced display. If available, students could use modeling software such as SolidWorks™ or TinkerCad™, depending on subscriptions and free versions available. Using the available technology provided, they could be in breakout rooms, rotating and demonstrating their creations, with different students taking the lead to enact the discussion and provide feedback for the prototypes.

SUMMARY AND REFLECTIONS

Upon reflection, an unintended outcome of the rapid and pervasive transition to online and hybrid learning is situating aspects of design thinking and maker education in the students' place. This addition aligns with the NGSS (Lead States, 2013) and *Frameworks* (National Research Council, 2012) call to situate students' lived experiences and relevancy in more inclusive and diverse science teaching. Although design thinking and mini-maker kits add another layer to teaching, it integrates into any subject matter and provides a framework and the tools to begin meeting the charge of more inclusive and relevant teaching.

Additionally, undergraduate peer teachers and those individuals who prepare teachers had the opportunity to embrace elements of design thinking themselves. They problem-solved how to meet the learning outcomes with outside constraints, which is relevant in an engineering design. The instructor is asking students to do this task, which places instructors in the space to understand the student perspective, helping them build the kind of empathy that is integral to the design thinking process.

TIPS AND ADVICE

- Consumable materials can be recycled from other projects and the maker kits do not have to be exactly uniform. However, ensure there a is a variety of consumable making supplies.
- There are several ways to distribute the maker kits to students, depending on the scenario. One way is to provide bags in a centrally located area for undergraduate students to pick one up. Another way is to deliver kits to undergraduate students or align with meal delivery and pick up if your context provides meal pick up/delivery. Additionally, volunteers may be used to deliver the kits to students. We have seen each of these delivery methods employed or combinations of the three.
- Please encourage students to use what is on hand in their environment but provide enough materials in the maker kit for students to complete the assignment(s).

RESOURCE NOTES

Name of Resource	Primary Website	How to Locate the Resource Online
CreatEdu	https://createdu.org/	Go to https://createdu.org/. The entire site is devoted to design thinking and education. A good place to start is to navigate to the green tab Design Thinking towards the top of the page to see in-depth resources. In addition, in the middle of the page, click on the individual tabs to see design thinking across subject matter and grade level.
dSchool, Stanford University	https://dschool.stanford.edu/programs/k12-lab-network	Go to https://dschool.stanford.edu/programs/k12-lab-network. Scroll down the page to explore a variety of resources for educators including the opportunity to sing up for learning projects and their periodic newsletter.
IDEO.org	https://www.designkit.org/resources/1	Go to https://www.designkit.org/resources/1. To access the downloadable text (due to limited print access) scroll to the tab toward the bottom of the page. In addition, the site includes resources on design thinking mindsets, resources, and case studies across broad topics of education and community projects.
MakerED	https://makered.org/blog/how-to-assemble-distribute-home-make-kits/	Although we used different materials, there is a useful picture of what take home mini-maker kits may look like. Go to https://makered.org/blog/how-to-assemble-distribute-home-make-kits/ to see a picture of one way to assemble kits. Navigate to the bottom of the article to click the link on making take home kits. The examples and lessons may not be in your content area, but how to assemble take home kits is applicable across many grade levels and content areas.

DISCUSSION QUESTIONS

1. In using the NGSS and *Frameworks* for science teaching and learning, how can you break down barriers to engineering design processes and associated stereotypes of who is and is not an engineer?
2. In science lessons you are currently using in your repertoire, how can you center student lived experiences and provide multiple approaches and answers, including failure and reiteration?
3. What challenges do you anticipate in working with design thinking and mini-maker kits in your context?

REFERENCES

CreatEdu. (2021). *Design thinking.* https://createdu.org/

IDEO.org. (2015). *The field guide to human-centered design.* https://www.designkit.org/resources/1

Lead States. (2013). *Next generation science standards: For states, by states.* National Academies Press.

Maker Ed Staff. (2020, June 26). *How to assemble & distribute home make kits.* Maker Ed. https://makered.org/blog/how-to-assemble-distribute-home-make-kits/

Moll, L. C., Amanti, C., Neff, D., & Gonzalez, N. (1992). Funds of knowledge for teaching: Using a qualitative approach to connect homes and classrooms. *Theory Into Practice, 31*(2), 132–141. https://doi.org/10.1080/00405849209543534

National Research Council. (2012). *A framework for K–12 science education: Practices, crosscutting concepts, and core ideas.* National Academies Press. https://doi.org/10.17226/13165

Stanford D. School. (2021). *Overview.* https://dschool.stanford.edu/programs/k12-lab-network

PART III

LESSON PLANS

CHAPTER 15

EXPLORING REGIONAL CLIMATES WITH 360-DEGREE PHOTO SPHERES

Matthew Clay

Fort Hays State University

LESSON PLAN OVERVIEW

In a push to prepare middle school students to be scientifically literate it is helpful to reflect on how words and ideas get their meaning in the first place. Cavell (1981) argued, "…the saying of something when and as it is said is as significant as the meaning and ordering of the words said" (p. 34). For science educators, that means that a concept or an idea really gains its meaning when placed and studied within a particular context. The explosion of 360-degree photo spheres available provides an incredible opportunity to place a number of earth and science concepts in a physical context, while educating from a distance. In this lesson, students will use photo spheres to explore the factors influence regional climates and to engage in scientific practices authentically with actual landscapes. Through the ability to move through an image, zoom in and out, adjust perspective, and even move to adjacent satellite images and photo spheres, students are able to engage and explore virtually as an active process. Moreover, as opposed to a single static photograph, there is the opportunity for discovery as students move through the

Teaching and Learning Online: Science for Secondary Grade Levels, pages 209–223.

FIGURE 15.1. Pegman logo located below other navigational buttons in the bottom righthand corner

virtual landscape. It is also worth noting this lesson has a complimentary elementary lesson available in *Teaching and Learning Online: Science for Elementary Grade* Levels (Allaire & Killham, 2022).

Although there are a variety of ways to access satellite imagery and photo spheres, the web-based Google Earth and Google Street View are described here. Coordinates are provided for all locations discussed in this lesson. To access satellite images via Google Earth, search the coordinates at google.com/maps and click on the box that says "Satellite" in the lower left-hand corner. To access the photo spheres for the location, search the coordinates at google.com/maps and drag the orange pegman (Figure 15.1) from the lower right-hand corner to the small blue circle that will appear at the coordinates. Releasing the pegman on the circle will enter you into the photo sphere. Google Street View photo spheres are crowd-sourced and constantly updated.

Discipline: Earth's Systems-Weather and Climate

Grade Level: Middle School

CONNECTIONS TO NGSS AND THREE-DIMENSIONAL LEARNING

Performance Expectation MS-ESS2-6: Students will use evidence from their observations of photo spheres to create a model of factors that influence regional climates. (NGSS Standards: MS-ESS2-6: Develop and use a model to describe how unequal heating and rotation of the Earth cause patterns of atmospheric and oceanic circulation that determine regional climates.)

Science and Engineering Practices:

Developing and Using Models

Modeling in 6–8 builds on K–5 experiences and progresses to developing, using, and revising models to describe, test, and predict more abstract phenomena and design systems.

- Develop and use a model to describe phenomena.

Engaging in Argumentation from Evidence

Engaging in argument from evidence in 6–8 builds on K–5 experiences and progresses to constructing a convincing argument that supports or refutes claims for either explanations or solutions about the natural and designed world(s).

- Construct, use, and/or present an oral and written argument supported by empirical evidence and scientific reasoning to support or refute an explanation or a model for a phenomenon or a solution to a problem.

Disciplinary Core Ideas:

ESS2.C: The Roles of Water in Earth's Surface Processes
- Variations in density due to variations in temperature and salinity drive a global pattern of interconnected ocean currents.

ESS2.D: Weather and Climate
- Weather and climate are influenced by interactions involving sunlight, the ocean, the atmosphere, ice, landforms, and living things. These interactions vary with latitude, altitude, and local and regional geography, all of which can affect oceanic and atmospheric flow patterns.

Crosscutting Concepts:

Systems and Systems Models

- Models can be used to represent systems and their interactions—such as inputs, processes and outputs—and energy, matter, and information flows within systems.

TEACHING AND LEARNING ONLINE 5E LESSON PLAN

Grade: Middle School   **Topic(s):** Earth's Systems: Climate

Guiding Question(s): How do different factors impact regional climates?

Performance Expectation(s):

Students will use evidence from their observations of photo spheres to create a model of factors that influence regional climates. (NGSS Standards: MS-ESS2-6: Develop and use a model to describe how unequal heating and rotation of the Earth cause patterns of atmospheric and oceanic circulation that determine regional climates.)

Science & Engineering Practices:	Disciplinary Core Ideas:	Crosscutting Concepts:
Developing and Using Models Argumentation from evidence	ESS2.C The Roles of Water in Earth's Surface ESS2.D Weather and Climate	Systems and System Models

BACKGROUND INFORMATION

Prior Student Knowledge:

- Students will need to be familiar with the concept of climate and what elements are including in discussing a region's climate.
- Students will need to be familiar with navigating Google applications, specifically Google Earth, and how to take screenshots on their particular electronic device. There are a number of helpful videos available on YouTube for introducing students to Google Earth which can be located by searching "Google Earth Tutorial."
- This lesson will potentially connect with social science standards related to geography and maps as well as the difference between longitude and latitude.

Possible Preconceptions / Misconceptions:

- Some students may struggle to distinguish between climate and weather. This difficulty could become particularly challenging when looking for evidence in photo spheres where students might think 'sunny day' would be a description of climate.
- Some students might think regional climate and habitat type are interchangeable concepts. This difference will be important to distinguish since most of the examples they will view are similar types of habitats but could still experience very different climates.
- A critical misconception that could develop as a result of this lesson is that changes in climate are always natural or that variation in climate in different locations indicates that climate change is not occurring. This misconception could potentially be addressed by discussing what an increase in temperature might look like in one or two of the example locations.

LESSON PLAN

ENGAGE:

The beginning of this lesson is best presented synchronously to allow students to ask questions and interact with each other to describe their observations. However, to deliver it asynchronously, the teacher dialogue can be recorded, and students can interact through an asynchronous discussion board such as Google Jam Board.

The practice observation location is located at 24°54'53.4"N 80°38'26.9"W (24.91483 N, 80.64081W)

1. Introduction

   We are going to investigate what factors influence climate in different regions. Before we can explore different example locations, we need to work as a group to decide what the climate of a location really means. Before we head off on our long virtual journey, we are going have a bit of a virtual vacation to practice observing characteristics of climate. Climates are the long-term averages and characteristics of the temperature, precipitation, wind, or other weather variables for an area. Climate is different from weather which are the daily conditions, so we will want to be careful to make claims about climate, but not weather.

2. Practice Observation

   For our practice, we are going to visit Islamorada Fish Company, a restaurant in the Florida Keys. As we look at this example, we are going to practice making claims and providing evidence. As you observe, you can either suggest a claim about the climate or provide evidence to support yours or a classmate's claim.

3. Discussion

   The goal in the discussion is to lead students toward thinking about the types of observations and evidence for which they will search in each example, as well as what type of evidence and data will support their claims about the regional climates. This discussion is going to be a key place to build a conceptual understanding of the difference between climate and weather.

   - What types of information did we make claims about? (e.g., temperature, precipitation, wind)
   - What types of evidence helped us support our claims?
   - How might the evidence have been different if we were looking at an example location with a very different climate?
   - Where else on earth do you think we could find similar climates?

4. Student Questions

   In remembering that this standard is asking for students to develop a model, it is key to direct students' questioning towards using evidence to support claims, rather than relying on existing knowledge or library type research. Some students may 'know' that a particular location has a certain climate, but the claim/evidence process is critical to help them better understand the mechanisms of why a region has a particular climate.

EXPLORE:

Students can complete the explore component of the lesson in breakout room small groups or individually. Coordinates are provided in the list below and photo spheres can be accessed by following the procedure in the Lesson Overview. Co-ordinates can be copied and pasted directly into Google Maps (Google, n.d.). They can also be typed with degrees and decimal minutes which are listed in parentheses. This approach avoids students needing to use the special character degrees symbol. It is also worth noting that you can locate each location on Google.com/maps and then simply provide a direct link for students to that page. The exploration journal pages can be provided as digital copies of a document or students can be given directions of information to include. It should be noted that there does not necessarily need to be a set number of claims or evidence for each location; however, requiring at least a handful will help students look more critically and carefully for evidence.

- Hachita, New Mexico 31°29'48.6"N 108°12'32.7"W (31.49683N, 108.2091W)
- Cañada de Olguin, New Mexico 36°27'51.8"N 106°05'03.2"W (36.46439N, 106.0842W)
- Stony Pass, Colorado 37°47'45.9"N 107°32'49.8"W (37.79608N, 107.5472W)
- Ptarmigan Pass, Rocky Mountain National Park, Colorado 40°18'39.7"N 105°41'47.7"W (40.31103N, 105.6966W)
- Pearl Lake, Colorado 40°47'11.1"N 106°53'13.0"W (40.78642N, 106.8869W)
- Sweetwater County, Wyoming 42°14'05.5"N 107°42'20.9"W (42.23486N, 107.7058W)
- Shoshone Lake, Yellowstone National Park, Wyoming 44°21'36.9"N 110°40'23.0"W (44.36025N, 110.6731W)
- Dubois, Idaho 44°28'57.1"N 112°04'47.1"W (44.48253N, 112.0797W)
- Saint Mary Falls, Glacier National Park, Montana 48°40'00.4"N 113°36'56.4"W (48.66678N, 113.6157W)
- Waterton Lake, Glacier National Park, Montana 48°59'54.5"N 113°54'21.1"W (48.99847N, 113.9059W)

We are going to explore climate by going on a virtual journey along the Continental Divide Trail. The Continental Divide Trail, or CDT, stretches from the US/Mexico border all the way into Alberta, Canada and is near the continental divide in the Rocky Mountains the entire way. The continental divide is the boundary on the map that separates streams and water that will eventually end up in the Atlantic Ocean from water that will end up in the Pacific. You are going to make 10 stops along the trail as you travel from south to north. For each stop, you are going to observe evidence of climate and then make claims and provide evidence to support what you believe the climate in that region is like.

Sample Exploration Journal Page

Student Name:

Location:

Claim 1:	Evidence to Support Claim 1:
Claim 2:	Evidence to Support Claim 2:
Claim 3:	Evidence to Support Claim 3:
Claim 4:	Evidence to Support Claim 4:

EXPLAIN:

As before, the discussion to launch the explain portion of the lesson would best be conducted synchronously. However, it also could be completed through asynchronous discussion boards by allowing each discussion question to be a thread topic.

> An important part of exploring is to report your findings. Since you have explored the length of the CDT, you now need to use your claims and evidence to start to explain why the differences exists between the different locations. Let's discuss a few questions to help us get started:

- What similarities and differences did you notice in comparing the locations?
- What patterns did you notice between the locations?
- What other data would be helpful in comparing the locations?

Vocabulary:

As students explore regional climates, there will be opportunities for 'just in time' vocabulary as students are describing observations. The terms included in this list are those words likely to be significant as students describe observations and create their models. Definitions are adapted from the Glossary of Meteorology from the American Meteorological Society. In both defining and discussing these terms, students should take notes in a science notebook to refer to as they create their models.

- Average Annual Temperature-Annual average of air temperature based on evenly spaced frequent measurements in a location

- Average Annual Precipitation-Average amount of all forms of precipitation that fall at a given point usually measured in millimeters or inches
- Elevation-Height of a point on the earth's surface above sea level
- Prevailing Winds-The wind direction most often observed in a location over a period of time
- Topography-Major physical features of the earth's surface
- Arid-A climate that does not have enough moisture to support significant plant life

ELABORATE:

Now that we have made claims and collected to evidence to explain the climate in each of these locations, we are going to look at other data to help us better understand why these climates are different. There are four types of data we are going to look at, including elevation (United States Geological Survey, n.d.), average temperature, average precipitation (Lindsey, 2021), and prevailing wind direction (Viegas & Wattenberg, n.d.). To look at average temperature and precipitation, we are going to look at maps. Some of the locations we observed do not have weather stations, so these maps can be a great tool to match the location to an approximate average annual temperature and annual precipitation. For each location we observed, use the maps to record temperature and precipitation. Remember you can search the location on Google Maps again if you are struggling to find its exact location.

Now we are going to collect elevation data for each of the locations. We are going to access the Elevation Point Service from the USGS. For each location you will need to enter the coordinates. There are a few key points to keep in mind when using the tool. First, the X should be the longitude and the Y will be latitude. This tool only wants a number input, so we are going to use the decimal coordinates. Also, since our longitudes are all 'West' we are going to put a negative sign in front. For example, for our first location, Hachita, New Mexico, the X value will be −108.2091 and the Y value will be 31.49683.

Finally, we are going to look at prevailing wind direction. We are going to use the live wind map for this step. This map uses different thickness of lines to show wind speed and direction. When we first go to the page it is going to show us what the wind is doing right now. You should also go to the gallery and choose a few days to see if the wind direction today seems normal for the location.

EVALUATE:

As is emphasized in the standard, evaluating students' learning in this lesson takes the form of them creating a model. Although there are a number of forms this model could take, realistically the simplest will be to have them draw a diagram or create one using software such as Google Slides. Ultimately, they will need to explain how different factors impact regional climate, but not necessarily the specifics of the climate for any one of their observed locations.

Formative Monitoring (Questioning / Discussion):

The observations students make of their locations will be a key indicator in understanding if students are making a clear distinction between climate and weather. Also, the number of factors they are considering in describing the climate will be an important indicator. A student who is struggling might record an observation such as "It looks like a hot day." On the other hand, students who are grasping the concept of climates might say: "The climate looks dry and hot, because…" In synchronous sessions it is also possible to gain insight using the discussion questions in the "Explain" portion of the lesson. If the teacher is concerned about specific individual student progress, then it might be helpful to turn one of those discussion questions into a digital exit ticket using Google Forms.

Summative Assessment (Quiz / Project / Report):

In the models students create, the key points of consideration are going to be if they represent how latitude, elevation, topography, and prevailing winds can all shape regional climate. Additionally, it is going to be essential that they recognize the interaction of these factors. If a student uses an absolute statement such as, "the further north you go the colder it is," then it is going to be important to refer them back to the locations they observed to ask if it always seemed to be colder the further north it went. In this type of assessment, it will likely be most beneficial to allow students to adapt and modify their models until they have reached mastery. Also, since models can be a difficult form of communication for students, it would be beneficial to allow them an opportunity to explain their model either in writing or through recording a short video.

ADDITIONAL LESSON INFO

Extension and Contingency Plans:

If students are struggling to make progress in observing their locations as in groups, then it can be beneficial to give them a set number of hints, like how escape rooms are structured. These hints can be used at points when the group is stuck and could include the teacher providing a specific example of a type of evidence for which students should search or by helping orient them in their photo sphere or satellite image. Providing hints can be accomplished via screen sharing in a video conferencing program or the teacher providing a screenshot of a particular portion of the location.

For students who finish quickly and have been thorough in identifying evidence from their location, it is possible to let them expand their area to search for additional evidence of the regional climate in surrounding areas. This step can be accomplished by allowing them to search surrounding photo spheres.

Accommodations and Modifications:

It is important to consider that with the given standard a model could take a number of forms. A student who struggles to express themselves in writing could explain a model orally or kinesthetically using a manipulative such as a ball to represent the globe or even in touring the teacher through one of the observed locations. In supporting English Language Learners, it is possible to allow students to make observations in whichever language they feel most comfortable and then provide support in using those observations to create explanations. Additionally, teachers could provide students with a list of 'look fors' if they struggle with the unstructured environment of a virtual landscape. This 'look for' could consist of prompts such as "How warm do you think the climate is in this location?" or "Do you think this location gets much precipitation?"

LESSON NARRATIVE

Although it is always a risk in teaching, a lack of interaction with the natural world can be a particular challenge in teaching online. David Orr (1992) argued "…experience in the natural world is both an essential part of understanding the environment, and conducive to good teaching" (p. 91). In this light, a main goal in this lesson is to allow as much interaction with the natural world as possible in an online setting. Additionally, in aiming to have students create models, it is essential that they understand concepts of climate as they occur in actual locations and not just as abstract ideas in a diagram. Although it might be easier to just allow students to compare vastly different climates, looking at several example locations along a relatively consistent longitude helps emphasize the importance of nuance and careful investigation in describing the factors impacting the climate of a location.

Engage

A key factor in ultimately introducing this lesson to students is to consider students' previous experiences in natural settings. For students who are more experienced in natural settings, this lesson presents a particular way to explore the natural world or a particular set of goals for exploring. However, students inexperienced in natural settings might need to be introduced to the concept of natural settings as a whole before being able to apply specific scientific skills. For students who do not have previous experiences exploring natural settings, it might be beneficial to introduce the tools of Google Earth and photo spheres in a context that might feel more familiar. Helping students become more familiar could potentially include using the tools to explore an area in their city or community.

Alternatively, in introducing the idea of climate, it might work well to have students observe evidence of climate in their own front yards, depending on the type of area. A few points to consider depending on the location is the impact of built environments on these observations. For example, cities located in arid regions might still have very lush vegetation because of irrigation.

Explore

During the 'Explore' portion of this lesson, it is important to remember that exploration as a scientific practice requires a range of characteristics. First, there must be an element of the unknown. Creating an element of the unknown requires purposefully providing rather sparse details for students as they explore their locations, such as not indicating what specific erosion evidence they might find. Although this is an inherently inefficient process, deciding what evidence is and is not of value is critical to developing students' ability to make scientific observations. It will probably be most effective to schedule meeting times with groups or individual students in an online setting. Students can then screenshare photo spheres to guide the teacher through their location and their evidence. It may be helpful to record these sessions for students to look back at input they receive from their teacher.

Although students can document observations in a number of different ways, it will likely be most effective if they have separate pages for each location. Students can use physical science notebooks or use separate pages in a Google Doc or Google Jam Board to record their observations, claims, and evidence. Given the inefficiencies of the exploration process, it is essential to allow plenty of time for this aspect of the lesson. It could easily take a couple hours to observe each of the locations. If it is needed to reduce this lesson into a shorter amount of time, then it would be better to remove a handful of the locations to observe, rather than allow students less time with each location.

Explain

The key point during the 'Explain' stage of this lesson is to help students start to transition from the descriptions of the individual locations' climates to a broader recognition of the patterns which can lead to an understanding of the factors which impact regional climate. The goal is to lead students toward considering what other types of data will be helpful, rather than directly instructing them to look for particular aspects. A way of framing these discussions and prompting can be to use students' own claims and evidence from their observations to suggest questions. For example, you might ask, "You said this looks like an arid climate, what data could help you confirm that?" or "You said this location looks like it gets a lot of precipitation, but some of the others get very little, what do you think is different between them?"

Elaborate

The 'Elaborate' aspect of this lesson is designed to make a critical transition which is important to students' scientific literacy which is to compare direct observations with existing data. There are a few points of emphasis in this part. First is that the data used is not necessarily to test if their claims and evidence from their observations were correct or not, but rather to update or refine their explanations. As a result, if students update their descriptions of the climate in a location, then it is important to help them frame that as revising their understanding based on new information rather than fixing an incorrect response.

At the elaborate stage it is again critical to emphasize the difference between climate and weather. Students might have some familiarity with one of the locations or might have experiences that vary from average patterns. For example, they may have an experience along the lines of "My family visited New Mexico once and it rained the entire trip." However, it is important to emphasize looking at data for larger patterns.

Another critical point of emphasis in accessing elevation data is that the National Map from USGS uses decimal degrees positive and negative in a coordinate plane. There is an opportunity to provide a math integration discussing why coordinates must be entered this way, or a computer science integration to discuss how algorithms need numerical inputs. However, at the very least it is critical to be very explicit in explaining how the coordinates must be entered.

Evaluate

Evaluation for this lesson lends itself particularly well toward teaching for mastery and allowing revision of models. The key point will be to have students describe in their models why each factor impacts regional climate. However, these models could take many forms. In order to support students, it will be important to be clear about the emphasis of evaluation on the evidence and scientific reasoning provided in the models rather than the aesthetics of the model. This point is particularly important for students for whom accommodations are provided to allow them to demonstrate their understanding in a form which best fits them. Accommodations in the format of the model for evaluation can be made without losing scientific rigor.

SUMMARY AND REFLECTIONS

In an educational system increasingly focused on outcomes, there is the potential for the wonder of the process of science, especially in environmental sciences, to be lost. For many of us that chose to be earth science educators, the initial draw was the fascination of exploring the natural world. Not only are there opportunities to use 360 photo spheres to improve scientific literacy through the process of observing, making claims, and providing evidence, but more importantly the opening is there to allow students to explore the world around them within the structure of online learning environments. The explosion of available information in online learning environments requires educators to emphasize a new set of skills to ensure students are successful. As the late biologist E.O. Wilson (1998) argued, "We are drowning in information, while starving for wisdom. The world henceforth will be run by synthesizers, people able to put together the right information at the right time, think critically about it, and make important choices wisely" (p. 294).

TIPS AND ADVICE

- Depending on the manner of online teaching, it can be highly advantageous to have the same type of device available in preparing for the lesson as students will be using. This tip can be particularly important in teaching asynchronously when students are not as readily able to ask questions if the way they are accessing Google Earth causes it to look slightly different than it did for the teacher in creating and providing instructions.
- Although the fundamental functions are identical, web-based and app-based versions of Google Earth function differently. It is beneficial to provide instructions to students that reflect the version of Google Earth you are asking them to utilize. Web-based versions are accessed through a web browser, typically on a laptop or Chromebook. The app-based version is downloadable and more effective on tablet computer and smartphones.
- It is also worth noting that Google Earth Pro, a downloadable desktop version of Google Earth with greater functionality, is available to educators at no cost. It also tends to work a little more seamlessly for screensharing.
- The desktop version of Google Earth allows for the permanent saving of waypoints, making it very quick for a teacher to locate each of the different locations students are exploring.
- It is beneficial to remember that photo spheres are generally crowd-sourced. As a result, it is best to preview each photo sphere before assigning it to a student to ensure they are appropriate and effective for the topic being taught.

RESOURCE NOTES

Name of Resource	Primary Website	How to Locate the Resource Online
Google Maps	https://maps.google.com	This link is the general Google Maps access point, which is used for accessing photo spheres and satellite images.
NOAA-Science and Information for a Climate-Smart Nation	https://www.climate.gov	Go to https://www.climate.gov. At the top righthand corner there is a search box. Searching the phrase "Average Annual Temperature" will lead to a page with current average annual temperature maps. At the bottom of the resulting page there is also options to download image files of the maps. https://www.climate.gov/news-features/featured-images/new-maps-annual-average-temperature-and-precipitation-us-climate
USGS-National Map	https://www.nationalmap.gov	Go to https://www.nationalmap.gov. Click on "3D Elevation Program (3DEP)" in the left-hand column. On the resulting page, scroll and click on "Learn About 3DEP Product and Services." From this page click on "Elevation Tools." Finally, select "Point Query Service." https://nationalmap.gov/epqs/
Wind Map	http://hint.fm/	Go to http://hint.fm/. Scroll down and click on "Wind Map." On the left-hand side of the resulting page there are red letters for a link that says "See the Live Map." It is worth noting that it is possible to zoom in on the map, but you must refresh the page to reset the zoom to its original size. To access the wind map gallery, scroll down and click on the small map images below the Gallery heading on the left-hand side of the page. http://hint.fm/wind/

DISCUSSION QUESTIONS

1. In what ways can we create opportunities for students to explore in virtual learning environments?
2. How should teachers balance using instructional time efficiently with allowing students opportunities to explore?
3. With what other scientific content areas and standards are there opportunities to utilize satellite imagery and photo spheres?
4. In what other science and engineering practices are there opportunities to allow students to engage through photo spheres?
5. In what ways can teachers increase the students' aesthetic experience in exploring virtual environments?
6. How can teaching strategies such as satellite imagery and photo spheres promote equity and inclusion in natural settings, particularly for students from marginalized populations?

REFERENCES

Allaire, F. S., & Killham, J. E. (Eds.) (2022). *Teaching and learning online: Science for elementary grade levels.* Information Age Publishing.

Cavell, S. (1981). *The senses of Walden.* North Point Press.

Google. (n.d.). *Google Maps.* www.google.com/maps

Lindsey, R. (2021, October 11). *New maps of annual average temperature and precipitation from the U.S. climate normal.* Climate.gov. https://www.climate.gov/news-features/featured-images/new-maps-annual-average-temperature-and-precipitation-us-climate

Orr, D. W. (1992). *Ecological literacy: Education and the transition to a postmodern world.* State University of New York Press.

United States Geological Survey. (n.d.). *Elevation point query service.* The National Map. https://nationalmap.gov/epqs/

Viegas, F., & Wattenberg, M. (n.d.) *Wind map.* Hint.FM. http://hint.fm/wind/

Wilson, E. O. (1998). *Consilience: The unity of knowledge.* Knopf.

CHAPTER 16

SCIENTIFIC MODELING IN A VIRTUAL SETTING

Floating and Sinking Pennies!

Sophia Jeong
The Ohio State University

David Pauli
Brenau University

LESSON PLAN OVERVIEW

Density is a concept vital to all aspects of science and engineering. This lesson provides the middle grades learner with a project-based opportunity to examine how mass and volume relate to the density of an object. Through a series of demonstrations, videos, and simulations, the concept of density is brought to life: Students can "see" the relationships of mass, volume, and density. Students can "experience" density through simulations. Students can "illustrate" their understanding through a scientific model. These methods are multi-dimensional and multi-modal ways that students can "learn" a difficult yet important science concept such as density. The unit culminates in an inquiry-based, scientific modeling activity where students apply their knowledge of mass and volume to create a

Teaching and Learning Online: Science for Secondary Grade Levels, pages 225–239.

penny floater. This lesson, which has been taught online both synchronously and asynchronously, challenges students to think critically.

Discipline: Physical Sciences

Grade Level: Middle Grades 6th–8th

CONNECTIONS TO NGSS AND THREE-DIMENSIONAL LEARNING

Students' Performance Expectations

- **Code: MS-PS1** (Matter and Its Interactions)
- **Domain:** Physical Sciences (PS)
- **MS-PS1-1:** Develop models to describe the atomic composition of simple molecules and extended structures.

Science and Engineering Practices

Developing and Using Models (MS-PS1-1)
- Develop a model to predict and/or describe phenomena.

Analyzing and Interpreting Data (HS-PS1-2)
- Analyze and interpret data to determine similarities and differences in findings.

Disciplinary Core Ideas

Structure and Properties of Matter (MS-PS1.A)
- Substances are made from different types of atoms, which combine with one another in various ways. Atoms form molecules that range in size from two to thousands of atoms.
- Solids may be formed from molecules, or they may be extended structures with repeating subunits (e.g., crystals).
- Each pure substance has characteristics physical and chemical properties (for any bulk quantity under given conditions) that can be used to identify it.

Chemical Reactions (MS-PS1.B)
- Substances react chemically in characteristic ways. In a chemical process, the atoms that make up the original substances are regrouped into different molecules and these new substances have different properties from those properties of the reactants.

Crosscutting Concepts

Scale, Proportion, and Quantity (MS-PS1.A)

* Time, space, and energy phenomena can be observed at various scales using models to study systems that are too large or too small.

Patterns (MS-PS1.B)

* Macroscopic patterns are related to the nature of microscopic and atomic-level structure.

TEACHING AND LEARNING ONLINE 5E LESSON PLAN

Grade: 6th to 8th   **Topic(s):** Density

Guiding Question(s):

* How does an object's density relate to whether it will float or sink?
* How can I create something that will float as many pennies as possible?

Performance Expectation(s):

* Students should be able to explain why some things float while some things sink using the concepts of density, mass, and volume.
* Students should be able to articulate the relationship between mass, volume and density.
* Students should be able to master the calculation of density.
* Students should be able to create a model using pennies to illustrate the density of pennies.

Science & Engineering Practices:	Disciplinary Core Ideas:	Crosscutting Concepts:
Developing and Using Models Analyzing and Interpreting Data	Structure and Properties of Matter Chemical Reactions	Scale, Proportion, and Quantity Patterns

BACKGROUND INFORMATION

Prior Student Knowledge:

* Academic: Students should be familiar with mass and volume. Students should have a basic concept of fractions and division
* Cultural: Students should be familiar with boats, typical materials they are made of, and their basic shape.

Possible Preconceptions / Misconceptions:

* Mass and density are the same.
* Mass and volume are the same.

- Heavy objects always sink.
- Light objects always float.

Source Notes:

- Density simulation on PhET. On Google, type in "Phet Density." Search result will show "Density—Mass | Volume | Archimedes' Principle—PhET." Click and enter the simulation.
- MITK12Videos, "How do ships float?" On Google, type in "MITK12Videos, 'How do ships float?'." The YouTube video will show up under the account of MITK12Videos. https://www.youtube.com/watch?v=pnIlE1xD-yM

LESSON PLAN

ENGAGE:

Introduction to the Unit

Asynchronous:
- Know-Want-Learn (KWL) Chart on density (Use a general KWL chart to modify as needed. Teachers should facilitate students to fill out this chart).

Synchronous:
- Pose the following question: Why do somethings float and some things sink?
- Teachers do a demo using blocks of wood.
- Teacher Explanation: In the demo, there are two identical looking blocks of wood and they are submerged into separate tanks. One of the pieces of wood floats, while the other sinks. Wood normally floats, so it is unexpected for one piece to sink (This event is called the discrepant event). The pieces of wood are then put in the opposite tanks, which will tell the viewer that it is in fact the wood, not the liquid that is causing the difference. Finally, the pieces of wood are put into the same tank. The viewer can observe that the wood is the same volume. Since densities are different, one of the pieces of wood must have more mass.

Discussion Questions Using Claims-Evidence Reasoning (CER):
- Teacher can facilitate class discussion in various ways such as board asynchronous, class discussion, or synchronous
- The discussion board asks the student to make a claim about why they think one piece of wood sinks and the other floats. They are then to provide evidence from the video then support their claim. Students then reason how the evidence shows their claim is valid. This activity is a classic Claims-Evidence-Reasoning (CER) activity.

Follow-up Using a Demo, "the Secret of the Block of Wood" video:
- Teacher does another demo. In this demo, teacher prepares one of the blocks of wood such that it has been hollowed out and filled with a piece of metal. Doing so increases its mass. This demo illustrates an important visual representation of density that there is more inside the one piece of wood even though they are the same size. This example illustrates the concept of density.

Discussion Questions
- Teacher can facilitate class discussion in various ways such as board asynchronous, class discussion, synchronous
- This discussion board asks the students to explain what the concept of density is in their own words based on the two videos.

EXPLORE:

Asynchronous:
- Review the concepts of mass and volume with the student.
- Teacher should find appropriate resources such as videos or other illustrative tools to review the concept of density.

Synchronous:
- Students will use the following PhET "Density" simulation to see how mass and volume are related to density.
- Phet "Density" simulation can be retrieved from their website and teacher should use the simulation to facilitate the activity and the resources that come with the simulation. https://phet.colorado.edu/sims/html/density/latest/density_en.html

Discussion Questions: Teacher should ask these questions and facilitate a class discussion, think-pair-share, or individual reflection.
- What are your observations?
- What type of materials were more likely to float? Sink?
- What did you notice about the mass compared to the volume of objects that floated? Sank?

EXPLAIN:

Asynchronous or Synchronous:
- Teacher instructs students to read the transcript of Dr. P's explanation using the weeds as an analogy in "Density with Weeds" (Appendix 1).
- Teacher instructs students to watch "Density with Legos" (Appendix 2)
- Reviewing these resources, students should be prepared to explain the concept of density.

Discussion Questions:
- Teacher facilitates with a question, "Now that you have read the explanation by Dr. P on "Density with Weeds" and "Density with Lego," reflect on Dr. P's explanation, by choosing only one of the two options to answer:
  - ○ Discuss how the density relates to social distancing.
  - ○ Give an example of density using the members of your family.
- For either topic, the teacher will look for two to four sentences.

Synchronous: Students will complete these activities
- "Calculate Density Video" (Appendix 3)
- "Calculate Density Worksheet" (Appendix 4)

Answers for Teachers:
1. 0.0096 g/ml
2. 1 g/cm^3
3. 5 g/ml
4. 8.96 g/cm^3
5. gold
6. benzene
7. 2.7 g/cm^3
8. 5 g/cm^3

Scaffolds for Students:
- If students cannot figure out how the teacher got these answers, then teacher should provide additional support on the problems and review the calculations.

Academic Vocabulary:
- Mass
- Volume
- Density

ELABORATE:

Introduction:
- In this section, students will create their own boat to float as many pennies (objects) as possible.

Asynchronous/Synchronous:
- Students will watch the following videos to prepare them for the challenge:
  - ○ MITK12Videos: https://www.youtube.com/watch?v=pnIlE1xD-yM

Discussion Questions:
- Teacher facilitates with an introduction, Now that you have seen the MITK12VIDEO" complete the discussion board as follows:

- ○ Identify one way the video helped you better understand Density. Discuss why and how they helped you understand Density.
- ○ Identify one way the video left you still wondering about Density. Explain what you are still wondering about Density, what questions you still have about Density, and how you would find answers to your lingering questions about Density.
- Teacher reminds students: "This discussion post should be a good, thoughtfully written paragraph."

Synchronous Activity:
- Students will create floating devices according to the following rules:
  - ○ Students will be building a floating device that will hold as many pennies as possible.
  - ○ Follow the requirements listed below:
    - – Must stay afloat in water for a minimum of 30 seconds.
    - – Must have a cargo area in which pennies can easily be added or removed.
    - – Constraints:
      - – Must not exceed 8" × 8" × 4."
      - – Must be made of at least three different materials.
      - – Must not have any toys.

Scaffolds for Students:
- Students should have several days to complete this Engineering-By-Design project. Students should learn to build a model within the requirements and constraints. Teachers should emphasize that any common household material will work. Typical materials include water bottles, Ziplock bags, aluminum foil, Tupperware lids or bowls, plastic cups, Styrofoam from packaging, bags from a cereal box, etc. The biggest issue is what the student should use to weigh down the boat. Pennies are the classic object but anything will work. The idea is for students to realize that the bigger the volume and lighter the materials, the better it will float.

EVALUATE:

Formative Monitoring (Questioning / Discussion):
- See discussion boards and formative assessments to check students' understanding throughout the lesson.

Summative Assessment (Quiz / Project / Report):
- Students will create a video of their floating device and explain how mass and density related to their success or failure.

ADDITIONAL LESSON INFO

Extension and Contingency Plans:

Extensions and various approaches have been included throughout the Density Lesson. Students who need additional time should be given the opportunity to work on the activities during extended time during the school day such as study-hall or virtual office hours in order to complete their work. Pedagogies and teaching strategies towards mastery learning model should be used so that all students can be successful and achieve the learning outcomes

Accommodations and Modifications:

Accommodations for students who are experiencing challenges and struggles should be invited for extended opportunities such as study hall or virtual office hours to complete their work. Students who are gifted and talented can be accommodated through implementing varying levels of inquiry throughout the activities. For example, modeling activity can be differentiated such that students have a varying degree of requirements and constraints. Students who are English Language Learners can be accommodated through the use of sentence starters, translation tools to translate activities, and resources to their native language. Teachers should use multimodal and multi-representational assessment where appropriate.

LESSON NARRATIVE

Engage

The Engage phase of the lesson is one of the most important phases in launching a unit. Engage is intended to not only focus on capturing students' attention on a problem or phenomenon of interests, but also elicit and reveal what students already know about the topic in order to build on their prior knowledge to develop their science and engineering practices. A Claims-Evidence-Reasoning (CER) approach, when used in the science classroom, provides students with an opportunity to make claims, support with evidence, reason, and participate in the process of productive dialogues and conversations that is at the heart of what scientists actually *do* (Jeong et al., 2020).

Starting with Engage, the teacher will begin with a series of essential or discussion questions for students to consider and reflect: Why do somethings float and some things sink? This classroom discussion and dialogues are intended to stimulate students' interest as they connect abstract science concepts such as density to their daily lives or what they observe in the teacher's demo. The "Secret of the Block of Wood" demonstration is a great opening to this unit on density. This demonstration using blocks of wood is a popular activity and feasible in both asynchronous and synchronous setting. Teacher prepares one of the blocks of wood such that it has been hollowed out and filled with a piece of metal. Doing so increases its mass. This demo provides an important visual representation of density and shows that there is more inside the one piece of wood even though they are the same size. This example illustrates is the concept of density.

Explore

The Explore phase of the lesson creates a "common, concrete experience" that will set the stage for further inquiry-based exploration in the rest of the lesson (5E Model of Instruction, 2002). Students will explore using the PhET simulation on Density. Grounded in the Next Generation Science Standards, we aim to provide opportunities for students to engage in Science & Engineering Practices (NRC, 2012). The CER approach we introduce in this lesson provides students an opportunity to continue exploring the concepts of density by first interacting with a PhET simulation, analyze and interpret the data, and use data as evidence to make and support their claims. Using the simulation, the teacher can facilitate a class discussion and scaffold students to begin constructing their explanations about why certain things float and why certain things sink, and about the relationships between mass, volume, and density.

Explain

The Explain phase of the lesson is intended specifically for the teacher to help students construct their explanation about the relationships between mass, volume, and density. Explain phase is where teacher should refrain from providing a teacher-led explanation as little as possible. Instead, this phase is where student-led explanation is produced.

Teacher will use various resources and representations of the concept of density, such as Dr. P's analogies, to help students make the connections between mass, volume, and density. We believe the Explain phase is empowering for students. Students will develop confidence in their ability to understand what density means as they connect between their prior knowledge and what they learned in previous instructional activities and scientific knowledge. Drawing on the CER approach, when the teacher asks students to "explain and discuss density" as it relates to the metaphors and analogies Dr. P used in his video, this discussion helps to grow confidence in students that they *can* learn difficult science concepts. CER approach allows us to continue to press students to construct their own explanation that shows their understanding.

In the Explain phase, we integrated a mathematical exercise. This approach is another way to introduce and illustrate the relationships between mass, volume, and density. This activity gives students a mathematical model of density that can be connected to their scientific model of a "floater."

Elaborate

In the Elaborate phase of the lesson, students will have the opportunity to create a "model" or a floater in order to hold as many pennies or other appropriate objects as possible. The teacher will facilitate this activity with an essential question after students have watched the MITK12VIDEO on density. At the core of this modeling activity is Engineering-by-Design. Students are provided requirements as well as constraints to build a model, which is what engineers and scientists *do* in real life to solve a problem. Do not forget that students worked on a mathematical problem and have been exposed to the mathematical model of density, which shows the relationship between mass, volume, and density. An effective teacher should help students make these connections between the mathematical model with the students' scientific model.

Evaluate

In the Evaluate phase of the lesson, teachers evaluate student learning by providing actionable and high-quality feedback on their models or "floaters." As teachers, we understand that informal or formative assessments that are implemented throughout the lesson can be more powerful at checking students' understanding. Teacher should plan for acceptable evidence for how students master the learning outcomes (McTighe & Wiggins, 2012). The Evaluate phase should allow students to feel confident that they achieve mastery of the content and topic as a result of the learning experience (Keller, 2010). The Evaluate phase is an opportunity for the teacher to reflect on implementing multi-dimensional and multi-modal assessment that yields in data on student learning to inform the next iteration of the instruction. For the students, the Evaluate phase is where they can experience what it feels to be successful in science learning.

Formative assessments are used throughout this lesson to check students' understanding about density on an ongoing basis during unit. On the other hand, for the summative assessment in this lesson, students have to produce a deliverable or a product in a modeling activity. Developing and using a model is one of the important Science & Engineering Practices (NRC, 2012). Performance-based task such as developing a scientific model or a "floater" is an effective method to evaluate whether students have mastered the key concepts in density, or else their floater device would not float.

SUMMARY AND REFLECTIONS

Students are often concerned with building the actual floater and how many pennies it can hold but, as the teacher, that is the last of the concerns. The key is to focus on any changes made to their design or their "scientific model" and how those changes relate to changes in mass or changes in volume. The ultimate goal is for the student to see that they can float more pennies if their floater has less mass and more volume which is the illustration of the concept of density that students should understand. If students can explain that to you in writing, verbally, in person, through a video explanation, or asynchronous discussion board, then they understand the concept of density.

Online and Remote Learning Environments

This lesson on Density has been designed with teachers who need to teach the content in a virtual setting. Teachers, students, parents, and school leaders must begin to accept that science instruction as we know it today will continue to evolve and virtual teaching may one day become the norm. As science educators, we know inequities exist in the face-to-face science classrooms, and so will inequities continue to exist in a virtual setting. Although the emphasis of this lesson was to facilitate the teaching of density in a virtual setting, this lesson draws on effective, equitable, and inclusive pedagogical approaches that are applicable in all types of settings in science teaching and learning. To this end, we should continue to reflect on our pedagogies and teaching practices to build on students' ideas, thinking, and prior knowledge as strengths and continue to provide an inclusive space where all students can learn science

Critiques and Considerations

Teachers around the world ask: "How can we effectively teach an inquiry-based science lessons in a virtual environment when we can't do hands-on activities?" We hope that our lesson provides insights and exemplars that would encourage science teachers to intentionally plan and integrate demos, simulations, and videos. Additionally, we hope science teachers consider various affordances of educational technology for creating an inquiry-based and hands-on learning environment.

TIPS AND ADVICE

- When doing the lesson in an asynchronous setting, do not worry about the materials they use for their floater or what they use for pennies during the modeling activity. Anything will work. Modeling activity is about illustrating the concepts, not the actual floater.
- Some students will complain that they do not have any materials at home, so you might have to be creative such as using aluminum foil, used water bottles, sandwich bags, cereal boxes (which can get yucky, but they work), or anything from a recycle bin.
- Allow time for students to revamp or recreate their floater. The power of the lesson is in the changes they make.
- Doing the mathematics problems using the formula only helps some students. However, you should still introduce it, but do not focus on the formula for density too much, especially for lower middle grades. When you

do use the formula, do not forget to relate it to the idea of fractions. This activity gives the students a concrete example of how fractions work.

RESOURCE NOTES

Name of Resource	Primary Website	How to Locate the Resource Online
Density	www.Phet.colorado.edu	On Google, type in "Phet Density." Search result will show "Density—Mass | Volume | Archimedes' Principle—PhET." Click and enter the simulation.
MITK12Videos, "How do ships float?"	www.Youtube.com	On Google, type in "MITK12Videos, 'How do ships float?'" The YouTube video will show up under the account of MITK12Videos. https://www.youtube.com/watch?v=pnlIE1xD-yM
Appendix 1	n/a	Density with Weeds Transcript (PDF)
Appendix 2	www.Vimeo.com	Density with Legos Video on Vimeo. On the Vimeo website, search for "density with Legos." Authors have uploaded and made the video available at https://vimeo.com/user166378105/review/676130321/8b8c1f3ae5
Appendix 3	www.Vimeo.com	Calculate Density Video on Vimeo. Authors have uploaded and made the video available at https://vimeo.com/user166378105/review/676131241/5b0edaa884
Appendix 4	n/a	Calculate Density Worksheet (PDF).

DISCUSSION QUESTIONS

1. How can we effectively create an inquiry-based science learning environment?
2. How can we effectively teach a difficult concept in science such as density through scientific modeling activity in a virtual classroom setting?
3. How can we foster productive classroom dialogue in a virtual classroom setting to engage students in evidence-based claims and constructing explanations about why certain things float while other things sink?
4. How do we use discrepant events in a virtual setting to help students make sense of what the observe in the demonstration with the wood blocks?

REFERENCES

Jeong, S., King, G., Pauli, D., Sell, C., & Steele, D. (2020). Conceptualizing multiplicities of scientific literacy from five theoretical perspectives. In T. W. Teo, A. L. Tan, & Y. S. Ong (Eds.), *Science education in the 21st century: Re-searching issues that matter from different lenses* (pp. 3–17). Springer Singapore. https://doi.org/10.1007/978-981-15-5155-0_1

Keller, J. M. (2010). *Motivational design for learning and performance: The ARCS model approach.* Springer.

McTighe, J., & Wiggins, G. (2012). *Understanding by design framework.* Association for Supervision and Curriculum Development.

National Research Council. (2012). *A framework for K–12 science education: Practices, crosscutting concepts, and core ideas.* National Academies Press. https://doi.org/10.17226/13165

San Diego County Office of Education. (2002). *5E Model of Instruction.* https://ngss.sdcoe.net/Evidence-Based-Practices/5E-Model-of-Instruction

APPENDIX 1

Hello, everyone, this is Dr. P.

I figured we'd start our discussion on density outside in my garden today. And I've read through all of your KWL charts to get an idea of what you know already. A lot of y'all have said that density has to do with how close molecules are together, how close things are together. And you're right, it has to do with that. A lot of the things y'all wanted to learn was about how to calculate it, and why it was important.

So we'll kind of start that discussion. Let's start back from the beginning of density, and what it means in the sense of how much stuff is packed into this particular space. What I have here is going to be a nice little square of weeds (Figure 1 Density Before Weeding).

Okay, Dr. P doesn't like weeds very much. But we can see that the weeds have taken over the square here. And that, that's pretty dense actually. In other words, there's a lot of weeds in that particular square.

Now, what I can do to make this less dense, is I can pull the weeds out. And as I pull the weeds out, there's more space in between each of the particular areas. So I keep pulling weeds out. And look, there's less weeds, meaning less dense (Figure 2 Density After Weeding).

And I can keep going and thinking this is easy. Okay. And you can see, as you go through that inside the square, there's a lot less weeds in the area. I'm taking molecules out of the given space. Now if we watch this for a long time, the weeds would probably grow back and its density would increase. But right now, I'm happy with taking the weeds out.

Okay. So why is this important? Aside from Dr. P having no more weeds in his yard?

Well, we think of this in the sense of population density, we use the word where things are a lot closer together, population, in this case, meaning animals or people. It might become important.

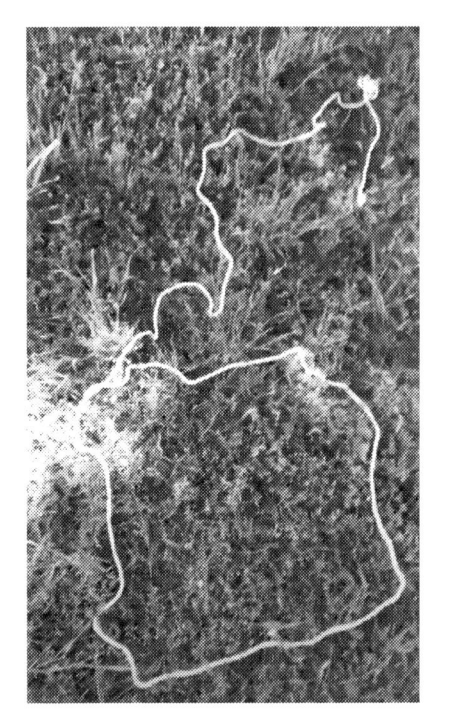 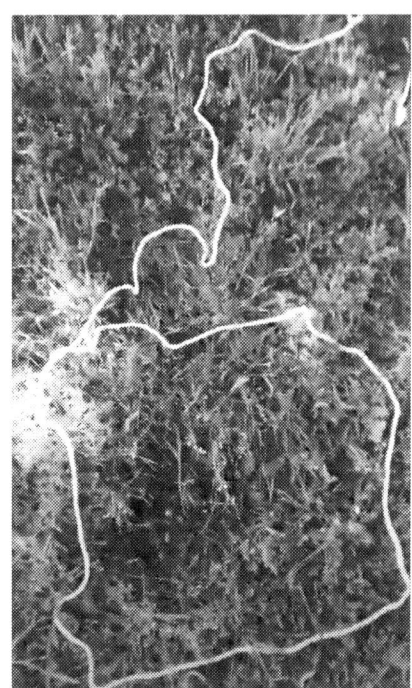

FIGURE 16.1. Density Before Weeding

FIGURE 16.2. Density After Weeding

If we think of those weeds as individual people, then the more dense they are far more likely to come into contact with each other. There are more people or more weeds, in this case shoved into a particular space. And I think that we can relate that to our current global pandemic pretty easily. In places that have a high population density, there's going to be more people in contact closer together, and so it'd be easier for our virus to spread.

Now, if we do things like social distancing, where we take those individual people, and we keep them apart from each other, then all of a sudden our population density starts to decrease, and it makes it harder for the virus to spread. So whether it's weeds or people, the idea of having fewer items in a particular space drives at the heart of what density is all about. Alright, this is enough for our first introduction video. In the next video, I'm going to do a different demonstration to talk a little bit more about some of the facts of density. See you then.

APPENDIX 2

Density with Legos Video on Vimeo. Authors have uploaded and made the video available at https://vimeo.com/user166378105/review/676130321/8b8c1f3ae5

APPENDIX 3

Calculate Density Video on Vimeo. Authors have uploaded and made the video available at https://vimeo.com/user166378105/review/676131241/5b0edaa884

Density Word Problems

Use the following formula to answer the problems. You must **SHOW** your work!

$$density = \frac{mass}{volume}$$

or, in short form:

$$d = \frac{m}{V}$$

1. What is the density of carbon dioxide gas if 0.196 g occupies a volume of 100 mL?

2. A block of wood **3.0 cm** on each side and has a mass of 27 g. What is the density of this block? (Hint, find the volume first)

3. An irregularly shaped stone was lowered into a graduated cylinder holding a volume of water equal to 2.0 mL. The height of the water rose to 7.0 mL. If the mass of the stone was 25 g, what was its density? (Hint: find the volume by seeing how much the water went up)

4. A 10.0 cm^3 sample of copper has a mass of 89.6 g. What is the density of copper?

5. Silver has a density of 10.5 g/cm^3 and gold has a density of 19.3 g/cm^3. Which would have a greater mass, 5 cm^3 of silver or 5 cm^3 of gold?

6. Five mL of ethanol has a mass of 3.9 g and 5.0 mL of benzene has a mass of 4.4 g. Which liquid is denser?

7. A rock occupies a volume of 20 cm^3 and has a mass of 54 g. Find the density of this rock.

8. A cube made of an unknown material has a **height of 9cm**. The mass of this cube is 3645 g. Calculate the density of this cube given this information. (Hint: Remember cubes have all three sides the same length)

CHAPTER 17

DIGGING INTO ROCKS & MINERALS THROUGH SCIENCE OLYMPIAD'S MY SO PROGRAM

Lucas Gobel
Indiana University

John Loehr and Katrina Pavlik
Science Olympiad

LESSON PLAN OVERVIEW

The following lesson is a modified version of the MY SO lesson plan on Rocks & Minerals. MY SO is a program developed by Science Olympiad that provides a 9-month, calendar-based set of supports to keep individuals engaged in science learning at home, at school, or after school. MY SO is available to students, families, afterschool providers and classroom teachers, regardless of whether they are involved in Science Olympiad. Each themed month is built from popular Science Olympiad events and offers free resources like this lesson plan that can be used at home or at school; Science Olympiad STEM Sessions, webinars, and interviews with leading experts in the field about careers and workforce (available on the Science Olympiad TV YouTube channel); and the option to participate in STEM Showdowns—national-level, online Science Olympiad tests. MY SO can be used as a standalone activity, a classroom activity, or to support a Science Olympiad team.

Teaching and Learning Online: Science for Secondary Grade Levels, pages 241–258.
Copyright © 2023 by Information Age Publishing
www.infoagepub.com
241

The lesson plan is written for middle school students who may be learning from home or school but it can be modified to fit the needs of high school students as well. Students will begin the lesson by reviewing previous knowledge about rocks and minerals. Next, students will extend that learning through an online activity to practice using different testing techniques to identify mystery rocks and minerals. Students will also have the opportunity for independent learning by reviewing and taking notes on slide shows with information about rocks and minerals. Then, students can choose from a variety of activities or additional resources for further exploration. Finally, tests are included as a learning assessment.

Discipline: Earth Materials and Systems

Grades: 6th through 9th grades

CONNECTIONS TO NGSS AND THREE-DIMENSIONAL LEARNING

Performance Expectations:
Middle School Physical Science
- **Code:** MS-PS1 (Middle School Matter and Its Interactions)
- **Domain:** Physical Science (PS)
- **MS-PS1-2:** Analyze and interpret data on the properties of substances before and after the substances interact to determine if a chemical reaction has occurred.

Middle School Earth and Space Science
- **Code:** MS-ESS1 (Middle School Earth's Place in the Universe)
- **Domain:** Earth and Space Sciences
- **MS-ESS 1–4:** Construct a scientific explanation based on evidence from rock strata for how the geologic time scale is used to organize Earth's 4.6 billion-year-old history.
- **Code:** MS-ESS2 (Middle School Earth's Systems)
- **Domain:** Earth and Space Sciences
- **MS-ESS 2–1:** Develop a model to describe the cycling of Earth's materials and the flow of energy that drives this process. MS-ESS 2–2. Construct an explanation based on evidence for how geoscience processes have changed Earth's surface at varying times and spatial scales.
- **MS-ESS 2–3:** Analyze and interpret data on the distribution of fossils and rocks, continental shapes, and seafloor structures to provide evidence of past plate motions.

High School Physical Sciences
- **Code:** HS-PS2 (High School Motion and Stability: Forces and Interactions)
- **Domain:** Physical Sciences
- **HS-PS 2–6:** Communicate scientific and technical information about why the molecular-level structure is important in the functioning of designed materials.

High School Earth and Space Science
- **Code:** HS-ESS1 (High School Earth's Place in the Universe)
- **Domain:** Earth and Space Sciences
- **HS-ESS 1–6:** Apply scientific reasoning and evidence from ancient Earth materials, meteorites, and other planetary surfaces to construct an account of Earth's formation and early history.
- **Code:** HS-ESS2 (High School Earth's Systems)
- **Domain:** Earth and Space Sciences
- **HS-ESS 2–1:** Develop a model to illustrate how Earth's internal and surface processes operate at different spatial and temporal scales to form continental and ocean-floor features.
- **HS-ESS 2–3:** Develop a model based on evidence of Earth's interior to describe the cycling of matter by thermal convection.

Science and Engineering Practices:

Constructing Explanations and Designing Solutions

Constructing explanations and designing solutions in 9–12 builds on K–8 experiences and progresses to explanations and designs supported by multiple and independent student-generated sources of evidence consistent with scientific ideas, principles, and theories.
- Design, evaluate, and refine a solution to a complex real-world problem based on scientific knowledge, student-generated sources of evidence, prioritized criteria, and trade-off considerations.

Disciplinary Core Ideas:

Ecosystem Dynamics, Functioning, and Resilience (LS2.C)
- Moreover, anthropogenic changes (induced by human activity) in the environment, including habitat destruction, pollution, introduction of invasive species, overexploitation, and climate change, can disrupt an ecosystem and threaten the survival of some species.

Biodiversity and Humans (LS4.D)
- Biodiversity is increased by the formation of new species (speciation) and decreased by the loss of species (extinction). *(secondary)*
- Humans depend on the living world for the resources and other benefits provided by biodiversity. However, human activity also has adverse impacts on biodiversity through overpopulations, overexploitation, habitat destruction, pollution, introduction of invasive species, and climate change. Thus, sustaining biodiversity so that ecosystem functioning and productivity are maintained is essential to supporting and enhancing life on Earth. Sustaining biodiversity also aids humanity by preserving landscapes

or recreational or inspirational value. *(secondary) (Note: This Disciplinary Core Idea is also addressed by HS-LS4-6).*

Developing Possible Solutions (ETS1.B)
• When evaluating solutions, it is important to consider a range of constraints including cost, safety, reliability and aesthetics and to consider social, cultural and environmental impacts. *(secondary)*

Crosscutting Concepts:

Stability and Change (HS-LS2-7)
• Much of science deals with constructing explanations of how things change and how they remain stable.

TEACHING AND LEARNING ONLINE 5E LESSON PLAN

Grade: 6th through 9th grades   **Topic(s):** Rocks and Minerals

Guiding Question(s): What are the identifying characteristics of different rocks and minerals? What tests can one perform to identify a rock or mineral?

Performance Expectation(s): Students will build knowledge and understanding around various rocks and minerals, including how they are formed, where they are found, and how they can be identified.

Science & Engineering Practices:	Disciplinary Core Ideas:	Crosscutting Concepts:
• Analyzing and Interpreting Data	• PS1.A: Structure and Properties of Matter	• Patterns
• Constructing Explanations and Designing Solutions	• PS1.B: Chemical Reactions	• Scale, Proportion, and Quantity
• Developing and Using Models	• PS1.C: Nuclear Processes	• Stability and Change
• Obtaining, Evaluating, and Communicating Information	• PS2.B: Types of Interactions	• Structure and Function
- -	• PS4.A: Wave Properties	• Energy and Matter
Connections to Nature of Science	• ESS1.C: The History of Planet Earth	- - - - - - - - - - - - - - - -
• Scientific Knowledge is Based on Empirical Evidence	• ESS2.A: Earth's Materials and Systems	*Connections to Engineering, Technology, and Applications of Science*
• Scientific Knowledge is Open to Revision in Light of New Evidence	• ESS2.B: Plate Tectonics and Large-Scale System Interactions	• Interdependence of Science, Engineering, and Technology
• Science Models, Laws, Mechanisms, and Theories Explain Natural Phenomena	• ESS1.C: The History of Planet Earth	
	• ESS2.C: The Roles of Water in Earth's Surface Processes	

BACKGROUND INFORMATION

Prior Student Knowledge:
This lesson was created for students with varying experiences and knowledge bases around rocks and minerals. The classroom teacher can gauge student understanding during the first two exercises to assess additional needs for resources.

Possible Preconceptions / Misconceptions:
- Students may assume that rocks and minerals are similar or are formed in similar ways.
- Students may assume that the only way to identify a rock is by looking at it.

Source Notes:
- Annenberg Learner. (n.d.). Rock Cycle Interactive. https://www.learner.org/series/interactive-rock-cycle/
- Bill Nye. (n.d.). Rocks and Soil. https://billnye.com/the-science-guy/rocks-and-soil
- ExploreLearning. (n.d.). Explorelearning Gizmos: Math & Science Virtual Labs and simulations. https://gizmos.explorelearning.com/
- Geology Kitchen. (n.d.). A Free Earth Science Video Resource for Educators. Esteem Education Co. https://www.esteemeducation.org/geology-kitchen/
- Poarch, M. (2003). Sugar Rock Cycle [worksheet]. Science-class.net. http://science-class.net/Geology/rocks/sugar_rock_cycle.pdf
- Poarch, M. (2007). Crayon Rock Cycle [worksheet]. Science-class.net. http://science-class.net/Geology/rocks/crayon_rock_cycle.pdf
- Rasmussen, Jan C. (2010). How to Identify Rocks and Minerals [booklet]. Arizona Mining and Mineral Museum. https://janrasmussen.com/pdfs/rock%20and%20mineral%20identification%202012.pdf
- Science Olympiad. (n.d.). MY SO. https://soinc.org/myso/
- Science Olympiad TV. (2021, December 15). Science Olympiad MY SO STEM Session—Rocks and Minerals [video]. YouTube. https://www.youtube.com/watch?v=b-MoNtkJGDs
- TeachEngineering. (n.d.). Rock Cycle. https://www.teachengineering.org/curricularunits/view/cub_rock_curricularunit

LESSON PLAN

ENGAGE:

This activity should take approximately 5–10 minutes from start to finish.

Activity Description
In this part of the lesson, the student will manipulate a Snickers bar in multiple ways which will allow them to make inferences about their observations and the

Rock Cycle. The Rock Cycle is a core concept for all of the following activities, so it is important that students have some base knowledge of the various processes and stages involved. This activity will allow students to develop and connect that knowledge to a hands-on activity.

Materials
- One (1) Snickers candy bar (Fun Size or Bite Size piece would work too)
- One (1) copy of the Student Instruction Sheet (in Appendix)
- One (1) copy of Student Instruction Sheet Answers (in Appendix)
- Napkin, Paper Towel, or Hand wipes
- Pen or pencil
- Access to a microwave oven

EXPLORE:

This activity should take most students between 30 and 45 minutes.

Activity Description
In this activity, the student will further explore minerals by performing a series of standard identification tests. While this activity can be done in person using a set of mineral specimens and the necessary tools, these items might not be available to everyone. For the purposes of this lesson, the experiment will be conducted online using the free Mineral Identification Gizmo from ExploreLearning (https://gizmos.explorelearning.com/). The teacher can sign up for a free trial account by visiting the website and clicking on the button "Sign Up Free."

Materials
- A computer with internet access and sound
- Headphones (optional)
- One (1) pencil or pen

Procedure:
1. Sign up for the Explore Learning Mineral Identification Gizmo: visit https://gizmos.explorelearning.com and click on "Find Gizmos" at the top of the page. In the search bar, type "mineral" and then click on the picture for the "Mineral Identification" activity to enter the introductory page.
2. Access the Student Exploration Sheet: within the introductory page, click on any type of document (Word, PDF, Google Doc, etc.) listed under "Student Exploration Sheet" on the right-hand side of the page. Print out or download the document.
3. Start the activity: Click on "Launch Gizmo" on the top right-hand side of the page. Follow the questions and practice activities listed on the "Student Exploration Sheet: Mineral Identification" worksheet.

Note: If a hands-on activity is preferred, Science Olympiad's partner, Ward's Science, sells the Elementary Science Olympiad: Rock Hound identification kit that can be used at school or home (https://www.ward-sci.com/store/catalog/product.jsp?catalog_number=470330-056). This kit contains a starter set of rocks and minerals, as well as the necessary testing and safety equipment and instructions.

EXPLAIN:

This activity should take between 30 minutes and 1 hour to complete.

Activity Description

In the **EXPLAIN** phase, students review the material to learn more about identifying various rocks and minerals and understanding how they are formed. It is recommended that the student takes notes on what he or she reads on the slide shows. There are many different note-taking systems in use. Students should use one that is supported by the school's teachers and/or a method with which they feel comfortable. Science Olympiad recommends Cornell Notes as it is widely used, offers great flexibility, and is supported by a wealth of training materials.

Materials

- MY SO Rocks & Minerals Slide Shows (available at soinc.org/MYSO)
- MY SO Rocks & Minerals Note Sheets (available at soinc.org/MYSO)
- Laptop or computer
- Paper
- Pencil or Pen

Procedure:

1. Download the MY SO Rocks & minerals Slide Shows & Note Sheets from soinc.org/MYSO.
2. Find a quiet place to sit and review the slide show taking notes on the material that you feel is important. If you do not already use a note-taking method, then Science Olympiad recommends the Cornell Note Taking System.
3. As you read through the slide shows and take notes, if there is something you don't understand, then write it down and use the recommended extension resources to find answers during the ELABORATE phase.

Vocabulary: Rock, Mineral, Inclusion, Streak, Sedimentary, Metamorphic, Igneous, Pressure, Hardness, Cycle, Mohs Scale, Weathering, Erosion, Elements, Acid, pH, Chemicals, Chemical Reaction, Luster

ELABORATE:

Activity Description
In the ELABORATE phase, students have the opportunity to deepen their knowledge, address remaining misunderstandings, and expand learning to new but related topics. All these things are accomplished through a mix of learning methods, such as readings, videos, hands-on activities, and online simulations, chosen by the students themselves to best meet individual learning needs.

The activity in the ELABORATE phase is student-directed, so there is no specific timeframe for how long any activities in this phase should take or how long students may spend on this phase at all. It is generally recommended that a student selects and completes at least one activity either from the list recommended here or of their own choosing. Once the student is ready to move on from the ELABORATE phase he or she should move to EVALUATE and complete one of the brief quizzes provided.

Materials
Since the ELABORATE phase can go in so many directions, we cannot provide a comprehensive and inclusive list of materials that will be used in this learning step as we have previously. Instead, what we have done here is to provide some recommendations of possible activities. These activities are divided into two broad categories: Videos and Readings and Hands-on Activities. For Videos and Readings, we have identified open-source online courses, lessons, textbooks, and videos that apply to the topic of Rocks & Minerals. For Hands-on Activities, we have identified simple activities that can be conducted at home using materials either found around the house, acquired from "Big Box" stores, or found in pharmacies. Additionally, we have listed free online learning activities.

Videos & Recordings
Geology Kitchen https://www.esteemeducation.org/geology-kitchen/

> This link is a free, twelve-episode, online video series that uses food metaphors to explain Earth Science concepts in a fun and entertaining way. There are also activities and other resources that the student should feel free to try out.

Bill Nye the Science Guy's Rocks and Soil Video https://billnye.com/the-science-guy/rocks-and-soil

> In this brief video clip, Bill Nye provides an entertaining overview of essential characteristics of rocks and the processes that convert them to soil.

How to Identify Rocks & Minerals by Dr. Jan C. Rasmussen https://janrasmussen.com/pdfs/rock%20and%20mineral%20identification%202012.pdf

Dr. Jan C. Rasmussen, an Arizona educator and former curator of the Arizona Mining and Mineral Museum, created this booklet regarding how to identify rocks and minerals. In addition to helping students understand the tests they need to perform and how to interpret data they collect, the book also identifies the key specimens that students and teachers will want to have on hand to create their own collection.

Hands-On & Simulation Activities

1. For this activity students roll a die and travel through different stations to learn about the rock cycle. After their journey, they use the information from the "trip" to create a comic strip (created by Stacy Baker, Pleasant Hill School, Peoria, IL). Student Worksheets posted on MY SO webpage (soinc.org/myso).
2. Science-class.net has provided a number of different Rocks and Mineral activities including this Crayon Rock cycle activity: http://science-class. net/Geology/rocks/crayon_rock_cycle.pdf and this sugar cube rock cycle activity: http://science-class.net/Geology/rocks/modeling_the_rock_ cycle_adv.pdf
3. Learner.org has a great interactive that helps students distinguish between the multiple different types of rocks: https://www.learner.org/series/interactive-rock-cycle/
4. TeachEngineering has a unit on the rock cycle that teaches students on how stress affects rocks and minerals: https://www.teachengineering. org/curricularunits/view/cub_rock_curricularunit

Projects & Culminating Activities

- Obtain 15 different types of minerals. Ask your teacher if you can borrow a streak plate. Make a data table of 15 minerals determining their color, luster, streak, specific gravity, cleavage, fracture, and hardness. In your write up include some uses for these minerals.
- Create a board game about minerals. Be sure to include critical vocabulary such as color, luster, streak, specific gravity, cleavage, fracture, and hardness. Also include common uses of minerals.
- Create a rhyme or rap about minerals. Include important vocabulary such as color, luster, streak, specific gravity, cleavage, fracture, and hardness. You might also include the properties of all minerals and/or the uses of some common minerals. Pick and choose on which to focus.
- Create a poster that helps students understand the processes involved in the formation of rocks.
- Create a video for your teacher that will help students understand the processes involved in the formation of rocks.
- Record a podcast where you are an Earth Science teacher. The podcasts need to help students understand the processes involved in the formation of rocks.

- Create a rock cycle poster that has four sections: igneous, metamorphic, sedimentary, and rock cycle. Have five facts about each type of rock in each section, and a diagram of the rock cycle drawn, labeled, and colored.

EVALUATE:

Formative Monitoring (Questioning / Discussion):

ENGAGE Phase
- Student Activity Worksheet—The objective of this sheet is to help the student make the connection from a rather common item like a Snickers bar, and the transformations that it can undergo, to the various types of rocks and the Rock Cycle. Since there a variety of observations that the student can make, any responses given are entirely formative since they represent the student's prior knowledge and the connection to the topic at hand.

EXPLORE Phase
- Rock and Minerals Gizmo Activity—As part of the ExploreLearning Gizmo, the students will not only have the opportunity to practice a variety of tests used to identify minerals but also there is a part of the activity where students will be expected to identify a series of unknowns. The process of unknown identification can serve as either a formative or summative evaluation depending on teacher needs. If more formative information is needed on the students, then initial unknowns can be solved as a whole group activity or in the presence of the teacher. If this tack is taken, then key questions to ask would include:
  - Why would you perform that test?
  - What might you expect to see?
  - How does that result influence the next test you want to perform?
  The goal here is to understand the students' thinking to see if they are truly understanding and recognizing patterns, thereby, limiting the tests conducted to only the ones necessary to identify the unknown versus running every possible test just to have "all the data."

EXPLAIN Phase
- Student Note Sheets—If the teachers choose to use the provided Student Note Sheets, then these documents could be reviewed as a Formative Assessment to see if the students are able to identify the key information from the presentations.
- Whip Around with Pass—At the end of each class the teacher could conduct a "whip around with pass" activity where each student offers up one new piece of information that he or she learned during the presentation. It is recommended that students be allowed the option to pass their turn if they feel they have nothing to contribute or are uncomfortable speaking.

- Exit/Entrance Ticket—Another possible formative knowledge check includes students completing either an exit or entrance ticket where they write down one piece of knowledge they have gained on the topic, along with one question that they still have. These tickets could be collected before the students leave class to help prepare the next lesson or could be submitted upon entry the next day.

ELABORATE Phase

- Depending upon how the ELABORATE Phase is structured, the assigned activities include formative items that can be used. If there is no common activity, then it is entirely appropriate to probe students with the following questions:
  - What was the most interesting thing you've learned so far?
  - What have you learned that surprised you the most?
  - Are you still confused by anything that you have learned?
  - Out of all the material you've looked at, what has been the hardest to understand?
  - What is the biggest question that you still have?

  These questions can be asked as the teacher circulates the room or serve as the basis of an Exit/Entrance Ticket.

Summative Assessment (Quiz / Project / Report):

Activity Description

In the EVALUATE phase, students can assess learning as well as areas for further study by taking either of the two brief tests: one for middle school students and one for high school students. Students may refer to notes they have previously taken during the lesson or try to answer as many of the questions as is possible without the use of notes, depending on the needs of the teacher.

Once tests have been graded, students may go through and review any questions that were wrong. This step is important in the learning process since it allows the student to examine mistakes to determine what led to the mistake. The EVALUATE phase should take about an hour to 90 minutes to take and grade the test.

Materials

The Middle School (Division B) Rocks & Minerals test and answer key can be accessed online at www.soinc.org/MYSO. The High School (Division C) Rocks & Minerals test and answer key can be accessed online at www.soinc.org/MYSO.

ADDITIONAL LESSON INFO

Accommodations and Modifications:

Various accommodations can be used, depending on the needs of the students, including printing, or using technology to increase print size of text, translating relevant vocabulary words into students' native language, scribing on behalf of a student, creating cue cards with pictures for multi-step directions, and allowing for open note tests or extra test-taking time. Please refer to students' learning plans for specific needs.

LESSON NARRATIVE

The purpose of the activities in this lesson plan is twofold: review and/or introduce students to the concept of the Rock Cycle and practice identifying rocks and minerals through a series of basic tests. The skills practiced in this lesson plan are useful for a variety of careers and educational pathways, in addition to being a handy skill when students are out in nature. Science Olympiad alumna and geotechnical engineer Tova Peltz works for the Oregon Department of Transportation and manages multi-million-dollar infrastructure projects. She still uses the knowledge and skills she developed in Science Olympiad as a student in her work analyzing soils and planning out projects. Students can learn more about Tova's work by watching the STEM Session on Rocks and Minerals on the Science Olympiad TV YouTube channel here: https://www.youtube.com/user/scienceolympiadtv.

This lesson can be used in a variety of ways, which will be explained below. The original intent of the MY SO program was to offer a STEM learning opportunity to students who were learning from home during the early months of the COVID-19 pandemic. As of the writing of this chapter, most schools across the country have returned to in-person learning and, as a result, we have seen an increase in the use of this curriculum in school by classroom teachers and Science Olympiad coaches and afterschool providers, in addition to students and their families who want to use it at home. The intention of the curriculum is to give students a glimpse into many different aspects of STEM, no matter where they are learning and no matter who might be helping to guide them.

In the **ENGAGE** portion of the lesson plan, students have the opportunity to review their knowledge of the Rock Cycle in a fun hands-on (and maybe delicious) activity with a Snickers bar. The different ingredients of the Snickers bar are good representations of the stages of rock formation, as well as a good visual when reviewing and connecting information later on in the lesson. This activity makes an excellent "Bell Ringer" or "Do Now" in a classroom setting as an individual activity or in pairs, depending on the availability of supplies. For the microwave portion of the activity, a pair of students can complete the activity (using the teachers' lounge microwave, for example) and then report back to the rest of the group. Have extra candy bars on hand so students can sample fresh ones as opposed to eating the ones they have been using to complete their tests but be aware of peanut allergies.

When students are finished with the activity, the worksheet can be self-graded or handed in for grading by the teacher. At this point in the lesson, it is not important that students have the "right" answers to the questions, but rather that they made their best effort to access prior knowledge and recognize the gaps in their current understanding. For students who struggled with all portions of this lesson, the teacher can provide books, websites, and other resources to review or introduce the concepts in the worksheet.

The ENGAGE phase at home: The activity can be done if students are learning from home, either synchronously or asynchronously. The teacher should communicate several days in advance to both students and families that students will need a Snickers bar, plate, knife, and access to a microwave. The worksheet can be printed out or loaded into a document sharing system for online completion (e.g., Google docs).

During the **EXPLORE** section of the lesson plan, students have the opportunity to develop their understanding of how rocks and minerals are categorized and identified. This activity can be done as a hands-on activity, if the appropriate samples and testing materials are available. However, this lesson was designed to work in the classroom or home, so even without hands-on materials, students can learn how attributes like density, acid reaction, and crystal shape contribute to identifying a rock or mineral.

If students will be using the Explore Learning Mineral Identification Gizmo, then the teacher can use the account they created to provide access to all students; individual students do not need to create individual accounts. If each student has access to their own computer, then walk through the worksheet and introductory activity together as a class and allow students to work at their own pace. Students can also work in pairs or the activity can be led by the teacher on an overhead projector as a whole group activity, depending on time, technology availability, and students' prior knowledge. If students are getting frustrated and discouraged, then use your judgement to monitor the students' engagement in the task to ensure that the goal is met without it becoming counterproductive. One option might be to have the students do something else and return to the activity after taking a break.

The EXPLORE phase at home: This activity can be done at home if students have reliable access to a computer and internet connection. The teacher can demonstrate the activity on their own computer by sharing their screen and then staying online while students work independently if students have questions. The worksheet can be printed out or loaded into a document sharing system for online completion (e.g., Google docs).

During the **EXPLAIN** portion of the lesson, the teacher may familiarize themselves with slide shows and "deliver" them as a lecture over the course of a class period or two while students take notes. Students can also break into small groups and tackle parts of the slideshow for note taking that they then share back to the larger group, also known as the jigsaw technique. Finally, students can independently review the slides and take their own notes.

More important than the approach to reviewing the slides is student reflection. The teacher should lead a discussion after the slide review that helps students assess their own understanding and areas for growth and further study. Questions might include:

- What was the most interesting thing you've learned so far?
- What have you learned that surprised you the most?
- Are you still confused by anything that you have learned?
- Out of all the material you've looked at, what has been the hardest to understand?
- What is the biggest question that you still have?

The EXPLAIN phase at home: This portion of the lesson plan can be done at home. If the teacher plans to use the slides in a lecture format, then they can share their screen and talk through the slides. If students are to work independently, then the teacher can send them the slide show files to download and review. Students can take notes in a document sharing platform (e.g., Google docs) or on paper and then scan or take a photo as evidence of their work for the teacher.

The **ELABORATE** phase is designed to facilitate individualized and/or small group learning and exploration. Students can use the activity suggestions in the lesson plan or design their own projects (with teacher approval). They can conduct these activities during the school day or as homework. If this portion of the lesson plan is being used as an assessment, then the teacher should provide a rubric to set expectations and grading. Alternatively, students could develop their own rubrics based on what they hope to learn from the activity.

The **EVALUATE** section of the lesson plan is the culmination of all that has been learned throughout the set of activities. If student work is graded, then the teacher should consider the breadth of work that was done in every phase of the lesson, in addition to student achievement on the final test. If the school's grading and evaluation system is competency-based, then the teacher may offer another chance at taking the test to students who want to improve their scores. The EVALUATE phase at home: This portion of the lesson can be done at home. Students should choose a project to complete based on the materials and equipment they have access to at home (e.g., computer with internet access, rocks and minerals kit).

SUMMARY AND REFLECTION

It is difficult to imagine all possible iterations of this lesson plan. However, we hope that we have helped to build a structure for teaching and learning that is inquiry-based and flexible enough that educators, families, and self-motivated students will find value and enjoyment in the activities. Rock and mineral identification can be a lifelong hobby or a career pursuit, as evidenced by many of our alumni.

TIPS AND ADVICE

- Even if students will be performing rock and mineral identification through an online platform (like ExploreLearning), it is a good idea to have some samples in the classroom so that students can handle them and feel the difference in attributes like smoothness, density, etc.

- Connect student learning to real-life materials that they may come into contact with daily, such as marble countertops, jewelry with stones, or landscaping embellishments that include rocks.

- Extend learning by visiting a local science or lapidary museum that features rocks and minerals. If needed, there may be virtual tours of exhibits available to the public.

- Seek out community volunteers who are jewelry makers or rock collectors and have them speak to the group about their interests and showcase their collections.

- Depending on the location of the school and climate, the class could take a short nature walk and collect rocks that appear to be native to the area. Afterwards, students can use the identification techniques to label them. Connect this lesson to known geologic history of the community.

RESOURCE NOTES

Name of Resource	Primary Website	How to Locate the Resource Online
Annenberg Learner	https://www.learner.org/	Go to https://www.learner.org/. In the search bar at the center of the screen, type in "rock cycle interactive" and click on the submit button. Click on the box with the same name to go to the interactive lesson. https://www.learner.org/series/interactive-rock-cycle/
Bill Nye	https://billnye.com/	Go to https://billnye.com/. At the top right-hand side of the screen, click on "Learn" and use the drop-down menu to select "Episode Guide." Scroll down the screen and click on "Rocks and Soil" under the "Planetary Science" column. https://billnye.com/the-science-guy/rocks-and-soil
Esteem Education Co.	https://www.esteemeducation.org/	Visit https://www.esteemeducation.org/. On the top of the screen, click on "Geology Kitchen." Choose from the available resources (videos, lesson plans, and experiments). https://www.esteemeducation.org/geology-kitchen/
Jan Rasmussen	https://janrasmussen.com	Visit https://janrasmussen.com. At the top of the screen, click on "Publications." Scroll down the screen to the section labeled "Popular Geology." Click on the hyperlink in the second listing, entitled "Rasmussen, Jan C. 2010, How to Identify Rocks and Minerals…" to access the PDF of the booklet. https://janrasmussen.com/pdfs/rock%20and%20mineral%20identification%202012.pdf

Name of Resource	Primary Website	How to Locate the Resource Online
ExploreLearning	https://gizmos.explorelearning.com/	Visit https://gizmos.explorelearning.com and click on "Find Gizmos" at the top of the page. In the search bar, type "mineral" and then click on the picture for the "Mineral Identification" activity to enter the introductory page. To access the Student Exploration Sheet—within the introductory page, click on any type of document (Word, PDF, Google Doc, etc.) listed under "Student Exploration Sheet" on the right-hand side of the page. Print out or download the document. To start the activity: Click on "Launch Gizmo" on the top right-hand side of the page. Follow the questions and practice activities listed on the "Student Exploration Sheet: Mineral Identification" worksheet. https://gizmos.explorelearning.com/index.cfm?method=cResource.dspDetail&ResourceID=640
Science-class.net	http://science-class.net/	Visit http://science-class.net/. On the left-hand side of the screen, click on "Geology." In the middle of that screen, you'll see a list of geology topics. Click on "Rocks and Minerals." In the middle of the page, under "Hands-on Lessons, Labs, & Activities," click on either "Crayon Rock Cycle" or "Another version of the sugar cube investigation" to access the suggested activities. http://science-class.net/Geology/rocks/crayon_rock_cycle.pdf http://science-class.net/Geology/rocks/sugar_rock_cycle.pdf
Science Olympiad	https://www.soinc.org/	Visit https://www.soinc.org/. Click on "Menu" at the top, left-hand side of the screen. A menu will drop down, and on the top right-hand side of the drop-down menu, under "Programs," click on "MY SO." To find relevant lesson plans and resources, you may need to scroll down the page for the 2021-2022 Resources list. Follow the directions to access the resources. https://soinc.org/myso/
Teach Engineering	https://www.teachengineering.org	Visit https://www.teachengineering.org. On the top right-hand side of the screen, click into the green search bar with magnifying glass. Type "rock cycle" in the box. Click on the top listed item "Rock Cycle—Unit" to access the lesson materials. https://www.teachengineering.org/curricularunits/view/cub_rock_curricularunit
YouTube (Science Olympiad TV channel)	https://www.youtube.com/	Visit https://www.youtube.com/. In the search bar at the top of the screen, type "Science Olympiad TV." Click on the Science Olympiad TV icon or title. Under the screen header, click on the magnifying glass search function. Type in the word "rocks." Click on the video labeled "Science Olympiad MY SO STEM Session—Rocks and Minerals" to view the video. https://www.youtube.com/watch?v=b-MoNtkJGDs

DISCUSSION QUESTIONS

1. For students who have not previously developed an interest in earth science, how might this lesson spark an interest for them?
2. Why is it important for students to be able to home in quickly on relevant tests to identify rocks and minerals? What are other applications for this skill?
3. How can this lesson contribute to future lessons on horticulture and agriculture?

REFERENCES

Annenberg Learner. (n.d.). *Rock cycle interactive.* https://www.learner.org/series/interactive-rock-cycle/

Bill Nye. (n.d.). *Rocks and soil.* https://billnye.com/the-science-guy/rocks-and-soil

ExploreLearning. (n.d.). *Explorelearning gizmos: Math & science virtual labs and simulations.* https://gizmos.explorelearning.com/

Geology Kitchen. (n.d.). *A free earth science video resource for educators.* Esteem Education Co. https://www.esteemeducation.org/geology-kitchen/

Poarch, M. (2007). *Crayon rock cycle* [worksheet]. Science-class.net. http://science-class.net/Geology/rocks/crayon_rock_cycle.pdf

Poarch, M. (2003). *Sugar rock cycle* [worksheet]. Science-class.net. http://science-class.net/Geology/rocks/sugar_rock_cycle.pdf

Rasmussen, Jan C. (2010). *How to identify rocks and minerals* [booklet]. Arizona Mining and Mineral Museum. https://janrasmussen.com/pdfs/rock%20and%20mineral%20identification%202012.pdf

Science Olympiad. (n.d.). *MY SO.* https://soinc.org/myso/

Science Olympiad TV. (2021, December 15). *Science Olympiad MY SO STEM session— rocks and minerals* [video]. YouTube. https://www.youtube.com/watch?v=b-MoNt-kJGDs

TeachEngineering. (n.d.). *Rock Cycle.* https://www.teachengineering.org/curricularunits/view/cub_rock_curricularunit

APPENDIX

Rock Cycle Student Worksheet

Name_____Period_____

Materials:
- A Snickers bar; Fun Size
- Access to a microwave
- Napkin, Paper Towel, or Hand wipes
- Pen or pencil

1. Cut the Snickers bar in half. Write down three observations about what you see:

   Answers may vary here but ideally you would see observations that indicate the student recognizes: different layers (i.e.; wrapped in chocolate, caramel) and inclusions (i.e.; peanuts, caramel which would allow them to connect what they are observing to a sedimentary rock.

2. Take the same bar and smash it with your hand. Write three observations about what you see:

   Answers may vary here but ideally you would see observations that indicate the student recognizes: that the different layers are no longer present (i.e.; flat, no layers, smooshed together) but some inclusions remain (i.e.; peanuts) which would allow them to connect what they are observing to a metamorphic rock.

3. Now place the Snickers bar and place it in a microwave for 30 seconds. Write down three observations about what you see:

   Answers may vary here but ideally you would see observations that indicate the student recognizes: that the different layers are no longer present (i.e.; flat, no layers, melted together, gooey, runny) and the inclusions have been "moved out" (i.e.; peanuts on top) which would allow them to connect what they are observing to an igneous rock.

4. What type of rock would the Snickers bar cut in half represent?
   Sedimentary

5. What type of rock would the smashed bar represent?
   Metamorphic

6. What type of rock would the melted bar represent?
   Igneous

7. What were the processes involved in making each rock model?

   Sedimentary – Depositing Layers
   Metamorphic – Pressure
   Igneous - Heat

 Science Olympiad, Inc. (c) 2021

5

CHAPTER 18

A LOOK INSIDE THE ATOM

The Basic Building Block of Matter and the Foundation in an Online Science Course

Natasha Hillsman Johnson
University of Toledo

Sophia Jeong
The Ohio State University

LESSON PLAN OVERVIEW

Atomic structure has always been one of our favorite topics to teach at the secondary level. It is often the first-time students have been exposed to key concepts related to the atom including models of the atom, electron configuration, and valence electrons. Many students are intimidated by the chemistry content, but we have found that a successful introduction to atomic structure opens the door for a positive experience in the chemistry course.

Our perspective on teaching online has shifted over the years based on the role. Between the two of us, we are fortunate to have experienced virtual instruction as a teacher, as a parent, as an administrator, and as an education professor. It is our belief that effective teachers are often able to easily transition their instructional practices into a virtual or blended format. While online instruction creates

Teaching and Learning Online: Science for Secondary Grade Levels, pages 259–279.
Copyright © 2023 by Information Age Publishing
www.infoagepub.com

a unique opportunity to highlight excellent teaching practices, it can also draw attention to any shortcomings at the district, school, or teacher level. Using a 5E Model of Instruction (SDCOE, 2002) on atomic structure for context, we will offer best practices in online science instruction that can benefit all stakeholders. The most important lesson of this chapter is that regardless of the learning environment, the elements of good teaching will always be the same (Teach Remotely, 2002). The Covid-19 global pandemic has forever changed the K-12 educational system; however, educators must continue to focus on their science content, pedagogical practices, and assessment methods. Our knowledge of the "educative" Teacher Performance Assessment, edTPA, has consistently demonstrated that the extent to which an educator can plan along these three dimensions will determine teaching effectiveness—both in-person and online.

The rationale for the instructional approaches selected in this lesson are based on a consistent barrier experienced by teachers in a virtual setting: student motivation. According to Pintrich and Schunk (2002), motivation is the process of instigating and sustaining goal-directed behavior. Motivation plays an important role in the learning process. While motivation cannot be directly observed as an individual characteristic, it can be inferred from behavior and academic choices (Schunk, 2008). It is an explanatory concept that facilitates better understanding of student behavior (Schunk, 2008). When faced with academic difficulty, a motivated student will expend greater effort rather than quit (Schunk, 2008). One theory that attempts to offer guidance to educators seeking to incorporate key elements of motivation design into their instruction is the ARCS model. The ARCS model, developed by John Keller, consists of four major categories: attention, relevance, confidence, and satisfaction. The ARCS model is closely aligned with the 5E Model of Instruction. Using the 5E Model of Instruction as a framework for this instructional sequence, this chapter will discuss how atomic structure can be taught online in a manner that captures students' attention, creates content relevance, builds confidence, and leads to a high level of satisfaction with learners.

CONNECTIONS TO NGSS AND THREE-DIMENSIONAL LEARNING

The Disciplinary Core Idea central to this lesson is Matter and Its Interactions (PS1), specifically Structure and Properties of Matter (PS1.A): Each atom has a charged substructure consisting of a nucleus, which is made of protons and neutrons, surrounded by electrons. (HS-PS1-1). This standard is addressed in middle/high school physical science and chemistry courses. Atomic structure is an essential concept to science learners. The extent to which students develop mastery of the structure of the atom will determine their ability to learn more advanced concepts related to the periodic table, bonding, nomenclature, and chemical reactions.

Students' Performance Expectations

- **Code:** MS-PS1 or HS-PS1 (Matter and Its Interactions)
- **Domain:** Physical Sciences (PS)
- **MS-PS1-1:** Develop models to describe the atomic composition of simple molecules and extended structures.
- **HS-PS1-1:** Use the periodic table as a model to predict the relative properties of elements based on the patterns of electrons in the outermost energy level of atoms.

Science and Engineering Practices

Developing and Using Models (MS-PS1)

- Develop a model to predict and/or describe phenomena.

Developing and Using Models (HS-PS1)

- Use a model to predict the relationships between systems or between components of a system.

Disciplinary Core Ideas

Structure and Properties of Matter (MS-PS1.A)

- Substances are made from different types of atoms, which combine with one another in various ways. Atoms form molecules that range in size from two to thousands of atoms.
- Solids may be formed from molecules, or they may be extended structures with repeating subunits (e.g., crystals).

Structure and Properties of Matter (HS-PS1.A)

- Each atom has a charged substructure consisting of a nucleus, which is made of protons and neutrons, surrounded by electrons.
- The periodic table orders elements horizontally by the number of protons in the atom's nucleus and places those with similar chemical properties in columns. The repeating patterns of this table reflect patterns of outer electron states.

Crosscutting Concepts

Scale, Proportion, and Quantity (MS-PS1.A)

- Time, space, and energy phenomena can be observed at various scales using models to study systems that are too large or too small.

Patterns (HS-PS1.A)

- Different patterns may be observed at each of the scales at which a system is studied and can provide evidence for causality in explanations of phenomena.

TEACHING AND LEARNING ONLINE 5E LESSON PLAN

Grade: 6–12   **Topic(s):** Atomic Structure

Guiding Question(s):
- Why is it important to understand atomic structure?
- What secrets can be revealed in the Periodic Table?
- What do we think an atom "looks like" now?

Performance Expectation(s):
- Students will be able to explain the role of atomic number in determining the identity of an atom.
- Students will be able to distinguish between the subatomic particles in terms of relative charge and mass.
- Students will be able to describe the structure of the nuclear atom, including the locations of the subatomic particles.
- Students will be able to calculate the number of electrons, protons, and neutrons in an atom given its mass number and atomic number.

Science & Engineering Practices:	Disciplinary Core Ideas:	Crosscutting Concepts:
Asking questions	Structure and Properties of Matter	Patterns.
Developing and using models		Scale, proportion, and quantity.
Constructing explanations		

BACKGROUND INFORMATION

Prior Student Knowledge:
- Chemistry is the study of matter, and matter is anything that has mass and takes up space.
- Atoms are the basic building blocks of matter.
- Electrons, protons, and neutrons are subatomic particles found in the atom.

Possible Preconceptions / Misconceptions:
- Only one model of the atom is correct.
- Electrons and protons are the only fundamental particles.
- Electrons are larger than protons.
- Electrons have no mass, just charge.

Source Notes:

- Bill Nye "Atoms" Video is available on School Tube. Search on Google and type "Bill Nye—Atoms, Schooltube." Choose the first search result that is on the SchoolTube site. https://www.schooltube.com/media/Bill+Nye+-+Atoms/1_k7dvbaam.
- Search on Google and type "Bill Nye 'Atoms' worksheet." Search result will bring up a live URL of the PDF version of the Worksheet. https://www.cusd80.com/cms/lib/AZ01001175/Centricity/Domain/6371/BillNyeAtoms.pdf
- Go to https://phet.colorado.edu click on "Simulations," click on "Chemistry," then scroll down and click on "Build an Atom."
- Go to https://phet.colorado.edu. Teachers may need to create an account for full access. Under Teacher Resources, the teacher will have access to Teacher Tips, Video Primer, and Alignment Documents. Under Activities, the teacher can sort student resources by Level, Type, Subject, and Language. Choose the worksheet titled "Build an Atom" created by Moore et al.
- On Google search, type "Flinn Scientific Flame Test Demonstration." Choose the result that is housed in the main FlinnSci website. https://www.flinnsci.com/api/library/Download/7cb7a26bedbb44e1adcef3177936f087
- Visit https://ptable.com/#Properties for an electronic version; or, https://www.sciencegeek.net/tables/tables.shtml for a printable/download version.

LESSON PLAN

ENGAGE:

Opening Activity—Access Prior Learning / Stimulate Interest / Generate Questions:

Question(s):

How many of you (students) cook on a gas stove? [Teacher can observe how many students raise their hand. It may be necessary to explain that gas stoves have an open flame and electric stoves have a heating element that glows orange.]

What happens when you spill a substance into an open flame? [Possible responses: The flame goes out. The flame gets bigger. The flame changes color.]

What would happen if you were boiling water for pasta or cooking pasta and water spilled over? Why does the flame change color? What color does it change? [Possible responses: Water droplets on the hot surface form and move around if you are using an electric stove. You would hear the water droplets "sizzle" as the water spills over.]

Teacher Explanation: The salted water will contain sodium chloride, NaCl. When the NaCl burns, the flame color turns a characteristic orange/yellow color. The color will return to normal when there is no more NaCl present. This phenomenon is the chemistry concept behind fireworks.

Flame Test Demonstration: If the teacher is delivering instruction from a science classroom, then a flame test demonstration could be performed using a variety of chloride salts. [Possible substances: Lithium chloride, sodium chloride, copper chloride, potassium chloride, strontium chloride, copper (II) chloride.] If the teacher is delivering instruction from home or an alternate location, then a flame test video is another option.

EXPLORE: Lesson Description:	**Probing Or Clarifying Questions To Ask While Students Explore:**	**Materials Needed**
Students will engage in a PhET Build an Atom Simulation. They will explore using the Atom portion of the simulation. This activity will allow students to explore the location of protons, electrons, and neutrons in the atom. It will also demonstrate how the number of particles influences the identity, charge, and mass of the atom.	• What happens when we add a proton to the model? • What happens when we add an electron to the model? • What happens when we add a neutron to the model? • What happens if you place a proton/neutron in the electron cloud? … an electron in the nucleus? • What makes an atom stable?… unstable?	Student Chromebooks PhET Lab found at https://phet.colorado.edu/en/simulations/build-an-atom

EXPLAIN:

Concepts Explained and Vocabulary Defined:
This portion of the lesson will begin with the students watching Atoms, a Bill Nye video (up to 10:35). [The entire video should be made available for students through your learning management system (LMS), but the students will only watch the first segment.]

Teacher will present a whole-group lesson on How Atoms Differ. Each student will need access to a periodic table of elements.

Students will learn:
- Atomic number is the number of protons in an atom. It determines the identity of an element. For a neutral atom, the atomic number always equals the number of protons and the number of electrons.
- The mass number represents the sum of the number of protons and neutrons in the nucleus.

- Example: Atomic number for gold, Au is 79. An atom of gold has 79 protons and 79 electrons. The mass number for gold is 197, so gold has 118 neutrons (197–79).
- *It is best to use a Round Robin Teaching Strategy to practice this skill in this sequence using a variety of students:
  - ○ Select an element from the periodic table. Other students should locate the element on the periodic table.
  - ○ What is the atomic number for this element?
  - ○ How many protons are there in this element?
  - ○ How many electrons are there in this element?
- Once the majority of the group has demonstrated proficiency, add the following questions:
  - ○ What is the mass number for this element?
  - ○ How many neutrons are there in this element?
    *Note: You will need to explain the difference between atomic mass and mass number. Additionally, students may need a review of the rules for rounding numbers.

Vocabulary: Atom, Atomic Number, Electron, Electron cloud, Ion, Mass Number, Neutron, Nucleus, Proton

ELABORATE:

Connecting Concepts to the CCC and SEP. Making sense through building models and constructing explanations
Students will complete the Build an Atom Simulation/Worksheet. Students will construct an explanation of how the number of particles influences the identity, charge, and mass of the atom, supporting their explanations with evidence from the PhET lab simulation.

EVALUATE:

Formative Monitoring (Questioning / Discussion):
Teacher observation of classwork.
- Atomic Structure Chart
- Build an Atom Simulation Worksheet
- *Atomic Structure Quiz

Summative Assessment (Quiz / Project / Report):
- Atomic Model Project
- *Atomic Structure Unit Test

ADDITIONAL LESSON INFO

Extension and Contingency Plans: Extensions and various approaches have been included in the Actual Lesson described above. Students who need additional time should be invited to work on the activities during teacher study hall or virtual office hours to complete their work. Approaches towards mastery learning model should be used so that all students can achieve mastery.

Accommodations and Modifications: Students who are struggling would be invited for teacher study hall or virtual office hours to complete their work. Students who are gifted and talented can be accommodated through implementing varying levels of inquiry throughout the activities. Students who are English Language Learners can be accommodated through the use of sentence starters, translation of activities into their native language, and multimodal/multi-representational assessment where appropriate.

LESSON NARRATIVE

Engage

The Engage phase of the lesson is intended to focus students' attention on a problem or phenomenon of interest. In the ARCS model, this correlates to the Attention phase. The goal is to "capture the interest of the learners" as the instructor asks: "How can I make this learning experience stimulating and interesting?" (Keller, 2010, p. 45).

The teacher will begin with a series of questions to the student audience: **How many of you cook on a gas stove? What happens when you spill a substance into an open flame? What would happen if you were boiling water for pasta and the water spilled over?** This discourse is intended to stimulate students' interest as they connect science concepts to their daily lives. Through this class discussion, students will learn that the flame color will sometimes change from blue to orange/yellow due to the presence of sodium chloride, $NaCl$.

A flame test demonstration is a natural transition from this lesson opener. Flame tests are a popular laboratory activity in general chemistry courses but work well as a demonstration in a virtual setting. A variety of chloride salts can produce a beautiful array of colors: calcium chloride (orange-red), copper(II) chloride (green), lithium chloride (pink), potassium chloride (purple), sodium chloride (orange), and strontium chloride (red). Fourth of July will never be the same once your students learn the chemistry behind fireworks. Note: If the flame test cannot be performed safely in the instructional setting, there are many high-quality videos (see Resource Notes) that can be shown or made available to students through the Learning Management System (LMS).

Explore

According to Keller's ARCS model, relevance is the ability to "meet the personal needs of the learner" (Keller, 2010, p. 45). The instructor seeks to answer the question: "In what ways will this learning experience be valuable for my students?" (Keller, 2010, p. 45). The connection between the flame test and fireworks is one method of creating relevance because it connects the lesson to "real life." Another approach is the goal-oriented approach which relates the benefits of this lesson to future success in the course. In order to establish this relevance, teachers should consistently communicate the importance of atomic structure to their ability to master future chemistry concepts.

The Explore phase of the lesson creates a common, concrete experience that will become the foundation for more formal instruction (SDCOE, 2002). Students will explore using the Phet *Build an Atom simulation*. The Build an Atom simulation includes three options: Atom, Symbol, and Game. Students will begin with the Atom portion of the simulation. Students will explore the location of protons, electrons, and neutrons in the atom. The simulation will demonstrate how the number of particles influences the identity, charge, and mass of the atom.

Students should be given time to explore the Build an Atom simulation independently on their iPad, chromebook, or one-to-one device. During this time, the students should be presented with a set of guiding questions:

- **What happens when we add a proton to the model?** When a proton is moved from the bucket to the model, the atom's identity will shift to the next element with an increase in atomic number.

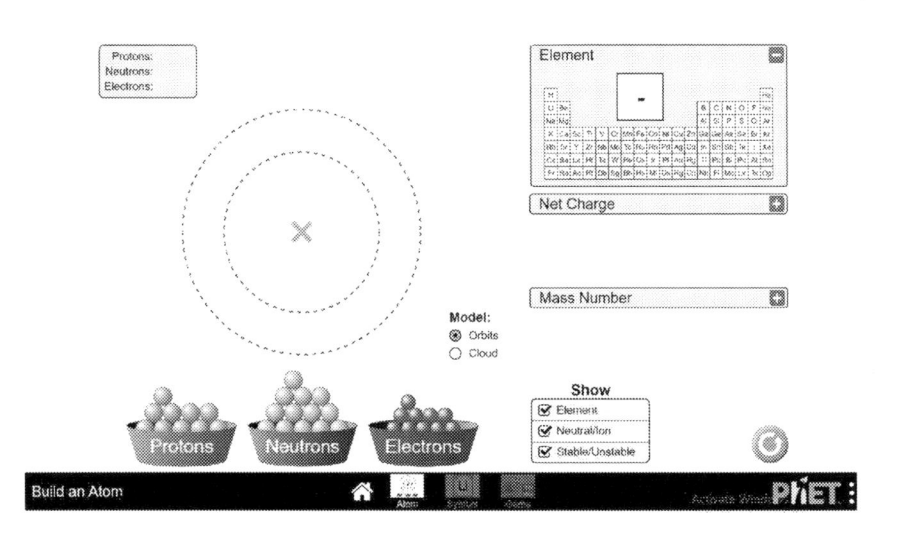

FIGURE 18.1. Screenshot of Building at Atom on PhET Interactive Simulations

- **What happens when we add a neutron to the model?** When a neutron is moved from the bucket to the model, the mass number will increase by one.
- **What happens when we add an electron to the model?** When an electron is moved from the bucket to the model, the charge will decrease by one.
- **What happens if you place a proton/neutron in the electron cloud? … an electron in the nucleus?** The simulation does not allow for the improper placement of subatomic particles. If a proton or neutron is placed on the second energy level, then it will fall back to the bucket. If a proton or neutron is placed on the first energy level, then it will be pulled into the atom's nucleus. If an electron is placed in the nucleus, then it will be pulled to the first available energy level.
- **What makes an atom stable?...unstable?** Students can investigate the stability of an atom as a preview to future lessons on isotopes and radioactive decay. Some students will recognize the relationship between stability and the ratio of protons to neutrons.

Explain

During the Explain phase of the lesson, the teacher will provide formal instruction on atomic structure to facilitate students' understanding of key definitions, explanations, and information (SDCOE, 2002). Students will develop confidence in their ability as they form connections between prior thinking and scientific knowledge. According to Keller's ARCS model, confidence is defined as the act of "helping the learner believe that they will succeed" (Keller, 2010, p. 45). The focus of the teacher should be this question: "How can I via instruction help the student succeed?" (Keller, 2010, p. 45).

The teacher will show the Bill Nye video, *Atoms*. This video is an excellent educational resource for students. It is recommended that the first segment be shown to students, approximately 10:35, but the entire video should be made available through the schools' LMS. The teacher could create a set of video questions to guide student learning and focus their attention on key concepts. Bill Nye videos are popular with students across the K–12 grade band. His instructional videos explain complex concepts in an entertaining and relatable way. This video includes two features that we have found particularly beneficial for learners. At 2:25, Bill Nye uses a bandsaw to cut a cheese wheel into successively smaller pieces. He explains the concept of atoms by saying that the cheese will eventually reach a point where it becomes "un-break-apart-able." Another visual that is especially helpful to learners relates to the relative size of the nucleus and electron cloud. The segment opens at 4:30 with a close-up shot of a bumble ball sensory learning toy as a visual representation of the atom's small densely packed nucleus. Next, Bill Nye runs 500 yards away from the bumble ball toy to show the vastness of the electron cloud.

Next, the teacher should facilitate a discussion of *How Atoms Differ* (Appendix 1) using NearPod, PowerPoint, or other presentation platform. Students will learn how to determine the number of protons, neutrons, and electrons in an atom. Each student will need access to a print or electronic version of the periodic table of elements. We provide an outline of the instructional sequence below. Teacher will present the following key concepts:

- Atomic number is the number of protons in an atom. It determines the identity of an element. For a neutral atom, the atomic number always equals the number of protons and the number of electrons.
- The mass number represents the sum of the number of protons and neutrons in the nucleus; the number of neutrons is the difference between the mass and atomic numbers.
- Example: Atomic number for gold, Au is 79. An atom of gold has 79 protons and 79 electrons. The mass number for gold is 197, so gold has 118 neutrons (197–79). [Note: The teacher can use any element for the example. It is best to use an element that is familiar to students.]

Successful implementation of this lesson will require instructors to use a "no opt-out" approach. Students should be informed at the beginning of this lesson that participation will be required for all students. The teacher can use a "round robin" teaching strategy to practice this skill, as exemplified below:

Teacher: Student A, can you select an element from the periodic table?
Student A: Hydrogen. [Students always choose hydrogen first. I typically ask for a higher element between 2 and 20.]
Teacher: Student A, can you pick an element between 2 and 20?
Student A: Lithium.
Teacher: Great! Lithium. Class…take a second and find lithium on your periodic table.
Teacher: Student B, can you tell me the atomic number for Lithium?
Student B: Three.
Teacher: Excellent! The atomic number for lithium is three.
Teacher: Student C, how many protons does a lithium atom have?
Student C: Three.
Teacher: You are correct! A lithium atom will have three protons.
Teacher: Student D, how many electrons does a lithium atom have?
Student D: Three.
Teacher: Good! A neutral lithium atom will have three electrons.

Once the majority of the group has demonstrated proficiency in determining protons and electrons for several elements, the teacher will add mass number and neutrons to the sequence.

Teacher: Student A, can you select an element from the periodic table?
Student A: Zinc.
Teacher: Great! Zinc. Class, take a second and find zinc on your periodic table.
Teacher: Student B, can you tell me the atomic number for zinc?
Student B: 30.
Teacher: Excellent! The atomic number for zinc is 30.
Teacher: Student C, how many protons does a zinc atom have?
Student C: 30.
Teacher: You are correct! A zinc atom will have 30 protons.
Teacher: Student D, how many electrons does a zinc atom have?
Student D: 30.
Teacher: Excellent! A neutral zinc atom will have 30 electrons.
Teacher: Student E, can you tell me the mass number for zinc?
Student E: 65.
Teacher: Yes, the mass number for zinc is 65.
Teacher: Student F, how many neutrons does a zinc atom have?
Student F: 35.
Teacher: Exactly. If you subtract the atomic number, 30 from the mass number, 65, you get 35 neutrons.

Note: It is important to practice some larger elements so that the number of neutrons will differ from the number of protons and electrons.

If a student is not able to successfully answer their question, then another student can be called on. It is important to communicate to the struggling student that you will ask them another question later. Once students have mastered the learning objectives, they can get additional practice using this *Atomic Structure Chart* (Appendix 2) or other practice activity.

Elaborate

For the Elaborate phase of the lesson, students will return to the Build an Atom simulation and complete the student worksheet. The structured simulation activity will allow students to make conceptual connections between information presented in the exploration and explanation phases. There are a number of high-quality resources available to teachers on the Phet website. Under Teacher Resources, the teacher will have access to Teacher Tips, Video Primer, and Alignment Documents. Under Activities, the teacher can sort student resources by Level, Type, Subject, and Language. The Build an Atom student handout and answer key developed by Emily Moore, Ariel Paul, Trish Loeblein, and Kathy Perkins work well with this lesson.

During this Elaborate phase, students will be able to increase their understanding of Cross-Cutting Concepts: Patterns; and Scale, Proportion, & Quantity. They will develop the Science and Engineering Practices (Nantional Research Council,

2012) as they manipulate the simulation. Students will ask questions such as: "What makes an atom stable?" Students will develop and use models to create atoms with a specific mass or charge. Students will construct explanations for how the addition of a proton will alter the identity, mass, and charge of the atom.

Evaluate

In the final phase of the lesson, teachers evaluate student learning by offering high-quality feedback through formative and summative assessments. The evaluation phase allows students to "feel satisfaction with the process of results of the learning experience" (Keller, 2010, p. 46). The teacher should strive to answer: "What can I do to help the students feel good about their experience and desire to continue learning?" (Keller, 2010, p. 45). For some students, this satisfaction is defined by intrinsic motivation, but other students require extrinsic rewards.

Formative assessments allow students and teachers to assess learning on an ongoing basis during instruction. The Atomic Structure Chart, Bill Nye Video Worksheet, and Build an Atom Simulation can all be used as formative assessments during this lesson. The Atomic Structure Chart provides feedback regarding the student's ability to determine the number of protons, neutrons, and electrons in an atom. The Bill Nye Video Worksheet communicates students' conceptual understanding of the atom including the relative location and size of the subatomic particles. The Build an Atom Simulation and related worksheet assess student understanding of the relationship between subatomic particles and the identity, charge, and mass of an atom. It would also be beneficial to develop an Atomic Structure quiz during this unit that could be administered using Google Forms, Illuminate, or similar tools.

Summative assessments are important tools to determine if key concepts have been mastered after instruction has occurred. Student mastery indicates the level of proficiency necessary to move on to the next unit or course. A lack of mastery is an indicator that one or more students will need remediation to be successful in the next unit or course. The level of student mastery can be determined using a unit test on the Structure of the Atom. Google Forms, Illuminate, and similar tools allow for powerful data analysis at the item and/or standard level. Multiple choice assessments are convenient tools for administering summative assessments, but teachers should also consider alternate assessments. The *Atomic Model Project* (Appendix 3) is an assessment that allows students to develop a three-dimensional model of an atom and a corresponding written assessment.

Online/Remote Learning Environments

While this lesson is designed to be delivered in a remote learning environment, the lesson includes the same basic elements that would be used for face-to-face instruction. Atomic structure is the ideal concept to teach in an online/remote learning environment for a variety of reasons. The topic is addressed early enough in the course to provide a positive experience for learners. When students experience success, they will be more likely to take academic risks with advanced concepts later in the course. Additionally, there is a wealth of high-quality educational resources available to support instruction of this concept.

Critiques and Considerations

This lesson plan is intended to offer guidance to pre-service and in-service teachers seeking additional support with online instruction. It is critical that teachers consider the unique needs of their student population and their context for learning when planning for instruction. Here are some additional considerations related to student participation, academic integrity, and students' misconceptions.

Student Participation

How do you facilitate student participation in a virtual classroom? This lesson includes a "no opt out" approach for students to learn how to determine the number of protons, electrons, and neutrons in an atom. Teachers should always weigh the risks and benefits of requiring student participation. The practice of "cold-calling" or calling on students in class can be very intimidating for many students. It can be more comfortable if students are equipped with the necessary tools for success. Many teachers prefer to ask for volunteers to participate in class discussions. Another creative tool is the practice of "warm" calls by sending students a private message so they have advanced knowledge and time to prepare their response. Other teachers prefer a buddy system that allows students to have a partner that can assist if they need additional support.

Academic Integrity

How can we ensure academic integrity in this setting? Available technology including computers, tablets, smart phones, smart watches, and cloud-based voice services like Alexa and Siri continue to create challenges for teachers attempting to maintain academic integrity of class work and assessments. Teachers can use software manager programs like GoGuardian or similar tools to set passwords, limit access, or randomize questions/answers. There will always be a population of students who will seek shortcuts to the learning process. As teachers, we must work to promote a culture that encourages academic honesty and creates multiple opportunities and methods for students to demonstrate mastery. This culture can be accomplished by shifting emphasis away from high-stakes testing, and to the development of creative and authentic assessments.

Students' Misconceptions

How can we elicit and build on students' misconceptions or alternative conceptions? A student misconception is defined as "an inaccurate or incomplete idea about scientific processes and phenomena before formal instruction" (Burgoon et al., 2011, p. 101). Even following formal instruction these ideas are often resistant to change and, as a result, these misconceptions can produce significant barriers to students' ability to learn chemistry concepts. Teachers' content knowledge and their awareness of student misconceptions are important factors in the successful implementation of any conceptual change approach (Burgoon et al., 2011). Common misconceptions associated with atomic structure include only one model of the atom is correct; electrons and protons are the only fundamental particles; electrons are larger than protons; and electrons have no mass, just charge (Intel®Teach Program, 2013). Through careful design and advanced preparation, instructors can develop informal and formal assessments to identify student misconceptions. Through early identification of student misconceptions, instructors have the capability to correct these alternative frameworks before they interfere with further learning.

SUMMARY AND REFLECTIONS

"The days are long, but the years are short."

This quote by Gretchen Rubin is often used in the context of parenthood, but here we will apply it to an educational setting. The last two years have created significant challenges for students, teachers, and parents. We would like to close this chapter by offering our encouragement to pre-service and in-service teachers struggling to meet the ever-changing demands of the classroom. It can be so difficult to maximize instructional time, teach to state standards, and engage students in the learning process. As you work to find creative ways to structure the online science course and effectively use educational technology, remember to enjoy your time with your students. The school year passes quickly, so take advantage of every opportunity to develop relationships with your students and create memorable learning experiences.

TIPS AND ADVICE

- Communication is critical in an online learning environment. The goal for response time should always be within 24 hours. It is important to communicate with students and parents in a consistent and predictable manner (weekly newsletter or email) and establish multiple methods of communication (phone, text, email, within LMS) to facilitate timely interactions.
- Focus on the quality and not the quantity of assignments. Online learning can be very monotonous for young learners. Students will be more engaged with creative activities, such as making videos, constructing models, or writing tasks.
- Maintain a visual of your students/student perspective by using multiple screens or a secondary device.
- Technical difficulties can create significant barriers to student learning and frustrate students. Be sure to troubleshoot assignments for technical issues by loading content in advance and checking links to instructional resources.
- Avoid or limit the use of third party or external websites. It is very common for issues to arise with logins, passwords, preferred browsers, etc.

RESOURCE NOTES

Resource	Primary Website	How to Locate the Resource Online
Bill Nye "Atoms" Video	https://www.schooltube.com	This video is available on School Tube. Search on Google and type "Bill Nye—Atoms, Schooltube." Choose the first search result that is on the SchoolTube site. https://www.schooltube.com/media/Bill+Nye+-+Atoms/1_k7dvbaam
Bill Nye Video Worksheet	https://www.cusd80.com	Search on Google and type "Bill Nye 'Atoms' worksheet." Search result will bring up a live URL of the PDF version of the Worksheet. https://www.cusd80.com/cms/lib/AZ01001175/Centricity/Domain/6371/BillNyeAtoms.pdf
Build An Atom Simulation	https://phet.colorado.edu	Go to https://phet.colorado.edu and click on "Simulations." Click on "Chemistry," then scroll down and click on "Build an Atom."
Build An Atom Student/Teacher Resources (Worksheet)	https://phet.colorado.edu	Go to https://phet.colorado.edu. Teachers may need to create an account for full access. Under Teacher Resources, the teacher will have access to Teacher Tips, Video Primer, and Alignment Documents. Under Activities, the teacher can sort student resources by Level, Type, Subject, and Language. Choose the worksheet titled "Build an Atom" created by Moore et al.
Flinn Scientific Flame Test Demonstration	https://www.flinnsci.com/	On Google search, type "Flinn Scientific Flame Test Demonstration." Choose the result that is housed in the main Flinn Scientific website. https://www.flinnsci.com/api/library/Download/7cb7a26bedbb44e1adcef3177936f087
GPB Chemistry	https://www.gpb.org/	On Google search, type "GPB Chemistry" and choose the search result that says "Chemistry: A study of matter." https://www.gpb.org/chemistry-study-of-matter or https://www.gpb.org/chemistry-matters. This link is a general resource helpful for teachers.
Periodic table	https://ptable.com	Visit https://ptable.com/#Properties for an electronic version; or, https://www.sciencegeek.net/tables/tables.shtml for a printable/download version.
The Science Spot	https://sciencespot.net	On Google search, type "The Science Spot." Go to the search result that takes you to the main page of "The Science Spot" and choose "Chemistry" under "Science Classrooms." https://sciencespot.net/Pages/classchem.html. This link is a general resource helpful for teachers.
Appendix 1. How Atoms Differ	n/a	See attached appendix 1 for the slides.

Resource	Primary Website	How to Locate the Resource Online
Appendix 2. Atomic Structure Chart	n/a	See attached appendix 2 for this chart.
Appendix 3. Atomic Model Project	n/a	See attached appendix 3 for this activity.

DISCUSSION QUESTIONS

1. How do we create and foster an engaging and interactive online learning environment when we are teaching challenging topics such as Atomic Structure in science?
2. How do we maximize the affordances of educational technology to facilitate student participation in an online science class?
3. How do we implement on-going, formative assessments that not only check for students' understanding but also elicit and reveal students' ideas and thinking in an online science class?
4. How do we as teachers effectively respond to and build on student thinking to create a productive dialogue in an online science class?

REFERENCES

Burgoon, J. N., Heddle, M. L., & Duran, E. (2011). Re-examining the similarities between teacher and student conceptions about physical science. *Journal of Science Teacher Education*, *22*(2), 101–114. https://doi.org/10.1007/s10972-010-9196-x

Intel*Teach Program. (2013). *Small, smaller, smallest: Misconceptions about the structure of atoms*. Intel Corporation. https://www.intel.com/content/dam/www/program/education/us/en/documents/project-design/atoms/small-misconceptions-about-the-structure-of-atoms.pdf

Keller, J. M. (2010). *Motivational design for learning and performance: The ARCS model approach*. Springer.

National Research Council. (2012). *A framework for K–12 science education: Practices, crosscutting concepts, and core ideas*. National Academies Press.

Pintrich, P. R., & Schunk, D. H. (2002). *Motivation in education*. Prentice Hall.

San Diego County Office of Education (SDCOE). (2002). *5E Model of Instruction*. https://ngss.sdcoe.net/Evidence-Based-Practices/5E-Model-of-Instruction

Schunk, D. H. (2008). Metacognition, self-regulation, and self-regulated learning: Research recommendations. *Educational psychology review*, *20*(4), 463–467.

Teach Remotely. (2002). *Pedagogical Best Practices: Residential, blended, and online*. https://teachremotely.harvard.edu/best-practices

APPENDIX 1

HOW ATOMS DIFFER

Mass number – represents the sum of the number of protons and neutrons in the nucleus

of = mass - atomic
neutrons   number   number

Atomic number – number of protons in an atom; determines the identity of an element.

Atomic =   # of   = # of
number   protons   electrons

EXAMPLE

Atomic number for gold, Au is 79. An atom of gold has 79 protons & 79 electrons. The mass number for gold is 197, so gold has 118 neutrons (197–79).

APPENDIX 2

Name _____   Date _____

Complete the Atomic Structure Chart

I. Fill in the remaining information for the element to complete the following chart.

	Name of the Element	Symbol	Atomic Number	Number of Protons	Number of Electrons	Mass Number	Number of Neutrons
1	Osmium	Os	76	76	76	190	114
2			6			12	
3		Cl			17		
4	Zinc			30			
5	Bismuth		83				
6						91	51
7		K			19		
8				27			32
9	Iridium		77			192	
10		Cu			29		
11			15				
12						48	
13			10				
14						84	
15	Gallium						
16		Pb					
17	Silver						
18			14				
19		Au					
20						195	

Johnson & Jeong, *A look inside the atom*

APPENDIX 3

Part one: Create 3D Model of the Atom (50 points)
Your task is to create a three dimensional (3D) model of an atom. Be sure to consider appropriate size of each particle and location in the atom. It should clearly show the major parts of an atom: the nucleus which is made up of protons and neutrons, and electrons which travel around the nucleus in a "cloud". Your model should show that there is empty space between the nucleus and the electrons. Be sure to include the element name, symbol, atomic number, atomic mass, number of protons, electrons, and neutrons. Label each part or make a key.

Use your imagination and creativity in selecting materials for this project. It can be presented as a free standing model, or suspended from something like a coat hanger, or mounted on a poster board. Feel free to use gumdrops, mini marshmallows, jelly beans, Styrofoam balls, paints, fabric, cut paper, etc. to represent the parts of an atom.

Part Two: Written Assessment(50 points)
Create a cover page for your report. Draw a colored diagram of your model and label all parts including the subatomic particles. Your name, class period, and due date must be included.
Write an analysis following the format below:

1. **Paragraph One**: State the purpose of this assessment and summarize what you did complete the task. (What is an atom? Why is it important to understand atomic structure? What is a model? What are the benefits of models? What are the limitations?)

2. **Paragraph Two**: Provide a brief overview of atomic theory as discussed in class. What contributions did Democritus, Dalton, Thomson, Rutherford, Millikan and Chadwick make to our knowledge of the atom?

3. **Paragraph Three**: What is the significance of the number of protons in an atom? How does a change in number of protons affect the atom? What is the significance the number of neutrons in an atom? How does a change in number of neutrons affe the atom?

4. **Paragraph Four:** What did you learn from this project? What challenges did you encounter? If you could make another model, what would you do differently?

5.
*REQUIRED VOCABULARY: Include the following key vocabulary in your analys atom, nucleus, cloud, proton, neutron, electron, mass number, isotope, average mass

"3D MODEL OF THE ATOM" RUBRIC

Dimension	Level 1 Below Expectations	Level 2 Approaching Expectations	Level 3 Meets Expectations	Level 4 Exceeds Expectations
Required Elements	The 3D Model is missing more than two required elements.	The 3D Model is missing two of the required elements.	The 3D Model is missing one of the required elements.	All required elements are included in the 3D Model.
Subatomic Particles	Model does not contain the appropriate numbers of subatomic particles. Respective locations and size of particles is not correct.	Model does include the correct numbers of each subatomic particle, but the respective size and location is not accurate.	Model includes the correct number of subatomic particles in the appropriate location, but relative size of particles is not correct.	Model includes the correct number of subatomic particles appropriately located and sized.
Accuracy of Model	The correct numbers of electrons are not included on each energy level, nucleus is not densely packed and neutrons are separated from protons in the nucleus.	The correct numbers of electrons are included on each energy level, but nucleus is not densely packed and neutrons are separated from protons in the nucleus.	The correct numbers of electrons are included on each energy level, nucleus is densely packed, but neutrons are separated from protons in the nucleus.	The correct numbers of electrons are included on each energy level; nucleus is densely packed with neutrons separating protons.
Creativity/Neatness/Visual	Not neatly assembled or visually pleasing, or creative	Neatly assembled, but not visually pleasing or creative in the selection of materials or display (Too small, not color coded, etc.)	Neatly assembled, visually pleasing, but no creativity displayed in of materials or display (ex. wire, Styrofoam balls, etc.)	Neatly assembled, visually pleasing, and creative in the selection of materials and display (WOW factor)

CHAPTER 19

WHEN THINGS MOVE WITH CONSTANT VELOCITY AND ACCELERATION

Philomena N. Agu

University of Houston-Downtown

LESSON PLAN OVERVIEW

A projectile is an example of a body that simultaneously moves in both the x and y direction. When things move, they can travel in a circle (planets orbiting the sun), travel in a horizontal direction (Cheetah chasing a prey), or move vertically (autumn leaves falling). They can also move in two dimensions—horizontal and vertical (human performing a long jump). A body thrown or launched into the air and subjected to gravitational force (gravity) is called a projectile (Serway & Faughn, 2015). Gravity accelerates the body in the vertical direction and causes the body to follow a parabolic trajectory in the absence of air resistance. The vertical velocity is solely influenced by gravity, causing velocity to change by 9.8 m/s each second. A projectile does not experience a force in the horizontal direction. Its inertia propels it once the body is launched. In the absence of air resistance, the horizontal velocity is considered constant (no acceleration) and this premise is assumed in this lesson plan. The time of flight for an object that moves in both

Teaching and Learning Online: Science for Secondary Grade Levels, pages 281–308.

the vertical and horizontal dimensions is always equal and this knowledge can be used to solve projectile problems since it provides a common variable that is constant in both dimensions (Mader & Winn, 2007, p. 109).

Students will discover the definition of a projectile, characteristics of its trajectory, variables that influence its trajectory, and apply kinematic equations to solve projectile problems by completing inquiry activities in the 5E learning cycle (i.e., Engage, Explore, Explain, Elaborate and Evaluate). The Engage phase introduces students to things that are usually thrown or launched and the characteristics of trajectory of fired objects. The student will use "throwing spears" in the Pheasant and Kingfisher children's literature book to learn about throwing and the paths of fired bodies. Then, they will fire a cannonball using "Projectile Motion" PhET simulation to discover the similarity between the trajectory of spears in the children's literature and the path of the launched cannonball. They will study the effect of air resistance on the fired cannonball and how the velocity vector splits into x and y components. In the Explore phase, the student will investigate how launch angles, launch speed, and launch height influence the trajectory of a projectile. In the Explain phase, the student will learn to use kinematic equations to calculate the displacement, velocity, and acceleration vectors in the vertical and horizontal directions. The student will then apply what was learned about projectiles and build a projectile that lands at a calculated target.

This lesson plan is created for an on-level physics course. You will teach this lesson fully synchronously online and hold virtual meetings via Zoom, Teams, or any platform with video, microphone, and chat features. You will also use the Learning Management System for the students to turn in their assignments. Have students use their science notebook to take notes, record observations and measurements, and open a "When Things Move" folder in their device and save their work inside this folder. Monitor student engagement with Popsicle Sticks and chat by (a) writing their names on Popsicle Sticks (one student per stick) and cold calling students from the stack (b) asking them to copy and paste their work in the chat and also answer formative assessment questions through the chat and orally. Finally, this lesson may take multiple days to complete. Continuously monitor students' understanding as you teach through formative assessment.

Discipline: Physical Science—Motion and Force

Grade Level: High School (9th to 12th)

CONNECTIONS TO NGSS AND THREE-DIMENSIONAL LEARNING

Students' Performance Expectations

- Code: HS-PS2-1
- Domain: Physical Science (PS)

- **HS-PS2-1:** Analyze data to support the claim that Newton's second law of motion describe the mathematical relationship among the net force on a macroscopic object, its mass, and its acceleration. (Clarification statements: Examples of data could include tables or graphs of position or velocity as a function of time for objects subject to a net unbalanced force, such as a falling object, object sliding down a ramp, or a moving object being pulled by constant force.)

Science and Engineering Practices:

Analyzing and Interpreting Data
- Analyze data using tools, technologies, and/or models (e.g., computational, mathematical) in order to make valid and reliable scientific claims or determine an optimal design solution.

Planning and Carrying Out Investigations
- Plan and conduct an investigation individually and collaboratively to produce data to serve as the basis for evidence, and in the design: decide on types, how much, and accuracy needed to produce reliable measurements and consider limitations on the precision of the data (e.g., number of trials, costs, risk, time), and refine the design accordingly.

Using Mathematics in Computational Thinking
- Use mathematical representations of phenomena to describe explanations.

Constructing Explanations and Designing solutions
Constructing Explanations and designing Solutions in 9—12 builds on K—8 experiences and progresses to explanations and designs that are supported by multiple and independent student-generated sources of evidence consistent with scientific ideas, principles, and theories.
- Apply scientific ideas to solve a design problem, considering possible unanticipated effects.

Disciplinary Core Ideas

Forces and Motion (PS2.A)
- Newton's second law accurately predicts changes in the motion of macroscopic objects.

Crosscutting Concepts:

Cause and Effect
- Empirical evidence is required to differentiate between cause and correlation and make claims about specific causes and effects.
- Systems can be designed to cause a desired effect.

TEACHING AND LEARNING ONLINE 5E LESSON PLAN

Grades: High School (9th–12th)   **Topic:** Force and Motion

Guiding Question(s):
- What is a projectile?
- How does air resistance influence the trajectory of a projectile?
- What are the characteristics of the trajectory of a projectile?
- How do mass, height, angle, and speed influence trajectory of a projectile launched horizontally or at an angle to the surface of the earth neglecting air resistance?
- How can you design a ramp that launches a projectile horizontally and allows it to land on a predicted target?

BACKGROUND INFORMATION

Prior Student Knowledge:
- Constant speed(velocity)
- Acceleration
- Free Fall
- Forces
- Force of gravity
- Acceleration due to gravity
- Kinematic equations
- Newton's Laws
- Inertia

Possible Preconceptions / Misconceptions:
- Free Fall objects fall faster than a projected object.
- Force is required to keep an object in motion hence a force maintains the horizontal motion
- Two forces are involved in the vertical motion—a force that keeps the object moving upward and a force that brings the object downwards.

LESSON PLAN

ENGAGE: Teach this phase synchronously online and use Zoom, Teams, or any platform with video, microphone, and chat to hold a synchronous virtual meeting. Have students create a "When Things Move" folder on their devices and save work inside this folder. Also, have them upload assignments to the Learning Management System and use their science notebook to write observations, notes, lab reports, and answer questions you ask in the class. Monitor students' engagement with Popsicle Sticks (random and cold calls), chat and discussion forums.

Use the sticks to call on students to answer questions. Have students use the Snipping Tool to cut images, post them in chat, write notes and observations inside their science notebook, and save word documents and pictures and When Things Move folder.

Guiding Question:
- What is a Projectile?
- What are the characteristics of the trajectory of a projectile?
- How does air resistance influence the trajectory of a projectile?

Teacher: To answer the guiding questions:
Read aloud Berndt (1994) Pheasant and Kingfisher children's literature book and record yourself reading this book. Share YouTube video link with students and have them watch the video on their devices and answer the following questions:

1. What are some actions you read or saw in the book?
2. What other things (bodies) are thrown, launched or fired?
3. Draw the path or trajectory of the spear and describe the shape.

Teacher Note:
Ask the questions in order and discuss answers to question one before proceeding to questions 2 and 3. For question 1, accept all responses but pay attention to "throwing spears." Kicking a football, firing a bullet, launching a rocket, and

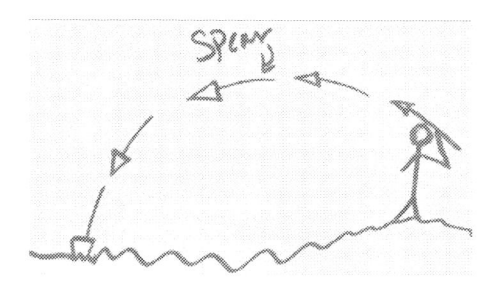

FIGURE 19.1.   Student on Drawing of Spear Thrown in the Air

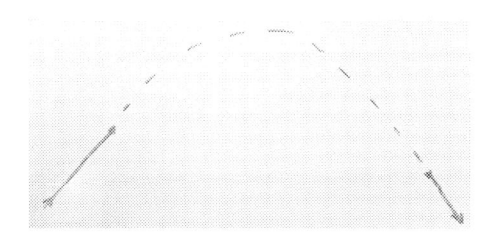

FIGURE 19.2.   Student 2 Drawing of a Spear Thrown in the Air

jumping frog are examples of bodies that are launched. For question 3, accept diagrams that make sense, such as Figure 19.1 and Figure 19.2, and reject shapes that do not resemble a parabola. Discuss the shape of the curve and introduce the concept of a projectile. Point out from their drawings two independent linear motions of a projectile, vertical and horizontal. Have students generate more examples and non-examples of a projectile.

Ask students:

1. Open "Projectile Motion" PhET simulation (see Source Note) and select "Intro."
2. Play with the simulation, record and report observations.
3. Fire an object from the drop-down menu in the presence and absence of air resistance. Record and report your observations.
4. Draw the trajectory of the projectile with and without air resistance.
5. Check "Total" velocity and acceleration vectors, fire an object, and observe the vectors. Draw and record observations.
6. Check "Total" and "Components" of velocity and acceleration vectors, fire an object, and observe the vectors. Draw and record observations.
7. Read "what is projectile" and "motion characteristics of projectile" from physicsclassroom.com (see source note) and take note.
8. Summarize what you learned.

Teacher Note:
After students have played with the simulation and discussed their observations, teach them how to run the simulation and point out trajectory characteristics. A projectile moves in two directions (vertical and horizontal) and traces a parabolic path in the absence of air resistance. Particles in the air slow down the motion of projectiles, as shown in Figure 19.3. Figure 19.4 shows that acceleration is constant but the total velocity vector changes vertically. The vertical component of the velocity also changes. It decreases as the projectile climbs up, reaches a minimum at the vertex of the parabola, and begins to increase to a maximum before landing. The horizontal velocity remained constant throughout the trajectory

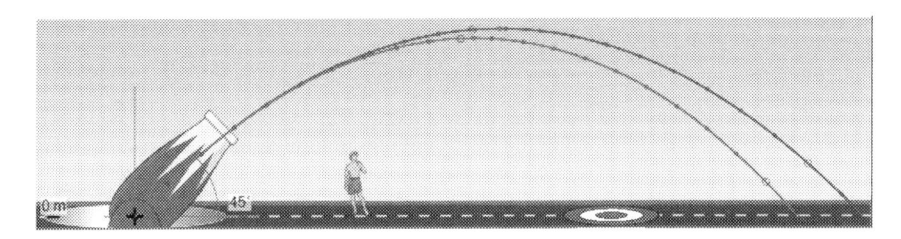

FIGURE 19.3.   Baseball Launched at an Angle of 45° in the Absence(Blue) and Presence (Neon) of Air Resistance

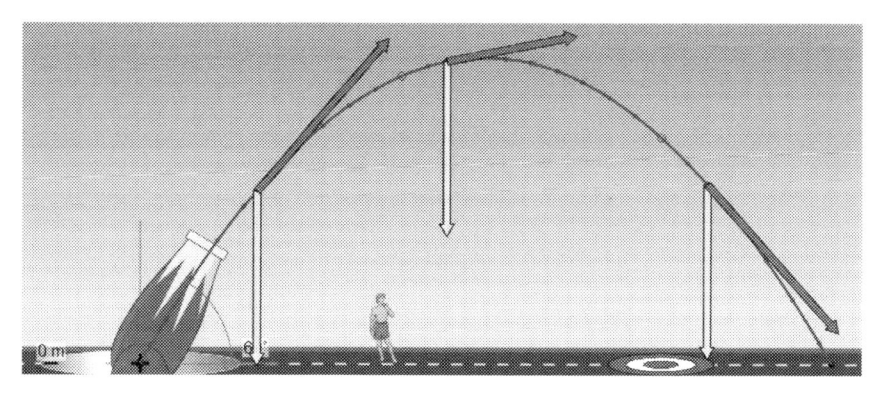

FIGURE 19.4. Total Velocity(Green) and Acceleration (Yellow) Vectors of a Projectile

(Figure 19.5). In Figure 19.6, the force of gravity changes the velocity of the projectile travelling upward and down and this force does not influence the horizontal component of the velocity vector.

Guiding Question: How do mass, height, and speed influence trajectory of a projectile fired horizontally?

EXPLORE: Teach this phase synchronously online and use Zoom, Teams, or any platform with video, microphone, and chat to hold a synchronous virtual meeting. Have students create a "When Things Move" folder on their devices and save work inside this folder. Also, have them upload assignments to the Learning Management System and use their science notebook to write observations, notes, lab

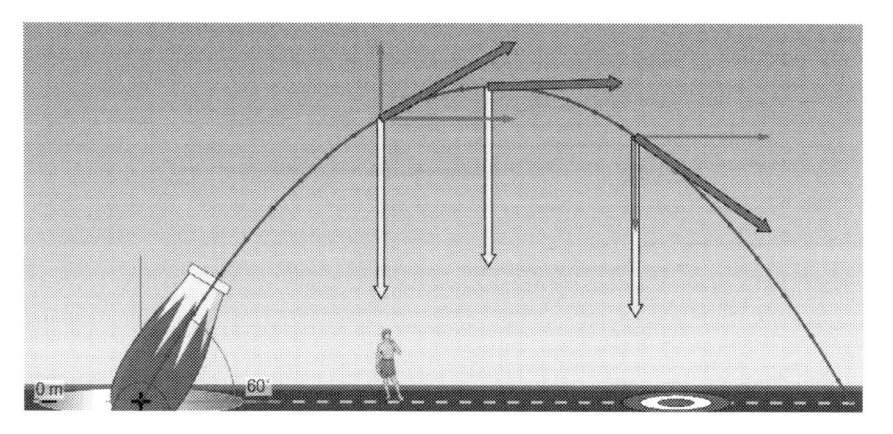

FIGURE 19.5. Acceleration (Yellow) Vector, Velocity (Green) Vector and Its Components in x and y Directions

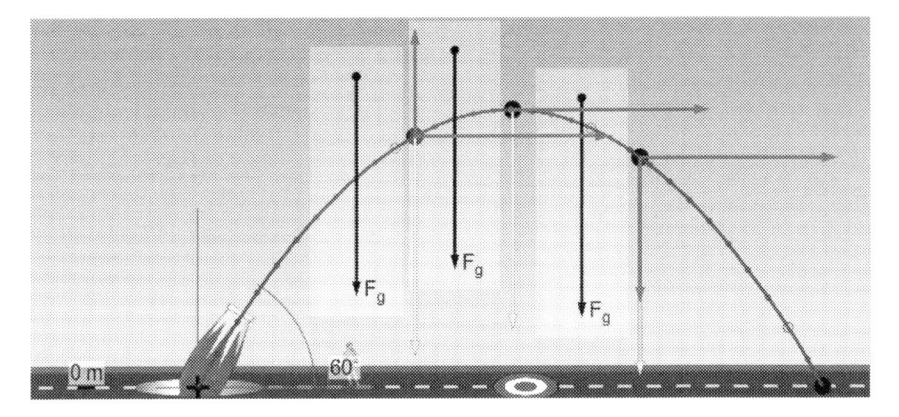

FIGURE 19.6. Force (Black), Acceleration (Yellow), and Component Velocity (Green) Vectors of Projected Cannonball

reports, and answer questions you ask in the class. Monitor students' engagement with Popsicle Sticks (random and cold calls), chat and discussion forums.

Guiding Question One: Neglecting air resistance, how does mass (type of object) influence the trajectory of a projectile if launch angle, speed, and height are kept constant?

Experiment One: Mass or Type of Object

Ask students:

1. Switch to "Lab." Keep the angle, height, and initial speed constant.
2. Do not check the air resistance button.
3. Fire a Cannonball. Draw its trajectory and measure range, time of flight, and its trajectory's maximum height and record data.
4. Predict the trajectory of a football.
5. Fire the football and compare your prediction with observation.

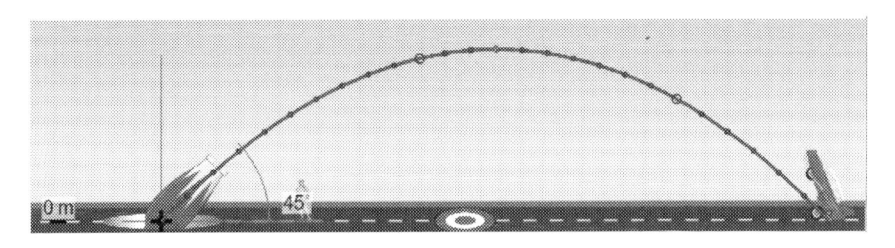

FIGURE 19.7. Cannonball, Football and Car Fired at Angle 45° to the Ground.

TABLE 19.1.   Influence of Mass on Trajectory

Object Type	Mass(kg)	Horizontal Distance or Range (m)	Maximum Height(m)	Time of Flight(s)
Cannonball	17.60	33.03	8.26	2.59
Tank Shell	18.00	33.03	8.26	2.59
Golf Ball	0.05	33.03	8.26	2.59
Baseball	0.15	33.03	8.26	2.59
Football	0.41	33.03	8.26	2.59
Pumpkin	5.00	33.03	8.26	2.59
Human	70	33.03	8.26	2.59
Piano	400	33.03	8.26	2.59
Car	2000	33.03	8.26	2.59

6.   Fire other objects from the drop-down menu.
7.   What do you conclude?

Teacher Note: Teach students how to take measurements with the measuring tools in the system. Discuss findings. Table 19.1 shows the range, maximum height, and time of flight data of objects of various masses launched with an initial speed of 18m/s at an angle 45° to the earth's surface (Figure 19.7), neglecting air resistance. In the absence of air resistance, mass or the type of object do not influence the trajectory of a projectile.

Guiding Questions Two: How does launch angle influence the trajectory of a projection, keeping height and speed constant and neglect air resistance?

Ask students:

1.   Keep height and initial speed constant.
2.   Do not check the air resistance button.
3.   Fire a Cannonball at angle 250°.
4.   Predict how a change in angle will influence its trajectory.
5.   Fire the cannon at a different angle and compare your prediction with observation.
6.   Measure range, time of flight, maximum height, and time to reach maximum height.
7.   Repeat step 5 until you obtain five sets of data.
8.   For a given angle, measure horizontal displacement (range), vertical displacement (height), and corresponding time every 0.1 seconds until you reach landing position.
9.   Graph horizontal displacement versus time and analyze the graph.

TABLE 19.2. Kinematic Equation of Projectiles Launched at Angle to Ground

Horizontal Motion	Vertical Motion
$v_x = v_i \cos\theta$ = constant	v_y, $f = v_i \sin\theta + g\Delta t$
$d_x = (v_i \cos\theta)\, \Delta t$	v_y, $f^2 = v^2_i\, (\sin\theta)^2 + 2g\Delta y$
$T = \sqrt{\dfrac{2dy}{g}}$	$\Delta d_y = v_i(\sin\theta)\, \Delta t + \tfrac{1}{2}\, g(\Delta t)^2$
	$T = \sqrt{\dfrac{2dy}{g}}$

10. Graph vertical displacement versus time and analyze the graph.
11. Give examples of projectiles launched at an angle to the ground.
12. Read "horizontal and vertical velocity" and "horizontal and vertical displacement" (see source note) from physicsclassroom.com and take note.
13. Summarize what you learned.

Teacher Note: Discuss with students what they discovered. Allow them to fire any object from the drop-down menu, choose different angles or use angles from Table 19.3. Have them launch at a complementary angle (two angles that add up to 90 degrees). Table 19.4 shows results of a cannonball launched at angle 18°

TABLE 19.3. Projectile launched at an Angle to the Ground

Projection Angle(degree)	Horizontal Distance(m)	Maximum Height(m)	Time of Flight (m)	Time to reach Maximum Height(m)
25				
30				
45				
60				
65				
75				

TABLE 19.4. Sample Data of Cannonball Launched at Different Angles to Earth's Surface

Projection Angle	Horizontal Distance(m)	Maximum Height(m)	Time of Flight (m)	Time to reach Maximum Height(m)
25	25.30	2.95	1.55	.78
30	28.60	4.13	1.83	.92
45	33.03	8.26	2.59	1.3
60	28.60	12.38	3.18	1.59
75	16.51	15.41	3.54	1.77

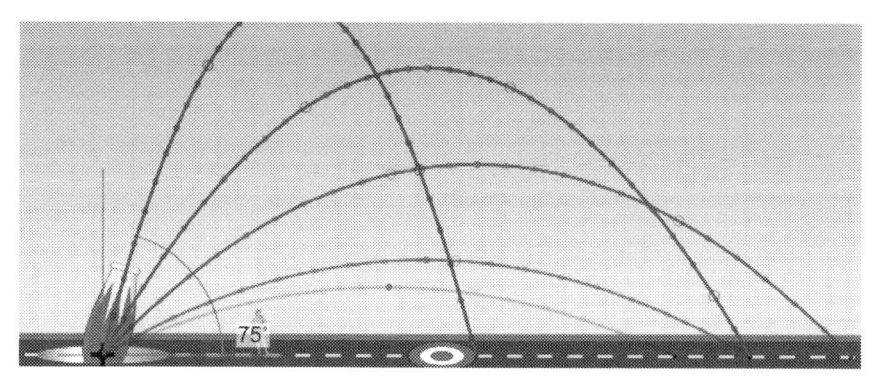

FIGURE 19.8.   Trajectory of Cannonball Launched at Different Angles to Earth's Surface

to the surface of the earth. A cannonball fired at complementary angles (30°and 60°) landed at the same position and covered the same horizontal distance, but the time of flight was different. At angle 30°, the cannonball spent less time in the air before landing at the same position with the larger complement. The cannonball covered the highest horizontal distance at an angle of 45°, as shown in Figure 19.8 and Table 19.4. This result is valid for projectile motion. Table 19.4 shows that the maximum height attained by the projectile and the time to reach the maximum height increases with angle. Baseballs, missiles, and golf balls are projectiles launched at an angle to the ground. Figure 19.9 shows the graph of horizontal displacement versus time has a constant slope supporting the premise that the velocity of a projectile in the horizontal direction does not change in the absence of air resistance. On the contrary, height (vertical displacement) versus time (Figure 19.8) is a parabola, indicating a constant change in velocity. Table 19.2 is kinematic equations for solving problems involving projectiles launched at an angle. You may teach advanced students who have taken trigonometry to solve problems on projectiles launched at an angle to the ground.

Guiding Question Three: How does height influence the trajectory of a projectile if launch angle and speed are kept constant, and air resistance is neglected?

Ask students:

1.   Keep launch angle and speed constant and do not check the air resistance button.
2.   Change the height until you obtain five sets of data (range, time of flight, and time to reach maximum height).
3.   What is the trend of data?
4.   What did you discover?

TABLE 19.5. Displacement of Cannonball Launched at Angle 45° to the Earth's Surface

Time(s)	Vertical Displacement or Height (m)	Horizontal Displacement or Range (m)
0	0	0
0.10	1.22	1.27
0.20	2.35	2.55
0.30	3.38	2.82
0.40	4.31	5.09
0.50	5.14	6.36
0.60	5.87	7.64
0.70	6.51	8.91
0.80	7.04	10.18
0.90	7.48	11.46
1.00	7.82	12.75
1.10	8.07	14.00
1.20	8.21	15.27
1.30	8.26	16.26
1.40	8.21	17.82
1.50	8.06	19.09
1.60	7.81	20.36
1.70	7.46	21.64
1.80	7.02	22.91
1.90	6.48	24.18
2.00	5.84	25.46
2.10	5.10	26.73
2.20	4.26	28.00
2.30	3.30	29.27
2.40	2.29	30.55
2.50	1.16	31.82
2.59	0	33.03

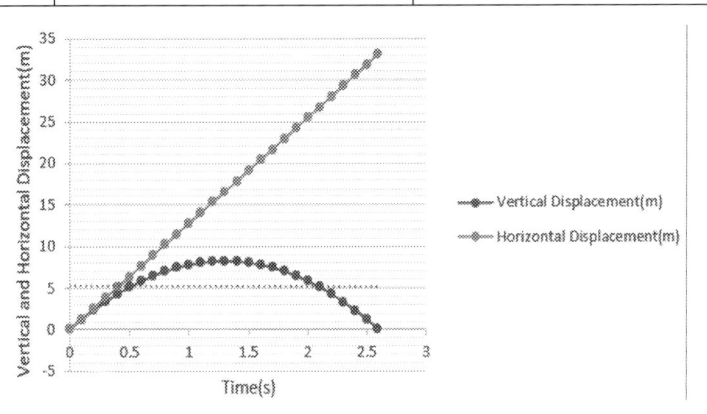

FIGURE 19.9. Horizontal and Vertical Displacement Plots

5. What do you discover about a quarter coin launched horizontally from a lab table and another quarter coin dropped from the same height simultaneously?
6. Read "horizontally launched projectile problems" from physicsclassroom.com and take note.
7. Summarize what you learned.

Teacher Note: Discuss with students their discoveries. Note that this lesson plan treats projectile fired from a height as horizontally launched projectile and Figure 19.10 shows the trajectory of a launched cannon at each height. The students may choose different heights from the values listed in the Table 19.7 or select different numbers. Table 19.7 shows that horizontal displacement (range) and time of flight increased with height. This time of flight, T, depends only on the height above the ground, dy, from which a project is launched and the acceleration due to gravity, g, ($T = \sqrt{\dfrac{2dy}{g}}$) revealing that the horizontal motion does not affect this time (Kiefer and Landa, p. 24).

A launched object and a body in free fall land on the ground simultaneously. Demonstrate to students that a projected coin and a free fall coin fall on the earth's surface together. Have the students repeat the demo, create a video of the coins, and share it with the class.

Procedure:
- Mark two quarters A and B with a marker. You may use different coins.
- Place coin A on the edge of a table and coin B a short distance behind it. Flicker Coin B with your index finger to push coin A off the table.
- Observe the projected coin (launched coin) and free fall coin (pushed coin) land on the ground simultaneously (See Madder & Winn, p. 110).
- You may also watch Paul Hewitt 2.23 minutes video demonstration about Free Fall and projectile on YouTube by searching "Conceptual Physics Projectile Motion."
- Use kinematic equations in Table 19.6 to solve problems about horizontally launched projectiles. Solve an example problem and have the students practice questions 1 and 2.

Example Problem: Calculate the landing position of a marble launched horizontally with a velocity of 1.50m/s from a table of 1.20m high.

Solution:

Vertical motion:

$v_y, i = 0$

TABLE 19.6. Kinematic Equation of Projectiles Launched Horizontally

Horizontal Component	Vertical Component
$a_x = 0$ (No acceleration in the horizontal direction)	$a_y = g = 9.8 m/s^2$ (Vertical motion acceleration is ca due to gravity)
	$v_y, f = vyi + g\Delta t$
v_x = Constant (Horizontal Velocity is constant)	$v_y, f^2 = vy, i^2 + 2g\Delta y$
$dx = v_x \Delta t$ (Horizontal distance = Horizontal Velocity times time)	$\Delta dy = vy, i\Delta t + \frac{1}{2} g(\Delta t)^2$
	When a projectile falls from rest (launched horizontally), $vy, i = 0$ and the first in the equation becomes zero.
$T = \sqrt{\frac{2dy}{g}}$	$v_{y, f} = g\Delta t$
	$v_{y, f2} = 2g\Delta y$
	$\Delta y = \frac{1}{2} g(\Delta t^2)$
	$T = \sqrt{\frac{2dy}{g}}$

$\Delta y = \frac{1}{2} g(\Delta t^2)$

$$T = \sqrt{\frac{2dy}{g}} = \sqrt{\frac{2(1.2m)}{9.8m/s^2}} = 0.49s$$

Horizontal motion:

dx = v_x Δt = 1.5m/s (0.49s) = .74m

The marble will land 74 cm away from the table top.

Practice Question 1: A Tennis ball projected off a 0.80m lab table landed on the floor 0. 35m away from the table. How fast was it traveling?

Practice Question 2: A plane traveling horizontally with a speed of 120 m/s drops a package from an altitude of 70 m high. What horizontal distance did the package travel before landing on the ground?

Guiding Question Three: How does launch speed influence the trajectory of a projectile if launch angle and height are constant and you neglect air resistance?

Ask students:

1. Keep launch height and angle constant and do not check the air resistance button.
2. Obtain five sets of data (range, time of flight, maximum height, and time to reach maximum height).

TABLE 19.7. Height Influence on Trajectory of Launched Cannon

Launch Height(m)	Horizontal Distance(m)	Time of Flight(s)	Time to Reach Maximum Height(s)	Horizontal Distance at Maximum Height(m)
3	35.80	2.81	1.3	16.51
6	38.21	3.00	1.3	16.51
9	40.39	3.17	1.3	16.51
12	42.38	3.33	1.3	16.51
15	44.23	3.47	1.3	16.51

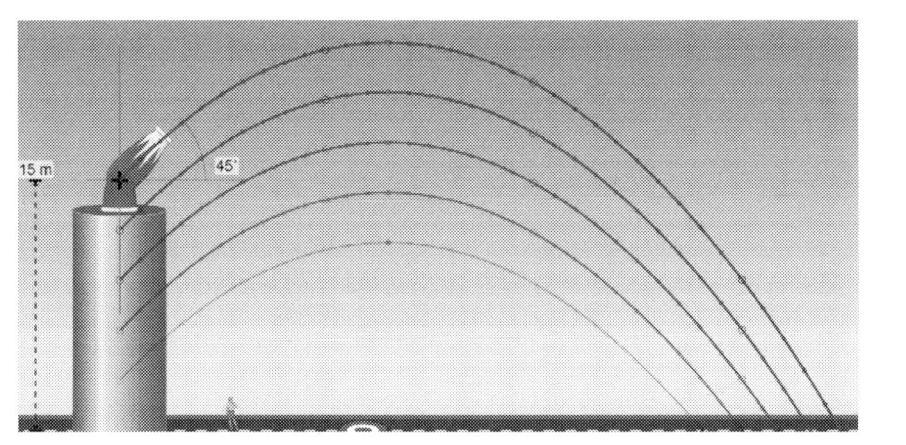

FIGURE 19.10. Height Influence on Trajectory

3. What is the trend of data?
4. What did you discover?
5. Summarize what you learned.

Teacher Note: Discuss with students their discoveries. Allow them to use the launch speed listed in Table 19.8 or choose a different initial launch speed. Table 19.9 shows speed influenced the trajectory of a cannonball. This discovery is valid for projectiles launched horizontally or fired at an angle to the earth's surface.

EXPLAIN: Teach this phase synchronously online and use Zoom, Teams, or any platform with video, microphone, and chat to hold a synchronous virtual meeting. Have students create a "When Things Move" folder on their devices and save work inside this folder. Also, have them upload assignments to the Learning Management System and use their science notebook to write observations, notes, lab

TABLE 19.8. Speed Influence on Trajectory of a Projectile

Speed (m/s)	Horizontal Distance(m)	Time of Flight(s)	Maximum Height(m)	Time to Reach Maximum Height(s)
6				
12				
18				
24				
30				

TABLE 19.9. Speed Influence on the Trajectory of a Launched Cannon

Angle(degree)	Horizontal Distance(m)	Time of Flight(s)	Maximum Height(m)	Time to Reach Maximum Height(s)
6	3.67	.86	0.92	.43
12	14.68	1.73	3.67	.86
18	33.03	2.59	8.26	1.30
24	58.72	3.46	14.68	1.73
30	91.74	4.32	22.94	2.16

reports, and answer questions you ask in the class. Monitor students' engagement with Popsicle Sticks (random and cold calls) chat and discussion forums.

Teacher Note:
1. Group students and ask each group to present a PowerPoint of what they learned about projectiles.
2. Uses Slide Deck (see source note, Henderson, 2022) from physicsclassroom.com to review projectile motion. Click on each hyperlink to access Slides:
   – Motion Characteristic of Projectiles
   – Velocity Components of a Projectile
   – X and Y Displacement for a Projectile
   – Mathematics of Projectile Motion
   – Solving Horizontally Launched Projectile Problems
3. Use Table 19.10 to review how to use kinematic equations to solve projectiles problems.

Vocabulary
- **Acceleration** is the rate of change of velocity.
- **Acceleration due to gravity** is the acceleration of an object in free fall.
- **Air Resistance** is a force that opposes the motion of bodies moving in the air.
- **Complementary Angle** is two angles that add to 90 degrees.

TABLE 19.10. Kinematic Equations of Projectiles Launched Horizontally and at an Angle

Horizontal Component	Vertical Component
Projectiles Launched Horizontal: $a_x = 0$ (No acceleration in the horizontal direction) v_x = Constant (Horizontal Velocity is constant) $dx = v_x \Delta t$ (Horizontal distance = Horizontal Velocity times time) **Launched at an angle to the Horizontal:** $v_x = vi \cos\theta$ = constant $dx = (vi \cos\theta) \Delta t$	**Projectiles Launched Horizontal:** $a_y = g = 9.8 m/s^2$ (Vertical motion acceleration is caused by force of gravity) $v_y, f = vyi + g\Delta t$ $v_y f^2 = vy, i^2 + 2g\Delta y$ $\Delta dy = vy, i\Delta t + \frac{1}{2} g(\Delta t)2$ When a projectile falls from rest (launched horizontally), $vy, i = 0$ and the first term in the equation is zero. $V_y, f = g\Delta t$ $Vy, f^2 = 2g\Delta y$ $\Delta y = -\frac{1}{2} g(\Delta t2)$ Launched at an angle to the Horizontal: $v_y, f = vi \sin\theta + g\Delta t$ $v_y, f^2 = v^2i (\sin\theta)^2 + 2g\Delta y$ $\Delta d_y = vi(\sin\theta) \Delta t + \frac{1}{2} g(\Delta t)^2$

- **Displacement** is the change in position of an object.
- **Free Fall** is the motion of a body acted upon by only the gravitational force.
- **Gravitational Force** is the force with which the earth attracts matter towards its center.
- **Inertia** is the tendency of a body to resist a change in velocity or rest.
- **Maximum Height** is the turning point of a projectile. At Maximum Height, the vertical component of the velocity equals the horizontal component.
- **Parabola** is the set of all points in a plane that are equidistant from a particular line, called the directrix, and a particular point, called the focus, in that plane.
- **Projectile** is an object moving in two dimensions under the influence of gravity.
- **Projectile motion** is the motion a body thrown or launched on earth's surface.
- **Range** is the horizontal distance a projectile cover, usually measured in the x-direction.
- **Time of Flight** is the time it takes a project fired horizontally or at an angle to land.
- **Trajectory** is the path a projectile takes to travel.
- **Velocity** is the rate of change of displacement.
- **Vector** is a physical quantity that has both a magnitude and a direction.

ELABORATE:

Teach this phase synchronously online and use Zoom, Teams, or any platform with video, microphone, and chat to hold a synchronous virtual meeting. Have students create a "When Things Move" folder on their devices and save work inside this folder. Also, have them upload assignments to the Learning Management System and use their science notebook to write observations, notes, lab reports, and answer questions you ask in the class. Monitor students' engagement with Popsicle Sticks (random and cold calls) chat and discussion forums.

Guiding Question: How would you design a horizontally launched projectile to hit a predicted target?

Teacher: Have students apply what they learned about how height and speed influence the trajectory of a projectile fired horizontally. This demonstration is on Mader and Winn, 2007, p. 115.

Title: Predicting a Target:

Materials:
- Marble or steel ball
- Cell phone stopwatch
- Meter stick
- Ramp
- Catch cup

Distribute a meter stick and a marble to each student or have students purchase the materials.

Teach students how to build a ramp with everyday items in their surroundings such as books, boxes, wood, gutter, etc.

Ask students:

Set up the experiment as shown in Figure 19.11.

Step 1: Horizontal Speed

1. Measure the table distance dx.
2. Time how long it takes the marble to travel from the end of the ramp to the edge of the table.
3. Repeat set 2 three times and obtain the average time, t.
4. Calculate the horizontal speed v_x by dividing the table distance d_x by average time, t. Note: Make the ramp low and d_x a distance student you can time. Release the ball each time from the same spot.

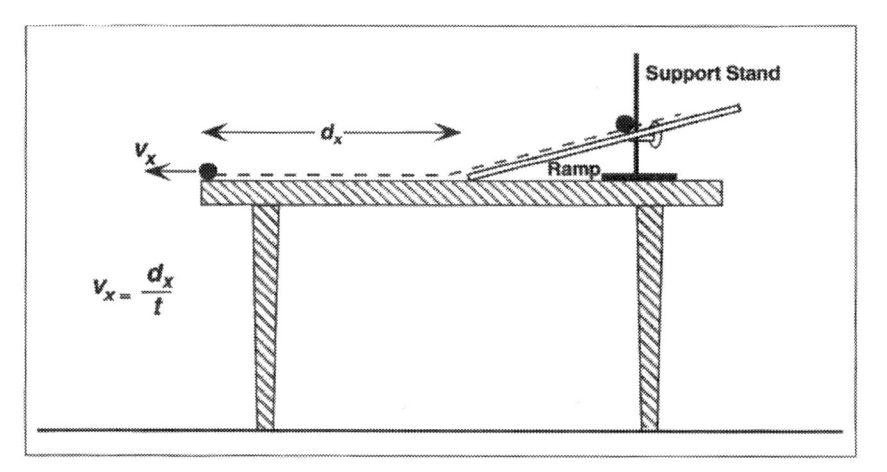

FIGURE 19.11. Experimental Setup Reproduced from Teaching Physics for the First Time (Mader & Winn, 2007, p.115), with the permission of the American Association of Physics Teachers.

Step 2: Time of Flight

1. Measure the height of the table dy.
2. Determine the Time of Flight (time taken the projectile to leave the edge of the table and land on the ground) using the equation, $T = \sqrt{\dfrac{2dy}{g}}$

Step 3: Floor Distance:

1. Predict the spot on the floor where the projectile will land. use equation $d_x = v_x T$ where T is the time of flight.
2. Measure the distance on the floor and keep the catch cup at this distance.
3. Share your calculation with your teacher before you launch the marble. The projected marble will land on the cup if timing and calculations are accurate.
4. Create a video of yourself performing this demonstration and discussing how you predicted the landing position. Convert the video to YouTube "unlisted" and share the link with your teacher.

EVALUATE:

Synchronous: The students will present their work in a synchronous virtual platform and turn in assignments in the Learning Management System.

Formative Monitoring (Questioning / Discussion) is embedded in each phase of the learning cycle.

Summative Assessment (Quiz / Project / Report):

1. A cannonball is projected from a height of 15m with a speed of 25m/s.
   a. Calculate how long it takes the cannonball to land on the ground.
   b. Calculate the horizontal velocity.
   c. If the speed or the height is changed, then would the time and range remain the same?
2. Have students share the link to YouTube video of the "Predicting a Target" demonstration and their calculations.
3. Read "Motion Characteristics of Projectile," "Horizontal and Vertical Displacement," and "Horizontally Launched Projectile Problems" at Physicsclassroom.com (see source note) and answer "Check Your Understanding" questions.

ADDITIONAL LESSON INFO

Extension and Contingency Plans:

Teacher: Ask students to write a research paper about how man uses knowledge of characteristics of the projectile and its trajectory in launching a missile, rocket, baseball, soccer ball, and football.

Accommodations and Modifications: Allow students extended time to complete each activity and assist a student who needs help.

Materials Required:

Quantity	Description	Potential Supplier (item #)	Estimated Price
1	pheasant and kingfisher	Amazon	$5.90
100	Popsicle Sticks	Amazon	$6.15
2	A pack of 10 Meter Sticks	Amazon	$28.99 x 2
1	A pack of 50 marbles	Amazon	$6.99
1	Teaching Physics for the First Time-Teacher's Edition	American Association of Physics Teachers (AAPT) store	$40.00

LESSON NARRATIVE

Clarification Statements of Performance Expectations HS-PS2-1 guided this lesson plan. Examples of data could include tables or graphs of position or velocity as a function of time for objects subject to a net unbalanced force, such as a falling object, object sliding down a ramp, or a moving object being pulled by constant force. The lesson analyzes the motion of a falling body and an object moving along the x-direction. When things move, bodies can accelerate or move at a constant speed. Falling objects accelerate naturally because of gravity and objects moving along the x-axis either accelerate or move at a constant speed. According to Newton's first law, a body continues to move at constant speed in the same direction in the absence of an external net force. On the other hand, an unbalanced force causes a mass to accelerate, as stated in Newton's second law of motion.

Scholars treat projectiles as simultaneous linear motion occurring in both the x-direction and y-direction (Henderson, 2022; Kiefer & Landa, 1995; Serway & Faughn, 2002, 2015). The body ascends and falls with a constant acceleration of 9.8 m/s^2. A plot of vertical displacement versus time graph shown in Figure 3.3 is a parabola depicting a continuous change in velocity and a constant acceleration. A dropped ball in free fall and a ball launched horizontally from the same height reach the surface of the earth at the same time in the absence of air resistance. The same force, the force of gravity, acts on both objects to cause a change in their velocities. Both objects begin falling with an initial velocity of zero.

The horizontal motion of a projectile is independent of the vertical motion. In the absence of air resistance, the horizontal component of the velocity does not change. A graph of horizontal displacement versus time is linear, indicating that the velocity is constant in the x-direction. If the projection speed and launch angle are kept constant, then a projected object will land at the same target each time it is launched. Also, in the absence of air resistance, the mass of the launched object does not influence the trajectory of a projectile. Using Projectile Motion PhET simulation, the students discover the properties of a projectile motion. This lesson plan begins with the students reading Pheasant and Kingfisher, a children's literature book, to discover that the common games they play at home such as throwing spears, a baseball, or a football, are games that use projectiles.

Engage

The students use PhET online lab simulation in an exclusively synchronous virtual space to study the properties of a projectile motion. The guiding questions for the Engage cycle are: What is a projectile and how does air resistance influence its trajectory? First, the students draw the trajectory of the spear launched into the air that they read from Pheasant and Kingfisher to have an idea of a parabola and observe that a moving object can cover a vertical and horizontal distance simultaneously. Second, students will use Projectile Motion PhET Online Lab simulation to discover:

- Air resistance slows down a projectile motion.
- A projectile traces a parabolic path.
- The velocity vector has a component in both x and y directions. While the y-component changes, the x-component remains constant.
- The force and acceleration vectors do not change.
- The force vector points only in the vertical direction, causing a change in the velocity in this y-direction.

- The acceleration vector points only in the vertical direction.
- There is no force to change the horizontal motion.
- A projectile does not accelerate in the horizontal direction.
- A projectile covers a constant horizontal distance in the absence of air resistance.

Explore

In the Explore phase, the guiding question is the following: How does each variable, mass, height, angle, and speed, influence the trajectory of a projectile launched horizontally or at an angle to the surface of the earth, neglecting air resistance? Again, through investigations with Projectile Motion PhET Lab simulations, students discover that mass or the type of object launched does not influence the trajectory of a projectile if there is no air resistance. The range a projectile attains is dependent on the height, speed, and angle of projection. Objects projected at complementary angles cover the same horizontal distance but spend different times in the air. Students also learn how to use kinematic equations to solve problems involving projectiles fired horizontally.

Explain

In the Explain cycle, the students will present a PowerPoint of what they learned about projectile motion and play videos of themselves explaining how they figured out the landing position of projected marble and performed the experiment. You will use Slide Deck from physicsclassroom.com to review important properties of projectile motion. You will also solve more example problems involving projectiles launched horizontally. If the students have taken trigonometry, then use the example problems at physicsclassroom.com under "non-horizontally launched projectile problems" to explain how to solve problems using the kinematic equations with cousin and sine functions shown in Table 19.10.

Elaborate

Have students build a ramp on top of a table and launch a marble horizontally, as shown in Figure 19.11. The students will determine the landing position through measurement and calculation and launch the marble to fall into the cup (target). See Engage phase for a detailed description of how to perform this demonstration.

SUMMARY AND REFLECTIONS

This lesson plan used mostly online simulations to teach projectile motion. Simulations enabled observation and visualization of how the velocity vectors change in the y-direction and remain constant in the x-direction. Mapping the displacement vector each 0.1s is daunting or not practical in a traditional high school experiment. Also, high school physics teachers and some university professors may not have the resources to create a vacuum and observe the influence of air resistance on projectile motion, a demonstration reported in this lesson plan. In other words, PhET simulations enabled conceptualization and understanding of complex concepts and illustrated terminologies and vocabularies associated with projectile motion. Amazingly, I used the simulations to produce the type of diagrams I see in physics textbooks. I thank the University of Colorado Boulder for providing PhET simulations and making them free to educators and students. I also thank Catherine Berndt, the author of Pheasant and Kingfisher, for bringing science material into children's books. We do not talk science; we do science. The everyday games students play involve projectiles.

TIPS AND ADVICE
- Engage students with hands-on activities.
- Have students share their work periodically as they engage in the learning process. The student may post their work on chat, share their screen, or turn their video on to show their notebook. They could discuss a question orally and use the discussion forum in the Learning Management System.
- Hold more synchronous sections and assign minimal asynchronous work.
- Write each student's name on a popsicle stick and use it for random name-calling.
- Use Padlet to elicit prior knowledge and collaborations.

RESOURCE NOTES

Name of Resource	Primary Website	How to Locate the Resource Online
Projectile Motion	https://phet.colorado.edu	Go to https://phet.colorado.edu. Located in the top right corner, use the search magnifying glass to search for "Projectile Motion" and click on "Projectile Motion(simulation)." https://phet.colorado.edu/en/simulations/projectile-motion
Projectile Motion Tutorial	https://www.physicsclassroom.com	Go to https://physicsclassroom.com. Click on "Physics Tutorial" located in the left panel and select "Vectors-Motion and Forces in Two Dimensions" and access "Lesson 2—Projectile Motions" tutorial: What is a projectile? Characteristics of a Projectile's Trajectory Horizontal and Vertical Components of velocity Horizontal and Vertical Displacement Horizontally Launched Projectile-Problem-solving Non-horizontally Launched Projectile Problem—Solving What is a projectile?: https://www.physicsclassroom.com/class/vectors/Lesson-2/What-is-a-Projectile Characteristics of a Projectile's Trajectory: https://www.physicsclassroom.com/class/vectors/Lesson-2/Characteristics-of-a-Projectile-s-Trajectory Horizontal and Vertical Components of velocity: https://www.physicsclassroom.com/class/vectors/Lesson-2/Horizontal-and-Vertical-Displacement Horizontal and Vertical Displacement: https://www.physicsclassroom.com/class/vectors/Lesson-2/Horizontal-and-Vertical-Displacement Horizontally Launched Projectile-Problem-Solving: https://www.physicsclassroom.com/class/vectors/Lesson-2/Horizontally-Launched-Projectiles-Problem-Solving Non-horizontally Launched Projectile Problem-Solving: https://www.physicsclassroom.com/class/vectors/Lesson-2/Non-Horizontally-Launched-Projectiles-Problem-Solv:

Name of Resource	Primary Website	How to Locate the Resource Online
Check Your Under-standing	https://www.physicsclassroom.com	Go to https://physicsclassroom.com, click on "Physics Tutorial," and select "Vectors—Motion and Forces in Two Dimensions." "Check Your Understanding" is towards the end of each page: Characteristics of a Projectile's Trajectory . Horizontal and Vertical Displacement Horizontal-launched Projectile Problems Characteristics of a Projectile's Trajectory: https://www.physicsclassroom.com/class/vectors/Lesson-2/Characteristics-of-a-Projectile-s-Trajectory Horizontal and Vertical Displacement: https://www.physicsclassroom.com/class/vectors/Lesson-2/Horizontal-and-Vertical-Displacement Horizontal-launched Projectile Problems: https://www.physicsclassroom.com/class/vectors/Lesson-2/Horizontally-Launched-Projectiles-Problem-Solving
Slide Deck	https://www.physicsclassroom.com	Go to https://www.physicsclassroom.com and click on "Video Tutorial" located in the left panel and select "Vectors and Projectiles" to access contents with slide deck: Components of a Projectile X and Y Displacement for a Projectile Mathematics of Projectile Motion Solving Horizontally-Launched Projectile Problems To access "Components of a Projectile," "Slide Deck," click on "Slides" located towards the end of the page. Repeat this procedure for items b-d. Components of a Projectile: https://www.physicsclassroom.com/Physics-Video-Tutorial/Vectors-and-Projectiles/Projectile-Displacement-Components/Slides X and Y Displacement for a Projectile: https://www.physicsclassroom.com/Physics-Video-Tutorial/Vectors-and-Projectiles/Projectile-Displacement-Components/Slides Mathematics of Projectile Motion: https://www.physicsclassroom.com/Physics-Video-Tutorial/Vectors-and-Projectiles/Mathematics-of-Projectiles/Slides Solving Horizontally-Launched Projectile Problems: https://www.physicsclassroom.com/Physics-Video-Tutorial/Vectors-and-Projectiles/Horizontally-Launched-Projectiles/Slides

Name of Resource	Primary Website	How to Locate the Resource Online
How to Plot Line Graph in Excel	Excel	Open Excel. Enter "Time" on the first column and Dependent variables (vertical and horizontal displacement) on the second and third columns. Highlight the three columns. Click on "Insert." Choose "Scatter." Click on "Quick Layout." Choose "Option 10" for a nonlinear and "Option 9" for linear graph. Label the axis.

DISCUSSION QUESTIONS

1. At what angle and height do you think David fired the slingstone that hit Goliath on the forehead and killed him? Explain using your knowledge of projectile motion.
2. At what angle do you think NFL player Justin Tucker of Baltimore Ravens kicked the football 66 yards (60.350 m) to break the NFL record on field goals?
3. Why do households use parabolic dish receivers to receive signals and watch television?
4. If you desire a projectile to reach a target quickly, then would you fire it at an angle 30° or 60° degrees to the surface of the earth? Explain.
5. What thoughts would you like to share about the online physics lab and instruction?

REFERENCES

Berndt, C. H. (1987). *Pheasant and kingfisher*. Mondo Publishing.

Henderson, T. (2022, April 18). *Projectile motion*. The Physics Classroom, LLC. https://www.physicsclassroom.com

Henderson, T. (2022, April 18). *What is a projectile?* https://www.physicsclassroom.com/class/vectors/Lesson-2/What-is-a-Projectile

Henderson, T. (2022, April 18). *Characteristics of a projectile's trajectory*. https://www.physicsclassroom.com/class/vectors/Lesson-2/Characteristics-of-a-Projectile-s-Trajectory

Henderson, T. (2022, April 18). *Horizontal and vertical components of velocity*. https://www.physicsclassroom.com/class/vectors/Lesson-2/Horizontal-and-Vertical-Displacement

Henderson, T. (2022, April 18). *Horizontal and vertical displacement*. https://www.physicsclassroom.com/class/vectors/Lesson-2/Horizontal-and Vertical-Displacement

Henderson, T. (2022, April 18). *Horizontally launched projectile-problem-solving*. https://www.physicsclassroom.com/class/vectors/Lesson-2/Horizontally-Launched-Projectiles-Problem-Solving

Henderson, T. (2022, April 18). *Non-horizontally launched projectile problem-solving*. https://www.physicsclassroom.com/class/vectors/Lesson-2/Non-Horizontally-Launched-Projectiles-Problem-Solv

Henderson, T. (2022, April 18). *Slide deck for components of a projectile*. https://www.physicsclassroom.com/Physics-Video-Tutorial/Vectors-and-Projectiles/Projectile-Displacement-Components/Slides

Henderson, T. (2022, April 18). *Slide deck for X- and Y- displacement of a projectile*. https://www.physicsclassroom.com/Physics-Video-Tutorial/Vectors-and-Projectiles/Projectile-Displacement-Components/Slides

Henderson, T. (2022, April 18). *Slide deck for mathematics of projectile motion*. https://www.physicsclassroom.com/Physics-Video-Tutorial/Vectors-and-Projectiles/Mathematics-of-Projectiles/Slides

Henderson, T. (2022, April 18). *Slide deck for solving horizontally-launched projectile problems.* https://www.physicsclassroom.com/Physics-Video-Tutorial/Vectors-and-Projectiles/Horizontally-Launched-Projectiles/Slides

Kiefer, D. R., & Landa J., (1995). *Reviewing physics with sample examinations.* Amsco School Publications, Inc.

Mader, J., & Winn, M. (2007). *Teaching physics for the first time.* AIP Publishing LLC.

Serway, R. A., & Faughn, J. S. (2002). *Holt physics.* Holt, Rinehart and Winston.

Serway, R. A., & Faughn, J. S. (2015). *Texas physics.* Houghton Mifflin Harcourt.

University of Colorado Boulder. (2021). *Projectile Motion.* PhET. https://phet.colorado.edu

CHAPTER 20

USING SCAFFOLDING TO DEVELOP EVIDENTIARY REASONING

A Simulation-Based Approach to Teaching Biological Evolution Online

Robert B. Marsteller
Delaware State University

Alec M. Bodzin
Lehigh Environmental Initiative

LESSON PLAN OVERVIEW

This lesson addresses the topic of biological evolution. For approximately five class sessions, students will complete several simulation activities and read authentic articles on mutations in genes involved in the digestion of lactose. While the original implementations of this lesson were asynchronous, this lesson could easily be implemented into a hybrid setting where teachers use synchronous video time to provide foundational knowledge or to model the use of the simulations. Natural selection will be presented as the primary driver of biological evolution,

---

Teaching and Learning Online: Science for Secondary Grade Levels, pages 309–330.

and other processes, such as artificial selection or contrasts between gradualism and punctuated equilibrium, will not be discussed. Students will learn about the process of natural selection and the evidence that natural selection has occurred in the past and continues to occur in the present.

Online simulations act as the centerpiece of this lesson. Simulations allow students to manipulate variables and collect data to answer questions about the process of natural selection. Students will explore simulations about predator-prey dynamics, Methicillin-Resistant *Staphylococcus aureus* (MRSA), and nest parasitism. In each simulation, a different environmental factor is used to drive changes in a population (predators, pollution, antibiotics, and nest parasites). Further, students will practice using evidence to argue for their scientific claims. Explicit modeling and instructional scaffolding ideas for the use of simulations are provided.

Discipline: Life Science—Evolution

Grade level: 9th–10th grade (high school life science/ biology)

CONNECTIONS TO NGSS AND THREE-DIMENSIONAL LEARNING

Students' Performance Expectations

- **Code:** HS-LS4 (Biological Evolution: Unity and Diversity)

Domain: *Life Science*

- HS-LS4-1 Communicate scientific information that common ancestry and biological evolution are supported by multiple lines of empirical evidence.
- HS-LS4-2 Construct an explanation based on evidence that the process of evolution primarily results from four factors: (1) the potential for species to increase in number, (2) the heritable genetic variation of individuals in a species due to mutation and sexual reproduction, (3) competition for limited resources, and (4) the proliferation of those organisms that are better able to survive and reproduce in the environment.
- HS-LS4-4 Construct an explanation based on evidence for how natural selection leads to adaptations of population.
- HS-LS4-5 Evaluate the evidence supporting claims that changes in environmental conditions may result in (1) increases in the number of individuals of some species, (2) the emergence of new species over time, and (3) the extinction of other species.

Science and Engineering Practices

Obtaining, Evaluating, and Communicating Information (LS4)

Obtaining, evaluating, and communicating information in 9–12 builds on K–8 experiences and progresses to evaluating the validity and reliability of the claims, methods, and designs.

Constructing Explanations and Designing Solutions (LS4)

Constructing explanations and designing solutions in 9–12 builds on K–8 experiences and progresses to explanations and designs that are supported by multiple and independent student-generated sources of evidence consistent with scientific ideas, principles, and theories.

Analyzing and interpreting data (LS4)
   • Analyzing data in 9–12 builds on K–8 experiences and progresses to introducing more detailed statistical analysis, the comparison of data sets for consistency, and the use of models to generate and analyze data.

Engaging in Argument from Evidence (LS4)
   • Engaging in argument from evidence in 9–12 builds on K–8 experiences and progresses to using appropriate and sufficient evidence and scientific reasoning to defend and critique claims and explanations about the natural and designed world(s). Arguments may also come from current or historical episodes in science.

Disciplinary Core Ideas

LS4.A Evidence of Common Ancestry and Diversity
   • Genetic information, like the fossil record, provides evidence of evolution. DNA sequences vary among species, but there are many overlaps; in fact, the ongoing branching that produces multiple lines of descent can be inferred by comparing the DNA sequences of different organisms. Such information is also derivable from the similarities and differences in amino acid sequences and from anatomical and embryological evidence.

LS4.B Natural Selection
   • Natural selection occurs only if there is both (1) variation in the genetic information between organisms in a population and (2) variation in the expression of that genetic information—that is, trait variation—that leads to differences in performance among individuals. The traits that positively affect survival are more likely to be reproduced, and thus are more common in the population.

LS4.C Adaptation

- Evolution is a consequence of the interaction of four factors: (1) the potential for a species to increase in number, (2) the genetic variation of individuals in a species due to mutation and sexual reproduction, (3) competition for an environment's limited supply of the resources that individuals need in order to survive and reproduce, and (4) the ensuing proliferation of those organisms that are better able to survive and reproduce in that environment.
- Natural selection leads to adaptation, that is, to a population dominated by organisms that are anatomically, behaviorally, and physiologically well-suited to survive and reproduce in a specific environment. The differential survival and reproduction of organisms in a population that have an advantageous heritable trait leads to an increase in the proportion of individuals in future generations that have the trait and to a decrease in the proportion of individuals that do not.
- Adaptation also means that the distribution of traits in a population can change when conditions change.
- Changes in the physical environment, whether naturally occurring or human-induced, have thus contributed to the expansion of some species, the emergence of new distinct species as populations diverge under different conditions and the decline–and sometimes the extinction–of some species.
- Species become extinct because they can no longer survive and reproduce in their altered environment. If members cannot adjust to change that is too fast or drastic, then the opportunity for the species' evolution is lost.

Crosscutting Concepts

Patterns (LS4)

Different patterns may be observed at each of the scales at which a system is studied and can provide evidence for causality in explanations of phenomena.

Cause and Effect (LS4)

Empirical evidence is required to differentiate between cause and correlation and make claims about specific causes and effects.

LESSON: TEACHING AND LEARNING ONLINE 5E LESSON PLAN

Grade: 9–10　　　　　　**Topic(s):** Evolutionary Biology

Guiding Question(s):
- How do we know that evolution occurs in the past and present?
- How do populations respond to environmental factors to survive and reproduce?

- What role do humans play in changing the environment and driving natural selection?

Performance Expectation(s):
- HS-LS4-1 Communicate scientific information that common ancestry and biological evolution are supported by multiple lines of empirical evidence.
- HS-LS4-2 Construct an explanation based on evidence that the process of evolution primarily results from four factors: (1) the potential for species to increase in number, (2) the heritable genetic variation of individuals in a species due to mutation and sexual reproduction, (3) competition for limited resources, and (4) the proliferation of those organisms that are better able to survive and reproduce in the environment.
- HS-LS4-4 Construct an explanation based on evidence for how natural selection leads to adaptations of population.
- HS-LS4-5 Evaluate the evidence supporting claims that changes in environmental conditions may result in (1) increases in the number of individuals of some species, (2) the emergence of new species over time, and (3) the extinction of other species.

Science & Engineering Practices:	Disciplinary Core Ideas:	Crosscutting Concepts:
• Analyzing and Interpreting Data • Constructing Explanations and Designing Solutions • Engaging in Argument from Evidence • Obtaining, Evaluating, and Communicating Information	• LS4.A Evidence of Common Ancestry and Diversity • LS4.B Natural Selection • LS4.C Adaptation	• Patterns • Cause and Effect

BACKGROUND INFORMATION

Prior Student Knowledge:

- Characteristics of living things
- Basic needs to sustain life
- Levels of biological organization (especially, species-population-community)
- Heredity (how do allele variations cause phenotypic variation)

Possible Preconceptions / Misconceptions:

- Evolution occurs at the individual rather than population level
- Confusion regarding human evolution and modern primates ("humans evolved from monkeys")

Resource Notes:

- MedlinePlus, National Library of Medicine: https://medlineplus.gov/genetics/understanding/mutationsanddisorders/evolution/
- MRSA simulation: https://www.lehigh.edu/~amb4/person/mrsa.html
- MRSA simulation scaffolding: See Appendix A.
- Nest Parasite simulation: https://www.lehigh.edu/~amb4/person/nestparasites.html
- NPR Lactose (in) tolerance https://www.npr.org/sections/thesalt/2012/12/27/168144785/an-evolutionary-whodunit-how-did-humans-develop-lactose-tolerance
- Predator-Prey simulation: https://phet.colorado.edu/en/simulation/natural-selection
- PhET Interactive Simulations University of Colorado Boulder: http://phet.colorado.edu/
- PhET simulation scaffolding See Appendix B.
- Understanding Evolution. 2021. University of California Museum of Paleontology. 22 August 2008 http://evolution.berkeley.edu/
- WGBH Educational Foundation and Clear Blue Sky Productions. (2001) Evolution of antibiotic resistance. https://www.pbs.org/wgbh/evolution/library/10/4/l_104_03.html
- Wilensky, U. (1999). NetLogo. http://ccl.northwestern.edu/netlogo/. Center for Connected Learning and Computer-Based Modeling, Northwestern University, Evanston, IL.
- Vocabulary definitions https://www.nationalacademies.org/evolution/definitions

LESSON PLAN

ENGAGE: Students watch a short video that introduces the concepts of life's diversity and the terminology used in subsequent task sets.

Foundational Knowledge, The Diversity of Life: Students investigate the source of genetic variation. Students are presented with the concept of diversity within a population. Review relevant genetics content knowledge to explain traits of individuals and diversity within a population.

EXPLORE: Students use the Predator-Prey simulation to model the effects of predation and ecological resources on survival. Students are allowed to manipulate several variables that impact a bunny population. Guided questions ensure that students attend to relevant features of the simulation.

Simulation Study, the Struggle for Survival: Students investigate factors that determine which individuals within a population will survive and reproduce. Students are presented with the concept of limited environmental resources (food, shelter, mates) and the resultant competition.

EXPLAIN: Students are asked to use their resources to critique human activities that either limit or promote the spread of MRSA and to evaluate possible outcomes.

Case Study, MRSA: Students explore the recent "appearance" of Methicillin-resistant Staphylococcus aureus (MRSA) and how scientists have traced its development and plan for its impact.

Vocabulary: antibiotic resistance, bacteria, mutation, selective pressure, virus

ELABORATE: Students are given resources from reputable sources to learn about the spread of genes allowing for the persistence of lactose tolerance beyond infancy in humans. Students are directed to think about how this scenario may or may not indicate that human evolution is an ongoing process and to think about other human traits that may be subject to selective pressure.

Case Study, Lactose (in)tolerance: Students investigate the genetic basis for lactose (in)tolerance and find out how scientists have traced the appearance and persistence of this mutation to specific regions of the world.

EVALUATE:

Formative Monitoring (Questioning / Discussion): Students are given daily question sets to review developing content knowledge and provide opportunities to practice applying knowledge to novel situations. Additionally, students contribute to discussion prompts in an online forum monitored and supported by the teacher.

Summative Assessment (Quiz / Project / Report): Students are asked to utilize a simulation that shows the impact of road-building on nesting bird populations. They are then able to propose modifications to the simulation that would allow them to collect other data. Students utilize data collected from the simulation and their speculations about other potential data that could be modeled, to propose how humans can balance economic growth with environmental stewardship.

ADDITIONAL LESSON INFO

Extension and Contingency Plans:

Accommodations and Modifications:
Formative assessment is required to ensure that appropriate levels of support are provided for all students. Students' ability to independently read and follow direc-

tions is a concern. Explicit modeling for using the simulations is recommended for classes with English learners, students with disabilities, and reluctant readers. It may be advantageous to provide directions in a stepwise fashion, rather than all at once. Additionally, students with limited language proficiency may require directions to be read to them by a peer or paraprofessional. Students who are unable to see the simulations would require descriptive assistance. Finally, consider reduced scaffolding for gifted and talented students.

LESSON NARRATIVE

Evolution is a central concept in the study of biology. However, it can be difficult to allow students to get involved with hands-on learning on this topic. In order to facilitate experiential learning, students will use three web-based simulations to explore the environment's role in natural selection. By manipulating variables within the simulations and analyzing the data they generate, students will be able to see relationships between the environment, natural selection, and evolution.

1. How do we know that evolution occurs in the past and present?
2. How do populations respond to environmental factors in order to survive and reproduce?
3. What role do humans play in changing the environment and driving natural selection?

Engage: Foundational Knowledge About the Diversity of Life

Start by activating students' prior knowledge about the wide variety of life on Earth. Students are prompted to think about the wide variety of plants and animals they are familiar with, as well as the abundance of microscopic life that may not be part of their everyday experiences. Engage students by bringing in meme-friendly animals like honey badgers, pangolins, narwhals, or aye-ayes. While this lesson was designed to use a video, this part could easily be a whole class activity in person or using a live web conference platform like Zoom. Be sure to have images ready to share! Once your students are thinking about all of the weird and wonderful things in the world, direct their thinking to prior knowledge about genetics. Ask the following: "Why does a honey badger look like a honey badger, rather than a pangolin or an oak tree?" If your students require further prompting, then refer to examples used in your class when exploring genetics. Did you examine student traits such as tongue rolling and widow's peaks? Did you compare pea plants? Students should all be able to explain that variations in traits (phenotype) are determined by genes.

Now that you have established a genetic basis for variation between species, ask about the differences within a species. Students should be able to recognize that interspecies and intraspecies variation are both due to genetic differences. Further, students should consider that all genetic variation is a product of mutation. Refer students to the MedlinePlus resource if they require background knowledge about mutations.

Explore: Simulation Study About the Struggle for Survival

Ask your students to explore the impact of phenotypic diversity with the Predator-Prey simulation. Depending on the ability of your students to read and follow directions, you can distribute the following written directions or read them aloud to your students. Teachers will need to determine how much explicit modeling is appropriate for their students. We recommend that you explicitly model how to use the simulation for classrooms that contain English learners and students with disabilities.

Explain: Case Study About MRSA

Vocabulary

- Antibiotic resistance: some bacteria develop mutations that make them less susceptible to the effects of antibiotics
- bacteria: single celled organisms without a nucleus or membrane bound organelles
- mutation: a change in the genetic sequence of an organism, sometimes resulting in new phenotypes
- selective pressure: factors in the environment that drive the spread of beneficial mutations through a population
- virus: a vehicle for transmitting and replicating genetic material with some of the features of living things

Direct students to the PBS resource about antibiotic resistance. Ask your students to respond to the questions below. Model responses have been included. Note: the term *selective pressure* does not appear in the PBS resource. Selective pressure is an environmental factor that drives evolution in populations. For example, there would not be any advantage to being a brown bunny who can hide in the desert without hungry wolves. Predators provide selective pressure on prey populations.

1. *What is the environment bacteria inhabit?* These bacteria live in and on humans.
2. *What selective pressure is placed on bacteria populations?* Antibiotics are driving the evolution of bacterial populations.
3. *How can you limit the dangers of the antibiotic paradox?* Do not ask for antibiotics unless they are necessary. You could also discuss hormone-free animal farming or vegetarianism if you have students who concern themselves with food politics or animal rights.

Next, direct students to the MRSA simulation. Provide students with a scaffolded activity to utilize this simulation. Following engagement with the scaffolded activity, students should be able to answer the questions included in Appendix A

Elaborate: Case Study About Lactose (in)tolerance

Have students read the NPR article about the development of the persistence of the lactose gene into adulthood. It may be surprising to discover that most of the world is lactose intolerant. There is a small portion of the world where a mutation occurred that allowed humans to digest milk after they were infants. This mutation must have provided a *selective advantage*, meaning that people with this trait survived and reproduced better than people that did not have this trait. However, this trait did not spread across all human populations because it developed relatively recently. An important point to take from this topic is that evolution occurs in humans, not just bacteria and bunnies.

Have your students respond to the following prompt in an online discussion forum or an in-class small group discussion:

> The ability to produce lactase and digest milk as an adult was subject to selective pressure in human history. Does that same pressure from natural selection exist today? Explain your reasoning and support your conclusion with evidence.

Students should recognize that there is little or no selective pressure to digest milk. We have many alternative sources of nutrition, even milk alternatives, such as soy, almond, or oat milk.

You could extend this discussion by asking students to consider if any selective pressures exist for humans now. Has our technological ability insulated us from our environment to the point where humans are no longer subject to natural selection? In an economically developed country such as the United States, students may not recognize that parasites such as malaria are responsible for hundreds of thousands of deaths each year. While not cured, other diseases, such as AIDS, are treatable in the U.S., but many countries do not have access to the resources to provide treatment. Hundreds of thousands of people die every year from AIDS. It may be worth considering how these devastating diseases may provide selective pressure in some local human populations but not others.

Evaluate

Formative Monitoring

Questions have been embedded in the lesson narrative and these questions could be extracted to produce individual assignments for students. Be sure to use data gathered during simulations as a source of evidence. Ensuring students refer to their data may be something you have to prompt, such as asking: "What data can you use to support a claim about selective pressure on bacteria to promote the spread of a mutation through a population?" Additionally, it is possible to create exit tickets or short multiple-choice assessments to measure the acquisition of vocabulary and content knowledge.

Summative Assessment

The summative assessment for this lesson asks students to demonstrate an understanding of evolutionary biology concepts and use simulations as a tool to test hypotheses. Provide students with access to the nest parasite simulation. Provide introductory information about nest parasites. Nest parasites are birds, like the cuckoo, that lay their eggs in the nests of other birds. When the cuckoo egg hatches, it pushes the other chicks out of the nest. The parent birds continue to feed the cuckoo chick while their chicks die. One other aspect of nest parasitism that is relevant to this simulation activity is that nest parasites tend to lay eggs in nests on the edges of forests. When a road is built, it creates open space and more exposed edges of the forest.

Have students set up and run the simulation without adding any roads. Use the default settings for nesters (100) and parasites (4). Nest parasites are red arrows. Other birds' nests are black arrows. When a parasite lays an egg in the nest, it changes color to red. Run the simulation for 500 ticks, then record the number of red arrows. Do a second trial with the same settings but add a road before clicking **go**. Let the simulation run for 500 ticks and click **go** again to stop the simulation. After recording the number of red arrows after this trial, set up a third trial. Add another road (the roads will intersect at right angles in the middle of the forest). Record the number of red arrows after 500 ticks. Have students compare results from the three trials to explain the effect of roads on nest parasites. Trials could be conducted individually, in small groups, or as a whole class. You may want to aggregate student data.

Now ask students to think about the concept of selective pressure relative to bird populations in this forest. What environmental factors impact the ability of nesting birds to survive and reproduce? The presence of nest parasites and the building of roads both impact the ability of nesting birds to survive and reproduce. How could nesting birds adapt to this situation to improve their ability to survive and reproduce? Allow students to consider creative ideas. Changing nest designs to camouflage or protect against nest parasites are possibilities. Only selecting nesting sites away from forest edges could be another. Students may come up with innovative solutions. Just make sure those variations can be explained by the emergence of a genetic mutation.

Next, have your students propose how they would add their new mutation to this simulation. Is there a button that adds another blue arrow variation that cannot be parasitized? You do not need your students to understand how to code a simulation or to get serious about designing these changes, but that is a possibility. The code is available under the Netlogo code tab below the simulation window. What is important here is that they describe a reasonable mutation that could provide a selective advantage and that they can describe how that mutation could be included in the simulation. You may want to ask your students to provide a hypothesis about how they would expect the data from the simulation to change based on their revisions.

This assessment is limited by the scope of the nest parasite simulation. It is hoped that by narrowing the scope of this activity, students will require less instructional scaffolding than if the simulation itself were more expansive. As with other sections of this lesson, adjust the amount of support your students require based on your experience and assessment of their capabilities.

SUMMARY AND REFLECTION

Evolutionary biology is complex and requires a depth of understanding. This complexity sets it apart from much of the material covered in typical high school science classrooms. If we want students to gain depth of understanding, then they will need time to engage with the content and the practices we want them to use. Students require both guidance and independence. Guidance will help them attend to relevant details and independence will allow students to evaluate their understanding. Simulations offer an engaging way to gather and interpret data and make sense of concepts through firsthand experience.

Simulations allow students to test ideas in a relatively short period of time. Further, simulations are a source of visual data representations that can be used to support or refute scientific claims. Providing instructional scaffolding helps students understand how to utilize simulation resources effectively. It is important to remember that an appropriate amount of instructional scaffolding will still provide students with some freedom to explore. The scaffolding sample provided above for the predator-prey simulation is probably more support than most students require. It may be helpful to engage students in modeling an example then to provide significantly less scaffolding for their independent work. The key is to provide the amount of support that is "just right." Ultimately, teachers should rely on formative assessments to determine the appropriate level of scaffolding for each of their students.

TIPS AND ADVICE

- Use inquiry to stimulate engagement: Put students in a position to explore with simulations and learn for themselves.
- Find the scaffolding sweet spot: Too much can be stifling, not enough can leave unprepared students directionless and dependent on their teacher.
- The simulations recommended in this lesson plan may have additional variables that can be manipulated. Consider how to prepare students to isolate variables in order to determine causality. How could you use additional variables to extend learning for some students?

- Provide opportunities for students to interact: Working independently in online learning environments can be isolating, but interactions must be meaningful and appropriate.
- Ask your students to make their thinking visible: Periodically asking your students to track their planning, monitoring, and evaluation processes will help you and them understand the processes students use to solve problems.
- Support evidentiary reasoning: Providing a written structure for evidence-based reasoning such as EBRF (Brown et al., 2010) or the Claim Evidence Reasoning framework (McNeil & Krajcik, 2011) can be effective. Structures like EBRF or CER can be presented in the form of graphic organizers for your students.

RESOURCE NOTES

Name of Resource	Primary Website	How to Locate the Resource Online
PhET Interactive Simulations	https://phet.colorado.edu/ selection	Go to https://phet.colorado.edu/. Located in the top right corner, use the search magnifying glass to search for "Natural Selection (simulation)." https://phet.colorado.edu/en/simulations/natural-selection
PBS Evolution	https://www.pbs.org/ wgbh/evolution/	Got to https://www.pbs.org/wgbh/evolution/. In the middle of the landing page, select "evolution library." From the topic menu, select "why evolution matters." Scroll through the topics to the "medicine" section. Select "Evolution of Antibiotic Resistance." https://www.pbs.org/wgbh/evolution/library/10/4/l_104_03.html
MRSA simulation	https://www.lehigh.edu/~amb4/person/	Go to https://www.lehigh.edu/~amb4/person/. Select mrsa.html. https://www.lehigh.edu/~amb4/person/mrsa.html.
NPR	https://www.npr.org/	Go to https://www.npr.org/. Located in the top right corner, use the search magnifying glass to search for "Evolutionary Whodunit." The recommended article will be the first option available. https://www.npr.org/sections/the-salt/2012/12/27/168144785/an-evolutionary-whodunit-how-did-humans-develop-lactose-tolerance
Nest Parasite Simulation	https://www.lehigh.edu/~amb4/person/	Go to https://www.lehigh.edu/~amb4/person/. Select nest parasites. https://www.lehigh.edu/~amb4/person/nestparasites.html

DISCUSSION QUESTIONS

1. This lesson is focused on using data from simulations as evidence to support scientific claims. How would you respond to a challenge from a student that simulations are not real and only report data according to their programming? Are simulations and models a valid source of scientific knowledge?

2. Evolution, while not controversial among most biologists, remains a topic that is disputed by many Americans. How will you address this issue with your students?

3. Using scaffolded activities in place of direct instruction could feel unusual for you and your students. What strategies could you use to acclimate your classroom to using a new approach to learning?

4. If your students do not have experience constructing scientific arguments, then how can you make sure they recognize the differences between arguing to support a scientific claim and having a disagreement?

5. Simulations may have an array of variables that can be manipulated. This lesson relies on a scaffolded approach to inquiry to ensure students focus on particular variables. What benefits could exist for students if you provide less scaffolding when using simulations? How could you prepare students for a more learner-centered approach to inquiry learning using simulations?

6. Students and teachers who are familiar with direct instruction methods may lack confidence in the quality of learning that occurs when using case studies and simulations. What assessment techniques could you use to both ensure students are learning and to make students aware of their success?

REFERENCES

Medicine Plus. (2020, Sep 18). *How are gene mutations involved in evolution?* National Institutes of Health. https://medlineplus.gov/genetics/understanding/mutationsand-disorders/evolution/

Marsteller. (n.d.). *MRSA simulation.* https://www.lehigh.edu/~amb4/person/mrsa.html

Marsteller. (n.d.). *Nest parasites simulation.* https://www.lehigh.edu/~amb4/person/nest-parasites.html

National Academies of Science, Engineering, and Medicine. (2021). *Definitions of evolutionary terms.* https://www.nationalacademies.org/evolution/definitions

Thompson, H. (2012, December 28). *An Evolutionary whodunit: How did humans develop lactose tolerance?* NPR. https://www.npr.org/sections/the-salt/2012/12/27/168144785/an-evolutionary-whodunit-how-did-humans-develop-lactose-tolerance

University of California Museum of Paleontology. (2008, August 22). *Understanding evolution.* http://evolution.berkeley.edu/

University of Colorado Boulder. (n.d.). *Natural selection*. PhET. https://phet.colorado.edu/en/simulation/natural-selection

WGBH Educational Foundation and Clear Blue Sky Productions. (2001). *Evolution of antibiotic resistance*. https://www.pbs.org/wgbh/evolution/library/10/4/l_104_03.html

Wilensky, U. (1999). *NetLogo*. http://ccl.northwestern.edu/netlogo/

APPENDIX A

Here is an example of how to present the MRSA simulation with some instructional scaffolding for students:

1. Go to the MRSA simulation.
   https://www.lehigh.edu/~amb4/person/mrsa.html.
2. This image is what you should see.

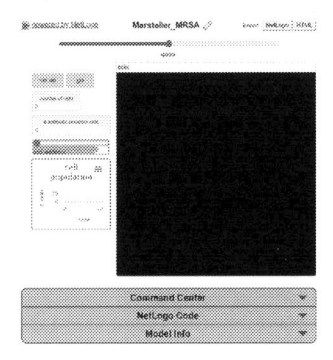

3. Click the setup button.

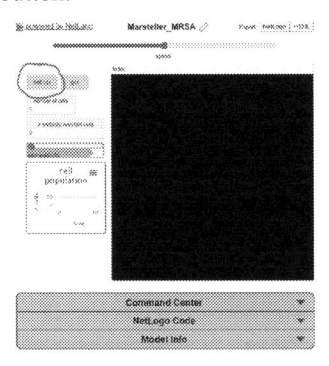

4. In this simulation, a single, non-resistant bacteria is present at the beginning. Bacteria appear as colorful dots. Different colors represent different mutations. Every time the "go" button is pressed, the bacteria divides.

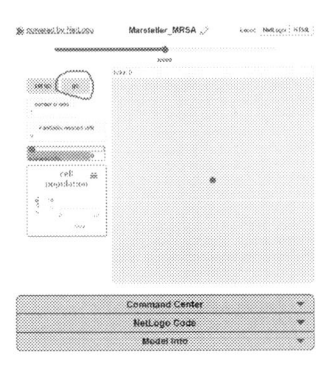

5. Immediately above the simulation image is a tick counter. Each time you press go it will register five ticks. The replication process introduces the possibility of a mutation that could cause antibiotic resistance.

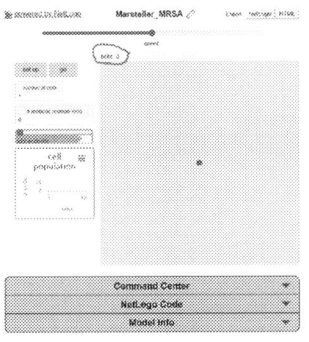

6. The other relevant variable to manipulate in this simulation is the ability to add antibiotics. Antibiotics appear as green squares. Bacteria that touch green squares die unless they have developed a mutation for antibiotic resistance.

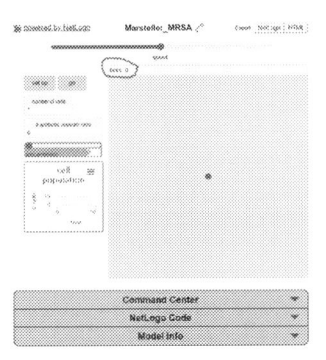

7. Have students try adding antibiotics at different times or in different amounts. Also, ask students to remove the antibiotics after a set period of treatment. Try to limit the number of bacterial generations to 100 ticks. Once you get past 150 ticks, the simulation can start to lag. We recommend trying the following trials with your students:

Control/Treatment Trial 1

Step 1: Press **set-up**, then **go** until the tick counter reads 100 ticks.
Step 2: Record the number of cells and the number of resistant cells.
record the number of cells _____
record the number of resistant cells _____
Step 3: Press **go** until the tick counter reads 150.
Step 4: Record the number of cells and the number of resistant cells.
record the number of cells _____
record the number of resistant cells _____

Control/Treatment Trial 2

Step 1: Press **set-up**, then add 25 antibiotics, then press **go** until the tick counter reads 100 ticks.
Step 2: Record the number of cells and the number of resistant cells.
record the number of cells _____
record the number of resistant cells _____
Step 3: Press **go** until the tick counter reads 150.
Step 4: Record the number of cells and the number of resistant cells.
record the number of cells _____
record the number of resistant cells _____

Dosage Trial 1

Step 1: Press **set-up**, then add 50 antibiotics, then press **go** until the tick counter reads 100 ticks.
Step 2: Record the number of cells and the number of resistant cells.
record the number of cells _____
record the number of resistant cells _____
Step 3: Press **go** until the tick counter reads 150.
Step 4: Record the number of cells and the number of resistant cells.
record the number of cells _____
record the number of resistant cells _____

Dosage Trial 2

Step 1: Press **set-up**, then add 25 antibiotics, then press **go** until the tick counter reads 100 ticks.

Step 2: Record the number of cells and the number of resistant cells.
record the number of cells _____
record the number of resistant cells _____
Step 3: Press **go** until the tick counter reads 150.
Step 4: Record the number of cells and the number of resistant cells.
record the number of cells _____
record the number of resistant cells _____

One thing students will notice is that once a resistant bacterium is present, it will multiply and cannot be destroyed by antibiotics. If this phenomenon occurs, students may want to modify the directions to add antibiotics before resistant bacteria spawn rather than rely on a set tick count. Questions are provided below, which may provide a fruitful classroom discussion. These questions could be posted to a discussion forum, further explored with students as group work, or could form the basis of a research project to follow up on the initial simulation work. Require your students to refer to evidence from the simulation to support their claims and communicate with their peers.

When does antibiotic resistance arise within the simulation?
Have the class collect data on this and compare results. It should be apparent that there is no set number of ticks where resistant bacteria are introduced. Based on foundational knowledge and their experience with this simulation, students should recognize that mutations occur randomly.

At what point would someone take an antibiotic?
We have bacteria present in and on our bodies all the time. We have more bacterial cells in and on our bodies than human cells! However, this fact rarely causes us to be ill. It is unlikely that we would take antibiotics every day, like a vitamin. Antibiotics require a prescription and can have side effects such as upset stomachs that we would not want if we were not ill. We do not take medicine of any kind, usually, unless we are symptomatic. We do not take medicine unless we feel sick. Have your students decide on several bacteria that would create symptoms (100? 1000?). Then, have them add antibiotics after their bacterial population reaches that threshold.

What happens if you stop taking antibiotics too soon?
Often people will stop taking medicine when they start to feel better and they assume that medicine has done its job and they no longer need it. When a doctor prescribes an antibiotic, they will provide directions explaining how long we should take this medicine. Have students create a trial where they use antibiotics for different periods of time and compare the outcomes.

This simulation seems rigged, do the resistant bacteria always win in real life?

Answering this question requires some sensitivity to the maturity of your students and their ability to grapple with concepts that may appear bleak. While pharmaceutical companies are trying to develop new antibiotics to treat resistant bacteria and have had some success, there can always be more mutations in the future. The issue to understand is that antibiotic resistance is a serious issue, and one of the most important medical tools we have may not be effective forever.

APPENDIX B

Here is an example of how to present the PhET Predator-Prey simulation with some instructional scaffolding for students:

1. Go to the Natural Selection simulation. https://phet.colorado.edu/en/simulation/natural-selection.
2. Click "play."
3. Click "lab."
4. This image is what you should see:

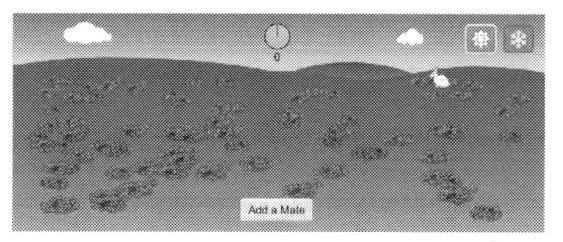

5. There will be one white rabbit present in the environment.
6. Look at the windows that provide information about this simulation. A graph plots population size against generations and this graph will initially appear blank.

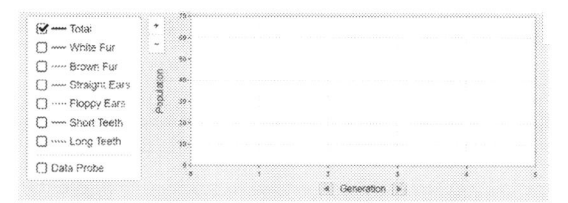

7. At the bottom center of the rabbit's environment is a yellow button labeled "Add a mate." Use your mouse to click that button one time. You should notice one new rabbit added to the environment.
8. Notice the pink circle in the top center of the environment. This circle marks the time for a generation. Each time the sweeping arm returns to the top of the circle, a new generation starts. Let the simulation continue uninterrupted.
9. Record the data from the population graph in Figure 20.1.

Generation	Total Population
1	
2	
3	
4	
5	
6	

FIGURE 20.1. Total Populations for Six Generations, Trial 1

10. How many bunnies were in each generation? How many generations does it take for bunnies to take over the world?

11. Since bunnies have yet to take over the world in real life, there must be factors limiting their population's growth. Look at the window on the right side of the simulation that is labeled *Environmental Factors*. What three factors can we add to our simulation?

12. Let us pick one environmental factor to add: wolves. Add a mate and let the simulation run for the same number of generations as step #6 above. Record the data from the population graph in Figure 20.2.

13. What happened to the bunnies when you added wolves to the simulation?

14. Let us try a third option. Start the simulation over. Do not add wolves yet. Add a mate, then let the simulation run for three generations. Then pause the simulation with the *pause button* in the lower right corner.

Generation	Total Population
1	
2	
3	
4	
5	
6	

FIGURE 20.2. Total Populations for Six Generations, Trial 2

Generation	Total Population
1	
2	
3	
4	
5	
6	

FIGURE 20.3.   Total Populations for Six Generations, Trial 3

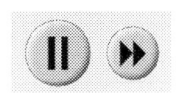

15. Now add the wolves and resume the simulation for another three generations. Resume the simulation by clicking the pause button one time.
16. Record the data from the population graph in Figure 20.3.
17. The wolves are still inhibiting the population growth of the bunnies, even with a head start. Perhaps we can use a mutation to provide some relief to the bunnies. In the section on the upper right side of the Web page, you will see three possible mutations, fur, ears, and teeth. Let us select fur as a dominant trait.

Add Mutations

Dominant Recessive

Fur

Ears

Teeth

Generation	Total Population
1	
2	
3	
4	
5	
6	

FIGURE 20.4.   Total Populations for Six Generations, Trial 4

Generation	Total Population	White Bunnies	Brown Bunnies
1			
2			
3			
4			
5			
6			

FIGURE 20.5. Total Population, with Sub-Populations for Six Generations, Trial 4

18. Now, run the simulation for three generations, pause, and add wolves back in for three more generations. Record the data from the population graph in Figure 20.4.
19. Notice that the population graph has become more complicated. There are now three lines charting population size, one for the total population, one for white bunnies, and one for brown bunnies. Let us revise our data table to include this new information for Trial 4.
20. First, let us compare our total population for this trial (#4) to the results from the previous simulation trial #3.

   In our previous trial, wolves were added after three generations.

   In our most recent trial, a mutation for brown bunnies was added to the population and wolves were added after three generations.
21. How do the total populations compare after three generations?
22. How do the total populations compare after six generations?
23. What claim can you make about bunnies with brown fur?
24. What evidence can you use to support your claim?
25. Explain how your evidence supports your claim.

Generation	Total Population, White Bunnies Only (Trial #3)	Total Population, White and Brown Bunnies (Trial #4)
1		
2		
3		
4		
5		
6		

FIGURE 20.6. Total Population Comparisons, trials 3 and 4

CHAPTER 21

CLIMATE CRISIS ISSUES IN OUR COMMUNITY

Amy Vo
University of Denver

LESSON OVERVIEW

The lesson plan, Climate Crisis Issues in Our Community, addresses one of the most pressing needs in the curriculum today. This past year we have had more extreme hurricanes, forest fires, and even a global pandemic. The planet's surface has increased in temperature 2.12 degrees Fahrenheit since the 19th century. The world's oceans have increased in temperature affecting plant and sea life globally. These climate-related events affect the polar ice caps, permanent ice fields, and ocean levels across the planet. The record high temperatures in the United States have increased the frequency of extreme weather events (i.e., heat waves, hurricanes, tornadoes, flooding, and forest fires; NASA: Climate, n.d.). Are students aware of how these events are related? Or how human choices have impacted these events? This lesson will address the essential question: "How do human choices affect climate crisis issues?"

In this online lesson, students will investigate climate issues that directly affect their community and develop solutions to address those issues. To engage in this lesson, students will become intimately aware of climate change, affecting their

Teaching and Learning Online: Science for Secondary Grade Levels, pages 331–346.

daily lives and the people around them. Each student will select one issue that is of particular interest to them and brainstorm possible solutions. Solutions could be simple, like organizing a clean-up day for the local park, or complex, like informing consumers of the environmental tradeoffs of electric vehicles.

The lesson may be implemented synchronously or asynchronously. In each of the 5E sections below and in the Lesson Narrative, teacher and student moves are described for both types of instruction. These modes of instruction may be modified to accommodate specific class needs.

The evaluative segment of the lesson requires students to identify an appropriate online platform to present their climate change issue and solution (e.g., using Tinkercad™, an engineering-based program for students to build a virtual model for presentation). The presentation will be given to peers for evaluation. Peers will provide feedback, thus allowing students the opportunity for refinement.

Discipline: Biology-Ecosystems

Grade Level: 10th

CONNECTIONS TO NGSS AND THREE-DIMENSIONAL LEARNING

Students' Performance Expectations

- **Code: HS-LS2-7 (High School Ecosystems: Interactions, Energy, and Dynamics)**
- **Domain: Life Sciences (LS)**
- **HS-LS2-7:** Design, evaluate, and refine a solution for reducing the impacts of human activities on the environment and biodiversity.

Science & Engineering Practices

Constructing Explanations and Designing Solutions (HS-LS2-7)

- Design, evaluate, and refine a solution to a complex real-world problem based on scientific knowledge, student-generated sources of evidence, prioritized criteria, and trade-off considerations.

Disciplinary Core Ideas

Ecosystem Dynamics, Functioning, and Resilience (LS2.C)

- Moreover, anthropogenic changes (induced by human activity) in the environment, including habitat destruction, pollution, introduction of invasive species, overexploitation, and climate change, can disrupt an ecosystem and threaten the survival of some species.

Biodiversity and Humans (LS4.D)

- Biodiversity is increased by the formation of new species (speciation) and decreased by the loss of species (extinction). *(secondary)*
- Humans depend on the living world for the resources and other benefits provided by biodiversity. However, human activity is also having adverse impacts on biodiversity through overpopulation, overexploitation, habitat destruction, pollution, introduction of invasive species, and climate change. Thus, sustaining biodiversity so that ecosystem functioning and productivity are maintained is essential to supporting and enhancing life on Earth. Sustaining biodiversity also aids humanity by preserving landscapes of recreational or inspirational value. *(secondary) (Note: This Disciplinary Core Idea is also addressed by HS-LS4-6).*

Developing Possible Solutions (ETS1.B)

- When evaluating solutions, it is important to consider a range of constraints including cost, safety, reliability, and aesthetics and to consider social, cultural, and environmental impacts. *(secondary)*

Crosscutting Concepts

Stability and Change

- Much of science deals with constructing explanations of how things change and how they remain stable.

TEACHING AND LEARNING ONLINE 5E LESSON PLAN

Grade: 10th   **Topic(s):** Ecosystems

Guiding Question(s):

1. Who benefits and who loses from the climate crisis?
2. Who owns the climate crisis? People? Governing bodies? Nature?

Performance Expectation(s): HS-LS2-7 Ecosystems: Interactions, Energy, and Dynamics: Design, evaluate, and refine a solution for reducing the impacts of human activities on the environment and biodiversity. **Students will be focusing on the design portion of the performance expectation.** See Resource Notes related to NGSS for possible design solutions expectations.

Science & Engineering Practices:	Disciplinary Core Ideas:	Crosscutting Concepts:
Constructing Explanations and Designing Solutions Constructing explanations and designing solutions in 9–12 builds on K–8 experiences and progresses to explanations and designs supported by multiple and independent student-generated sources of evidence consistent with scientific ideas, principles, and theories. • Design, evaluate, and refine a solution to a complex real-world problem, based on scientific knowledge, student-generated sources of evidence, prioritized criteria, and trade-off considerations.	**LS2.C: Ecosystem Dynamics, Functioning, and Resilience** • Moreover, anthropogenic changes (induced by human activity) in the environment - including habitat destruction, pollution, introduction of invasive species, overexploitation, and climate change - can disrupt an ecosystem and threaten the survival of some species. **LS4.D: Biodiversity and Humans** • Biodiversity is increased by the formation of new species (speciation) and decreased by the loss of species (extinction). (secondary) • Humans depend on the living world for the resources and other benefits provided by biodiversity. However, human activity also has adverse impacts on biodiversity through overpopulation, overexploitation, habitat destruction, pollution, introduction of invasive species, and climate change. Thus, sustaining biodiversity so that ecosystem functioning and productivity are maintained is essential to supporting and enhancing life on Earth. Sustaining biodiversity also aids humanity by preserving landscapes of recreational or inspirational value. (secondary) (Note: This Disciplinary Core Idea is also addressed by HS-LS4-6). **ETS1.B: Developing Possible Solutions** • When evaluating solutions, it is important to consider a range of constraints including cost, safety, reliability, and aesthetics and to consider social, cultural, and environmental impacts. (secondary)	**Stability and Change** Much of science deals with constructing explanations of how things change and how they remain stable.

BACKGROUND INFORMATION

Prior Student Knowledge:

- Students will most likely have background information regarding climate change. It would be beneficial to gather information from students concerning their depth of knowledge in this area.

Possible Preconceptions / Misconceptions:

- Students may believe that climate change does not exist, is exaggerated, or is a political stunt. It is essential to set a safe environment in the classroom where students do not feel attacked for their beliefs. An unsafe educational/social/emotional environment in the classroom will not be conducive to learning.

Resource Notes: *see detailed navigation descriptions for each website below in the Lesson Narrative.

Climate Crisis Websites:

- Pollution problems in the U.S. Website: Environmental Protection Agency
- Pollution problems in the U.S. Website: United States Government
- Environment America-Clean Air, Clean Water, Open Space
- The World Counts-counting deforestation, overfishing, arctic ice melting includes resources.
- NASA-Evidence and facts about climate change.
- UNFCCC-United Nations Climate Change agreement between participating countries.

TED-EdTM videos:

- The Tragedy of the Commons. Nicholas Amendolare
- Climate Change: Earth's Giant Game of Tetris. Joss Fong
- Why the Arctic is Climate Change's Canary in the Coal Mine? William Chapman
- How Big is the Ocean? Scott Gass
- Can Wildlife Adapt to Climate Change? Erin Eastwood
- Underwater Farms vs. Climate Change. Ayana Elizabeth Johnson & Megan Davis

Readings:

- Ted Ed: Climate Crisis Reading List, 15 essential reads.
- List of essays, poems, quotes, and illustrations related to the climate crisis.

Model Building Online:

- TinkercadTM: Online format for building/designing models or prototypes.
- CanvaTM: Graphic design program available online

LESSON PLAN

ENGAGE: Synchronous-You choose a Ted-Ed video for the entire class to watch. Asynchronous-Provide a list of Ted-Ed videos for students to select from.

- Questions for students: What do you know about climate change? How does climate change affect us locally? Can you think of recent events in our community that might be connected to climate change?
- View 2 Ted-Ed videos (choose from list). Ask students if they are aware of the ways climate change affects the local community.
- Ask for several students to share their thoughts concerning climate change and the local community.

EXPLORE: Synchronous

- You should be available for student questions/concerns while students explore the material. Asynchronous-provide students with the list of chosen resources for the Explore portion of the lesson. *See Source Notes list.
- Students will use the Source Notes list to dig into climate change issues.
- During the explore portion of the lesson, encourage students to explore all the resources to find one climate change issue that interests them.

EXPLAIN:

- Synchronous: You should be available for student questions.
- Asynchronous: Students may use the same Source Notes list to gather information for a climate change issue of their choice.
- Students will choose one climate change issue, of interest to them, that affects the local community and gather more in-depth information about the issue.

Questions students should be able to answer concerning the local issue chosen:

1. What is the issue?
2. How does it affect the local community?
3. Why is this issue considered a climate change issue?
4. How does this issue affect the climate?

Once students have gathered the above information for the climate change issue chosen, you should share the vocabulary below and ask students to determine which definition best fits the climate change/crisis issue they chose.

Ask several students to share their conclusions concerning the class's classification (climate change, climate crisis) of their chosen issue.

Vocabulary:
- **Climate Crisis:** A situation characterized by the threat of highly dangerous, irreversible changes to the global climate.
- **Climate Change:** A change in global or regional climate patterns, attributed mainly to the increased levels of atmospheric carbon dioxide produced by fossil fuels.

ELABORATE:
- Synchronous: You should introduce this portion of the lesson and be available for student questions concerning solutions to climate issues and how to use CanvaTM/TinkercadTM.
- Asynchronous: Students will be given instructions for the project.

Instructions: Students will brainstorm a possible solution to the local/community climate issue chosen. The government websites provided in the source notes help provide information concerning climate issues/causes/solutions. Use an online platform appropriate for the solution and develop a presentation on the chosen platform showcasing the climate issue and solution. See rubric in Table 1 for presentation requirements in the Lesson Narrative. See Modifications and Accommodations for addressing the diverse needs of students.

See Lesson Narrative for a description of different online platforms.

Resources for possible design solutions according to NGSS: See Resource Notes for navigation.

EVALUATE: Synchronous-Students will share their presentations with peers in an online small group format. Asynchronous-Students will post their presentations to an online platform (the preferred choice of school/district) for teacher/peers to view and assess according to the presentation rubric in Table 1 and peer presentation questions.

Students will share their presentations with peers. Peers will observe each other's presentations and answer the Peer Presentation Questions in the Lesson Narrative.

Formative Monitoring (Questioning / Discussion): See above.

Summative Assessment (Quiz / Project / Report): Teacher presentation assessment according to Climate Change/Crisis Solution Presentation rubric in Table 1 and peer assessment according to Peer Presentation Questions.

ADDITIONAL LESSON INFO

Extension and Contingency Plans:

Extensions: Students may be challenged to research the underlying purpose(s) that contributed to the climate issue they chose. This extension aims to provide the students with an understanding of all sides of an issue. The resources provided (source notes) will help students extrapolate the causes behind the climate issue chosen.

Students can determine who the stakeholders are in their chosen climate issue and develop a proposal for presenting their solution to the stakeholders.

Contingency: If students do not have reliable internet to view resources, then you could email the Ted-Ed videos' scripts and produce printer-friendly versions of the websites for students to view via email. If in-class synchronous presentations are not possible, then students could post their presentations on a school/district-approved online platform for everyone in the class to view. Students could also develop a poster board presentation for their climate issue.

Accommodations and Modifications:
Accommodations: Students may be provided a template for their presentation in addition to the rubric in Table 1. You could narrow down the number of choices for online resources and platforms for students. All of the Ted-Ed videos are animations to aid in understanding through context. Videos can be watched and re-watched as many times as students need. Closed captioning is also available in 25 languages for the Ted-Ed videos. All the websites in the Resource Notes can be translated on Google TranslateTM, which is free for all.

Modifications: You can provide ideas for how climate change issues affect the local community or hints for solutions to different climate change issues.

LESSON NARRATIVE

This lesson will address the guiding questions through student-driven research into a climate issue that affects the local community. Students will have the opportunity to dive deep into one issue to determine the causes, contributors, and possible solutions. By developing a presentation showcasing a proposed solution, students become agents of change, thus encouraging action and continued learning.

Guiding Questions
1. Who benefits and who loses from the climate crisis?
2. Who owns the climate crisis? People? Governing bodies? Nature?

Engage

Synchronous Learning: Choose two Ted-Ed videos (viewed prior to class to ensure appropriateness for the audience) for the entire class to watch. Asynchronous Learning: Provide a list of chosen Ted-Ed videos for students to choose from to watch. The remaining Engage content is the same for synchronous and asynchronous learning. If asynchronous, then you should provide the below information on an approved school/district platform, so students know the expectations for this section.

Questions for students: What do you know about climate change? How does climate change affect us locally? Use these questions to generate interest in the topic and engage the students in a class discussion. Possible Responses: Students will most likely have a wide range of background information and opinions regarding climate change. It is essential to start this lesson with a conversation about respectful language/actions. Emphasize the importance of valuing everyone's contributions to the conversation. These questions can provide a valuable resource for you in determining the extent of students' knowledge and opinions in the subject area.

View two Ted-Ed videos (choose from resource list). Ask students if they are aware of the ways the climate crisis affects the local community. Use the videos as a jumping-off point to connect climate change issues to the local community. Ask for several students to share their thoughts concerning climate change and the local community.

Explore

Synchronous Learning: You should be available for student questions/concerns while students explore the material. Asynchronous Learning: Provide students with chosen resources from the source notes portion of the lesson. Make sure you are available for student questions/concerns while students explore the material asynchronously.

Students will use the Source Notes list to dig into climate change issues and explore different climate issues or crises. Students should watch additional Ted-Ed videos, peruse the government websites, and read excerpts from the Ted-Ed blog. Students should begin narrowing down a climate change issue of interest to them and focus their exploration time on that issue. Encourage students to consider different geographic locations within their community or focus on how a climate issue might be affecting a specific group of people (e.g., indigenous, low-income populations, people in close vicinity to harmful emissions). Students may need some guidance in determining how a climate change issue might be affecting the local community. This guidance can take the form of group discussions and brainstorming or individual discussions between you and the student concerning the climate change issue of choice.

Explain

Synchronous Learning: Be available for student questions. Asynchronous Learning: Students may use the same source notes list to gather information for a climate change issue of their choice. Make sure to provide the questions below for students as they gather information about the climate change issue of choice.

Students will gather more in-depth information about the issue chosen using the provided resources on the source list.

Questions students should be able to answer concerning the local issue chosen:

1. What is the issue?
2. How does it affect the local community?
3. Why is this issue considered a climate change issue?
4. How does this issue affect the climate?

Students should collect the information related to the above questions on a note-catcher or other format commonly used for information gathering in class. After exploring the evidence individually, break the students into small groups according to chosen climate crisis issue. Students should share their findings and answers to the above questions in their groups. Once students have gathered the above information for the climate change issue chosen, share the vocabulary below and ask students to determine which definition best fits the climate change/crisis issue they chose. Ask several students to share their conclusions concerning the class's classification (climate change or climate crisis) of their chosen issue.

Vocabulary
- **Climate Crisis:** a situation characterized by the threat of highly dangerous, irreversible changes to the global climate.
- **Climate Change:** a change in global or regional climate patterns, mainly attributed to the increased levels of atmospheric carbon dioxide produced by fossil fuels.

Elaborate

Synchronous Learning: Introduce this portion of the lesson and be available for student questions concerning climate change/crises and how to use Canva™/Tinkercad™. Asynchronous Learning: Students will be given instructions for the project via the school/district's chosen online communication platform. Instructions: Students will brainstorm a possible solution to the local/community climate change/crisis issue chosen. Use an online platform appropriate for the solution and develop a presentation on the chosen platform showcasing the climate change/crisis and solution.

Platforms
- Tinkercad is a free, easy-to-use app for 3D design, electronics, and coding. Students should use this platform if they are designing a model as part of their solution.
- Canva is a free graphic design platform used to create presentations, posters, and other visual content. Students should use this platform if they de-

sire to present an artistic/creative or visually appealing solution that may not require a model.

- Prezi™ is a free, virtual presentation software program with interactive visuals. Students should use this platform if they desire for the solution presentation to be interactive for the viewers.

Use the rubric in Table 21.1 to guide students' presentation expectations.

Evaluate

Synchronous Learning: Students will share their presentations with peers in an online small group format. Asynchronous Learning: Students will post their presentations to an online platform (the preferred choice of school/district) for everyone in the class to view. Students will share their presentations with peers, addressing each of the categories on the rubric in Table 1. Peers will observe each other's presentations and answer the Peer Presentation Questions for each presentation viewed. You may develop a worksheet, note-catcher, or any form familiar to students for collecting feedback from peers for the questions.

TABLE 21.1. Climate Change/Crisis Solution Presentation Rubric

	Unsatisfactory	Basic	Proficient
Explains how climate change/crisis affects the local community.	-Does not answer a majority of the questions in the Explain portion of the lesson. -Answers are not correct or do not provide enough information.	-Answers most of the questions in the Explain portion of the lesson. -Answers are correct but may not provide a thorough explanation.	-Addresses all questions in Explain portion of the lesson thoroughly and succinctly.
Provides a solution to climate change/crisis issues.	-Does not provide a solution to the issue or provides a solution that is not possible in the community.	-Provides a solution to the issue that might be feasible in the community. -The solution description lacks some details for implementation.	-Provides a feasible solution for the issue that could be carried out in the community. -The solution description is explained thoroughly and succinctly.
Chooses appropriate online platform for the solution.	-Does not choose a platform to present a solution. -Chooses a platform that is not appropriate for the presentation of the solution.	-Chooses a platform that could be appropriate (other platforms might work better).	-Chooses a platform appropriate for the solution presentation (i.e., Tinkercad™ for models or engineering-type solutions).
Overall presentation	The presentation is full of errors.	The presentation has a few errors.	The presentation is free of errors and looks professional.

Peer Presentation Questions

1. Did the presenter explain the climate change/crisis issue in a way you understood? Provide evidence:
2. Did the presenter explain how the climate change/crisis issue affects the local community? Provide evidence:
3. Did the presenter provide a workable solution for the climate change/crisis issue? Provide evidence:
4. Did the presenter choose a platform that effectively showcases the solution? (e.g., Tinkercad for engineering-type solutions) Provide evidence:

Summative Assessment (Quiz / Project / Report)

Teacher assessment of presentation is according to Climate Change/Crisis Solution Presentation rubric in Table 1. Peer assessment is according to Peer Presentation Questions. See *Modifications and Accommodations* for addressing diverse needs of students for an evaluative portion of the lesson.

SUMMARY AND REFLECTIONS

This lesson, "Climate Crisis Issues in our Community," has shed light on the overarching purpose of allowing students the opportunity to experience the curriculum in an online environment. Students will choose issues that have meaning or value, develop a solution, build an interactive presentation detailing the problem and solution, and share their presentations with peers. This fundamental approach to learning through issues that affect a community allows inquiry to be the driver of the lesson.

TIPS AND ADVICE

- Make sure to view the videos, websites, and blog prior to implementation to ensure correct website addresses and determine appropriateness for the target audience.
- Students may struggle to determine how a particular climate issue might be affecting the community. Providing a few examples specific to the community surrounding the school can provide context for the students.
- Students may struggle to determine solutions for climate issues. Providing examples or small group discussion time centered around this topic can be helpful.
- Allow students to peruse credible online news outlets for recent articles about climate issues to aid in idea generation for their specific climate issue.
- Use the school/district's chosen online communication platform for group discussions centered around different climate issues.

RESOURCE NOTES

Name of Resource	Primary Website	How to Locate the Resource Online
Graphic Design Program: Canva	www.canva.com	Go to www.canva.com. You may begin developing a presentation or for ideas and help peruse the links at the top of the page: Design, Templates, Features, Learn & Plans. www.canva.com
Environment America: Clean Air, Clean Water, Open Space	www. environmentamerica. org	Go to www.environmentamerica.org. Located at the top of the page, click on the "About" drop-down menu, and choose "About Us" for information about Environment America and their work. Feel free to peruse the entire website for information and ideas related to climate issues. https://environmentamerica.org/feature/ame/about-us
Environmental Protection Agency: Pollution Problems in the U.S.	www.epa.gov	Go to www.epa.gov. Located in the top right corner, use the search magnifying glass to search for "Clean Air Act Overview." Select the choice titled "Air Pollution Current and Future Challenges." https://www.epa.gov/clean-air-act-overview/air-pollution-current-and-future-challenges
NASA Global Climate Change: Vital Signs of the Planet	https://climate.nasa. gov	Go to https://climate.nasa.gov. In the top right corner, use the search magnifying glass to search for "Evidence." Choose the first search result: "Evidence Facts-Climate Change: Vital Signs of the Planet." https://climate.nasa.gov/evidence/
Prezi: Free, virtual presentation software with interactive visuals	https://.prezi.com	Go to https://prezi.com. In order to access the free education software, click on the "Education" tab at the top of the page. On the "Education" page, click on the "Try Prezi for free" button and fill in the information to access the Education presentation software. https://prezi.com/education/?click_source=logged_element&page_location=header&element_text=education
Ted Education videos. What is the Tragedy of the Commons? Nicholas Amendolare	https://ed.ted.com	Go to https://ed.ted.com. Located in the top right corner, use the search magnifying glass to search "What is the Tragedy of the Commons?" Choose the first result under the Science & Technology category. https://ed.ted.com/lessons/what-is-the-tragedy-of-the-commons-nicholas-amendolare
Ted Education videos. Climate Change: Earth's Giant Game of Tetris. Joss Fong	https://ed.ted.com	Go to https://ed.ted.com. Located in the top right corner, use the search magnifying glass to search "Climate Change: Earth's Giant Game of Tetris." Choose the first result under Science and Technology. https://ed.ted.com/lessons/climate-change-earth-s-giant-game-of-tetris-joss-fong
Ted Education videos. Why the Arctic is Climate Change's Canary in the Coal Mine. William Chapman	https://ed.ted.com	Go to https://ed.ted.com. Located in the top right corner, use the search magnifying glass to search "Climate Change Canary in a Coal Mine." Choose the first result under Science and Technology. https://ed.ted.com/lessons/why-the-arctic-is-climate-change-s-canary-in-the-coal-mine-william-chapman

Name of Resource	Primary Website	How to Locate the Resource Online
Ted Education Videos. How Big is the Ocean? Scott Gass	https://ed.ted.com	Go to https://ed.ted.com. Located in the top right corner, use the search magnifying glass to search "How Big is the Ocean." Choose the first result under Science and Technology. https://ed.ted.com/lessons/how-big-is-the-ocean-scott-gass
Ted Education Videos. Can Wildlife Adapt to Climate Change? Erin Eastwood	https://ed.ted.com	Go to https://ed.ted.com. Located in the top right corner, use the search magnifying glass to search "Can Wildlife Adapt to Climate Change." Choose the first result under Science and Technology. https://ed.ted.com/lessons/can-wildlife-adapt-to-climate-change-erin-eastwood
Ted Education videos. Underwater Farms vs. Climate Change. Ayana Elizabeth Johnson & Megan Davis	https://ed.ted.com	Go to https://ed.ted.com. Located in the top right corner, use the search magnifying glass to search "Underwater Farms vs. Climate Change." Choose the first result under Science and Technology. https://ed.ted.com/lessons/could-underwater-farms-help-fight-climate-change-ayana-elizabeth-johnson-and-megan-davis
Ted Education Blog Climate Crisis Reading List	https://ed.ted.com	Go to https://ed.ted.com. Located in the top right corner, use the search magnifying glass to search "Climate Crisis Reading List." Choose the result titled "Your Climate Crisis Reading List: 15 Essential Reads." https://blog.ed.ted.com/2020/10/05/your-climate-crisis-reading-list-15-essential-reads/
Tinkercad: Online Format for building/ designing models or prototypes	https://tinkercad.com	For educators, go to https://tinkercad.com and choose the "Educators Start Here" button. Fill in the information for a free account. Students will go to https://tinkercad.com and choose the "Students, join a Class" button and fill in the information for a free account for the class. https://www.tinkercad.com/join
UNFCCC: United Nations Framework Convention on Climate Change	https://unfccc.int	Go to https://unfccc.int. Located in the top right corner, use the search magnifying glass to search "Paris Agreement." Choose the first result: "The Paris Agreement	UNFCCC." https://unfccc.int/process-and-meetings/the-paris-agreement/the-paris-agreement
Pollution Problems in the U.S.: United States Government	https://usa.gov	Go to https://usa.gov. Located in the top right corner, use the search magnifying glass to search "USA government pollution." Choose the first result: "Pollution-USA.gov." https://www.usa.gov/pollution
The World Counts—Counts deforestation, overfishing, arctic ice melting, and much more.	https:// theworldcounts.com	Go to https://theworldcounts.com. Located at the top of the website, choose the "Global Challenges" tab. This will direct you to the counters for the global climate crisis. https://www.theworldcounts.com/challenges

Note: TED employs a science curator as well as fact-checkers and topic-specific advisors. Before a speaker is invited to the TED stage, they strive to ensure that their work has been peer-reviewed and well regarded by other scientists. https://www.ted.com/about/our-organizattion/our-policies-terms/ted-science-standards

DISCUSSION QUESTIONS

1. How does this lesson encourage students to become advocates for the environment?
2. In what ways does the lesson effectively allow students to be the drivers of the inquiry?
3. What sort of additional resources could be used in this lesson to encourage student discussions in a digital space?
4. How would you implement this lesson in a digital space synchronously? Asynchronously?

REFERENCES

Amendolare, N. (n.d.). *The tragedy of the commons.* TED-Ed. https://ed.ted.com/lessons/what-is-the-tragedy-of-the-commons-nicholas-amendolare

Canva. (n.d.). *Canva for education.* www.canva.com/education.

Chapman, W. (n.d.). *Why the Arctic is climate change's canary in the coal mine.* TED-Ed. https://ed.ted.com/lessons/why-the-arctic-is-climate-change-s-canary-in-the-coal-mine-william-chapman

Eastwood, E. (n.d.). *Can wildlife adapt to climate change?* TED-Ed. https://ed.ted.com/lessons/can-wildlife-adapt-to-climate-change-erin-eastwood

Environment America. (2021, July). Action for a greener, healthier America. https://environmentamerica.org/feature/ame/about-us

Environmental Protection Agency. (2020, November). *Air pollution: Current and future challenges.* https://www.epa.gov/clean-air-act-overview/air-pollution-current-and-future-challenges

Fong, J. (n.d.). *Earth's giant game of tetris.* TED-Ed. https://ed.ted.com/lessons/climate-change-earth-s-giant-game-of-tetris-joss-fong

Gass, S. (n.d.). *How big is the ocean? 4 lessons to help you save the world.* TED-Ed. https://ed.ted.com/lessons/how-big-is-the-ocean-scott-gass

Johnson, A. E., & Davis, M. (n.d.). *Underwater farms vs. climate change.* TED=Ed. https://ed.ted.com/lessons/could-underwater-farms-help-fight-climate-change-ayana-elizabeth-johnson-and-megan-davis

Johnson, A. E., & Wilkinson, K. (2020, October 5). *Climate crisis reading list: 15 essential reads.* TED-Ed. https://blog.ed.ted.com/2020/10/05/your-climate-crisis-reading-list-15- essential-reads/

National Aeronautics and Space Administration. (n.d.). *Global climate change: Vital signs of the planet.* https://climate.nasa.gov/evidence/

Next Generation Science Standards. (n.d.). *Performance expectation HS-LS2-7.* https://www.nextgenscience.org/sites/default/files/evidence_statement/black_white/HS-LS2-7%20Evidence%20Statements%20June%202015%20asterisks.pdf

Prezi. (2009). *Prezi: Virtual presentations and interactive presentation software.* www.prezi.com

Tinkercad. (2011). *Tinkercad: Create 3D digital designs with online CAD.* Tinkercad.com

United Nations Framework Convention on Climate Change (UNFCCC). *United Nations: Climate change, The Paris Agreement.* https://unfccc.int/process-and-meetings/the-paris-agreement/the-paris-agreement

United States of America Government. (2019, July). *Pollution issues.* https://www.usa.gov/pollution

The World Counts. (2021). *Global challenges.* https://www.theworldcounts.com/challenges

CHAPTER 22

EXPLORING DIGITAL INCLUSIVE PEDAGOGY IN ACTION IN A HIGH SCHOOL PHYSICS CLASS

Analyzing and Interpreting Force and Motion

Jessica F. Riccio, Amanda L. Mazin, and Ibrahim Dincer
Teachers College, Columbia University

LESSON PLAN OVERVIEW

The lesson plan presented was created for a hybrid, online-in-person, 11th grade, high school physics classroom with a portion of the class attending live and in person with the teacher in the physical school building and a portion of the class learning remotely. While teaching one-dimensional motion, we realized that students were having difficulty understanding the phenomenon of constant speed, constant acceleration, distance, and position. The following misconceptions were identified for this lesson plan as the most common: 1) A constant force is needed to keep an object moving at a constant speed; 2) A force is required to keep an object moving; and 3) Objects slow down and stop if a force is not maintained (Champagne et al., 1980; Osborne, 1985; Sadanand & Kess, 1990; Twigger et al., 1994; Watts, 1983).

Teaching and Learning Online: Science for Secondary Grade Levels, pages 347–361.
Copyright © 2023 by Information Age Publishing
www.infoagepub.com

One of the essential parts of learning forces and motion is analyzing and interpreting graphs to understand main concepts. An example is looking at position-time graphs where the position is on the y-axis and time is on the x-axis. If there is a horizontal line, then most students stated that the object was moving at a constant speed. When they were asked to explain their reasoning, they said that the object was moving to the right because the line started from the y-axis and moved to the right direction. The correct answer was that the object is at rest or stationary, not moving at all, or at the same position as time 0.

We used the *Graphs and Ramps* simulation from www.physicsclassroom.com, where students could choose between position (distance)-time and velocity-time graphs. The simulation shows a graph first and students create a ramp or flat surface to match the first graph. Students could change the initial velocity (force) or add no initial velocity and create an inclined plane (use gravity) to get the object started.

Discipline: Physics (Physical Science)—Motion

Grade Level: 11th Grade (but variable to setting)

CONNECTIONS TO NGSS AND THREE-DIMENSIONAL LEARNING

This lesson is designed around NGSS standard HS-PS2-1, emphasizing clarifying misconceptions related to the Disciplinary Core Idea of Force and Motion in the vertical alignment of this curricular topic. We assert that the benefit of NGSS is that the continuous representation of content as students cognitively develop presents opportunities to clear misconceptions that would otherwise persist. Specifically, for this topic, 43% of students in 6th through 8th grade present difficulty with the Key Idea: A moving object will maintain the same speed and direction of motion unless a force acts on it (AAAS, 2021), and 40% of 9th through 12th grade students remain with some level of misconception of this idea. If we look to the specifics of NGSS, at the middle school level, students explore:

> The motion of an object is determined by the sum of the forces acting on it; if the total force on the object is not zero, its motion will change. The greater the object's mass, the greater the force needed to achieve the same change in motion. For any given object, a larger force causes a larger change in motion.

Moreover, in high school, students will explore the following. Newton's second law accurately predicts changes in the motion of macroscopic objects. The Science and Engineering Practice focuses on Analyzing and Interpreting Data, and the Cross-Cutting Concept is Cause and Effect. We will be explicitly employing strategies designed and utilized for inclusive digital learning to address these practices specifically. Our lesson is designed to meet the evidence standards in NGSS explicitly, and as a result, our lesson works through the 5E model to accomplish these performance expectations. As a note, many of us have been using Cross-Cutting Concepts like the "spices" to the "main ingredient," the DCIs, and the "cooking methods" or science and engineering practices. As such, our "spicing" in the lesson is basic as we put forward more weight to the strategies for meeting the needs of diverse learners, students new to the English language, and those needing meta-cognitive support in general.

Overview and Description of the Guiding Questions

This lesson was developed with two overarching guiding questions: 1) Using online simulations, how can we break down the parts of motion in the data we will collect? and 2) How can we create a scientific explanation linking your analysis of the artifacts from your data collection to identify trends evidenced by consensus with your research partner. The pillars of our pedagogical philosophy are inspired by three lenses; curriculum, inquiry, and social justice. At the practical level of making our lessons accessible for others, we used the gradual release of responsibility model (Fisher & Frey, 2008). These pillars are represented in the displayed in Figure 22.1.

We utilized explicit instruction unfolding in four steps: describing the skill and its value, modeling the skill, providing guided practice in the skill, and facilitating independent practice. In each lesson, the skill can be defined as measurable and observable by the objective. Self-Regulated Strategy Development (SRSD) was a framework into which numerous specific reading and writing strategies were incorporated throughout our lessons. The teacher does the following: discusses the strategy that will be taught; states its purpose and benefits; introduces any mnemonic(s) to be used; models the strategy; provides guided practice and then

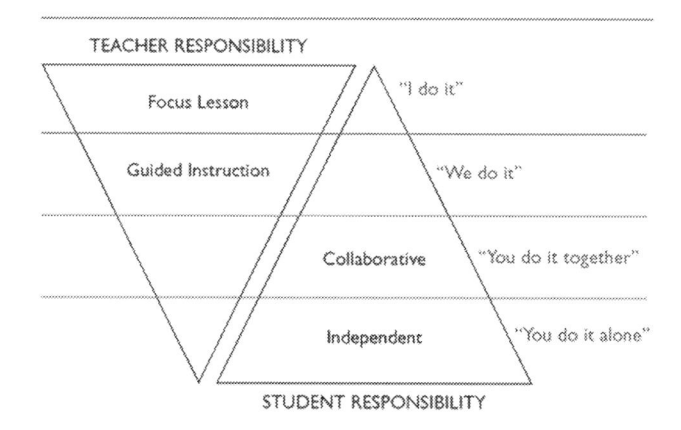

FIGURE 22.1.   Gradual Release of Responsibility Model

independent practice. Self-regulation techniques are embedded in the strategy: goal-setting, self-monitoring, self-instructions, and self-reinforcement.

This strategy is essential for inclusive digital settings because so much independent performance may be required in asynchronous tasks, even if they are short in duration. The lack of in-person teacher formative assessment to keep students prompted and on task presents us with challenges to seek alternative strategies to meet similar goals (https://iris.peabody.vanderbilt.edu/module/sr/cresource/q2/p04/). In creating an inclusive lesson plan where all learners are successful, we employed many universal teaching strategies to meet the individual and collective needs of the students in the class.

Students' Performance Expectations

- **Code:** HS-PS2-1
- **Domain:** Force and Motion
- **HS-PS2-1 Evidence Statement:** Analyze data to support the claim that Newton's second law of motion describes the mathematical relationship among the net force on a macroscopic object, its mass, and its acceleration.

Science and Engineering Practices

Analyzing and Interpreting Data
- Analyze data using tools, technologies, and/or models (e.g., computational, mathematical) in order to make valid and reliable scientific claims or determine an optimal design solution.

Disciplinary Core Ideas

Forces and Motion (PS2.A)
- Newton's second law accurately predicts changes in the motion of macroscopic objects.

Crosscutting Concepts

Cause and Effect
- Empirical Evidence is required to differentiate between cause and correlation and make claims about specific causes and effects.

LESSON PLAN

Grade: 11th Grade Hybrid, ONLINE, and In-Person Student Population
Topic(s): Physics: One Dimensional Motion

Guiding Question(s):

1. Using online simulations, how can we break down the parts of motion in the data we will collect?

2. Create a scientific explanation linking your analysis of the artifacts from your data collection to identify trends evidenced by consensus with your research partner.

Performance Expectation(s): from the Evidence Statement NGSS HS-PS2-1

1. **Organizing data** a) Students organize data that represent the net force on a macroscopic object, its mass (which is held constant), and its acceleration (e.g., via tables, graphs, charts, vector drawings).
2. **Identifying relationships** a) Students use tools, technologies, and/or models to analyze the data and identify relationships within the datasets, including i. A more massive object experiencing the same net force as a less massive object has a smaller acceleration. A larger net force on a given object produces a correspondingly larger acceleration; and ii. The result of gravitation is a constant acceleration on macroscopic objects, as evidenced by the fact that the ratio of net force to mass remains constant.

To support all learners in achieving these performance expectations in a digital learning environment, the following supports will be used:

1. Provide students with the organizational structure
2. Use contrasting and boundary cases to highlight organizing features
3. Provide authentic, real-world tasks
4. Offer multiple ways to demonstrate mastery of the skills
5. Peer-teaching

Science & Engineering Practices:	Disciplinary Core Ideas:	Cross-cutting Concepts:
Analyzing and Interpreting Data	Force and Motion PS2.A	Cause and Effect

BACKGROUND INFORMATION

Prior Student Knowledge:
Students will come to this lesson with prior knowledge learned in middle school to perform the following motion of an object is determined by the sum of the forces acting on it; if the total force on the object is not zero, its motion will change. The greater the object's mass, the greater the force needed to achieve the same change in motion. For any given object, a larger force causes a larger change in motion. However, middle school's science and engineering focus is constructing explanations and designing solutions, and the cross-cutting theme is systems and systems and system models.

Possible Preconceptions / Misconceptions:
- A constant force is needed to keep an object moving at a constant speed.
- A force is required to keep an object moving. Objects slow down and stop if a force is not maintained (Champagne et al., 1980; Osborne, 1985; Sadanand & Kess, 1990; Twigger et al., 1994; Watts, 1983).
- Moving objects stop when they run out of force (Twigger et al., 1994).
- An object's force can be used up and must be replenished to maintain activity (Watts, 1983)
- A moving object has a force within it that keeps it moving (McCloskey, 1983; Osborne, 1985; Viennot, 1979).

Source Notes:
- Graphs and Ramps Activity
- NGSS STEM Teaching Tool #28
- So you want to be a race car driver?
- Senses Formative Assessment Tool
- Bugatti Speed Analysis
- DSET Tool
- Self-Monitoring Resource

LESSON PLAN

ENGAGE

Objective: The students will ENGAGE with media, brainstorming, peer conversation, consensus building, and initial data analysis using virtual learning platforms.

I do it (teacher-led instruction): NGSS Anchoring Phenomena, NGSS STEM Teaching Tool #28

Goal to engage students in activating background knowledge on motion

So you want to be a race car driver? What about this video is exciting?

We do it (whole group modeled by teacher):

As you watch the video, **choose one** of your body senses from the following:
    VISION, HEARING, or FEELING/VIBRATING; fill out the handout to record your ideas.
    This video is 2:22 long.

You do it together (guided practice and collaborative group work):
After completing the task, students will use the breakout room feature on Zoom with randomly selected pairings created by the teacher to allow for a quick Think-

Pair-Share. This formative tool will enable students to share with a classmate the sense they used to watch the video and the observations they recorded.

You do it alone (independent practice):
We will ask students to prepare to share the answer to the following question: In what ways did our senses impact our data collection? Share two things you noticed.

Assessment: Student pairs will share the findings of their work in a (1) class discussion, (2) visual presentation/video, or (3) submission of notes to an online drive folder.

EXPLORE

Objective: The students will EXPLORE media using visual and auditory cues as evidence to create a representative graph.

I do it (teacher-led instruction): NGSS Anchoring Phenomena + simple graph paper activity
The students will work with the teacher to identify the x- and y-axis of a graph for motion. The teacher will demonstrate how to set up the graph paper using a document camera projected onto the screen. Color will be used to highlight key features.

We do it (whole group modeled by teacher): Students will be asked to identify features that they noticed were important after analyzing their first viewing of the video. These features, such as (speed, distance, acceleration, position, time) can be factors that a student can choose as an independent or dependent variable on their graph.

You do it together: Students will locate peers with the same interests in labeling their graph. Using the teacher-provided sentence starters "I choose this dependent variable because" and "I choose this independent variable because," the dyads will provide 1-2 sentences detailing their agreement on selecting these variables.

You do it alone (independent practice): The dyads will watch the video and use auditory and visual cues as evidence. They will collect data from the video to construct a graph.

Assessment (baseline assessment): The students will create a graph representing the vehicle's motion using their chosen variables.

EXPLAIN

Objective: The students will EXPLAIN essential vocabulary to demonstrate mastery of force and motion.

I do it (teacher-led instruction): NGSS Anchoring Phenomenon themed article https://www.wired.com/story/bugatti-chiron-speed-analysis/

We do it (whole group modeled by teacher): The teacher will begin the L-G-L strategy (https://www.readingrockets.org/strategies/list_group_label) by introducing the strategy and explaining the process. The teacher will present the vocabulary in a list.

L: velocity, speedometer, change, linear, motion, time, stopping, force, friction, distance, rest, constant, acceleration, position, plot, data, method, video, segment, part, slope

You do it together: The class will be divided into small groups.

G: The teacher will visually display the vocabulary words. Some words may not reflect the central concept, but hopefully, students will realize this as they begin grouping them in the next step.

You do it alone (assessment);

L: Each group will work to cluster the class list of words into subcategories. As groups of words emerge, the teacher will challenge students to explain their reasoning for placing words together or discarding them.

ELABORATE

Objective: The students will ELABORATE their developing understanding of constant motion.

I do it (teacher-led instruction): The teacher will reactivate the NGSS Anchoring Phenomenon notes taken during the VISION, HEARING, or FEELING/VIBRATING activity to identify and compare common vocabulary from the L-G-L activity recently completed.

We do it (whole group modeled by teacher): The teacher will reinforce an asset-based learning community by highlighting students' funds of knowledge on the topic of motion. The teacher will connect student work to learning objectives, and the work will highlight student growth in knowledge and practice.

You do it together: The teacher will model using a Graphs and Ramps simulation, https://www.physicsclassroom.com/Physics-Interactives/1-D-Kinematics/Graphs-and-Ramps/Graphs-and-Ramps-Interactive

You do it alone (independent practice): Students will investigate and continue to inquire about the variables represented in linear motion at constant velocity. https://www.physicsclassroom.com/Physics-Interactives/1-D-Kinematics/Graphs-and-Ramps/Graphs-and-Ramps-Interactive

Students will be paired for this activity. Using a series of three sticky notes (or Google Slides), students will evaluate each other on mastery of NGSS Performance Expectations (HSPS 2-1).

Assessment: The students will use each sticky note/Google Slide to write one skill related to (HSPS 2-1) that their partner has mastered. Each will write one way their partner demonstrates knowledge and skill in:

1. Organize Data
2. Identify Relationships about linear motion
3. One unexpected new concept learned

EVALUATE

Objective: The students will complete an interactive portfolio highlighting their data to EVALUATE its quality, the nature of its source, the completeness of its information, and the relationship to learning goals.

Instructions:
- Find your partner from EXPLORE
- With your partner, find your artifacts from previous activities:
- ENGAGE: brainstorm drawing, student pair findings
- EXPLORE: dyad sentence starter, baseline graph
- EXPLAIN: L-G-L Strategy
- ELABORATE: Graphs and Ramps Simulation and sticky notes

Identify:
- 1-2 artifacts that accurately describe constant velocity. Examples of data should include tables and graphs.
- Provide a rationale using the DSET tool provided. https://www.urbanadvantagenyc.org/wp-content/uploads/2018/04/Developing-a-Scientific-Explanation-Tool-DSET-Evidence_Claims_Reasoning-ECR.pdf

ADDITIONAL LESSON INFO

Extension and Contingency Plans:

Peer-teaching strategies can also be used. Every group can have an expert student so students can ask questions in a friendly environment. https://www.teachthought.com/pedagogy/the-definition-of-peer-teaching-a-summary-of-existing-research/

Utilize a combination of digital text resources like https://www.sciencenewsforstudents.org and literacy strategies https://www.readingrockets.org/strategies to engage learners in content development.

Asynchronous unit of study for students who need additional practice/support:
We head to the Porsche test track https://youtu.be/R8m9VJfwYrc to learn about the difference between speed and velocity. Different types of velocity are explored, and we investigate how to find information from a position versus time graph. (Other great lessons too at https://www.gpb.org/physics-in-motion.)

Practice Graphing: Uniform Acceleration Motion Graphs: Change all variables to observe changes on the graph. Best to keep acceleration constant first to observe other variables. For example: Set it to a gravitational constant to create freefall https://ophysics.com/k4.html

Position, Velocity, and Acceleration vs. Time Graphs: Interactive graphs; change position and velocity to observe changes in acceleration and motion https://ophysics.com/k4.html

Accommodations and Modifications: This inclusive lesson plan contains multiple means of representation and multiple opportunities for students to demonstrate knowledge and skill. Differentiated instruction and select modifications through the lesson provide access to a high-level science curriculum. Visual tools for students who require or prefer this means of presentation are provided. Active simulation for students who need or prefer to learn by doing is available. Leveled responses for multiple means of demonstrating goal attainment, skill acquisition, and mastery of information are modeled in assessments. Universal Design for Learning is an effective strategy to reach and teach all learners. (CAST, 2018). If you would like to engage more with UDL principles, please explore the link provided.

LESSON NARRATIVE

Students **ENGAGED** at the initiation of the lesson. The presentation of multiple modes of instructional technologies including media, brainstorming, peer conversation, consensus building, and initial data analysis using virtual learning platforms set the stage for student involvement throughout the lesson. Using a consistent demonstrative instructional model that began with teacher completion of the problem allowed students to see the expectation before participating in the activity. This increased student engagement and confidence at the onset of instruction.

Students knew the lesson process and expectations by actively engaging with the organizational structure and breaking down expectations into clear and measurable steps (task analysis) during **EXPLORE**. By following the same, predictable format each session, the students could focus on academics and not pragmatics and executive functioning skills. The students were able to work together to complete part of this project. This can be done in online groups (break-out rooms) when engaging in synchronous teaching or students can be provided with a format such as a shared document to use to collaborate. The videos used are open source and easily available for students to review as needed to complete all parts of the lesson. The guided notes provided a structure to help the students focus on the key vocabulary introduced in the L-G-L during the **EXPLAIN** portion of the lesson. Providing students with a vocabulary list is a helpful way to reduce student stress in recalling the terms used. The lesson goals are not related to vocabulary instruction and by providing this resource, students can focus on the goals and objectives of the lesson.

In each section, digital environments were expected as learning spaces. Document cameras, slide decks, and dyad learning all occurred in virtual or hybrid environments. All visuals were presented with key elements highlighted. Simulations and gamification were all accessed online through open-source websites. Using the graphing simulation "Graphs and Ramps" as a formative assessment of how the shape and slope of a position-time and velocity-time graph relate to the motion of an object was completed on a website, accessible from school and home. The gamification nature of this tool is employed to provide learners an opportunity to interact with these principles as they explore the parts of motion represented in the graph. Students were able to reflect on their knowledge to reinforce growth during these activities in the **ELABORATE** portion of the lesson. The use of peer-mediated learning and gamification added a new element to how students access information. This section of the lesson plan was essential to reinforce the asset-based learning community by highlighting students' funds of knowledge on the topic of motion. The teacher will connect student work to learning objectives, and the work will highlight student growth in knowledge and practice. This section allows students to really think deeper about the applications of what they have learned. The use of multiple open sourced websites promotes both group work and independent work. The students can access the websites for the class activities (group work) and for independent work. The students can also review and revisit the websites to gain a deeper understanding or address misconceptions in their learning at this point in the lesson. It is important for the teacher to address misconceptions by this point in the lesson.

Finally, students were able to curate a portfolio to culminate their learning and reflect on changes in mindset and misconceptions during the **EVALUATE** section of the lesson. A culminating portfolio allows students to demonstrate their knowledge in a way that highlights strengths. This strength-based approach aligns with the goals and objectives of the lesson. The portfolio brings the lesson full circle by connecting the students with their original learning partner. This can be done online or in person and synchronously or asynchronously.

SUMMARY AND REFLECTIONS

Teachers report they wish they had more time to learn and work with co-teaching special education partners to meet the needs of diverse learners, especially in co-teaching formats present in many schools. Co-teaching cannot be successful by placing two teachers in a room with no expectations or professional development to help them with expectations, no time to help them with planning, and no rapport to help them with their day-to-day efforts (Murawski & Dieker, 2013). This lesson employed many strategies to promote equitable access and learning opportunities for all students. Co-instructional techniques were employed in the development and implementation of the lesson. At the center of this lesson was differentiation. The use of synchronous and asynchronous teaching and learning tools is an effective way to allow students to access materials at their own pace. The materials chosen for this lesson allow students to revisit and reuse the simulations for practice and reflection. Shared document use is an effective tool for students who are better at writing or who need additional processing time to complete the task. Again, asynchronous and synchronous online learning can provide this time. The mix of teacher-led, small group, and independent activities was very intentional in the lesson. This capitalizes on learning style and preference and can increase student engagement. This begins at the start of the lesson, by making the lesson not only accessible, but relevant to the students' lives. When implemented, there is flexibility built into the lesson, but after reflecting on teaching, more can be added. Students may need additional time to complete the tasks. Some students may not work well with other students and should be afforded the opportunity to complete all tasks independently. The lesson is intended to be sequential, but multiple days may be needed for one activity and others may be able to be combined for one teaching session. The biggest takeaway from this lesson should be to meet the learners where they are at in terms of content and attention. Knowing your students and how to change the lesson structure while keeping the rigor essential for a quality implementation of these activities.

TIPS AND ADVICE

- Provide students with the organizational structure
- Break the skill into its smallest part for presentation (SEP= analyze)
- Give students guided notes that contain spaces for comments and questions (sentence starters)
- Use contrasting and boundary cases to highlight organizing features (frequently done in teacher "I do" modeling); present data in contrasting colors and highlighting, boxing, and circling important information
- Provide authentic, real-world tasks (using videos of sports cars, gamification in simulations); connect content to real life, make it meaningful for the students, and make connections among concepts explicit

- Offer multiple ways to demonstrate mastery of the skills (providing multiple choices for assessment completions and portfolios); multiple forms of assessment linked to the objectives
- Peer-teaching ("We Do" activities throughout the lesson facilitated through cooperative groupings in a virtual space); students will have the opportunity to teach and learn from each other

RESOURCE NOTES

Name of Resource	Primary Website	How to Locate the Resource Online
Bugatti Speed Analysis	https://www.wired.com/story/bugatti-chiron-speed-analysis/	To find the article google "RHETT ALLAIN SCIENCE10.06.2017 Wired Magazine."
Digital text resources	https://www.sciencenews-forstudents.org	Excellent open source site for text in science
DSET Tool	https://www.urbanadvan-tagenyc.org/wp-content/uploads/2018/04/Developing-a-Scientific-Explanation-Tool-DSET-Evidence_Claims_Reasoning-ECR.pdf	If the link does not work, then google "urban advantage and the DSET tool."
Extension Activities	https://ophysics.com/k4.html https://www.gpb.org/physics-in-motion https://youtu.be/R8m9VJf-wYrc	These links are to be used if you want to extend the learning. They are not designed to be part of this explicit plan.
Graphs and Ramps Activity	https://www.physicsclass-room.com/Physics-Interactives/1-D-Kinemat-ics/Graphs-and-Ramps/Graphs-and-Ramps-Interactive	Go to https://www.physicsclassroom.com/Physics-Interactives/1-D-Kinematics/Graphs-and-Ramps/Graphs-and-Ramps-Interactive. Located right at the center, look for the two activities that focus on "constant speed." You can also select to also navigate to https://www.physicsclassroom.com/Physics-Interactives/1-D-Kinematics/Graphs-and-Ramps/Graphs-and-Ramps-Notes for teacher notes about the interactives suggested.
Literacy Strategies (LGL)	https://www.readingrockets.org/strategies	Google reading rockets and "list group label strategy."
NGSS STEM Teaching Tool #28	http://stemteachingtools.org/brief/28	Go to http://stemteachingtools.org/brief/28. Just click on the link to navigate to this resource. If needed, you can go to http://stemteachingtools.org and look for Brief 28.
Self-Monitoring Tools	https://iris.peabody.vanderbilt.edu/module/sr/cresource/q2/p04/	Go to https://iris.peabody.vanderbilt.edu and search on the right for "self-monitoring." It will be the first resource.

Name of Resource	Primary Website	How to Locate the Resource Online
Senses formative Assessment Tool	https://drive.google.com/ file/d/1ez-ZOabUh8wIX- Qy5FxpNhWt0ubC- NV9v0/view	If you need help, then email the author at riccio@tc.edu.
So you want to be a race car driver?	https://www.youtube.com/ watch?v=PkkV1vLHUvQ	Go to www.youtube.com. Search: "BUGATTI Chiron 0-400-0 km/h in 42 seconds—A WORLD RECORD #IAA2017"
Universal Design for Learning Principles	www.cast.org	Scroll to the bottom middle of the page and click on the link "UDL guidelines."

DISCUSSION QUESTIONS

1. What additional ways can you provide access to this curriculum for students with diverse needs while continuing to focus on a high school-level science curriculum?

2. Physics is currently one of the sciences least accessible to ALL students. How do you think lessons like these could change students' opportunities to engage in rigorous science curricula like this?

3. How can this lesson be taught using additional technology? What else could we have considered? Are there additional resources or tools that could have been used?

4. In what ways could this graphing and multimedia technology be used to allow students to explore the concepts differently?

REFERENCES

American Association for the Advancement of Science. (2021). *Science assessment.* http://assessment.aaas.org/topics/1/FM/260#/2

CAST. (2018). *Universal Design for Learning Guidelines.* UDL Guidelines. http://udl-guidelines.cast.org

Champagne, A. B., Klopfer, L. E., & Anderson, J. (1980). Factors influencing the learning of classical mechanics. *American Journal of Physics, 48*, 1074–1079.

Fisher, D., & Frey, N. (2008). *Better learning through structured teaching: A framework for the gradual release of responsibility.* ASCD.

McCloskey, M. (1983). Intuitive physics. *Scientific American, 248*(4), 114–122. https://www.jstor.org/stable/10.2307/24968881

Murawski, W. W., & Dieker, L. (2013). *Leading the co-teaching dance: Leadership strategies to enhance team outcomes.* Council for Exceptional Children.

Osborne, R. (1985). Building on children's intuitive ideas. In R. Osborne & P. Freyberg (Eds.), *Learning in science: The implications of children's science* (pp. 41–50). Heinemann.

Sadanand, N., & Kess, J. (1990). Concepts in force and motion. *The Physics Teacher, 28*(8), 530. https://doi.org/10.1119/1.2343138

Twigger, D., Byard, M., Driver, R., Draper, S., Hartley, R., Hennessy, S., Mohamed, R., O'Malley, C., O'Shea, T., & Scanlon, E. (1994). The conception of force and motion of students aged between 10 and 15 years: An interview study designed to guide instruction. *International Journal of Science Education, 16*(2), 215–229. https://doi.org/10.1080/0950069940160209

Viennot, L. (1979). Spontaneous reasoning in elementary dynamics. *European Journal of Science Education, 1*(2), 205–221. https://doi.org/10.1080/0140528790010209

Watts, D. M. (1983). A study of schoolchildren's alternative frameworks of the concept of force. *European Journal of Science Education, 5*(2), 217–230. https://doi.org/10.1080/0140528830050209

CHAPTER 23

STABILITY AND CHANGE

Wildfires and Ecosystem Succession

Marissa Murdock
Rockdale County Public Schools, Georgia

Scott Cohen and Patrick Enderle
Georgia State University

LESSON PLAN OVERVIEW

Australia experienced devastating wildfires in the fall/winter of 2019, where some of its ecosystems were severely disturbed. The wildfire will be introduced as an anchoring phenomenon involving ecological succession for this lesson plan. Your students will explore the patterns of ecological succession to the ecosystem after a disastrous event such as a wildfire. The phenomenon has visual representations and educational YouTube videos to prompt the students' thinking on the core idea on human's interaction with the ecosystem (AsapSCIENCE, 2020).

This sequence focuses on making the crosscutting concept of *Stability and Change* explicit throughout the lesson as your students construct their understanding of how ecological succession changes the dynamic of the ecosystem before it restores to equilibrium. Your students will use the digital whiteboard to share their science ideas throughout the lesson. As they continue to update their white-

Teaching and Learning Online: Science for Secondary Grade Levels, pages 363–383.

board with new information, they will engage in arguing from evidence on how they can mediate human impact on ecosystems. Your students will use various online resources throughout the lesson, including Howard Hughes Medical Institute (HHMI) and BBC (BBC News, 2020; HHMI BioInteractive, 2014a, 2014b, 2015). These resources locate the context of the anchoring phenomenon in different parts of the world to identify potential connections to phenomena happening closer to their hometown. You have the flexibility to implement your lesson as a synchronous, asynchronous, or hybrid model as best suits your course. You can have your students upload video/text responses to the whiteboard or participate in a class discussion synchronously on a virtual platform as long as you provide the space for your students to communicate their understanding of the phenomenon to you and their peers.

Discipline: Biology, Environmental Science or HS Life Science

Grade Level: 9th–12th Grades

CONNECTIONS TO NGSS AND THREE-DIMENSIONAL LEARNING

Students' Performance Expectations

- **Code: 9-12-LS2 C**
- **Domain:** Life Science

NGSS HS Life Science

- **HS-LS2-6.** Evaluate the claims, evidence, and reasoning that the complex interactions in ecosystems maintain relatively consistent numbers and types of organisms in stable conditions but changing conditions may result in a new ecosystem. [*Clarification Statement: Examples of changes in ecosystem conditions could include modest biological or physical changes, such as moderate hunting or a seasonal flood, and extreme changes, such as volcanic eruption or sea-level rise.*]

Science and Engineering Practices

Obtaining, Evaluating & Communicating Information
- Obtaining, evaluating, and communicating information in 9–12 builds on K–8 experiences and progresses to evaluating the validity and reliability of the claims, methods, and designs.

Engaging in Argumentation from Evidence
- Engaging in argument from evidence in 9–12 builds on K–8 experiences and progresses to using appropriate and sufficient evidence and scientific reasoning to defend and critique claims and explanations about the natural

and designed world(s). Arguments may also come from current scientific or historical episodes in science.

Constructing Explanations and Designing Solutions
- Constructing explanations and designing solutions in 9– 12 builds on K–8 experiences and progresses to explanations and designs that are supported by multiple and independent student-generated sources of evidence consistent with scientific ideas, principles, and theories.

Developing and Using Models
- Modeling in 9–12 builds on K–8 experiences and progresses to using, synthesizing, and developing models to predict and show relationships among variables between systems and their components in the natural and designed world(s).

Disciplinary Core Ideas

Ecosystem Dynamics, Functioning, and Resilience (LS2C.)
- A complex set of interactions within an ecosystem can keep its numbers and types of organisms relatively constant over long periods of time under stable conditions. If a modest biological or physical disturbance to an ecosystem occurs, then it may return to its more or less original status (i.e., the ecosystem is resilient), as opposed to becoming a very different ecosystem. Extreme fluctuations in conditions or the size of any population, however, can challenge the functioning of ecosystems in terms of resources and habitat availability. (HS-LS2-2), (HS-LS2-6)
- Moreover, anthropogenic changes (induced by human activity) in the environment—including habitat destruction, pollution, the introduction of invasive species, overexploitation, and climate change—can disrupt an ecosystem and threaten the survival of some species. (HS-LS2-7)

Crosscutting Concepts

Primary:
Stability and Change
- Much of science deals with constructing explanations of how things change and how they remain stable.
- Change and rates of change can be quantified and modeled over very short or very long periods of time. Some system changes are irreversible.

Secondary:
Cycling of Matter & Flow of Energy
- Changes of energy and matter in a system can be described in terms of energy and matter flows into, out of, and within that system.

- Energy drives the cycling of matter within and between systems.

Cause and Effect
- Cause and effect relationships can be suggested and predicted for complex natural and human designed systems by examining what is known about smaller scale mechanisms within the system.
- Changes in systems may have various causes that may not have equal effects.

LESSON PLAN

Grade: Biology, Environmental /HS Life Science

Topic(s): Ecological Changes/Ecological Succession

Guiding Question(s):

1. How can an ecosystem recover from large-scale environmental disturbance?
2. What will happen to Australia's forest ecosystem over the next ten decades?

Performance Expectation(s): NGSS HS Life Science
HS-LS2-6. Evaluate the claims, evidence, and reasoning that the complex interactions in ecosystems maintain relatively consistent numbers and types of organisms in stable conditions but changing conditions may result in a new ecosystem. [Clarification Statement: Examples of changes in ecosystem conditions could include modest biological or physical changes, such as moderate hunting or a seasonal flood, and extreme changes, such as volcanic eruption or sea-level rise.]

BACKGROUND INFORMATION

Prior Student Knowledge: Background (Learning Progression):
Before this lesson, students received instruction on ecosystems, food, webs, food chains, the flow of energy, and the cycling of nutrients. Students would have already mastered these elements in the learning progression. This lesson series below would take place over three virtual class periods, and worksheets and digital resources would be provided on the virtual platform.

Possible Preconceptions / Misconceptions:
- An ecosystem can recover in less than a year when disturbed: Students may not understand the complexity of an ecosystem and may assume that once plants begin to grow, the ecosystem may recover within a year. However,

some disturbances can cause significant shifts in populations and the abiotic environment, such that the ecosystem might be permanently altered.

Vocabulary:

- **succession:** a predictable series of changes that occur over time in an ecosystem after an ecological disturbance (p. 149).
- **primary succession:** occurs when a community is built after a bare expanse of rock, sand, or sediment is exposed for the first time (p. 150).
- **secondary succession:** begins when a disturbance, such as a fire, logging, or farming, dramatically alters an existing community but does not destroy all living things or all organic matter in the soil (p. 151).
- **pioneer species:** species that colonize the newly exposed land first (p. 150)
- **intermediate species:** species that replace the pioneer species and organic matter increases in the ecosystem (p. 153).
- **climax community:** a stable community that completes the succession process, often the final stage in succession (p. 153).
- **ecosystem stability:** a community that is in equilibrium and generally balanced (p. 149).
- **disturbance:** any change in a community's environment, large or small, that may be naturally occurring or human-caused (volcanoes, hurricanes, floods, wildfires, farming; p. 149).

Source: Withgott, J. (2011). Environmental science: Your world, your turn. Savvas.

LESSON PLAN

ENGAGE: LESSON 1
Day 1 Opening: Phenomena—Australia's Wildfires

 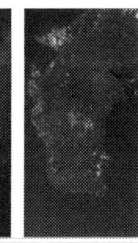

Students are presented with the images above, along with a short introduction by the instructor. Students are then directed to answer the questions below. (*Students can answer all questions, or the instructor may direct each student to answer a particular question.*)

1. What do you think resulted in these extensive wildfires in Australia?
2. What have you heard about these bush fires?
3. What event can you compare it to in the US?
4. What impact do you think the fires will have on the ecosystem now and in the long run?
5. Finally, what questions do you have about Australia's wildfires?

ENGAGE: LESSON 2
Day 2 Opening: Digging Deeper – How will *Australia's Forest Ecosystem Change?*

Students will watch the videos below that detail some of the impacts of the Wildfires and take short notes. If delivering synchronous instruction via a live virtual session, then students can discuss what they noted in the video.

• The Australia Fires Will Have This Impact
• How Climate change has intensified Australia's Wildfires

ENGAGE: LESSON 3
Day 3: Opening Activity:
Students will view the *Visual Guide to the Bushfire Crisis.* The instructor will pre-select a few images and have students discuss what is happening in each one. The instructor should also allow time for students to ask questions and engage in discussion.

Questions:
What event in the US is similar to the situation in Australia?
Why is it important for us to study these occurrences?

Students will submit their responses on a Padlet (*a Google Jamboard, Whiteboard, or any other discussion forum can be utilized*). Students will then respond to *ONE* other post. After responding to the questions, students will read the article on The Impact of Australia's Wildfires on the Forest Ecosystems. *[This activity can also be done under 'Explore' in the 5E model].*		

EXPLORE: LESSON 1
Day 1: Ecosystem Changes
• Students will watch the video *Think Like a Scientist,* which discusses how the **Gorongosa Game Reserve in Mozambique** was brought back from the brink of destruction.
• **Direct students to ask themselves:**
  – What is the role of the scientist in this situation?
  – How can humans positively impact the ecosystem?
• Have students view the *Gorongosa Timeline Interactive* to see the changes in the reserve over the last 180 years.
	EXPLORE: LESSON 2
	Day 2: Ecological Succession
	After an ecosystem is disturbed, it will go through several stages in order to regain stability. This process is called ecological succession, and there are two types: ***Primary and Secondary Succession.***
	
	• Students will watch the tutorial video on *Ecological Succession.*
	
	On the worksheet (MS Word document), students will make short notes of:
	  – What are the two main types of succession?
	  – What are the three main stages of succession?
	  – What does each stage typically look like?
	  – What types of organisms do you find in each stage?
	• Students will then be directed to go through the steps for the *Succession Interactive Simulations* using the link provided.
		EXPLORE: LESSON 3
		Day 3: Gathering Evidence for your argument.
		• After completing the main activities, students will read the short article on How Australia's Wilderness is Recovering from Wildfires.
		• Then students will use the *Visual Guide to the Bushfire Crisis to grab images* to serve as evidence in their arguments.

EXPLAIN: LESSON 1	EXPLAIN: LESSON 2	EXPLAIN: LESSON 3
Day 1: Ecosystem Changes Cont'd • Allow students to complete the HHMI Activity. They will use the *Gorongosa Ecosystem Cards* along with the *worksheet* to answer the questions. If delivering during a live lesson, then the instructor may walk students through an example. Additionally, providing worked examples can serve as a scaffold for students.	*Day 2: Ecological Succession Cont'd:* **On the worksheet provided, students should answer these questions:** • Which process is slower: *Primary or Secondary Succession?* Explain why. • Which type of succession will Australia's forests go through? Justify your answer.	*Day 3: Predicting the Future of Australia's Forests:* Students will construct their arguments using the CER template as directed below: **Final Task - Argumentation** Using the models of succession, your graphic organizer, evidence that you have gathered from the text, and videos on the state of Australia's forest, construct an argument that answers the question: *GUIDING QUESTION: What will happen to Australia's forest ecosystem over the next 10 decades?* Your argument will take the form of a: • **Claim:** Direct Response to the guiding question. Predict what will happen next. • **Evidence:** Gather evidence from the article, the videos, the succession model and use it to predict what will happen in stages. In this section, you can include the model, your CCC graphic organizer, cite evidence from the text, and draw a parallel with the videos.

		• **Reasoning**: Explain how your evidence is linked to scientific principles and supports your claim. Remember to discuss the role of several different organisms: the producers, the primary, secondary and tertiary consumers, decomposers, and humans! Also, remember to discuss the impacts that other factors, such as climate change, may have when justifying your claim.
ELABORATE & EVALUATE: LESSON 1 *Day 1: Reflection – What have we learned?* • Students will return to their Padlet post and add any new information they have learned to their original post as well as any of their questions that they have answered. Instructors may also discuss responses with students.	**ELABORATE & EVALUATE: LESSON 2** *Day 2: CCC Graphic Organizer* • Students will fill out the *'Stability and Change' crosscutting concepts graphic organizer* using the information they have gathered so far from videos and articles about the cause and effect of the Australian Wildfires. • Teachers will guide students as they complete the graphic organizer as a summarization tool and a thinking tool.	**ELABORATE & EVALUATE: LESSON 3** *Day 3: Critiquing Arguments* • During the next live session, students will share their arguments with the class and explain their reasoning. Students will critique the argument, and the teacher will provide feedback on the arguments in real-time.

Formative Monitoring (Questioning / Discussion):

As students move through the lesson series, there are questions that can help them self-assess, as they learn independently. During the live sessions, the teacher will facilitate discussions around the activities and will ask probing questions such as:

- How might this system be affected in the long term by [gradual changes not described in the scenario]?
- How is the effect of succession offset by the effect of climate change in this system?
- How would Australia's forest ecosystem look like if it were to be made stable (again)?

These questions would segue excellently into helping students complete the CER, which is a more summative-type task. Here, students can start thinking about which factor will win out and justify why this factor will have the most impact on the ecosystem. Will the succession model fit, or will the impact of climate change prove to be too devastating for the ecosystem ever to recover? What about human impacts? These impacts can be positive or negative. These questions will guide and scaffold as students complete the culminating task.

Summative Assessment (Quiz / Project / Report):

- The final argument will serve as the summative-type assessment for this lesson. A graphic organizer and CER Analytic Rubric help students through the exercise as the success criteria.

Crosscutting Concepts Exit Tickets.

CER Analytic Rubric.pdf

CER GO.docx

ADDITIONAL LESSON INFO

Extension and Contingency Plans:

- Likely, the lesson may well extend past three 90-minute periods or five 50-minute periods. In this case, the lesson can be adapted to focus on pertinent activities.

Accommodations and Modifications:

- Teachers may use extended time and small groups as necessary to support the students. Small groups may involve break-out rooms where students can collaborate in homogenous/heterogeneous groupings.
- Depending on the schedule, most parts of the lesson may be taught/completed both synchronously and asynchronously.
- Students may be provided with a choice board for the tasks listed in the lesson.

- Teachers may also tier the lesson. For example, gifted/advanced students may use the Gorongosa timeline interactive to map the changes in the ecosystem over time as they prepare to construct their argument about the impact of the Australia Wildfires. On-level students or those students needing extra support may complete the worksheet's food chains/ecosystem section to reinforce prior knowledge WHILE learning about ecosystem disturbances.
- Consider presenting text (articles in multiple languages to support the language needs for ELL).
    Note: This section is optional, depending on the structure and nature of your lesson.

Materials Required for This Lesson / Activity			
Quantity	Description	Potential Supplier (item #)	Estimated Price
1	Padlet Subscription	padlet.com	$69.99 per year for unlimited. (Free for 4 Padlets)

LESSON NARRATIVE

This lesson series examines the crosscutting concept of Stability and Change in the context of large ecosystem dynamics. In life sciences, students must understand the complex interactions between the biotic and abiotic factors within an ecosystem that can either help it remain stable or result in a significant shift or change in its structure. This 3-Dimensional science lesson is built around the phenomenon of Australia's recent wildfires (late October 2019—January 2020). The event made headlines across the world in January of 2020 when it became clear that it would impact more than 1 billion animals and several native species and was a clear signal of the impact of climate change. As we work to make science relevant and meaningful to students, we must take every opportunity to frame the learning experiences around real-life and real-time issues as we engage them in authentic problem-solving.

Lesson 1 (90 minutes): A Tale of Australia and Gorongosa

Engage (20 minutes)

Lesson 1 begins with a quick engage piece. Students may or may not have heard about the Australian wildfires. This 'engage piece' provides an excellent opportunity to present either a short clip or have one student share what they have seen and heard and inform the other students. Students should be presented with the images and allowed to think about what they notice/see. There are question prompts that relate directly to these photos, but students may not answer them yet. This strategy just allows them to start thinking about what they may be learning. Inform students that there are no right/wrong answers here. Students may capture their responses on a Padlet, Google Jamboard, or Whiteboard. This section can be done either synchronously or asynchronously. Students will then read the short article *The Impact of Australia's Wildfires on the Forest Ecosystems* (Machemer, 2020). Students are provided with key information regarding what has happened since the Wildfires began without giving away too much.

Explore (20 minutes)

We want students to understand that although this event may seem unique, ecosystems worldwide undergo several changes due to either natural occurrences (wildfires) or human activities. For the explore section, students are allowed to examine the Gorongosa National Park in Mozambique, Africa (BioInteractive, 2016). The short video discusses how scientists were able to bring back the forest from the brink of extinction. Here, we want students to think about how humans can impact an ecosystem both positively and negatively. We also want students to begin thinking like scientists, essentially stepping into the role of an ecologist/conservationist and thinking about how they could use this information and transfer it to the case of the Australian wildfires. This activity is best done synchronously.

Explain (25 minutes)

After watching the video and discussing their role as scientists, students will have the opportunity to use the Gorogosa Ecosystems cards and worksheet to explain how disturbances in the natural environment can affect the ecosystem (HHMI BioInteractive, 2014a, 2014b, 2015). Here they essentially select a disturbance card, determine the part of the ecosystem that will be impacted (a particular food chain or population), and then describe the impact. The worksheet also consists of other sections that review food chains and food pyramids. These sections would have been addressed in the lessons prior to this series; however, it can be used as a tiered lesson for differentiation to reinforce concepts that some students may not have mastered. Alternatively, for those students who are advanced/gifted, the Gorongosa timeline interactive and worksheet could be used. This activity will prepare those students for the culminating assessment, where students will have to predict (using past evidence) what could happen to Australia's Forests in the next 20–100 years. This activity is best done synchronously.

Elaborate and Evaluate (25 minutes)

For this section, students are allowed to reflect on their responses in the opening. What have we learned? They can then update or add to their responses on the Padlet. It will be interesting to see what students have learned over the class period as they reflect on the prompts. This section of the lesson may be done asynchronously or synchronously.

Lesson 2 (90 minutes): Succession

Engage (15 minutes)

Lesson 2 begins with a continuing examination of the phenomenon: The impact of the Australian wildfires. Students can discuss what they remember from the previous class and then watch the two news clips about the possible causes of the sustained wildfires (AsapSCIENCE, 2020; CBS This Morning, 2020). At this point, students need to have a small discussion (either in groups or whole class) about climate change, what they know and understand (cause and effect). This part of the lesson is best done synchronously but may be done asynchronously.

Explore (30 minutes)

Here, we introduce the concept of ecological succession. In this particular lesson, students will be introduced to several new vocabulary terms. A word wall, word bank, or anchor chart must be created for students to go through the day's activities. Students will first watch a quick video on the two types of succession (primary and secondary; Khan Academy, 2016). They are also provided with a note/worksheet with key questions about information from the video. Here the students engage directly in the practice of obtaining information. Next, students will work through the *Succession Interactive Simulations* (Bioman, 2015). This interactive allows students to create scenarios and add or remove species/events and see how the ecosystem changes. The interactive also provides vital information on both types of succession. This section can be done asynchronously.

Explain (15 minutes)

After working through the interactive, students will answer the questions on the second half of the note/worksheet provided. It is important now for students to start making connections between the scientific theory/principle of succession and how it relates to the case of Australia's ecosystem and even the Gorongosa reserve. In addition to the questions provided, a class discussion may provide some great insight on student understanding and may highlight any student misconceptions:

1. Which process is slower: Primary or Secondary Succession? Explain why.
2. Which type of succession will Australia's forests go through? Justify your answer.
3. How is the effect of succession offset by the effect of climate change in this system?
4. How would Australia's forest ecosystem look if it were to be made stable (again)?

Elaborate and Evaluate (30 minutes)

Students will complete the CCC graphic organizer as a closing/reflective activity. For this section of the lesson, students must use all the information they have gathered to understand how the scientific principles and knowledge relate to the real world. Here, students will examine the two major system components interacting and how the ecosystem will react to a change. It is highly suggested that this activity be done **with** the students to make sense of how everything is connected. It is recommended that this portion of the lesson be done synchronously with the students.

Lesson 3 (90 minutes): The Specialists Weigh In

Engage (15 minutes)

For Lesson 3, students will begin the culminating activity. Students are informed that they are **conservation ecologists** hired to predict what will happen to Australia's forest ecosystem over the next 20–100 years. The ecologists must present a claim supported with evidence (data, photos, graphs, and a model of succession) and provide a reasoning/explanation of their predictions based on evidence. For the engage piece, students can examine the *Visual Guide to the Bushfire Crisis* (BBC News, 2020). This article provides several photographs that students may use as evidence to support their arguments. Teachers may also select some of these photos/images for a short discussion or gauge student understanding. This portion of the lesson should be done synchronously.

Explore, Explain & Elaborate (60 minutes)

For the explore and explain, students will begin constructing their argument using the CER graphic organizer and analytic rubric to guide their work. Students may use information from their notes and graphic organizer from lesson 2, the images/photos, and information from the additional articles provided. Students also must include a model of (secondary) succession in either the evidence or reasoning portion of the argument. This section may be done asynchronously or synchronously. If done synchronously, then it is important to reinforce that the reasoning portion of the lesson must draw on scientific principles, which must then be applied to the current situation.

Evaluate (15 minutes)

During the last 15 minutes, allow students to reflect/summarize their thoughts. Here, a few students can be selected to present their arguments on the screen. Using sentence starters, students can provide critiques or feedback (*I agree with...*, *but I disagree with...*). Students can be provided extended time, as necessary, to complete their arguments. This section is best done synchronously.

SUMMARY AND REFLECTIONS

From my own classroom experiences, this lesson can be very powerful. Students were immediately engaged in the phenomenon. It was real-time, relevant, and deeply tied to the scientific concepts and big ideas embedded in the standards/ learning expectations. Schedules and class time may be challenging to work around. As such, many of the activities had to be shortened or skipped altogether. As teachers, we can use our professional judgment to decide which activities provide the best experiences for the students to engage deeply with the content. Overall, the experience was very enriching and students were able to learn beyond the requirement of the standard. More importantly, students could think like scientists and essentially become the scientist and the expert. This opportunity, in turn, made it an invaluable experience for students who had never imagined themselves in this role before.

For future consideration, it is suggested that other phenomena be used in conjunction with the Australian wildfires. The California wildfires can be compared to Australia's fires with regards to scope and impact. Several measures, such as controlled burning, are used to manage wildfires in the western portion of the United States. This concept can add depth to the discussion and be considered an adaptive mechanism since it is uncertain how many more events like this example could occur in Australia.

TIPS AND ADVICE

- The pacing of the lesson may need to be adjusted depending on the needs of the students, the class schedule, and the amount of time available. Fortunately, many of the sections are flexible and can be done synchronously or asynchronously.
- Some worksheets may need to be modified to meet the needs of the students. All the resources provided can be edited relatively easily or scaffolded. There may be answer sheets for the HHMI activities online. Check before deciding on whether to do that portion of the lesson synchronously or asynchronously.
- Allow students several opportunities for whole group discussions. Students will readily engage in talking about real-life issues with their classmates. As they examine the phenomena, ask probing questions that redirect the students to discuss the event in terms of the science and the crosscutting concepts.
- Allow students to fully embrace the idea that they are the scientists in this learning experience. Since the phenomena are relatively recent, students work like scientists to problem-solve and apply scientific concepts, allowing them to engage authentically in the science.

RESOURCE NOTES

Name of Resource	Primary Website	How to Locate the Resource Online
How do wildfires affect animals?—Video	https://www.youtube.com	Go to https://www.youtube.com. In the search bar, type "How do wildfires affect animals? ASAP Science." Press enter and select the first option in the search results. https://www.youtube.com/watch?app=desktop&v=jRdP6n1V2yU&feature=emb_logo
Australia Fires: A Visual Guide to the Bushfires—Article.	https://www.bbc.com/news	Go to https://www.bbc.com/news. Go to tab 'News' then tab 'World' then tab 'Australia'. At the bottom of page, use the arrow to navigate to the last page (page 30), then select the article. https://www.bbc.com/news/world-australia-50951043
Think Like a Scientist—Gorongosa | HHMI BioInteractive Video.	https://www.youtube.com	Go to https://www.youtube.com. In the search bar, type in the title of the video and press enter. https://www.youtube.com/watch?app=desktop&v=eRybWjD59oo
How climate change has intensified Australia's Wildfires.—Video	https://www.youtube.com	Go to https://www.youtube.com. In the search bar, type in the title of the video and press enter. https://www.youtube.com/watch?app=desktop&v=sGx6P2UR8Ig
Gorongosa Ecosystem Cards—HHMI Biointeractive	https://www.biointeractive.org	Go to https://www.biointeractive.org. In the top right-hand corner, click on the magnifying glass. In the search bar that appears on the left, type in "Gorongosa Ecosystem Cards" and select the third option that appears in the search results. All downloadable resources are on the right-hand side of the page. https://www.biointeractive.org/sites/default/files/Gorongosa-cards-SS.pdf
Gorongosa Ecosystem Worksheet—HHMI Biointeractive	https://www.biointeractive.org	Go to https://www.biointeractive.org. In the top right-hand corner, click on the magnifying glass. In the search bar that appears on the left, type in "Gorongosa Ecosystem Worksheet" and select the first option that appears in the search results. All downloadable resources are on the right-hand side of the page. https://www.biointeractive.org/sites/default/files/Food-Chains-Student.pdf\

Name of Resource	Primary Website	How to Locate the Resource Online
Gorongosa Timeline Interactive—HHMI Biointeractive	https://www.biointeractive.org	Go to https://www.biointeractive.org. In the top right-hand corner, click on the magnifying glass. In the search bar that appears on the left, type in "Gorongosa Timeline Interactive" and select the first option that appears in the search results. Click on "Launch Interactive." https://www.biointeractive.org/classroom-resources/gorongosa-timeline
Ecological Succession—Khan Academy Video	https://www.youtube.com	Go to https://www.youtube.com. In the search bar, type in "Ecological Succession Khan Academy" and select the first option that appears in the search results. https://www.youtube.com/watch?app=desktop&v=d7xbyNSxxrI
Smithsonian Magazine—How Australia's Wilderness is Recovering from Wildfires.—Article	https://www.smithsonianmag.com/	Go to https://www.smithsonianmag.com/. Look for a magnifying glass in the top left-hand corner of the page. In the search bar that appears (powered by Google), type in "How Australia's Wilderness is Recovering from Wildfires." Select the first option in the search result. https://www.smithsonianmag.com/smart-news/how-australias-wilderness-recovering-wildfires-180974464/
Bioman—Succession Interactive	https://biomanbio.com/	Go to https://biomanbio.com/ On the right-hand side of the page, select "Ecology." Under Ecology Video Games, Virtual Labs & Activities, select the "Succession Interactive" and start a new game. https://biomanbio.com/HTML5Gamesand-Labs/EcoGames/succession_interactive.html

DISCUSSION QUESTIONS

1. Consider the role of the anchoring phenomenon of the Australian wildfires. How does that event shape all of the activities in this lesson sequence? What are the benefits of consistently incorporating an anchoring phenomenon throughout a lesson?

2. In what ways do the science and engineering practices students engage during the lesson look different in online learning environments compared to face-to-face classrooms?

3. Stability and Change is the focal crosscutting concept for the lesson sequence. What function does this concept serve in support of students'

learning? Are there ways that this function could be further enhanced explicitly?

4. How can this lesson be modified for a middle-school context? What central themes and ideas would be the focus? Would another crosscutting context provide a more fitting lens to learn this content?

REFERENCES

AsapSCIENCE. (2020, January 8th). *How do wildfires affect animals?* [Video]. YouTube. https://www.youtube.com/watch?app=desktop&v=jRdP6n1V2yU&feature=emb_logo

BBC News. (2020, January 31). *Australia fires: A Visual Guide to the Bushfires*. https://www.bbc.com/news/world-australia-50951043

Biointeractive. (2016, January 22). *Think* Like a Sc*ientist—Gorongosa | HHMI BioInteractive Video* [Video]. YouTube. https://www.youtube.com/watch?app=desktop&v=eRybWjD59oo

Bioman. (2015, August). *Succession Interactive*. https://biomanbio.com/HTML5GamesandLabs/EcoGames/succession_interactive.html

CBS This Morning. (2020, January 3). *How climate change has intensified Australia's Wildfires* [Video]. YouTube. https://www.youtube.com/watch?app=desktop&v=sGx6P2UR8Ig

HHMI BioInteractive. (2014a, September 25). *Gorongosa ecosystem cards*. https://www.biointeractive.org/sites/default/files/Gorongosa-cards-SS.pdf

HHMI BioInteractive. (2014b, September 25). *Gorongosa timeline*. https://www.biointeractive.org/classroom-resources/gorongosa-timeline

HHMI BioInteractive. (2015, August). *Gorongosa ecosystem worksheet*. https://www.biointeractive.org/sites/default/files/Food-Chains-Student.pdf\

Khan Academy. (2016, August 19). *Ecological succession* [Video]. YouTube. https://www.youtube.com/watch?app=desktop&v=d7xbyNSxxrI

Machemer, T. (2020, March 23). *How Australia's wilderness is recovering from wildfires*. Smithsonian Magazine. https://www.smithsonianmag.com/smart-news/how-australias-wilderness-recovering-wildfires-180974464/

APPENDICES

Claim-Evidence-Reasoning (C-E-R)
Student Graphic Organizer

☆ Question: _____

(provided by teacher)

C **(Claim)** Write a statement that responds to the question.	
E **(Evidence)** Provide scientific data to support your claim. Your evidence should be appropriate (relevant) and sufficient (enough to convince someone that your claim is correct). This can be bullet points instead of sentences.	
R **(reasoning)** Use scientific principles and knowledge that you have about the topic to explain <u>why</u> your evidence (data) supports your claim. In other words, explain how your data proves your point? (paragraph format)	

CLAIMS-EVIDENCE-REASONING

ARGUMENTATION (CER) RUBRIC

SCORE	0-1	2-3	4-5	
CLAIM *A statement that answers the original question/problem.*	Does not make a claim or makes an inaccurate claim.	Makes an accurate but incomplete or vague claim.	Makes an accurate and complete claim.	**X**
SCORE	0-1	2-4	5-7	8-10
EVIDENCE *Scientific data that supports the claim. Data needs to be appropriate and sufficient to support the claim.*	Does not provide evidence, or only provides inappropriate evidence (evidence that does not support claim).	Provides appropriate but insufficient evidence to support claim. May include some inappropriate evidence.	Provides appropriate and sufficient evidence to support claim	Provides adequate and detailed evidence that in support of claim. The quality of the evidence may also be evaluated.
REASONING *Explain why your evidence supports your claim. This must include scientific principles/knowledge that you have about the topic to show why the data counts as evidence.*	Does not provide reasoning or provides reasoning that does not link evidence to claim using scientific principles.	Provides reasoning that links claim to evidence, but does not include scientific principles.	Provides reasoning that links the claim and evidence using scientific principles, but not sufficient.	Provides reasoning that links evidence to claim. Includes appropriate and sufficient scientific principles.

Points Earned	Percentage Grade	Letter Grade	Proficiency (Mastery)
23-25	92-100	A+	Distinguished
20-22	80-88	A	Proficient
17-19	68-76	B	Proficient
14-16	56-64	C	Developing
12-13	48-52	D	Developing
0-11	0-44	F	Beginning

Points Earned	
Total Possible Points	25
Percentage Grade	

CER Rubric – Adapted from http://hgms.psd202.org/documents/scolsant/1535034077.pdf

Applying Stability & Change to the Phenomenon of
Australia's Recent Wildfires

Biology SBS: Obtain, evaluate, and communicate information to assess the interdependence of all organisms on one another and their environment

c. Construct an argument to predict the impact of environmental change on the stability of an ecosystem.

- 1) Describe the system & complete the flowchart.
- **Australia's forest ecosystem runs along its continental coastline. Further inland, in the 'Australian Outback', are desert-like conditions.**

Describe Component A:
Robust and more-or-less balanced forest ecosystem.
Australia has the 7ᵗʰ largest forest area in the world and makes up 3% of earth's total forest (125 million hectares of land)

- 2) Over what timescale does the system change?
- **The system has changed over the timescale of 3 months from October to January due to the Wildfires.**

Describe Connection 1
(Event? +/-? Mechanism?)
Ecosystem damaged due to wildfires, the intensity and longevity of which was negatively impacted by climate change and variability

Describe Component B:
Wildfires which have spread around the country. Majority of the ecosystem destroyed. Trees have been burnt, estimated over 1 billion organisms killed, Habitats are destroyed, trophic cascades may result.

Describe Connection 2
(Event? +/-? Mechanism?)
Ecological succession: over a period of time (10–100 years), the ecosystem will recover. If allowed to: successive species will replace the ones lost and the ecosystem will eventually regain stability after several transitions!

- 3) Under what conditions is the system stable?
- **The system is stable when the ecosystem is healthy: adequate rainfall, and warm temperatures of, on average, 26°C. The system retains stability when population numbers remain stable for each trophic level and when there is high biodiversity.**

- 4) Under what conditions does the system change?
- **Due to sustained hot dry weather (extreme conditions due to climate change), and stronger trade winds, conditions have been more than suitable for the starting and spreading the wildfires.**

CHAPTER 24

HOW DOES CO$_2$ INTERACT WITH WATER TO MAKE IT MORE ACIDIC?

**Lorna Otero, Juliet Octavius,
Amanda L. Mazin, and Jessica F. Riccio**
Teachers College, Columbia University

LESSON PLAN OVERVIEW

In this lesson students will experience virtual model creation, virtual laboratory activity, deep analysis, and critical thinking through a 5E lesson plan model. They will engage, explore, explain, elaborate, and evaluate. The students will explore the PHET simulation to engage in balancing chemical reactions in an online environment. For analysis and critical thinking, students will do individual research. They will use reliable resources to inquire about the implications of ocean acidification on our planet and possible solutions to the challenges.

Discipline: Chemistry

Grade Level: 9th Grade

Teaching and Learning Online: Science for Secondary Grade Levels, pages 385–397.
Copyright © 2023 by Information Age Publishing
www.infoagepub.com

CONNECTIONS TO NGSS AND THREE-DIMENSIONAL LEARNING

LESSON PLAN

Grade: **9th**   **Topic(s):** How is CO_2 making water more acidic?

Guiding Question(s): What is happening to the oceans and what is the impact of this change on the environment?

Learning Objectives:
- Students will show balanced chemical reactions increase the concentration of H_3O^+ ions in water.
- Students will create an ocean acidification scenario through virtual laboratory experience.
- Students will analyze impact of human generated CO_2 on the environment

Performance Expectation(s):
- **HS-PS1-5.** Apply scientific principles and evidence to provide an explanation about the effects of changing the temperature or concentration of the reacting particles on the rate at which a reaction occurs.
- **HS-PS1-6.** Refine the design of a chemical system by specifying a change in conditions that would produce increased amounts of products at equilibrium.
- **HS-PS1-7.** Use mathematical representations to support the claim that atoms, and therefore mass, are conserved during a chemical reaction.

Science & Engineering Practices:	Disciplinary Core Ideas:	Crosscutting Concepts:
• Constructing Explanations and Designing Solutions. • Using Mathematics and Computational Thinking	• PS1.B: Chemical Reactions • ETS1.C: Optimizing the Design Solution	• Patterns • Stability and Change • Energy and Matter

BACKGROUND INFORMATION

Prior Student Knowledge:
- CO_2 interacts with ocean water making it more acidic.
- A system of reactions needs to occur in order to produce H_3O^+, which is what is generating ocean acidification.
- The system of reactions is a dynamic equilibrium.
- Observe, understand and balance the chemical reactions: CO_2 interacts with water to produce H_2CO_3. H_2CO_3 interacts with water and produces HCO_3 and H_3O^+.

- ○ $CO_2 + H_2O \rightarrow H_2CO_3$
- ○ $H_2CO_3 + H_2O \rightarrow H_3O^+$

Possible Preconceptions / Misconceptions:
- At equilibrium everything is still.
- The pH scale is linear
- Ocean acidification is caused by global warming

SOURCE NOTES:

- YouTube Video #1: https://www.youtube.com/watch?v=g9qRS_FjWLg— Google search as Blowing carbon dioxide into a slightly basic sol'n containing red cabbage juice.
- PhET simulator: https://phet.colorado.edu/sims/html/balancing-chemical-equations/latest/balancing-chemical-equations_en.html - Google search - balancing chemical equations phet simulation
- YouTube Video #2: https://www.youtube.com/watch?v=PJ2Lv_GKazY - Google search as $CO_2 + H_2O$ (Carbon dioxide + Water)
- YouTube Video #3: https://www.youtube.com/watch?v=blT7-GTzKiA - Google search Ocean acidification in a cup
- Possible Research Websites:
- Smithsonian—Ocean Acidification: https://ocean.si.edu/ocean-life/invertebrates/ocean-acidification
- NOAA—Ocean Acidification: https://www.noaa.gov/education/resource-collections/ocean-coasts/ocean-acidification
- Youtube Video: Acidifying waters corrode Northwest shellfish https://www.youtube.com/watch?v=x7MpI9dZIjk&t=367s
- Seattle Aquarium: https://www.seattleaquarium.org/blog/local-oysters-ocean-acidification-and-spat-whats

LESSON PLAN

ENGAGE:

Introduction/Do Now:
Students will watch a video (https://www.youtube.com/watch?v=g9qRS_FjWLg) of someone blowing (exhaling CO_2) into a glass with a basic solution (Windex and water) and. cabbage juice as a pH indicator.

Students will answer a prediction question regarding a demonstration. Pause the video before the color change in the substance is observed.

What do you think will happen if we blow CO_2 into cabbage juice (pH indicator)?

This introduction will introduce the concept of acidification with CO_2 interaction with a basic solution.

In-person modification: Have every student participate in a lab by blowing into cabbage juice and observing change in color.

After the video, discuss with students: Why do you think that blowing into the pH indicator made the color change?

EXPLORE:

- Have students use a PhET simulation to demonstrate how to balance various chemical reactions/equations: https://phet.colorado.edu/sims/html/balancing-chemical-equations/latest/balancing-chemical-equations_en.html
- Allow students to explore how to balance equations so they can familiarize with the idea. *Teachers can demonstrate with a personal video or online class how a balls and sticks model looks like. Build a model and show the exact reaction of $H_2O + CO_2$.
  - **In-person modification: Use balls and sticks models (option to use marshmallows and toothpicks if ball and stick models is not available).
- Have students draw the reaction of $H_2O + CO_2$. Answer the question: What would the product be?

EXPLAIN:

- Explain and improve models by group discussion and participation. Divide in smaller groups (e.g., breakout rooms) to generate discussion regarding the chemical reaction. Have students share their initial drawings/annotations about the reaction product and come up with different possible ideas. Gather back as a whole group to come to consensus about the balanced chemical reaction and product.

Vocabulary:
- Systems of reactions
- Ocean acidification
- Conservation of mass

ELABORATE:

- **Elaborate** in the interaction of carbon dioxide with ocean water and why this interaction makes ocean water more acidic. Show once more the interaction, reaction, and product of CO_2 & H_2O. Make sure to explain there are different molecules of water interacting in the reactions.
- Students will watch a video, https://www.youtube.com/watch?v=PJ2Lv_GKazY, to deepen the chemical interaction/reaction.
- Students will receive a worksheet that they will answer after watching the lab: Ocean acidification in a cup. https://www.youtube.com/watch?v=blT7-GTzKiA

*Find worksheet in Appendix 1. Worksheet used and adapted from https://www.exploratorium.edu/snacks/ocean-acidification-in-cup.

- Students will do research and read/study about ocean acidification. Suggested links for research are listed in the Sources Notes segment.

EVALUATE:

- Evaluate with discussion questions and the worksheet provided in Appendix.

Formative Monitoring (Questioning / Discussion):

- Initial discussion/prediction of what will happen if we blow CO$_2$ into a pH indicator solution like cabbage juice and why do you think that blowing into the pH indicator made the color change?
- Students draw the reaction H$_2$O + CO$_2$. and identify what the product of this reaction is; then discuss with peers and come to a consensus to identify the accurate balanced reaction and product.
- Research.
- Discuss synthesis questions: Why does it matter? How does this reaction affect us?

Summative Assessment (Quiz / Project / Report):

- Lab worksheet: in person, do the lab; online, watch the lab video and answer the following questions:
  - What do you see?
  - Where is the color change taking place?
  - What do you think is happening? How would you compare this reaction to a real environment (outside of this small scenario)?
  - How do you think CO$_2$ interacts with the ocean and what effects does this interaction have?
  - If CO$_2$ is making the ocean more acidic, then what changes can this acidification have in the ocean and what are the implications for the rest of the environment?
- Jot down three things you didn't know, two things you were intrigued by, and one thing that you would like to understand more.
- Answer the questions: How does other organisms being affected by ocean acidification affect humans directly or indirectly? Why should we be concerned about coral reefs being negatively affected by ocean acidification?

ADDITIONAL LESSON INFO

Extension And Contingency Plans:

- Learn what specific organisms are affected by ocean acidification and how it affects the environment, therefore affecting us.

- Take an advocate role. Identify how your community is contributing to ocean acidification and carbon dioxide emissions and what can you do to prevent or minimize it.
- Call for a rally, create posters, or get people involved to address the issue.
- Share and communicate your findings.

Accommodations and Modifications:
- Every video must include subtitles and translation as needed.
- Provide alternative resources for research and diverse reading levels material.
- Provide books and/or printed copies for students without access to internet or devices.
- Have peer to peer discussions and interactions to help students' understanding.
- Allow asynchronous and/or additional time for reading.
- Suggest text to speech voice reader app if needed.
- Allow for questions to be answered orally if necessary.

LESSON NARRATIVE

This section will contain the ways the lesson can be implemented in an online setting. There are modifications available for a hybrid or in person component to the lesson. The overall lesson will be completed in five separate class periods. It is assumed that most class periods will be approximately 45 minutes. The actions of the teacher and students will be explained.

Overview and Description of the Guiding Question and Performance Expectations

The students will explore the PHET simulation to engage in balancing chemical reactions in an online environment. For analysis and critical thinking students will do individual research. They will use reliable resources to inquire about the implications of ocean acidification on our planet and possible solutions to the challenges of these implications. The guiding question asks students to explore more global applications of the concepts taught in the lesson. The question, *what is happening to the oceans and what is the impact of this change on the environment?* is essential to understanding one of the biggest environmental changes currently impacting the oceans.

Lesson Plan Narrative 5Es

The lesson includes the 5Es as a blueprint for exploring the concepts. First, students will ENGAGE in the initial concepts by watching a video that uses household items. Watching such a video creates a relatable simulation. The teacher will pause the video and allow students to make predictions about what will happen during the demonstration. If this lesson is being implemented in an asynchronous session, then students will be reminded to pause and hypothesize prior to the simulation occurring. If synchronous, then students can write their answers in a chat or a Padlet/Jamboard. If the lesson is asynchronous, then students can use a Padlet/Jamboard or answer the question on a worksheet. Teachers should pause the video before the color change in the substance is observed. Students will EXPLORE the topics using a PhET simulation to demonstrate how to balance various chemical reactions/equations. The simulation allows for repetition and individuality while students explore the topic. If the lesson is synchronous, then the students can comment in real time on their observations. If the lesson is asynchronous, then the students can write their comments on a Padlet/Jamboard. There should be time for students to explore. This part of the lesson will need to be flexible and student-driven. Teachers can demonstrate a ball and stick model with a pre-recorded video or live during an online class. Teachers should build and show the exact reaction of $H_2O + CO_2$.

The next part of the lesson will involve small group discussions to EXPLAIN in breakout rooms. Students will discuss the different chemical directions and generate new questions about the processes observed. After meeting in small groups, the students will come back together as a whole to come to a consensus about the balanced chemical reactions and product.

Next, the students will focus on a more specific interaction. The students will ELABORATE on their previous experiences with simulations by using different websites to see carbon dioxide interacting with ocean water making it more acidic. Teachers will show once more, the interaction, reaction, and product of CO_2 and H_2O. The use of multiple simulations and multiple visual resources will help students see the interactions in different ways. The ability to explore the online resources in a guided synchronous or asynchronous way promotes more student engagement.

The students will complete an independent worksheet to EVALUATE their overall understanding of the concept of CO_2 interaction with water to make it more acidic. The worksheet contains not only a reading on a real application of the information, but a supplemental section where the students can explore the topic further. The end of the evaluation worksheet contains a chart where the students can write about new concepts learned, interesting new ideas, and concepts that need further elaboration. This worksheet provides a starting point for the next lesson series.

SUMMARY AND REFLECTIONS

Teaching online can be challenging. In order to increase engagement, teachers should work on building a class community environment and consider factors that may affect students' learning in a negative way (e.g., online fatigue, need for manipulatives for better understanding, etc.). Online community building activities will vary depending on each group's needs. Teachers can research activities that would be suitable for their own group. Some examples would include social, individual, and movement breaks. A social event would include discussing their day or any personal matter. In terms of access, each video should have a transcript, translation, or closed caption. In order to assist students that need individual support, they will be given specific reading resources to scaffold their learning. For ENL learners, peer tutoring in the subject will be an option as opposed to individual research. Assistive technology can be provided if needed. For this lesson, it is important to transmit the urgency of the impact ocean acidification has in the environment.

Students may feel overwhelmed with the individual research aspect of the lesson. This part can be modified as a group study session or group discussion. Additionally, students can be encouraged to create a presentation based on their research and give an oral report to their peers. Other evaluating strategies may be implemented in this lesson. It is important to give students hope. Let students know that there are solutions for this issue. Have them brainstorm possible solutions and what we can start doing today to contribute. In order to encourage engagement, teachers may want to make the material relevant to the students' circumstances and current events. Leave with the question: *Is there something I can do to contribute to the stop of ocean acidification?*

TIPS AND ADVICE

- Consider modeling as much as possible, in person and in online scenarios.
- Understand the content before teaching.
- Explain as much as possible.
- Motivate by encouraging students to do simple home experiments. Teachers can also model these experiments in person and/or online.
- Understanding may be reinforced with additional videos, articles, books, research, or projects.
- In order to make the activity culturally relevant to your students, use local resources and data.
- This lesson can be expanded into community work, field trips, law making, etc.

DISCUSSION QUESTIONS

1. Is it our work as educators to encourage students to be environmentally literate regardless of our professional expertise?
2. How are we [as educators] scaffolding students' learning to think critically about the environment and put into action strategies learned to address environmental issues?
3. What can be modified or adapted in this lesson to make it relevant to your students?

4. How can this lesson be expanded into a bigger project or PBL integrating other science disciplines and/or other courses like math, languages, social studies, etc.?
5. How can we make this lesson culturally relevant for our students in our community?
6. Is ocean acidification an important issue that should be addressed seriously?

SUGGESTED READINGS

Breslyn, W. (2018, September 19). CO₂ + H₂O *(Carbon dioxide + Water)* [Video]. YouTube. https://www.youtube.com/watch?v=PJ2Lv_GKazY

Exploratorium. (2021, October 8). *Ocean Acidification in a Cup.* https://www.exploratorium.edu/snacks/ocean-acidification-in-cup

Lancaster, K., & Carpenter, Y. (2021) *Balancing Chemical Equations* [Video]. PhET University of Colorado Boulder. https://phet.colorado.edu/en/simulations/balancing-chemical-equations

Moyer, D. (2020, May 18). *Video 38 Honors—Blowing carbon dioxide into a slightly basic sol'n containing red cabbage juice* [Video]. YouTube. https://www.youtube.com/watch?v=g9qRS_FjWLg

National Oceanic and Atmospheric Administration. (2020, April 1). *Ocean acidification.* https://www.noaa.gov/education/resource-collections/ocean-coasts/ocean-acidification

PBS News Hour. (2012, December 5). *Acidifying Waters Corrode Northwest Shellfish* [Video]. YouTube. https://www.youtube.com/watch?v=x7MpI9dZIjk&t=367s

Seattle Aquarium. (2018, June 21). *Local oysters, ocean acidification and spat (what's that?)* https://www.seattleaquarium.org/blog/local-oysters-ocean-acidification-and-spat-whats

Smithsonian Ocean. (2019, June 20). *Ocean Acidification.* https://ocean.si.edu/ocean-life/invertebrates/ocean-acidification

Timms, M. (2021, October 10). *Ocean Acidification in a cup* [Video]. YouTube. https://www.youtube.com/watch?v=blT7-GTzKiA

University of Colorado Boulder. (2021, October 19). *inquiryHub Chemistry.* (2021, October 19). https://www.colorado.edu/program/inquiryhub/curricula/inquiryhub-chemistry

APPENDIX 1: OCEAN ACIDIFICATION IN A CUP

The following lab and information were used and adapted from the *Science Snacks-Ocean Acidification in a Cup* (2021, October 8). Exploratorium. See references for full link. This model of ocean-atmosphere interaction shows how carbon dioxide gas diffuses into water, causing the water to become more acidic. Through the lab and readings, students will understand that ocean acidification is a change that can have big consequences.

Materials:

- Acid-base indicator such as bromothymol blue or cabbage juice. If using cabbage juice, then it should be made in advance.
- Two clear tall plastic or glass cups
- 3-oz size paper cup
- Masking tape
- Plain white paper to use as a bottom and back drop
- Baking soda
- White vinegar
- Two lids to cover the cups
- Graduated cylinder
- Gram scale (optional)

Followed Procedure:

1. Pour 40–50 mL of acid-base indicator solution into each of the two clear cups.
2. Add 1/2 teaspoon (2 grams) of baking soda to the paper cup.
3. Tape the paper cup inside one of the clear cups containing the indicator solution so that the top of the paper cup is about 1/2 inch below the top of the clear cup. The paper cup will appear to be suspended in the middle of the clear cup. Make sure the bottom of the paper cup is not touching the surface of the liquid in the clear cup—you don't want the paper cup to get wet. The second plastic cup containing indicator solution will be your control.
4. Place a white paper under and behind the cups (as a bottom and backdrop, making it easier to see the change).
5. Carefully add about 5–6 mL of white vinegar to the paper cup containing the baking soda. Be very careful not to spill any vinegar into the indicator solution. Immediately place a lid over the top of each clear cup.
6. Make and annotate your observations.

Notice Changes and Answer Questions:

- Look closely at the reaction in both cups. What do you see?

- Where is the color change taking place?
- What do you think is happening?
- *After a few minutes have passed, you should notice a distinct color change at the surface of the liquid and eventually in other parts of the cup. This change happens because the CO_2 gas is interacting with the pH indicator and making it more acidic.
- How would you compare this reaction to a real environment (outside of this small scenario)?
- How do you think CO_2 interacts with the ocean and what effects does this interaction have?
- If CO_2 is making the ocean more acidic, then what changes can this acidification have in the ocean and what implications does it have on the rest of the environment?

What's Going On?

Mixing vinegar and baking soda together in the paper cup creates carbon dioxide gas (CO_2). The CO_2 gas then *diffuses* into the liquid below. When CO_2 gas diffuses into water, the following chemical reaction takes place and results in carbonic acid (H_2CO_3):

$$CO_2 \text{ (aq)} + H_2O \rightarrow H_2CO_3$$

Carbonic acid dissociates into H^+ and HCO_3^-. The increase in H^+ causes the solution to become more acidic.

Even though carbonic acid is a weak acid, its presence has the ability to affect the pH of solutions. Thus, after a short time, the surface of the indicator solution changes color: from blue to yellow if you're using bromothymol blue or from purple to pale pink if you're using cabbage-juice indicator. This color change indicates a pH change caused by the diffusion of CO_2 gas into the liquid.

In the environment, atmospheric CO_2 diffuses into the oceans. Human activities such as burning fossil fuels and changes in land use have increased the amount of carbon dioxide (CO_2) in the atmosphere from 540 gigatons of carbon (Gt C) in pre-industrial times to 800 Gt C in 2015.

Current atmospheric CO_2 levels are greater than they have been in 800,000 years and, as a result, the fast carbon cycle is no longer in balance. Oceans are constantly absorbing CO_2 from the environment through diffusion. As the amount of CO_2 increases due to human activities, the levels of CO_2-ocean interaction also increase. Therefore, the ocean's pH reduces, making it more acidic. The ocean's pH appears to be changing [lowering] in a very small scale (from 8.2 in the 1900s to 8.1 currently). However, the pH scale is measured logarithmically. This measurement means that the ocean is approximately 30% more acidic than a century ago.

Additional information

In March 2015, the global monthly average of the atmospheric concentration of CO_2 was around 400 parts per million (ppm), or 0.04%. It is a small amount, but it is increasing by more than 2 ppm every year due to the combustion of fossil fuels such as oil, gasoline, natural gas, and coal, as well as land-use changes such as deforestation.

Increases in the concentration of atmospheric CO_2 have led to increases in the concentration of CO_2 and other carbon-containing molecules in seawater.

The CO_2 added to seawater reacts with the water molecules to form carbonic acid in a process known as *ocean acidification*. The oceans are absorbing about 25% of the CO_2 we release into the atmosphere each year. Additionally, as more CO_2 gas enters the atmosphere, the atmosphere gets warmer, causing global temperatures to rise.

Ocean acidification is expected to impact ocean species to varying degrees. Photosynthetic algae and seagrasses may benefit from higher CO_2 conditions in the ocean since they require CO_2 to live (just like plants on land). On the other hand, studies have shown that a more acidic ocean environment has a dramatic effect on some calcifying species including oysters, shellfish, clams, sea urchins, shallow water corals, deep sea corals, and calcareous plankton. When shelled organisms are at risk, the entire food web may also be at risk.

Lab and information from: *Ocean Acidification in a Cup.* (2021, October 8). Exploratorium. https://www.exploratorium.edu/snacks/ocean-acidification-in-cup **(See references).**

APPENDIX 2.   HOW DOES CO_2 MAKE WATER MORE ACIDIC?

Background Information

Read the article at the following link to deepen your knowledge on how CO_2 interacts with water to make it more acidic: https://www.noaa.gov/education/re-source-collections/ocean-coasts/ocean-acidification

Supplemental Information:

In the following chart, jot down three things you didn't know, two things you were intrigued by, and one thing that you would like to understand more.

I didn't know...	I was intrigued by...	I would like to understand

Synthesis questions: Why does it matter? How does it affect us?

Ocean acidification leads to species of animals like seashells, oysters, crustaceans, and others to be affected negatively and decline their population. When shelled organisms are affected by ocean acidification, larger species that need them for food may decline in number. How does ocean acidification affect humans directly or indirectly?

Coral reef ecosystems may decline [are declining] because of increasing ocean acidity. If coral reef quality is poor, then the entire marine ecosystem will be negatively affected. Why should we be concerned about this negative impact? *Hint: research benefits of healthy coral reef for the environments and coral reef declining health effects on the environment.

CHAPTER 25

A CASE OF VIOLET'S GLUT1

What is Wrong with Violet?

Sophia Jeong
The Ohio State University

Jennifer Yauck
Oglethorpe County High School

Sarah Robinson
University of Georgia

Patricia Zagallo
University of Wasington

Paula Lemons
University of Georgia

LESSON PLAN OVERVIEW

The unit is designed to be taught to high school students using an approach known as case-based learning (CBL), which is a "long established pedagogical" approach and is based on real-life patient cases (Thistlethwaite et al., 2012, p. 421). Case-based learning is an effective learning and teaching method to engage learn-

Teaching and Learning Online: Science for Secondary Grade Levels, pages 399–419.
Copyright © 2023 by Information Age Publishing
www.infoagepub.com

ers (Jeong et al., in press). As students take on the role of a health professional to problem-solve and critically think through the patient's case, they not only learn Disciplinary Core Ideas on protein structure and function but also engage in multiple Science and Engineering Practices and Cross Cutting Concepts (NRC, 2012). A group of science educators, discipline-based education researchers, and teacher-scholars collaborated in a year-long professional development and developed this case and focused on ways to elicit and build on students' ideas. We know from our previous work that collectively reflecting on pedagogical approaches aimed at eliciting and revealing student thinking leads to improved teaching (Jeong et al., in press). With the goal of foregrounding the importance of eliciting and building on student thinking, the instructional activities were designed to view students' ideas and resources from an asset-perspective and as strengths that they bring to the science classroom. This case-based unit is intended to be useful for science teachers to effectively teach challenging topics in science such as protein structure and function.

In this unit, students investigate the case of Violet, an infant having seizures. Through data analysis involving medical tests, students develop and construct explanations for the cause of Violet's symptoms and discover that the cause is related to a transport protein mutation. Students develop models to understand how patterns in chemical interactions influence protein structure and function. Through the use of models, students analyze evidence to construct an explanation of Violet's symptoms. In conclusion, students develop recommendations to help eliminate Violet's seizures.

Discipline: Life Sciences or Biology

Grade Level: Upper-level high school, 11th, 12th

CONNECTIONS TO NGSS AND THREE-DIMENSIONAL LEARNING

Students' Performance Expectations

- **Code: HS-LS1** (From Molecules to Organisms: Structures and Processes)
- **Domain:** Life Sciences (LS)
- **HS-LS1-1:** Construct an explanation based on evidence for how the structure of DNA determines the structure of proteins which carry out the essential functions of life through systems of specialized cells.
- **HS-LS1-2:** Develop and use a model to illustrate the hierarchical organization of interacting systems that provide specific functions within multicellular organisms.
- **HS-LS1-3:** Plan and conduct an investigation to provide evidence that feedback mechanisms maintain homeostasis.

- **HS-LS3-1:** Ask questions to clarify relationships about the role of DNA and chromosomes in coding the instructions for characteristic traits passed from parents to offspring.
- **Code: HS-PS1** (Matter and Its Interactions)
- **Domain**: Physical Sciences (PS)
- **HS-PS1-1:** Use the periodic table as a model to predict the relative properties of elements based on the patterns of electrons in the outermost energy level of atoms.
- **HS-PS1-2:** Construct and revise an explanation for the outcome of a simple chemical reaction based on the outermost electron states of atoms, trends in the periodic table, and knowledge of the patterns of chemical properties.
- **HS-PS1-3:** Plan and conduct an investigation to gather evidence to compare the structure of substances at the bulk scale to infer the strength of electrical forces between **particles.**
- **HS-PS1-4:** Develop a model to illustrate that the release or absorption of energy from a chemical reaction system depends upon the changes in total bond energy.

Science and Engineering Practices

Asking Questions and Defining Problems (HS-LS3-1)
- Ask questions that arise from examining models or a theory or to clarify relationships.

Developing and Using Models (HS-LS1-2)
- Develop and use a model based on evidence to illustrate the relationships between systems or between components of a system.

Planning and Carrying Out Investigations (HS-LS1-3)
- Plan and conduct an investigation individually and collaboratively to produce data to serve as the basis for evidence. In the design, decide on types, how much, and accuracy of data needed to produce reliable measurements and consider limitations on the precision of the data (e.g., number of trials, cost, risk, time), and refine the design accordingly.

Analyzing and Interpreting Data (SEP4)
- Analyze data using tools, technologies, and/or models (e.g., computational, mathematical) in order to make valid and reliable scientific claims or determine an optimal design solution.
- Evaluate the impact of new data on a working explanation and/or model of a proposed process or system.

Constructing Explanations and Designing Solutions (HS-LS1-1)

- Construct an explanation based on valid and reliable evidence obtained from a variety of sources (including students' own investigations, models, theories, simulations, peer review) and the assumption that theories and laws that describe the natural world operate today as they did in the past and will continue to do so in the future.

Engaging Argument from Evidence (SEP7)

- Compare and evaluate competing arguments or design solutions in light of currently accepted explanations, new evidence, limitations (e.g., trade-offs), constraints, and ethical issues.
- Evaluate the claims, evidence, and/or reasoning behind currently accepted explanations or solutions to determine the merits of arguments.
- Construct, use, and/or present an oral and written argument or counter-arguments based on data and evidence.
- Make and defend a claim based on evidence about the natural world or the effectiveness of a design solution that reflects scientific knowledge and student-generated evidence.
- Evaluate competing design solutions to a real-world problem based on scientific ideas and principles, empirical evidence, and/or logical arguments regarding relevant factors (e.g., economic, societal, environmental, ethical considerations).

Obtaining, Evaluating, and Communicating Evidence (SEP8)

- Compare, integrate and evaluate sources of information presented in different media or formats (e.g., visually, quantitatively) as well as in words in order to address a scientific question or solve a problem.
- Gather, read, and evaluate scientific and/or technical information from multiple authoritative sources, assessing the evidence and usefulness of each source.
- Communicate scientific and/or technical information or ideas (e.g., about phenomena and/or the process of development and the design and performance of a proposed process or system) in multiple formats (i.e., orally, graphically, textually, mathematically).

Disciplinary Core Ideas

Structure and Function (LS1.A)

- Systems of specialized cells within organisms help them perform the essential functions of life.
- All cells contain genetic information in the form of DNA molecules. Genes are regions in the DNA that contain the instructions that code for the formation of proteins, which carry out most of the work of cells.

- Multicellular organisms have a hierarchical structural organization, in which any one system is made up of numerous parts and is itself a component of the next level.
- Feedback mechanisms maintain a living system's internal conditions within certain limits and mediate behaviors, allowing it to remain alive and functional even as external conditions change within some range. Feedback mechanisms can encourage (through positive feedback) or discourage (negative feedback) what is going on inside the living system.

Inheritance of Traits (LS3.A)

- Each chromosome consists of a single very long DNA molecule and each gene on the chromosome is a particular segment of that DNA. The instructions for forming species' characteristics are carried in DNA. All cells in an organism have the same genetic content, but the genes used (expressed) by the cell may be regulated in different ways. Not all DNA codes for a protein; some segments of DNA are involved in regulatory or structural functions, and some have no as-yet known function.

Structure and Properties of Matter (PS1.A)

- Each atom has a charged substructure consisting of a nucleus, which is made of protons and neutrons, surrounded by electrons.
- The periodic table orders elements horizontally by the number of protons in the atom's nucleus and places those with similar chemical properties in columns. The repeating patterns of this table reflect patterns of outer electron states.
- The structure and interactions of matter at the bulk scale are determined by electrical forces within and between atoms.
- A stable molecule has less energy than the same set of atoms separated; one must provide at least this energy in order to take the molecule apart. (HS-PS1-4)

Crosscutting Concepts

Patterns (PS-PS1.A)

- Different patterns may be observed at each of the scales at which a system is studied and can provide evidence for causality in explanations of phenomena.

Cause and Effect (HS-LS3.A)

- Empirical evidence is required to differentiate between cause and correlation and make claims about specific causes and effects.

Systems and System Models (HS-LS1.A)
- Models (e.g., physical, mathematical, computer models) can be used to simulate systems and interactions—including energy, matter, and information flows—within and between systems at different scales.

Structure and Function (HS-LS1.A)
- Investigating or designing new systems or structures requires a detailed examination of the properties of different materials, the structures of different components, and connections of components to reveal its function and/or solve a problem.

Stability and Change (HS-LS1.A)
- Feedback (negative or positive) can stabilize or destabilize a system.

ACTUAL LESSON
TEACHING AND LEARNING ONLINE 5E LESSON PLAN

Grade: 9–12   **Topic(s):** Biology

Guiding Question(s):
- What is wrong with Violet?

Performance Expectation(s):
- The students should be able to construct an explanation based on evidence for how the structure of DNA determines the structure of proteins, which carry out the essential functions of life through systems of specialized cells.
- The student should be able to use representations and models to pose scientific questions about the properties of cell membranes and selective permeability based on molecular structure.
- The student should be able to construct models that connect the movement of molecules across membranes with membrane structure and function.
- The student should be to use representations and models to analyze situations or solve problems qualitatively and quantitatively to investigate whether dynamic homeostasis is maintained by the active movement of molecules across membranes.
- The student should be able to create a visual representation to illustrate how changes in a DNA nucleotide sequence can result in a change in the polypeptide produced.
- The student should be able to explain the connection between the sequence and the subcomponents of a biological polymer and its properties.
- The student should be able to refine representations and models to explain how the subcomponents of a biological polymer and their sequence determine the properties of that polymer.

- The student should be able to use models to predict and justify that the changes in the subcomponents of a biological polymer affect the functionality of the molecule.

Science & Engineering Practices:	Disciplinary Core Ideas:	Crosscutting Concepts:
Asking Questions and Defining Problems	Structure and Function	Patterns
Developing and Using Models	Inheritance of Traits	Cause and Effect
Planning and Carrying Out Investigations	Structure and Properties of Matter	Systems and System Models
Analyzing and Interpreting Data		Structure and Function
Constructing Explanations and Designing Solutions		Stability and Change
Engaging Argument from Evidence		
Obtaining, Evaluating, and Communicating Evidence		

BACKGROUND INFORMATION

Prior Student Knowledge:
- Students should have mastered the following grade band end points for LS1.A:
- All living things are made up of cells, which is the smallest unit that can be said to be alive. An organism may consist of one single cell (unicellular) or many different numbers and types of cells (multicellular). (MS-LS1-1) Organisms reproduce, either sexually or asexually, and transfer their genetic information to their offspring. (Secondary to MSLS3-2) Within cells, special structures are responsible for particular functions, and the cell membrane forms the boundary that controls what enters and leaves the cell. (MS-LS1-2) In multicellular organisms, the body is a system of multiple interacting subsystems. These subsystems are groups of cells that work together to form tissues and organs that are specialized for particular body functions. (MS-LS1-3)
- Students should have mastered the following grade band end points for PS1.A:
- Substances are made from different types of atoms, which combine with one another in various ways. Atoms form molecules that range in size from two to thousands of atoms. (MS-PS1-1) Each pure substance has characteristic physical and chemical properties (for any bulk quantity under given conditions) that can be used to identify it. (MS-PS1-2), (MS- PS1-3) Gases and liquids are made of molecules or inert atoms that are moving about relative to each other. (MS-PS1-4) In a liquid, the molecules are constantly in contact with others; in a gas, they are widely spaced except when they

happen to collide. In a solid, atoms are closely spaced and may vibrate in position but do not change relative locations. (MS-PS1-4) Solids may be formed from molecules, or they may be extended structures with repeating subunits (e.g., crystals). (MS-PS1-1) The changes of state that occur with variations in temperature or pressure can be described and predicted using these models of matter. (MS-PS1-4)

Possible Preconceptions / Misconceptions:
- Genes only control individuals' visible traits.
- Dominant traits are stronger than recessive traits.
- Dominant traits are better than recessive traits.
- Offering get all their traits from only one parent.
- Offspring look just like their parents.
- One set of alleles is responsible for determining each trait and there are only two different alleles (dominant and recessive) for each gene.
- Your genes determine all of your characteristics and cloned organisms are exact copies of the original.
- All mutations are harmful.
- A dominant trait is the most likely to be found in the population.
- Genetics terms are often confused.
- Once a mutation is discovered, it can be "fixed."

Source Notes:
- All resource notes are referenced in the resource notes table.

LESSON PLAN

ENGAGE:

Essential Question:
- What is Violet's problem?

Practices:
- Obtain, evaluate, and communicate information to analyze the nature of the relationships between structures and functions in living cells.
- Construct arguments supported by evidence to relate the structure of macromolecules (carbohydrates, proteins, lipids, and nucleic acids) to their interactions in carrying out cellular processes.
- Plan and carry out investigations to determine the role of cellular transport (e.g., active, passive, and osmosis) in maintaining homeostasis.

Learning Outcomes:
- Construct an argument based on data analysis.
- Obtain and evaluate different explanations based on data analysis.

Anchoring Phenomenon of the Case:

- Violet, an infant, is experiencing unusual tremors and seizures. Her parents rush her to the doctor to determine the cause of her illness.

Asynchronous and Synchronous Lesson Sequence and Tasks:

- Teachers shares the following story with students and asks them to put on a hat of a health professional (such as a medical doctor, nurse, physician assistant) to help Violet and find out what is wrong with Violet. (Students can read the story as an asynchronous activity if needed.) We suggest using an educational platform such as Flip Grid for students to share their reactions in a virtual setting and response to each other's reactions about Violet's illness.

Violet's Story:

Christina has just come home from school and greets her mother, who is holding her 6-month-old, little sister, Violet. Christina offers to watch her sister while her mother starts making dinner. Christina takes Violet and sets her down on her activity mat and gives her a toy keyboard. Violet loves the keyboard and pushes at the keys randomly with her chubby fingers as she smiles wide. Christina notices that Violet's right leg is shaking a little bit. She's about to call her mom when it subsides.

Christina: "Hmm, I'll ask mom about that at dinner."

Christina thinks to herself. Violet suddenly stops grabbing at the piano and goes into a blank stare. Her lips jerk slightly.

Christina: "Mom!!! Come here quick! Something is wrong with Violet!"

FIGURE 25.1.   Violet, 6-month-old

Christina's mother rushes from the kitchen. Just after she arrives, Violet is back to normal, playing with her piano as if nothing happened. "What was that?" Christina asks, freaked out.

Mom: "I have no idea, but I'm going to schedule an appointment to see Dr. Ramirez. It might have been some kind of seizure. I noticed earlier today she was having a tremor in her leg."

Christina: "Mom, that happened a few minutes before I called you! I hope Violet is okay. What is wrong with Violet?"

Activities and Tasks:
- Once the anchoring phenomenon has been introduced, teacher can facilitate the instructional activity by having students either work on the case study worksheet independently, in-pairs, or in groups. Then teacher facilitates a class discussion to review the Case Study Worksheet (Appendix 1) with the appropriate reports for students to examine:
  ○ Appendix 2a:
  ○ Appendix 3a:
  ○ Appendix 4a:
- Teacher's guide for each of the appendices are Appendix 2b, 3b, 4b, and 5.

EXPLORE:

Essential Question:
- How are proteins structured differently?

Practices:
- Obtain, evaluate, and communicate information to analyze the nature of the relationships between structures and functions in living cells.
- Construct arguments supported by evidence to relate the structure of macromolecules (carbohydrates, proteins, lipids, and nucleic acids) to their interactions in carrying out cellular processes.
- Plan and carry out investigations to determine the role of cellular transport (e.g., active, passive, and osmosis) in maintaining homeostasis.

Learning Outcomes:
- List and identify the components of an amino acid.
- List the categories of amino acids.
- Construct arguments supported by evidence to relate the structure of macromolecules.
- Differentiated learning outcomes for higher students:
  ○ Categorize amino acids based upon functional groups of side chains.
  ○ Construct arguments supported by evidence to relate the structure of macromolecules.

Asynchronous and Synchronous Lesson Sequence and Tasks:
- Teacher has the flexibility to implement these tasks either asynchronously or synchronously.
- Students observe different photographs of proteins with the names of the proteins and pose ideas regarding the function of the protein. We suggest using an educational platform such as Flip Grid for students to share their reflections as they review different proteins. Providing an asynchronous opportunity for students to reflect independently prior to coming to a synchronous session allows for a richer classroom discussion.
- Then, students observe the behavior of peeled and unpeeled grapes to predict the behavior of polar and nonpolar molecules. These activities will culminate with students classifying amino acids based on polar or nonpolar chemical behaviors to predict folding patterns in protein structures.

Activities and Tasks:
- Task 1 Investigating Protein Images: Students observe different photographs of proteins (which can be completed asynchronously or synchronously). Teacher can find any stock images of proteins with a specific function. We recommend finding images of proteins such as: 1) eye protein; 2) hemoglobin, myoglobin, leghemoglobin; or 3) collagen. Molecular Cell Biology has good figures in their protein chapter (Lodish et al., 2008).
- During a synchronous session, teacher facilitates a Think-Pair-Share Strategy for making claims about the photos. Students observe and review the photographs individually and write proposed functions. Then, in their pairs, students share their claims and ideas with a partner.
- Finally, during the sharing component, pairs can be called on to share their claims and ideas with the class. Then, teachers can give the function of each protein and may ask questions to summarize the activity:
  o What did you see in common with the proteins?
  o What did you notice that seemed to be different?
  o Based on what you have learned about transcription and translation, what might explain the differences you observe as you look at different proteins?
- Task 2 Grape Phenomenon (Appendix 6): Floating and Sinking Grapes (adapted from "A Demo a Day"TM by Borislaw Bilash II and Martin Shields which is published by Flinn Scientific, Inc.). Teacher can use this investigative phenomenon to introduce the concept of hydrophilic and hydrophobic interactions. Students can observe the graphs in the phenomenon and begin to understand the concepts of polar and nonpolar molecules.
  o This activity can be done in either asynchronous or synchronous session. Teacher can use the activity as a demonstration during a synchronous session. Teacher can also video tape the demonstration and instruct students to watch the video as an asynchronous activity. Students

can also perform the activity at home with everyday household items such as grapes and a plastic 1L soda bottle and complete the activity at home. Results of the demonstration can be shared out during a synchronous session.

- Task 3 Amino Acid Categorization (Appendix 7): Amino Acid Categorization (adapted from Khan Academy's "Classifications of amino acids") is an activity where students look at the chemistry of the amino acids and be able to tell why non-polar is nonpolar and polar is polar. At the end, give two additional amino acids and have students to classify why one is polar, while the other is nonpolar using evidence from the structure of the amino acid.
  - ○ This activity can be done as an independent activity asynchronously or facilitated by the teacher during a synchronous session.

EXPLAIN:

Essential Question:
- How do the concepts of polar and nonpolar molecules help us understand protein structure?

Practices

- Obtain, evaluate, and communicate information to analyze the nature of the relationships between structures and functions in living cells.

- Construct arguments supported by evidence to relate the structure of macromolecules (carbohydrates, proteins, lipids, and nucleic acids) to their interactions in carrying out cellular processes.

- Plan and carry out investigations to determine the role of cellular transport (e.g., active, passive, and osmosis) in maintaining homeostasis.

Learning Outcomes
- List at least five different classifications of proteins, based upon their functions.
- List and identify the components of an amino acid.
- List the categories of amino acids.
- Describe/explain how proteins get their shape in terms of interactions between amino acid R groups 5. Describe environmental changes (pH and temperature) on protein structure and function.
- Differentiated learning outcomes for higher students:
  - ○ List at least five different classifications of proteins, based upon their functions.
  - ○ List and define the four levels of protein structure.
  - ○ Categorize amino acids based upon functional groups of side chains.

○ Apply knowledge about amino acids (such as the components of an amino acid and categories of amino acids).
○ Discriminate between the four levels of protein structure.
○ Identify the four levels of protein structure within a visual representation of a protein.
○ Develop a visual representation for any level of protein structure.
○ Construct an explanation how the bonds (i.e., peptide, disulfide, hydrogen bonds) and forces (i.e., hydrophobic, dipole-dipole, van der Waals, electrostatic interactions) contribute to the conformation of proteins and interaction of proteins with other biomolecules.
○ Construct an explanation for how a folded polypeptide assumes a shape with a hydrophilic surface and a hydrophobic core.

Asynchronous and Synchronous Lesson Sequence and Tasks:
• Teacher has the flexibility to implement these tasks either asynchronously or synchronously.

Activities and Tasks:
• Task 1: This task is a formal instruction on "Protein Structure" (Appendix 8) that can be audio or video taped over Flipgrid or conducted in a synchronous session. Using notes, teachers and students can discuss the four levels of protein structure. Building from the amino acid, students can describe the behavior of bonds at each level of structure. Notes and images are adapted from Biology (Campbell et al., 2008).
• Task 2: This activity "Template for Student Amino Acid Models" (Appendix 9) can be done in a synchronous session or students can video tape themselves completing the activity with a pair at home and share the video on an educational platform such as Flip Grid. This activity is mainly to get students moving and engage in a fun activity that illustrates the structure of an amino acid. In a synchronous session, students can perform an activity where they pose as an amino acid. Ensure that there is enough space for students to move around. Their right arm represents the amine group, the left arm is the carboxyl group, their chest is the alpha carbon, and their head is the R group (side chain). Students would need to join together (with their pair) by holding hands to demonstrate the peptide bonds between amino acids. Their model also allows students to see the N-terminus and C-terminus of a protein. Then, students are asked to arrange themselves without breaking peptide bonds so that the R groups interact appropriately (which could bond and which would be hydrophobic). In the synchronous class session, teacher facilitates the discussion of why the order of R groups is critical to protein structure. Then, the teacher poses the following questions:
○ What would happen if the protein was place in a solution with a different pH? In a hydrophobic solution? In water?

- Task 3: This task is an activity called "Interactive Protein Model" from Concord.Org. Students are given different sequences of amino acids to model how protein side chains interact in a variety of solutions using the interactive computer resource. See differentiated note below.
- Teacher can check the student's work. Then, each student can pair up with another student who has an amino acid theirs can form a tertiary interaction with (hydrogen bond or ion-ion or ion-dipole interaction). Students can draw this interaction at pH 7. Next, the pair can join with another pair and they can work together to draw a tetrapeptide with their four amino acids.
  - The students will need to link the amino acids correctly with peptide bonds, with all ionizable groups at pH 7, and then label the N terminus and C terminus of the peptide. Teacher can check the students' work. Once finished, teacher can draw another example if needed, and then pose the following questions:
    - What class of amino acid have I left out of the cards? (answer: nonpolar)
    - What type of tertiary interaction can this group participate in? (answer: van der Waals)

Teacher's Annotations for Differentiation and Explanation:
- Task 3 can be differentiated
  - High School Biology classes may not talk about levels of structure of proteins. In this case, students learn the shape of the proteins by amino acid behaviors based on polar and nonpolar. However, they can still look at the lab. They can still talk about hydrophilic and hydrophobic shift and that is what is causing a change. AP Biology extends the knowledge of protein structure by discussing the levels of structure in proteins and interactions between amino acids. AP Biology or higher students can learn the ionization states of amino acids at a given pH. Each student can be given a card with a polar amino acid in its neutral form. The students will then draw that amino acid at pH 7.

ELABORATE:

Essential Question:
- How does glucose cross the membrane?
- How would Violet be able to survive and reduce abnormal brain activity due to the effects of the GLUT1 transport protein?

Practices
- Obtain, evaluate, and communicate information to analyze the nature of the relationships between structures and functions in living cells.

- Construct arguments supported by evidence to relate the structure of macromolecules (carbohydrates, proteins, lipids, and nucleic acids) to their interactions in carrying out cellular processes.
- Plan and carry out investigations to determine the role of cellular transport (e.g., active, passive, and osmosis) in maintaining homeostasis.

Learning Outcomes
- Analyze data to evaluate protein function.
- Evaluate and predict the effect that a given mutation would have upon the rate of ligand binding or transport.
- Analyze DNA sequence data to predict the effects of mutation on protein structure.
- Differentiated learning outcomes for higher students:
  - Analyze data to evaluate protein function.
  - Evaluate and predict the effect that a given mutation would have upon the rate of ligand binding or transport.
  - Analyze DNA sequence data to predict the effects of mutation on protein structure.

Asynchronous and Synchronous Lesson Sequence and Tasks:
- Teacher has the flexibility to implement these tasks either asynchronously or synchronously.
- Students will complete the Violet case study by analyzing data from a glucose uptake test and a DNA sequencing test. Through the data analysis, students will analyze the effects of mutations on the function of the GLUT1 transport protein. Students will conclude the case study by designing a solution to decrease Violet's symptoms.

Activities and Tasks:
- Students return to the case study involving Violet. With their understanding of protein structure, students use the handout to learn about a transport protein known as GLUT1. The glucose uptake test discusses how Violet's cells are getting glucose compared to a normal person (Appendix 10, 11a, 11b, and 12).
- Since there is a problem with Violet's GLUT1 transport protein, students then analyze the DNA sequencing results to see how a different nucleotide can substitute a different amino acid. Students should understand the concepts of transcription and translation before analyzing the DNA sequencing data. They should also be familiar with translating mRNA into an amino acid sequence. The emphasis should be on the chemistry change of the amino acid and how they would alter the structure and function of the GLUT1 transport protein as glucose tries to cross the cell membrane (Appendix 13a, 13b, and 14). Teacher should also reference the amino acid categorization chart in Appendix 9.

Teacher's Annotations for Differentiation and Explanation:
- Teacher can provide a complete chart of all amino acids and its abbreviations as reference to students.

EVALUATE:

Essential Question:
- What recommendations would a doctor make to help eliminate Violet's seizures?

Activities and Tasks:
- To conclude the case study, students recommend a solution to Violet's illness. This discussion can be facilitated in a synchronous session as way to encourage students compare and contrast their solutions.
  - How would Violet be able to survive and reduce abnormal brain activity due to the effects of the GLUT1 transport protein?
- Teacher have students read the following dialogue after a synchronous discussion is completed. Dr. Ramirez meets with the Sanders family to discuss Violet's DNA sequencing results:

Family Dialogue with Dr. Ramirez:

"Mrs. Sanders, sequencing results have confirmed what I suspected. Your daughter has GLUT1 deficiency syndrome. It is a rare autosomal dominant disorder. The mutation in just one copy of GLUT1 is sufficient to significantly decrease the transport of glucose across the blood brain barrier into the brain. There is good news. A change in her diet can reduce her symptoms. From now on, she needs to follow a ketogenic diet—very low in carbohydrates and high in fats."

Formative Monitoring (Questioning / Discussion):
- Discussion questions have been used to monitor and check students' understanding throughout the unit.
- Activities and deliverables provide a way to assess students' understanding for the instructional tasks.

Summative Assessment (Quiz / Project / Report):
- Although we are not providing a summative exam, a teacher is free to create a test or quiz which assesses students on the content and core ideas.
- Students' final solutions can be assessed as a summative assessment which can be extended into writing or a report.

ADDITIONAL LESSON INFO

Extension and Contingency Plans:

- Teachers should make the appropriate pedagogical decisions to teach the tasks and instructional activities either synchronously or asynchronously. All activities can be modified to be taught 100% asynchronously if needed.
- Students' final solutions can be assessed as a summative assessment which can be extended into writing or a report.

Accommodations and Modifications:
- The unit is designed with strategies for differentiation throughout the lesson. Learning outcomes are differentiated for higher level biology students who might be taking Advanced Placement (AP) level courses.

LESSON NARRATIVE

Engage

In Engage, students are given the story about Violet and her Glut-1 deficiency to hook and engage students in a real-life problem. Students can read the story either asynchronously or during a synchronous session. In the story, students will be given the narrative with her problems and symptoms. They will evaluate her symptoms and lab work. As students compare Violet's lab work, students should analyze what variables in her lab work are outside of the normal range. Since glucose levels are outside of the normal range, students then ask questions regarding the transport of glucose across the cell membrane and what's causing her lab work to be outside of the normal range.

Each handout has both a student and teacher version. The teacher notes are provided to show the relevant data points and to give some context for developing discussion questions. A sample handout for questions a teacher may ask students is provided for guidance. Teachers may choose to have students look at reports separately or collectively. A summary of all important lab findings and background is provided.

Explore

In Explore, the goal is for students to understand the ideas of polar and nonpolar interactions. This lesson assumes that students have no prior knowledge concerning polarity, so the investigative phenomenon for this lesson is used to explore the activities in the Explore phase. If the topic of polarity has been taught, then the phenomenon may be a review of previous material. Students observe photographs of proteins with the names of the proteins and pose ideas regarding the function of the protein. Then, they observe the behavior of peeled and unpeeled grapes to predict the behavior of polar and nonpolar molecules. These activities culminate with students classifying amino acids based on polar or nonpolar chemical behaviors to predict folding patterns in protein structures

Explain

In Explain, students observe polypeptide folding and examine patterns of chemical bonding across the four levels of protein structure. Students examine how changes in a system's environment alter a protein's structure and function and analyze data to evaluate protein function. Students analyze models of proteins to determine how bonds occur between different side chains. Students develop predictions about the effects of the environment and effects of changing polypeptide structure on protein folding by analyzing data.

Elaborate

In Elaborate, students complete the Violet case study. They analyze data from a glucose uptake test and a DNA sequencing test. Through the data analysis, students analyze the effects of mutations on the function of the GLUT1 transport protein.

Evaluate

In Evaluate, students conclude the case study by designing a solution to decrease Violet's symptoms. This lesson is a case-based approach. Thus, students should have learned not only the content but also various skills, practices, and abilities to engage in real-world, problem-solving, and critical thinking.

SUMMARY AND REFLECTIONS

Teachers should continuously strive to see their teaching through the lens of student learning, especially when the lesson is implemented in the asynchronous or synchronous format. The landscape of science teaching and learning is changing as science teachers meet the demands of virtual instruction. We should try new approaches such as case-based pedagogies to effectively facilitate how students construct meaning and learn science through problem-solving a real-world issue. Developing and working on the case study with the co-authors of this lesson changed how we as science educators viewed the application of content in science and how we could help students conceptualize an abstract and challenging idea like protein structure and function. We believe that our best professional learning occurs as we work with our teacher-colleagues to provide students with more inquiry-based, authentic, and improved experiences.

TIPS AND ADVICE

- This unit focuses on "protein structure and function" and we use a case-based approach to making the content more meaningful and relevant. Don't skip the Engage phase where we share the story of Violet. It is a critical step in "hooking" students' interests.
- Teachers can take apart and use different topics of the unit as they see fit. We designed the unit with clusters of science topics related to "protein

structure and function" and the appropriate instructional activities. The sequencing and scoping of these clusters can be changed.

- Teachers can take apart and choose to teach the different phases of the unit either asynchronously or synchronously. This unit is intended for upper-level high school students taking biology or AP biology. We assume a certain level of maturity in students and the activities can be done independently in an asynchronous or synchronous format.

RESOURCE NOTES

Name of Resource	Primary Website	How to Locate the Resource Online
Appendix 1	n/a	Case study worksheet called "What is wrong with Violet?" Appendix is provided by authors at the end of lesson.
Appendix 2a and 2b	n/a	2a is the student-facing worksheet: A report on complete blood count (CBC). 2b is the teacher-facing worksheet: A report on complete blood count (CBC). Appendix is provided by authors at the end of lesson.
Appendix 3a and 3b	n/a	3a is the student-facing worksheet: A report on cerebral spinal fluid (CSF). 3b is the teacher-facing worksheet: A report on cerebral spinal fluid (CSF). Appendix is provided by authors at the end of lesson.
Appendix 4a and 4b	n/a	4a is the student-facing worksheet: A report on Electroencephalo-gram (EEG). 4b is the teacher-facing worksheet: A report on Electroencephalo-gram (EEG). Appendix is provided by authors at the end of lesson.
Appendix 5	n/a	This document is the "Instructional Support Materials for the Patient Report Handouts." This document provides additional background information for the teacher. Appendix is provided by authors at the end of lesson.
Appendix 6	n/a	This activity, "Grape Questions! Will They Float or Sink?" is adapted from "A Demo a Day"TM by Borislaw Bilash II and Martin Shields which is published by Flinn Scientific, Inc. Appendix is provided by authors at the end of lesson.
Appendix 7	n/a	This activity, "Amino Acid Categorization," is adapted from Khan Academy's "Classifications of amino acids." Appendix is provided by authors at the end of lesson.
Appendix 8	n/a	This activity, "Protein Structure," is a formal instruction Slide Deck adapted from Biology (Campbell et al., 2008) which provides their Slide Deck. Authors provide an outline of the adapted Slide Deck for teachers to reference when they create their own Slide Deck to use. Appendix is provided by authors at the end of lesson.

Name of Resource	Primary Website	How to Locate the Resource Online
Appendix 9	n/a	This activity is "Template for Student Amino Acid Models." Appendix is provided by authors at the end of lesson.
Appendix 10	n/a	This activity is "Student Discussion: How does glucose cross the membrane?" Appendix is provided by authors at the end of lesson.
Appendix 11a and 11b	n/a	11a is the student-facing report on glucose uptake results. 11b is the teacher-facing report on glucose uptake results. Appendix is provided by authors at the end of lesson.
Appendix 12	n/a	This activity is "Glucose Uptake Report Questions." Appendix is provided by authors at the end of lesson.
Appendix 13a And 13b	n/a	13a is the student-facing report on DNA sequencing. 13b is the teacher-facing report on DNA sequencing. Appendix is provided by authors at the end of lesson.
Appendix 14	n/a	This activity is "DNA Sequencing Report Questions." Appendix is provided by authors at the end of lesson.
Flinn Scientific	n/a	On Google search, type in "Flinn scientific, demo a day, biology." Click on the appropriate search results to access the book. Teachers can use this book if they want to look at the original source of "Demo a Day"TM by Borislaw Bilash II and Martin Shields.
Interactive Molecular Models	www.Concord.org	On Google search, type in "interactive molecular models" and "concord." Next-generation molecular workbench will be available to access this online activity. The link is https://lab.concord.org/embeddable.html#interactives/samples/5-amino-acids.json
Khan Academy— "Classifications of Amino Acids"	khanacademy.org	On Google search, type in "Khan Academy, classifications of amino acids." Click on the first search result under the domain of Khan Academy.
Protein Functions	www.Sciencelearn.org	On Google search, type in "Role of proteins in the body, science learn." Click on the first search result under the domain of ScienceLearn.Org. The link is https://www.sciencelearn.org.nz/resources/209-role-of-proteins-in-the-body

DISCUSSION QUESTIONS

1. How can we effectively create an authentic, real-world, problem-based science learning environment?
2. How can we effectively teach a difficult concept in science such as protein structure and function using a case-based pedagogy in a virtual classroom setting?

3. How can we encourage student participation and foster engaging classroom dialogue about a case of Violet and her illnesses in a virtual classroom setting?

4. How do we implement multi-dimensional, formative assessments that not only check for students' understanding of "protein structure and function" but also their science and engineering practices and cross cutting concepts related to the unit in a virtual setting?

ACKNOWLEDGEMENT

This material is based upon work supported by the National Science Foundation under Grants No. DRL 1350345. Any opinions, findings, and conclusions or recommendations expressed in this material are those of the author(s) and do not necessarily reflect the views of the National Science Foundation.

REFERENCES

National Research Council. (2012). *A framework for K–12 science education: Practices, crosscutting concepts, and core ideas.* National Academies Press. https://doi.org/10.17226/13165

Bilash, B., & Shields, M. (2001). *A demo a day: A year of biological demonstrations.* Flinn Scientific.

Campbell, N., Reece, J., Urry, L. A., Cain, M. L., Wasserman, S. A., Minorsky, P. V., & Jackson, R. (2009). *Biology.* Pearson Benjamin Cummings.

Jeong, S., Bryan, L., Tippins, D., & Sexton, C. (Eds.). (in press). *Navigating elementary science teaching and learning: Cases of classroom practices and dilemmas.* Springer Nature.

Jeong, S., Clyburn, J., Bhatia, N. S., McCourt, J., & Lemons, P. P. (2022). Student thinking in the professional development of college biology instructors: An analysis through the lens of sociocultural theory. *CBE—Life Sciences Education, 21*(2). https://doi.org/10.1187/cbe.21-01-0003

Khan Academy. (n.d.). *Classification of amino acids* [Video]. YouTube. https://www.khanacademy.org/test-prep/mcat/biomolecules/amino-acids-and-proteins1/v/classification-amino-acids

Lodish, H., Berk, A., Kaiser, C.A., Kaiser, C., Krieger, M., Scott, M. P., Bretscher, A., Ploegh, H., & Paul Matsudaira, P. (2008). *Molecular cell biology.* Macmillan.

Thistlethwaite, J. E., Davies, D., Ekeocha, S., Kidd, J. M., MacDougall, C., Matthews, P., Purkis, J., & Clay, D. (2012). The effectiveness of case-based learning in health professional education. A BEME systematic review: BEME Guide No. 23. *Medical teacher, 34*(6), e421-e444. https://doi.org/10.3109/0142159X.2012.680939

BIOGRAPHIES

ABOUT THE EDITORS

Franklin S. Allaire is an assistant professor of science education in the department of urban education at the University of Houston-Downtown where he brings over 20 years of experience in formal and informal PreK-16 science education undergraduate and graduate courses in elementary and secondary science methods. He earned his master's and Ph.D. in educational foundations from the University of Hawai'i at Mānoa. Prior to that, he was a high school science teacher in Hawai'i Public Schools and served as the state director for the Hawai'i State Science Olympiad. His interests focus on issues impacting the success of historically marginalized groups in STEM-related fields and the innovative use of technologies and pedagogies in science teaching and teacher preparation. His research, publications, and presentations explore the lived experiences of historically marginalized members of the STEM community and investigate how teacher and teacher candidates' positive and negative emotions impact the quality and quantity of science teaching. Franklin is an active member in several state and national organizations including the American Association for Teaching and Curriculum (AATC), the Association for Science Teacher Education (ASTE), and the Science Teacher's Association of Texas (STAT). He currently serves as a reviewer for sev-

Teaching and Learning Online: Science for Secondary Grade Levels, pages 421–430.
Copyright © 2023 by Information Age Publishing
www.infoagepub.com
421

eral journals and is the assistant editor of *Curriculum & Teaching Dialogue* and the co-editor of the *Journal of Behavioral and Social Sciences*. He has presented on and published multiple articles and book chapters related to his work. @misterallaire; linkedin.com/in/franklin-allaire; allairef@uhd.edu

Jennifer E. Killham is an assistant professor of child and adolescent development and the co-director for the Center for Learning Innovation at the LaFetra College of Education, University of La Verne. She earned her master's and Ph.D. in social and cultural foundations of education from the University of Cincinnati. She has a strong belief in what Sara Lawrence-Lightfoot refers to as "seeing the good" in students, collaborators, and communities. Adopting an asset-based mentality, her curriculum has the special aim of sparking intellectual curiosity and nurturing high-impact engagement. For the last 10 years, she has taught online, combining the use of technology, critical pedagogy, and relational-cultural theory. Prior to teaching at the University of La Verne, she was an online course coordinator with the Early Childhood Education Online program at the University of Cincinnati, a nationally ranked program. As a technology optimist, her research focuses on the culture of online collaborative learning environments. She is also a longtime collaborator with the Interactive Communications & Simulations at the University of Michigan, the Institute of Innovation in Education, and has served on several technology advisory boards. Jennifer has presented her research nationally and internationally and has authored more than 20 publications appearing in a variety of peer-reviewed journals, such as the *International Journal of Game-Based Learning*, *Journal of Natural Inquiry & Reflective Practice*, and *Journal of Research on Technology in Education*. @rogueclone1138; linkedin.com/in/jenniferkillham; jkillham@laverne.edu

ABOUT THE AUTHORS AND CONTRIBUTORS

Philomena N. Agu is an adjunct professor of science education in the urban education department at the University of Houston-Downtown. She also teaches physics in high school at the Houston Independent School District. Her current research interests focus on science teacher certification and influence on the underrepresentation of minorities in STEM fields, science teaching efficacy, science teacher beliefs, and integration of science with other content areas. agup@uhd.edu

Alec M. Bodzin is a professor in the Teaching, Learning, and Technology program and is a core faculty member of the Lehigh Environmental Initiative. He is the Primary Investigator of Socio-environmental Science Investigations (SESI) and Environmental Literacy and Inquiry (ELI), an inquiry-based secondary school curriculum that uses geospatial technologies including Web GIS to investigate environmental issues in the areas of energy, climate change, and land use change.

Dr. Bodzin's research interests involve the design of immersive virtual reality learning environments, Web-based inquiry learning environments, learning with spatial thinking tools including GIS, the design and implementation of inquiry-based environmental science curriculum, visual instructional technologies, and the use of instructional technologies to promote learning. amb4@lehigh.edu

Kaitlin Campbell is an assistant professor at the University of North Carolina at Pembroke, where she teaches courses including environmental science, entomology, beekeeping, and invertebrate zoology. Community engagement, citizen science, scientific communication, and service-learning are important focuses of her courses. Her research focuses on invertebrate conservation and biodiversity with a special focus on pollinators, acarology, community ecology, and agroecology. kaitlin.campbell@uncp.edu

Tina Cheuk is an assistant professor of elementary science education at California Polytechnic State University in San Luis Obispo. Her research focuses on language and literacy practices in K–12 science education settings for culturally and linguistically diverse learners. tcheuk@calpoly.edu

Gina Childers is an assistant professor of STEM education in the Department of Curriculum & Instruction at Texas Tech University and serves as the STEM Education Track Program Coordinator. Currently, her research areas are focused on STEM learning opportunities in non-formal and informal learning spaces as well as cybersecurity education initiatives and adults' perceptions of cybersecurity awareness. gina.childers@ttu.edu

Matthew Clay is an assistant professor in the Department of Teacher Education at Fort Hays State University. Prior to coming to FHSU, he taught middle school and high school science, primarily in rural Western Kansas. His research interests are focused on environmental science education and rural educational equity. maclay@fhsu.edu

Scott D. Cohen is a Dean's Fellow for the College of Education and Human Development at Georgia State University working on his Ph.D. in science education. His research focuses on teachers' professional knowledge and skill in teaching science to Deaf students where he explores ways to support the growth of pre-service and in-service science teachers' Pedagogical Content Knowledge to improve the science learning experiences for Deaf students. scott_dcohen@yahoo.com

Isaiah Darden is an undergraduate student studying Game/Graphic Design at The University of Tulsa. He is also an online tutor with Tutoring Club. He relates to students as a near-peer and gets to know them as individuals. By working collaboratively, Isaiah leads students to think critically, create academic solutions, and increase their content knowledge in science and mathematics. isaiahdarden736@gmail.com

Ibrahim Dincer is an MA and EdM graduate of the Teachers College, Columbia University Program in science education. He teaches Physics and algebra to newcomer students in a Bronx NY High School. idd2108@tc.columbia.edu

Helen Douglass is an assistant professor of science education at the University of Tulsa. Her research interests include the intersections of formal and informal science and STEM teaching and learning. She examines learning spaces and equitable and inclusive teaching and learning practices. Additionally, using visual methodology, she investigates experiences women in science and engineering identify as early as elementary-aged years as important to their practices, and how to include those experiences in elementary educator preparation. She is curious about the affordances makerspaces and design-based pedagogy provide to students, teachers, and communities. hed2054@utulsa.edu

Leslie Ekpe is a third-year Ph.D. student in the Higher Educational Leadership program at Texas Christian University. Ekpe is an alumna of Alabama A&M University, where she earned her B.S. in Management, the University of Alabama at Birmingham, where she obtained her M.A. in Communication Management, and Sam Houston State University, where she received her M.B.A. Her research seeks to promote access for marginalized students in education, specifically focusing on college access policies and racial politics in education.

Patrick Enderle is an associate professor of science education at Georgia State University. Enderle leads graduate-level teacher preparation courses focused on preparing practice-focused science teachers who teach for social justice, including a newer course focused on exploring the Crosscutting Concepts. He also teaches doctoral courses focused on teacher learning about argumentation and other science practices. Enderle's research interests align with these areas and include several efforts exploring the impact of different professional development models in supporting teacher learning. penderle@gsu.edu

Kelly Feille is an assistant professor of science education in the Jeannine Rainbolt College of Education at the University of Oklahoma. Dr. Feille has worked in public education teaching science in grades Pre-K through sixth. At the University of Oklahoma, Dr. Feille continues her passion for science education through her work with pre-service elementary teachers. She seeks to ensure that her students leave the University of Oklahoma with the confidence and tools to teach science in ways that engage students to ask important questions, think critically, and collect, evaluate, and argue from evidence. Her research focuses on the development of elementary science teachers and, in particular, how to encourage the development of schoolyard pedagogy, which takes advantage of the learning moments in and out of the traditional classroom. feille@ou.edu

Lucas Gobel has a BS degree in Wildlife Management and his teaching license from Indiana University. He currently teaches middle school science at Raymond Park Intermediate and Middle School in Indianapolis, Indiana. He coaches both the Science Olympiad and Academic Teams. LGobel@warren.k12.in.us

Rita Hagevik is the Director of Graduate Programs in science education in the Biology Department and a professor at the University of North Carolina at Pembroke. Dr. Hagevik teaches courses to preservice and in-service teachers and conducts research on sustainability, STEAM curriculum, and professional development in the outdoor learning environment in K–12 schools, the use of geospatial technologies in education, and on STEM and nature identity. Her current funded research is on garden-based learning in schools and on climate change and civic engagement. rita.hagevik@uncp.edu

Stephanie Hathcock is an associate professor of science education at Oklahoma State University. She teaches undergraduate and graduate courses in science education and works with science educators in elementary schools. Dr. Hathcock's primary research interests include teacher change, outdoor education, and creativity in science teaching and learning. stephanie.hathcock@okstate.edu

Rebecca Hite is an associate professor of STEM education in the Department of curriculum and instruction at Texas Tech University in Lubbock, Texas, USA. Dr. Hite received her Ph.D. in science education from North Carolina State University and presently teaches graduate courses in personalized learning and STEM Education. One of Dr. Hite's research foci explores the affordances of emerging technologies in formal and informal science and engineering education. rebecca.hite@ttu.edu

Amal Ibourk is an assistant professor in science education in the School of Teacher Education at Florida State University. Her research encompasses the three areas of (1) science learning, (2) science teaching, and (3) identity. Under the umbrella of science learning and teaching, she looks at how they both take place in classrooms and across different settings as students and teachers engage with three-dimensional science learning and learning technologies. Dr. Ibourk is interested in how preservice teachers (PSTs) navigate their roles as science learners and teachers.

Sophia Jeong is an assistant professor of STEM education at The Ohio State University. Her scholarly work focuses on issues of equity and social justice in science education from a post-human lens. jeong.387@osu.edu

Natasha Hillsman Johnson is an assistant professor of science education in the Department of Teacher Education in the Judith Herb College of Education at the University of Toledo. Dr. Johnson has worked in the science education field as a K–12 teacher, virtual instructor, instructional supervisor, and education professor. The overarching goal of her scholarship is to increase interest, access, and achievement in the sciences for all students. Issues related to equity, social justice, and the amplification of marginalized voices continue to be the focus of her research interests in the area of science education. natasha.johnson@utoledo.edu

M. Gail Jones is an Alumni Distinguished Graduate professor of science education and Senior Research Fellow, Friday Institute for Educational Innovation at North Carolina State University, Raleigh. Dr. Jones teaches preservice and in-service teachers and conducts research on teaching and learning science, concepts of size and scale, and the development of science career aspirations. Dr. Jones' research is currently identifying factors and strategies to enhance science career aspirations and studying new approaches to convergence science education.

Paula Lemons is a professor of biochemistry and molecular biology and Associate Dean in Franklin College of Arts and Sciences at the University of Georgia. She has a Ph.D. in biochemistry from the University of Kentucky and completed postdoctoral work at Duke University in the Department of Biology. She conducts discipline-based education research focused on biochemistry learning and instruction as well as the thinking and practices of college biology instructors who engage in professional development. She also promotes discipline-based education research and its applications through her leadership of the Scientists Engaged in Education Research Center at the University of Georgia. plemons@uga.edu

Stephen T. Lewis received his Ph.D. in STEM education from The Ohio State University and is currently a secondary mathematics teacher at Northland High school, working with English Language Learners (ELLs). His scholarly work focuses on mathematical modeling in K–12 students. slewis10342@columbus.k12.oh.us

Trish Loblein was on the PhET team for 12 years while she also taught high school science and math. She wrote, used, and shared over 120 lessons using the PhET sims. In 2020, to help teachers who had to move to online learning, the PhET team developed strategies for writing online labs and Trish wrote 36 online PhET labs. patricia.loeblein@colorado.edu

John Loehr is the Vice President of STEM education at Science Olympiad where he works with the program's volunteers across the country to support the ongoing administration, development, and evolution of Science Olympiad events and competitions. Prior to joining Science Olympiad, he has worked as a classroom teacher, educational researcher, science leader, district administrator, test developer, and school principal. jfloehr@soinc.org

Brittany Lovest is a graduate student of child and adolescent development at the University of La Verne in the LaFetra College of Education. She is currently an early childhood educator and teacher assistant at Pasadena City College. Her research focuses on the pedagogical practices that promote the advancement of students in under-served communities.

Anne Mangahas is an assistant professor in teacher education and the director for the Center for Learning Innovation at the LaFetra College of Education, University of La Verne. Her research and work are in the area of culturally responsive practices, multicultural education, and comparative educational models in STEM.

Robert B. Marsteller is an assistant professor at Delaware State University. His research seeks ways to promote higher-order thinking skills in online environments for P16 students. Dr. Marsteller teaches assessment and research courses at Delaware State University. rmarsteller@desu.edu

Lisa Martin-Hansen is professor and chair of science education at California State University, Long Beach. She has experience working in K–12 schools and higher education in science education, program evaluation, educational technology and UX design, instructional design, professional development in science education, and volunteer management.

Amanda L. Mazin is faculty at Teachers College, Columbia University. She teaches and supervises graduate-level, special education preservice, and in-service teachers in high-need, urban environments. Dr. Mazin's research seeks to promote access to educational opportunities for all learners through the use of research-based, equitable, and inclusive practices. amanda.mazin@tc.columbia.edu

Preetha K. Menon is a researcher and an academic program professional at the Center to Support Excellence in Teaching at the Graduate School of Education, Stanford University. Her research interests include supports for multilingual learners, especially in science education, as well as in-service teacher professional development in language-integrated teaching and learning, using mixed methods. pkmenon@stanford.edu

Marissa Murdock currently serves as the Secondary Science Academic Coach and a High School Science in Rockdale County Public Schools in Georgia. She writes 3D aligned curricula for all 6–12 science courses and serves as a teacher mentor and professional developer within the school district. She is also a doctoral student in the College of Education and Human Development (CEHD) at Georgia State University. As a nod to her STEM background and prior work in the field of Climate Science, her research will focus on the efficacy of various teaching methods and STEM curriculum in facilitating equity, diversity, critical consciousness, and excellence among minority students in the contemporary world. mmurdock@rockdale.k12.ga.us

Juliet Octavius is a special education teacher and graduate of Columbia University's Teachers College Program in Intellectual Disabilities and Autism. As a culturally responsive special education teacher in New York City's classrooms, it has always been important for her to include conversations of identity with her students, helping them understand themselves in this society. Her goal is to have underrepresented and marginalized students see themselves as part of families, schools, and communities. jo2639@tc.columbia.edu

Cynthia Olivas is an associate professor in the undergraduate child development program at the University of La Verne. She teaches early childhood mathematics and cultural parenting courses. As a childhood education consultant, she trains preservice and in-service teachers in developmentally appropriate approaches for teaching mathematics to pre-k through second-grade students. Her research interests focus on teachers' attitudes toward teaching mathematics and the implications they have on student motivation and learning, as well as teachers' perceptions of parents' self-efficacy toward assisting their children with homework. colivas@laverne.edu

Lorna Otero is a doctoral student in the Science Teacher Education Specialization at Teachers College, Columbia University. She has been a science teacher for the past 10 years in New York and Puerto Rico, responsible for teaching bilingual science to first through 12th grades. She is a founding member of the first Montessori public high school in Puerto Rico and has been a long-term cooperating teacher for preservice students working towards science licensure. lvo2102@tc.columbia.edu

David Pauli is a middle school engineering teacher and an adjunct faculty member at Brenau University. A classroom educator for over 25 years, he focuses on integrating science, math, and writing into engineering curriculum. As a professor, he enjoys preparing future mathematics and science educators and helping prospective doctoral students through their research. davidleepauli@hotmail.com

Katrina Pavlik is an educator and non-profit administrator. Her experience spans K–12 and higher education, as well as non-profit organizations, focusing on expanding STEM access and leveraging partnerships. https://www.linkedin.com/in/katrina-pavlik/

John L. Pecore is a professor and Askew institute research fellow in STEM education for the school of education at the University of West Florida. His current research includes situational learning in contextualized experiences with an emphasis in project-based learning and instruction. jpecore@uwf.edu

Katherine Perkins is director of the PhET Interactive Simulations project at the University of Colorado Boulder and a faculty member in the physics education research group. Her work focuses on advancing the design and classroom use of interactive simulations to increase engagement and learning in STEM, and on scaling impact with open educational resources. Her work and research in STEM education also include sustainable course reform, students' beliefs about science, and institutional change. kathy.perkins@colorado.edu

Amber Purnell is a graduate student of child and adolescent development at the University of La Verne in the LaFetra College of Education where she aspires to teach undergraduate courses at the community college level. She currently serves as a child observation laboratory coordinator at a large community college.

Jessica F. Riccio is a senior lecturer and program director of the masters degrees in science education in the Department of Mathematics, Science and Technology at Teachers College, Columbia University. Dr. Riccio has worked for the last 18 years in the preservice, in-service, and residency master's programs in biology, chemistry, earth science, and physics teacher certification for secondary school grades 7–12. She serves as the Women in Science Forum Chair at the Association for Science Teacher Education, and past Teacher Education Policy Chair at Columbia. jf293@tc.columbia.edu

Sarah Baas Robinson is a lecturer in the Department of Biochemistry and Molecular Biology at the University of Georgia. She teaches Introductory Biochemistry courses. Her research focuses on how concept maps and drawing impact students' learning and motivation. srobinson@uga.edu

Isabella Sebastiani is a graduate student studying child and adolescent development with a concentration in early childhood at the University of La Verne. She is an early childhood educator and preschool dance instructor with a passionate commitment to diversity, social equity, and serving the communities around her.

Sarah Toutant is a fourth-year Ph.D. Candidate in Urban Education Policy at the University of Southern California's Rossier School of Education and Researcher at the USC Race and Equity Center. She also holds a B.A. in Sociology and Critical Diversity Studies from the University of San Francisco and an M.Ed. from USC Rossier. Her research investigates Black undergraduate women's experiences with their external environments outside the confines of college and university life. toutant@usc.edu

Amy Vo is a Ph.D. candidate at the University of Denver, in the Morgridge College of Education. She teaches graduate-level courses in secondary science methods and is a graduate research assistant in the Teaching and Learning Sciences department, focusing on elementary mathematics. Her research focuses on professional development in STEM education and culturally responsive pedagogies for K–12 educators. amylynn733@hotmail.com

Jennifer Yauck graduated from Oglethorpe County High School in 1997 and earned a Bachelor of Science in Plant Biology, a Bachelor of Science in Horticulture, and a Master's in Science Education from the University of Georgia. This year is Ms. Yauck's 18th year in education. She has taught at Washington-Wilkes Comprehensive High School, Oconee County High School, and has served as the director of 6–12 Science at Northeast Georgia RESA. She has also taught environmental education at the Rock Eagle 4-H Center and internationally in Kolkata, India. Currently, she is a science instructional coach and science teacher at Oglethorpe County High School. jenni.b.lance@gmail.com

Patricia Zagallo is a STEM instructor for TRIO SSS at the University of Washington. Her scholarly work focuses on developing a deep understanding of how students learn science concepts and skills and how learners develop problem-solving and critical thinking skills. In her teaching, she implements student-centered teaching approaches and technologies such as interactive computer simulations and activities to promote student learning. Her expertise areas include Curriculum and Assessment designs for Science Practices in Next Generation Science Standards (NGSS) and in AAAS Vision and Change for Undergraduate Education. pzagallo@uw.edu

We would like to thank Justine Diener O'Leary for her expertise and assistance in the production of this book.

We would also like to acknowledge George, Jacquie, and Jayme for their inspiration, vision, and unwavering support.